The Atlas of U.S. and Canadian Environmental History

Editor Char Miller received his Ph.D. from Johns Hopkins University in 1981, and is chair of the department of history and the interim director of the urban studies program at Trinity University in San Antonio, Texas. He was named a 2002 Piper Professor, a state-wide award for excellence in teaching and service to higher education. In 1997, he won Trinity University's Dr. and Mrs. Z. T. Scott Faculty Fellowship for excellence in teaching.

Editorial Adviser Jennifer Read is the assistant director of the Michigan Sea Grant College Program. She previously served as a research associate at the Great Lakes Institute for Environmental Research at the University of Windsor in Ontario, Canada.

The
Atlas of U.S. and Canadian Environmental History

CHAR MILLER, EDITOR

ROUTLEDGE
NEW YORK AND LONDON

© 2003 by The Moschovitis Group, Inc.

Published in 2003 by
Routledge
29 West 35th Street
New York, New York 10001
www.routledge-ny.com

Published in Great Britain by
Routledge
11 New Fetter Lane
London EC4P 4EE
www.routledge.uk.co

Routledge is an imprint of the Taylor & Francis Group.
Printed in Hong Kong on acid-free paper.

Produced by The Moschovitis Group, Inc.
339 Fifth Avenue
New York, New York 10016
www.mosgroup.com

Publisher	Valerie Tomaselli
Executive Editor	Hilary W. Poole
Senior Editor	Stephanie Schreiber
Associate Editor	Sonja Matanovic
Editorial Coordinator	Nicole Cohen Solomon
Design and Layout	Annemarie Redmond
Illustrator and Cartographer	Richard Garratt
Production Coordinator	K. Nura Abdul-Karim
Editorial Intern	Jessica Rosin
Researcher	Alison Quito Ziegler
Photo Research	Gillian Speeth
Copyediting	Carole Campbell
Proofreading	Paul Scaramazza
Index	Barber Indexing

2 4 6 8 10 9 7 5 3 1

Library of Congress Cataloging-in-Publication Data is available

ISBN: 0-415-93781-7

Table of Contents

Preface

In the 1970s, a small group of scholars launched the field of environmental history. These pioneers practiced a new approach to the study of history by considering humans' relationship to their environments and the effect that humans' interactions with their environments has had on historical developments. From its awkward beginnings to its transformation into a sophisticated academic field, environmental history has offered an important lens through which to view the past. Taking an interdisciplinary approach to the study of history, environmental historians investigate economic, political, scientific, technological, social, and cultural trends throughout history as they relate to both the natural and built environment. *The Atlas of U.S. and Canadian Environmental History* reflects the origins of the field, examining the role of the environment in our social institutions, political spheres, popular imagination, and daily life.

The Atlas of U.S. and Canadian Environmental History focuses on both Canada and the United States. With one of the longest borders in the world, these two nations share a remarkable landscape—including the Atlantic and Pacific Oceans, the Great Lakes and riparian watersheds, prairies and mountain chains, marine habitats and urban space. Since the first Europeans arrived in the New World, the environments and histories of Canada and the United States have been intertwined. These interactions date back even further, of course, given the intense interactions between native peoples over a landscape unmarked by our current political boundaries.

The North American environment—and American and Canadian attitudes toward nature—have developed and shifted throughout time. The continent's landscape has evolved continuously, from the establishment of farms in the colonial period, to the construction of rail networks across both nations in the nineteenth century, to the cleanup of toxic waste sites in the twentieth century. To best demonstrate these developments, the atlas has been arranged in seven chronological chapters, spanning the precolonial period to the present day.

Because environmental history is interdisciplinary, it often overlaps in focus with environmental science, which examines the relationship between humans and natural systems, and environmental policy, which considers legislation and current issues relating to the management of the environment. To help emphasize the recurring topics that appear in these interconnected fields, each chapter has been divided into six thematic categories: Agriculture; Wildlife and Forestry; Land Use Management; Technology, Industry, and Pollution; Human Habitats; and Ideology and Politics.

Maps, charts, tables, and photographic images illuminate many of the topics discussed in the articles. Some maps point out the specific location of geographic features, for example, mining regions, western dams, or public lands, that have been discussed in a particular article. Other maps show demographic changes, such as urbanization patterns during the late nineteenth and early twentieth centuries, or shifts in agricultural trends, such as the production of corn, wheat, and cotton before and after the Civil War. When appropriate, historical maps include present-day boundaries—even if the states, provinces, or countries did not exist at that point— to offer users a better sense as to how historical trends impacted current geographic areas. Charts and tables provide statistical information, for instance, timber production or levels of smoke pollution. Photographs and illustrations accompany many of the articles to document particular events, such as the first Earth Day in 1970, or offer readers a sense of a society's attitudes toward the environment, such as the Romantic painters' depiction of idyllic natural settings during the nineteenth century.

The atlas also features sidebars that highlight a particular subject related to the topic or, in some instances, provide excerpts of passages from books or documents. Many of the historical and environmental topics covered in the atlas recur within and across the various chapters, offering a sense of the interconnectedness of events, trends, and themes throughout U.S. and Canadian history. For this reason, the atlas includes in-text cross-references that will direct readers to pages with additional information on the topic. Each article also includes a distinct Further Reading section that directs readers to important literature, such as books or scholarly journal articles, on the subject.

Measurements are given in English units, followed by their metric equivalents in parentheses. As the metric ton is almost equal to the English ton, we have not provided a conversion in an effort to conserve space. In statistical charts and tables, we have left the data in their original form. However, where the information in a chart or table is provided for comparative purposes, we have converted the data to equivalent units.

At the end of the book is a timeline spanning the pre-Columbian period to the present day; it highlights important events, legislation, and trends that relate to the environmental history of Canada and the United States. An extensive bibliography offers readers a list of sources that will provide further reading on various topics. To make this list accessible to users, it has been divided into the following sections: general titles, sources dealing with the United States, sources dealing with Canada, an era-by-era section that mirrors the chapter divisions of the book, and a thematic section that reflects the six major categories repeated in each chapter. A list of contributors displays the vast range of expertise that has contributed to the production of this atlas. A detailed name, place, and concept index offers users an additional means of locating topics of interest.

The Atlas of U.S. and Canadian
Environmental History

CHAPTER ONE

European Exploration and the Colonial Era
(1492–1770s)

John Smith, an English explorer who journeyed to the New World in the early seventeenth century, was a legend in his own mind. His *General History of Virginia* (1624) offers a much-revised account of how he led his fellow Jamestown, Virginia, colonists through the many hardships they endured to establish the settlement in the early 1600s. Despite its vainglorious quality, Smith's book, which he wrote after he returned to England in 1609, is a firsthand and vivid depiction of the interactions between indigenous peoples and the invading English settlers. As he identifies the sharp disparities between the two peoples' civilizations and level of technological development, he also catalogs the region's astonishing wealth of natural resources. He mapped many of its rivers and bays, noted the rich, well-watered soil, and praised the thick stands of timber.

The book's descriptions of the economic wealth of the landscape were designed to appeal to English readers who might invest in or immigrate to the colony. This appeal was heightened by Smith's mouthwatering descriptions of the natural abundance of food. As winter approached, he wrote, "the rivers became so covered with swans, geese, ducks and cranes that we daily feasted with good bread, Virginia peas, pumpkins, and persimmons, fish, fowl, and divers sorts of wild beasts as fat as we could eat them."

In dangling such sumptuous fare before his readers, Smith was contributing to the emergence of a colonial literature that contrasted New World vitality with Old World weariness. His claims would be confirmed by subsequent generations of settlers in British North America, New France, and New Spain. Along the Atlantic seaboard, hundreds of settlements would spring up that

would enjoy rapid and consistent population growth, develop a very productive agricultural and commercial economy, and build busy port cities whose trade networks extended around the globe.

Natural Resources. Early English and French colonists were both overwhelmed by and eager to exploit the vast forests they encountered and the variety of wildlife that lived within North America's woods. As with the indigenous peoples of the continent, the settlers made full use of this great plenty, searching for berries and nuts, hunting game, and burning and logging forests to create more open space. Unlike Native Americans, they let their domesticated animals, cattle, hogs, and sheep, forage freely in the woods, an easy way to feed the expanding numbers of animals and to eliminate forest cover.

Despite their cultural differences, all Europeans believed in the concept of private property and the necessity of constructing agricultural landscapes. The key material for their built environments was wood. Because of their large numbers, the English colonists consumed vast quantities for housing, fencing, and fuel. This demand sparked the development of a complex lumber business that cleared lands far beyond the population centers. The profit from this trade was reinvested in new lands, contributing to rapid deforestation and the spread of a farm-based economy in what is now the eastern United States and Canada.

European Settlements. The English communities grew swiftly; by the mid-eighteenth century, more than 1.5 million English lived in the New World, compared with seventy thousand French settlers, and even fewer Spanish. Each group established different patterns of land use. The "Little Commonwealths" of New England were small towns built on the open-field system that granted individual settlers house lots, as well as rights to and responsibilities for common meadows and woodlots. Few towns existed in the southern Chesapeake Bay tobacco colonies, which developed around large-scale plantation agriculture that used slave labor to plant and harvest the crop, and river transportation to take it to market. Dependent on rivers, too, were the New France settlements in Canada. Under the feudal seigneurial system, narrow strips of land along the riverfront were parceled out to the Roman Catholic church and to elite individuals, who could either sell the property or rent it to tenants.

Far to the south and west, Spanish settlements formed around Roman Catholicism had also been established. Missionaries and civilian leaders worked with military forces to conscript local Native American populations into the labor force to clear agricultural land, dig irrigation ditches, and construct communal and religious buildings. The physical expanse of New Spain, which stretched from present-day California to Florida, resulted in the Spanish towns often being so far from one another, and from the larger

A European view of the New World from Franciscan missionary Louis Hennepin's 1697 Nouvelle Decouverte. *(From the collections of the Library of Congress)*

cities of central Mexico, that they remained small in population and limited in economic import.

Interactions with Native Americans. Unlike other European New World settlers, the Spanish interacted more freely with indigenous peoples, culturally and sexually, leading to the creation of a mestizo, or mixed, population. The English, by contrast, had no desire to mix with members of local Native American tribes; they saw themselves as a more advanced culture that was in direct competition with indigenous peoples for land and resources. Open conflict between these settlers and Native Americans intensified by the mid-eighteenth century as the English pushed beyond the Appalachian Mountains, where they replicated patterns of settlement and resource exploitation that they had employed along the Atlantic seaboard. The French, whose numbers were smaller and expansionary desires more muted, did not come into as much conflict with Native Americans.

Regardless of their motives or perspectives, the three major colonial powers in the New World forever changed Native American culture. The swelling European birthrate and immigration to the New World, when combined with the superiority of Europe's military technology, enabled settlers to extend their control over the land and its many resources. Despite the destructive impact of immigration and settlement on the indigenous human populations and on native flora and fauna, the Europeans brought different foods and animals that "Europeanized" North America, while concurrently influencing the cultures and diets of England, France, and Spain.

This so-called Columbian Exchange was not equal in its impact. Even before large-scale settlement, Old World diseases that European explorers and fishermen brought with them had devastated indigenous peoples who lacked immunity to measles and smallpox. Had the daring Captain John Smith been able to return to Virginia at the close of the eighteenth century, he would have been astounded by how thoroughly his dream of continental conquest had come to pass.

—*Char Miller*

Columbian Exchange

The Columbian exchange refers to the exchange of plants between the Old and New Worlds and the introduction of animals from Europe to the Western Hemisphere following the arrival of Europeans in the fifteenth century. By introducing a host of crop plants and domesticated animals to their new environment, the Spanish, French, and British settlers attempted to "Europeanize" the North American continent. Beginning with the second voyage of Columbus in 1493, the Spanish introduced wheat, melons, onions, sugarcane, grapevines, radishes, chickpeas, cauliflowers, cabbages, and lettuce, as well as horses, cattle, swine, sheep, goats, and chickens. This voyage began the exchange of plants and animals between the New and Old Worlds that would have significant effects on the environments and ecologies of both worlds.

Diseases. The Columbian exchange also spread Old World diseases, such as smallpox, influenza, and measles, among the indigenous populations—none of which had immunity to those diseases. Along the Atlantic coast of Canada, for example, fishermen and fur traders exposed indigenous peoples to European diseases during the early sixteenth century. During the seventeenth century, diseases decimated Native American populations in present-day New England, while during the eighteenth century Russian explorers spread diseases among the Aleut, Eskimo (Inuit), and Tlingit in the Pacific Northwest. Although the Old World diseases introduced in the New World were often catastrophic to indigenous populations, the Columbian exchange brought nutritional benefits and improved food supplies with the addition of new crops and new animal species.

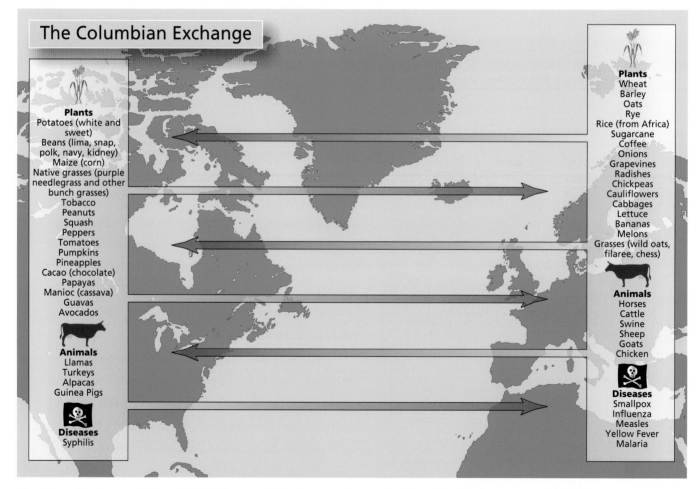

The exchange of flora between the New and Old Worlds was extensive by the seventeenth century. By the late eighteenth century, many agricultural plants had been traded, particularly between the Western Hemisphere and Europe and Africa. Although some native animals from the New World, such as turkeys and llamas, were introduced in Europe, the exchange of fauna for agricultural purposes was primarily from Europe to the New World.

Sources: James Lang, Notes of a Potato Watcher (College Station: Texas A & M University Press, 2001), 21; Elaine N. McIntosh, American Food Habits in Historical Perspective (Westport, Conn.: Greenwood Press, 1995), 65; and The Columbian Biological Exchange. Dr. Harold D. Tallant, Department of History, Georgetown College. 3 Dec. 1998. <http://spider.georgetowncollege.edu/htallant/courses/his111/columb.htm>.

Plants. By 1500, the Spanish (*see also* 16–17) had made considerable progress in their attempt to transform the New World into the Old World; by the mid-sixteenth century the process was irreversible. Spanish settlers at St. Augustine in present-day Florida raised oranges by 1579. By 1660, Spanish farmers or their subjects in Mexico cultivated nearly all of the most important food plants from the Old World, including wheat, barley, oats, and rye. Slaves or slave traders introduced the African crop of rice to the Carolina lowlands by the early 1670s. Rice enabled white planters on the sea islands and low coastal plain to cultivate swamplands, while wheat and barley permitted settlers in the present-day United States and Canada to cultivate lands too high, dry, or cool for growing maize (corn) and other native crops in significant quantity.

Animals. The introduction of animals from the Old World was more significant in the use of the environment than the influx of new plants. By 1500, the major breeds of cattle and horses had arrived from Spain, which enabled New World people to use the environment in a different way by converting grass grazed by animals into meat, milk, and cheese. Spanish hogs and cattle readily adapted to their new environment. In 1539 Hernando de Soto began exploring present-day Florida, taking thirteen hogs to help feed his men. By the time of his death in 1542, they had multiplied to a herd of seven hundred.

Spanish horses also bred rapidly and, along with disease, moved faster across the North American continent than the people who brought them. By 1700, the Plains tribes south of the Platte River in present-day Nebraska were familiar with horses; by 1750, the tribes north of the river were also routinely using horses. During the mid-1780s, horses grazed on the banks of the Saskatchewan River in

Further Reading
Crosby, Alfred W., Jr. *The Columbian Exchange: Biological and Cultural Consequences of 1492.* Westport, Conn.: Greenwood Press, 1972.
Lang, James. *Notes of a Potato Watcher.* College Station: Texas A & M University Press, 2001.

McIntosh, Elaine N. *American Food Habits in Historical Perspective.* Westport, Conn.: Praeger, 1995.
Smith, Andrew F. *The Tomato in America: Early History, Culture, and Cookery.* Urbana: University of Illinois Press, 2001.

present-day Saskatchewan. On the North American plains horses revolutionized transportation, hunting, and war, particularly for Native Americans like the Sioux, Cheyenne, and Comanche.

Concurrently, sheep arrived in the American Southwest, soon outnumbered cattle, and became important sources of food and skins. The Navajo were particularly successful at adapting sheep into their culture and environment, and they became great herders on the arid grazing lands of the Southwest. By the early eighteenth century Spanish longhorn cattle roamed the grasslands of present-day southern Texas, easily adapting to the hot, dry climate. Cattle also became a new food source for some Apache bands that stole them from the Spanish ranchers in that region. In some areas, cattle, horses, and sheep required large grazing areas and frequently strayed into Native Americans' fields and damaged crops.

Impact. Although Old World diseases decimated native populations in the New World, the introduction of Old World plants and animals, particularly horses and cattle, and the adoption of New World corn by European settlers contributed to population growth and more extensive use of the land for agricultural purposes. European plants and animals significantly increased food variety, supply, and nutrition, particularly in the addition of animal protein, to New World populations. The great variety of European food plants enabled settlers to adapt quickly to their new environment.

In the New World, these plant and animal introductions readily adapted to the environment. Horses, cattle, and particularly sheep enabled Native Americans and immigrants

to use the lands of the arid Southwest and semiarid Great Plains. However, in the absence of natural predators, cattle, horses, and sheep occasionally overgrazed grasslands, eventually contributing to soil erosion, the elimination of native grasses, and the invasion of weeds such as dandelions. Newly introduced Spanish grasses had a high tolerance for drought and overgrazing, which made them perfectly suited for the dry Southwest. Eventually these grasses, for example, wild oats, filaree, and chess, competed with and forced out native grasses like purple needlegrass and other bunch grasses. Although Spanish grasses contributed to greater flora diversity on the North American continent, some native grasses became threatened with extinction.

The Columbian exchange had other environmental consequences. Many indigenous New World plants that had been domesticated by Native Americans were abandoned as crops. When found in fields of European crops, the settlers considered them weeds. European farmers plowed the land for their crops, rather than using hoes and digging sticks, which exposed more soil and made it susceptible to wind and water erosion. European sheep and Native American sheepherders also pushed the native bighorn sheep into higher elevations. Domestic sheep often grazed slopes too steep for plowing and destroyed plants that prevented soil erosion. Although the introduction of European plants and animals enabled the use of soils and seasons heretofore unavailable, the Columbian exchange often upset the balance of nature, a matter that future generations would accept and perpetuate.

—*R. Douglas Hurt*

Domestication of the Land: From Wilderness to Farmland

European settlers in the early seventeenth century encountered a North America covered with forests (*see also* 8–9) that were home to abundant wildlife, including deer, turkey, beaver, bear, wolf, cougar, and many smaller mammals. The Native American population had been significantly reduced over the previous century by diseases introduced by the early explorers (*see also* 4–6), leaving abandoned fields and clearings scattered along the Atlantic coast and major rivers. Most successful European settlements before 1650 made use of these clearings, but soon the growing population needed more land and domestication of the continent began in earnest.

Wilderness. New settlements were increasingly carved entirely from the forest wilderness. Tree species were used as an indicator of land quality. Basswood, sugar maple, walnut, ash, and cherry were thought to indicate the best soils; oak, hickory, red maple, and beech indicated intermediate soils; and hemlock and pitch as well as other pines indicated poor soils. By the late eighteenth century most of the continent east of the Appalachian Mountains plus the Northeast, with the exception of the higher mountains, had been settled and transformed to farmland. Settlements spread from the coast up major rivers and streams to the rolling uplands and foothills (piedmont). The process differed somewhat among regions, but in all cases resulted in vast areas of forest being converted to agricultural use and the remaining woodlots being repeatedly harvested for timber, fuel, and many other uses. Habitat loss and hunting pressure significantly reduced or eliminated most large mammals and game species, turkey, for example, in settled regions.

Settlements. The kinds of settlements varied: In the Northeast (*see also* 18–19), most early towns followed the English open-field model, in which settlers, or proprietors, were granted large house-lots along a main street, plots in common fields and woodlots, and rights to common pastures. By the early eighteenth century the open-field system was less common in new towns. Proprietors received larger, often contiguous properties, but individual fields and pastures remained small and communities remained largely self-sufficient. In the South the plantation system was common (*see also* 20–21), with grants of one to several thousand acres allotted to an individual owner and large areas cleared for a single, valuable commercial crop. Agricultural patterns in the middle colonies often fell between these extremes.

Forest Clearing. Clearing forest was an arduous task. In the New England and Midatlantic colonies settlers often cleared only a few acres a year. The ability to clear and subsequently farm large tracts often depended on family size. Without easy access to water transportation, wood had little value beyond what was needed for local use, including construction, fencing, and, most important, fuel for heating and cooking. A typical New England household consumed 20 to 25 cords of fuel wood annually. Where river transport was available timber was harvested commercially, and towns at the mouths of larger rivers such as Portsmouth, New Hampshire, became lumber ports. As early as the mid-seventeenth century towns in outlying coastal areas were supplying wood for fuel to growing populations in Boston, New York, and Philadelphia.

Although certain crops, especially European grains, required clearing the land of stumps and plowing, most clearance was accomplished by simply felling the trees, using what wood was needed and piling and burning the rest. Farmers then employed

A photograph of a diorama built in the 1930s portraying typical land use in Massachusetts in the early eighteenth century. When new towns were established in the uplands, the new settlers slowly cleared forestland for their homes, fields, pastures, and commons. (Fisher Museum Dioramas, Harvard Forest, Petersham, Massachusetts; John Green, photographer)

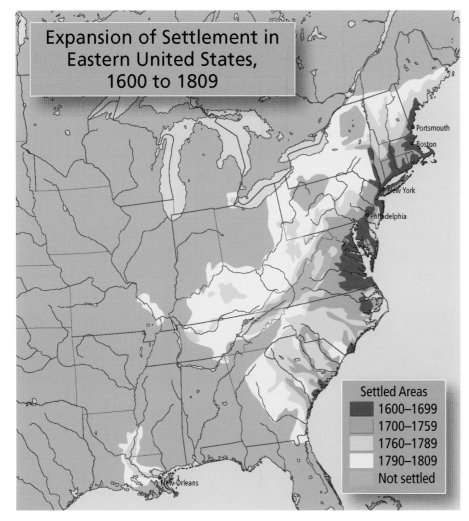

Expansion of Settlement in Eastern United States, 1600 to 1809

Portsmouth
Boston
New York
Philadelphia
New Orleans

Settled Areas
1600–1699
1700–1759
1760–1789
1790–1809
Not settled

The original coastal settlements in the eastern United States slowly moved upriver and inland through the eighteenth century. As populations grew and agriculture became progressively more commercial, vast areas were cleared for crops and pasture and much of the remaining forest was harvested for fuel and timber. Most areas west of the Appalachian Mountains were not settled until the nineteenth century.
Source: Michael Williams, *Americans and Their Forests: A Historical Geography* (Cambridge and New York: Cambridge University Press, 1989), 54. Adapted with the permission of Cambridge University Press.

to roam the woods feeding on tree nuts and young roots. An expanding trade in beef with the West Indies and other colonies in the eighteenth century made domesticated animals more important commercially, which greatly increased the clearing of upland pasture. This clearing would accelerate in the early 1800s across much of New England to provide pasture for sheep producing wool for the developing textile mills.

Impact. As settlements spread across the land, little forest was spared. The best land became productive fields, rougher land became pasture, and woodlots on the poorest sites were harvested repeatedly for fuel, creating persistent young stands of saplings. In the Northeast stone walls replaced wooden fences as wood became more valuable as fuel than fencing. By the early nineteenth century crops and domesticated animals dominated an open landscape and the few remaining wild animals were either hunted as game or exterminated as predators. Ironically, today forests have reclaimed much of this landscape, especially in the Northeast, as agriculture has shifted westward, and deer, moose, bear, beaver, and coyote haunt the maturing forests, which many newcomers now mistake for wilderness.

—*John F. O'Keefe*

hoe agriculture to work around the stumps or used the land for pasture. This method of felling and burning, which worked well for corn, also produced potash from the piles of burned wood; this potash could be spread on the fields as fertilizer or collected and sold (it had a variety of chemical uses).

The less labor-intensive method of girdling (cutting a notch around the trunk) was used to kill trees without felling them; the trees eventually had to be removed when they rotted and fell several years later. Girdling was most commonly used in the South, often by slaves, for preparing large acreages of plantations for tobacco. This

very valuable crop depleted the soil of nutrients so quickly that planting had often moved to newly cleared areas before the girdled trees rotted and fell. On southern tobacco or cotton plantation fields, crops might be grown for only five to seven years, with the field then abandoned to regrow to forest for twenty to thirty years before being prepared for crops again.

Forest clearing accelerated in the middle and late eighteenth century, moving into the hills as populations grew and new homesteads and settlements were formed. Woodlands had traditionally been used for rough day pasture for cattle, with swine left

Further Reading

Foster, David R., and John F. O'Keefe. *New England Forests Through Time: Insights from the Harvard Forest Dioramas.* Petersham, Mass.: Harvard Forest, Harvard University, 2000.

Russell, Howard S. *A Long, Deep Furrow: Three Centuries of Farming in New England.* Hanover, N.H.: University Press of New England, 1982.

Whitney, Gordon Graham. *From Coastal Wilderness to Fruited Plain: A History of Environmental Change in Temperate North America, 1500 to the Present.* Cambridge and New York: Cambridge University Press, 1994.

Williams, Michael. *Americans and Their Forests: A Historical Geography.* Cambridge and New York: Cambridge University Press, 1989.

Early American and Canadian Forests

Prior to European settlement, forests covered about 1 billion acres (0.4 billion hectares), or about half of what was to become the United States, including Alaska. About three-quarters of that forest was in the eastern third of the country. Of Canada's nearly 2.5 billion acres (1 billion hectares) of land, just 48 percent was forest. Trees stretched from coast to coast below the Arctic Circle. Fire, disease, and wind created open areas that extended for miles, and the areas near many rivers and salt marshes were also naturally clear.

Forest Types. Two types of forests have dominated the United States and Canada since the pre-Columbian era. Temperate forests, which stretch from the southern United States into southern Canada, contain both broadleaf (oak, maple, and beech, for example) as well as coniferous (pine) trees. They receive about 30 to 60 inches (0.8 to 1.6 meters) of rain annually, with rainfall distributed evenly throughout the year. The second forest type is the boreal forest, which lies in a wide swath across the middle of Canada and on into Alaska. The boreal forest receives 12 to 40 inches (0.3 to 1.2 meters) of precipitation annually, much of it in the form of snowfall. Conifers, such as spruce, larch, and fir, predominate because they can survive and grow in a short growing season and in poor sandy soil with relatively little water.

Native Practices. The population of pre-Columbian North America (*see also* 14–15) is estimated to have been between 9.8 and 12.5 million. Although these figures are regularly revised, any sizable population would have had a noticeable impact on the land. Contrary to the popular myth of Native Americans living lightly on the land, they did, in fact, clear land and alter the landscape around them to suit their needs. At the time of European settlement, Native American agriculture and use of fire for clearing and hunting had changed portions of the woodlands to a more open, park-like vegetation where populations of deer, rabbits, and wild turkey thrived. Native Americans felled trees for housing and fuel, and also used them for fibers, foods, and medicines. Native Americans hunted black bear and used that animal's fat in ointments as protection against winter winds and summer insects like mosquitoes. They burned the understory and ground cover adjacent to settlements to reduce insect problems, to improve the habitat of the game animals they hunted for food, to clear the land to plant crops, and to remove protective cover that could be used by enemies for concealment. About every ten to fifteen years, a typical Native American settlement would be abandoned because the resources of the surrounding land had been exhausted. With the majority of game either consumed or driven off and the soil no longer as fertile as it had been, the entire village would move to a new location, leaving behind large clearings that early European settlers used. As Europeans moved westward in the 1600s and 1700s, they regularly found open patches of land in the forests that indicated the former presence and industriousness of Native Americans.

European Practices. Like Native Americans, early European farmers also found the dense forests of the New World to be a major source of sustenance. The forest provided berries, nuts, and maple sap from which to make maple syrup, and also forage

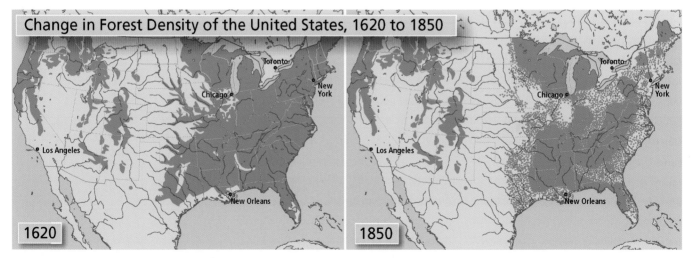

Change in Forest Density of the United States, 1620 to 1850

1620

1850

Note: Each dot represents 25,000 acres (10,000 hectares). Some variations in forest density from 1620 to 1850 reflect the increasing accuracy of land surveys in later periods. In 1620, during the early settlement of the New World, forests covered the eastern United States. By 1850, however, the land clearing practices of colonists (who desired both farmland and timber) had caused the edges of the forests to start to recede as settlers moved westward.
Source: Michael Williams, *Americans and Their Forests* (New York: Cambridge University Press, 1989), 436. Underlying data from W. Greeley, "The Relation of Geography to Timber Supply" *(Economic Geography* 1, 1925), 4, 5. Adapted with the permission of Cambridge University Press.

Forest Distribution and Loss in Canada, c. 1867

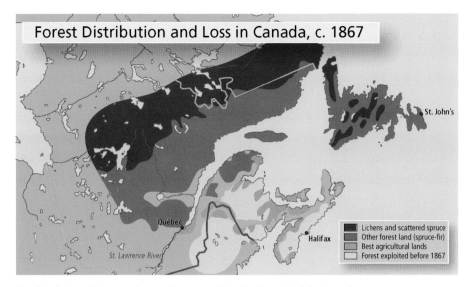

Lichens and scattered spruce
Other forest land (spruce-fir)
Best agricultural lands
Forest exploited before 1867

The distribution of forests and areas that were exploited in Canada's Atlantic region.
Source: Robert D. Mitchell, and Paul A. Groves, eds., *North America: The Historical Geography of a Changing Continent* (Totowa, N.J.: Rowman & Littlefield, 1987), 231. Adapted with the permission of Rowan & Littlefield.

for cattle and hogs. Additionally, it was the source of wood for utensils, tools, and furniture, as well as potash (fertilizer) for farming. Like Native Americans, settlers burned trees to clear land for farming or for safety. They abandoned farms when they had exhausted the land's fertility and cleared new forests to start the process over again. Unlike Native Americans, however, Europeans established permanent settlements. After using all the timber in surrounding areas, the settlers imported wood from the frontier for fuel and construction rather than moving on.

Consumption of Wood. Other cultural differences meant colonists consumed more wood than Native Americans. Native Americans did not fence in land because they did not believe in private ownership of land; colonists usually delineated their property with wooden fences—in part to prevent other farmers' animals from trampling their crops. A square 40-acre (16-hectare) field enclosed by a wooden split-rail fence required about eight thousand rails. (A mile of that fence represented enough timber to saw 75,000 feet [23,000 meters] of boards, according to historian Hu Maxwell.) The United States had about 3.2 million miles (5.1 million kilometers) of wooden fence by 1850.

Home construction used wood extravagantly. A simple one-room log cabin required eighty logs of 20 to 30 feet (6 to 9 meters) in length for the walls, plus additional logs for the gable and roof. Once a sawmill was established in a settled area and could produce clapboards for siding, housing styles began to change to reflect a desire for a more "English" or sophisticated type of home. Wealthier colonists built frame houses with siding to replace the log cabin, whereas less affluent settlers simply nailed clapboards over the logs to "modernize" their homes. Still, the log cabin remained the dominant style. As late as 1855, New York state had 33,092 log cabins housing roughly one-fifth of all farm families.

As the United States grew, the demands it placed on the environment increased. In the eighteenth century the establishment of ironworks would put heretofore unknown pressure on the forests. Furnaces used to produce iron, a critical industry for the U.S. economy, required huge quantities of wood charcoal to smelt the iron ore. A 1,000-ton ironworks, of which there were many by the late 1700s, required between 20,000 and 30,000 acres (8,000 and 12,000 hectares) of forest over a twenty-year period to sustain itself. Iron furnace operators found themselves competing with urban households for fuel wood. Between 10 and 20 acres (4 and 8 hectares) of forest were needed to supply the wood burned by one fireplace annually. By the 1780s, competition between iron furnaces and home consumption in urban areas drew farmers into the lumber supply trade, and provided them with an extra source of income.

Europeans in the 1600s and 1700s rapidly decimated the forests of the eastern seaboard. Cities and towns dotting the map from the St. Lawrence River to Georgia had consumed surrounding woodlands and began importing wood from the interior of the continent. By the mid-1700s, colonists had cleared forests for agricultural lands as far west as the Appalachian Mountains and now looked to the Great Lakes region (*see also* 34–35) and the southern colonies for new sources of timber as well as farmland. After the American Revolution, with the British government no longer restricting movement, the expansion westward accelerated.

—*James G. Lewis*

Further Reading

Apsey, Mike, et al. *The Perpetual Forest: Using Lessons from the Past to Sustain Canada's Forests in the Future.* Vancouver: FORCAST, 2000.

Cox, Thomas R., Robert S. Maxwell, Phillip Drennon Thomas, and Joseph J. Malone. *This Well-Wooded Land: Americans and Their Forests from Colonial Times to the Present.* Lincoln: University of Nebraska Press, 1985.

Halliday, W. E. D. "Forest Regions of Canada: Their Distribution and Character." *Canadian Geographical Journal* 19 (October 1939): 228–243.

Maxwell, Hu. "The Uses of Wood: Fencing Materials from Forests." *American Forestry* 25 (March 1919): 923–930.

Merchant, Carolyn. *Ecological Revolutions: Nature, Gender, and Science in New England.* Chapel Hill: University of North Carolina Press, 1989.

Walker, Laurence C. *The North American Forests: Geography, Ecology, and Silviculture.* Boca Raton, Fla.: CRC Press, 1999.

Williams, Michael. *Americans and Their Forests: A Historical Geography.* Cambridge: Cambridge University Press, 1992.

European Exploitation and Mapping the Land

From the late fifteenth through the late eighteenth centuries, European explorers and others sailed to North America, known as the New World. While the explorers provided first-hand accounts of the territory and the continent's rich resources, cartographers in Europe painstakingly pieced together a jigsaw of geographical information, converting this mythic region into a tangible territory ready to be settled and exploited. Thus began the transformation of a romantic and bountiful wilderness into a rapidly populated and commercially important continent.

Early Explorations. A handful of Europeans have been credited for what was, in reality, the collective effort of thousands of explorers, cartographers, missionaries, traders, and land speculators. Credit for discovering the New World is popularly given to Italian-born mariner Christopher Columbus, whose four voyages across the Atlantic Ocean between 1492 and 1504, under the sponsorship of the Spanish monarchy, began the European conquest of the Americas. Claims that Italian navigator Amerigo Vespucci reached the mainland first are generally disputed by scholars, but Vespucci is credited as the namesake of "America" and with charting much of the northern coast of South America. Neither Columbus nor Vespucci was the first European to reach North America: Icelandic explorer Leif Ericson is believed to have reached the coast of Labrador in about 1000 A.D.

Columbus's explorations led to Spain's domination of the southern part of the North American continent during the 1500s (*see also* 16–17); other explorers, including John Cabot, explored the north. Cabot was an Italian navigator sailing under the mandate of England's King Henry VII "to seeke

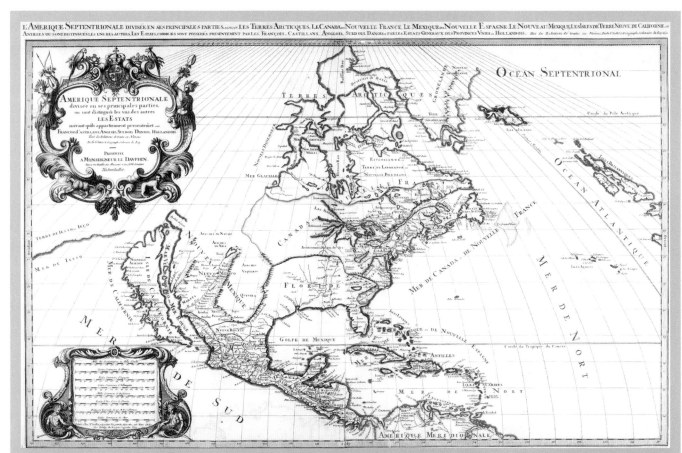

Working for France's King Louis XIII, Nicolas Sanson was one of the most influential of the early European cartographers. In a series of maps called Amerique Septentrionale (North America), drawn from 1650 onward, he recorded the emerging understanding of the New World. In this map, dated 1692, the Atlantic coast of North America and the Gulf of Mexico are charted in some detail; the rest of the territory is divided into the largely unknown regions of Canada, Mexico ("Mexique"), and Florida ("Floride"). California is depicted as an island ("Isle de Californie"); the map suggests the existence of a northwest passage, connecting the Atlantic and Pacific oceans via Hudson Bay. (Courtesy of Hargrett Rare Book & Manuscript Library/University of Georgia Libraries)

out, discouer, and finde whatsoeuer isles, countreys, regions or prouinces of the heathen and infidels whatsoeuer they be, and in what part of the world soeuer they be." When he reached the North American mainland in 1497, Cabot established England's claim to the entire northern continent. The claim to such a vast area was tenuous, not least because French and Dutch mariners were also actively exploring the region. Some, such as Italian navigator Giovanni da Verrazano and Frenchman Jacques Cartier, both of whom sailed on behalf of King Francis I of France, were seeking a westward route to Asia with its lucrative spice trade. The quest for this fabled "northwest passage" inspired others, including English navigators Martin Frobisher, who explored the Canadian Atlantic coast, and Henry Hudson, who charted the Atlantic coast as far north as Greenland and Svalbard (in the Arctic Ocean). The existence of the northwest passage was disproved only in the 1770s by the voyages of England's Captain James Cook, who explored both the Atlantic and Pacific coasts of North America.

Commercial Ventures. Searching for a northwest passage to Asia was only one of the driving forces behind European exploration. While Spain aimed to expand its empire by claiming territory, many English, Dutch, and French expeditions were commercial ventures, often sponsored by private companies. The English Muscovy Company (formed by English merchants in 1555 to improve trade with Russia) funded the early voyages of Hudson, for whom the Hudson Bay was named. The Dutch East India Company (founded by the Dutch in 1602 to advance trade in the Indian Ocean region) underwrote Hudson's later explorations. Cabot's voyages led to the development of the bounteous Newfoundland fisheries (*see also* 178–79), following reports from his sailors that "The sea is swarming with fish, which can be taken not only with the net but

in baskets let down with a stone." Exploring for gold and spices, Cartier laid the basis of the French government's claims to Canada. Cartier also began the lucrative fur trade (*see also* 32–33) along the St. Lawrence River; from the 1670s onward, the fur trade was controlled by the English Hudson's Bay Company. Distracted from his quest for the northwest passage, Frobisher sought gold, but found only fool's gold in the bay—now named for him—near Baffin Island, Canada.

Cartography. Charting seas and mapping land were central to the idea of possessing and exploiting the New World. But maps of the territory were usually produced by European cartographers who seldom saw the lands they charted, relying instead on often highly romanticized letters and journals of individuals like the Franciscan missionary Louis Hennepin, who brought his religion to the Great Lakes and Mississippi regions. The sensational accounts were sometimes the reflection of equally sensational discoveries. Hennepin, the first person to reach the Niagara Falls, described it as "a vast and prodigious cadence of water, which falls down after a surprising and astonishing manner, inasmuch that the Universe does not afford its parallel. . . . "

European cartographers slowly pieced together maps of North America from the sixteenth century onward. German cartographer Martin Waldseemüller drew the first map to separate America properly from Asia and gave the country its name (after Amerigo Vespucci). The first atlas devoted exclusively to the New World, produced in 1597 by Flemish cartographer Cornelius Wyfliet, contained nineteen regional maps. Although later explorers used these maps during their North American voyages, the maps were far from complete or accurate. The maps had more than one purpose; some showed not only the actual geographic features of the New World, but also what explorers hoped might be found in unexplored territories.

Another purpose was to convince potential sponsors that future explorations would be financially worthwhile. Mistakes on early maps of the continent commonly showed a "Sea of Verrazano" off North Carolina, depicted California as an island, and included a northwest passage to the Pacific via the St. Lawrence or Hudson rivers.

Impact. European explorers and mapmakers were not responsible for the first settlements in the New World; Native American peoples had lived in the region for fifteen thousand to twenty thousand years before Columbus arrived (*see also* 14–15). By charting the romantic ideas and hopes of the explorers and making clear how much more land remained to be explored, settled, and exploited, mapmakers helped make possible sponsorship of further expeditions. In addition, by charting the limits of the continent, the resources it could offer, and the best navigation routes, they made the decision to sail to and settle in the New World more realistic to the average person. Settlers and adventurers did not begin just the exploitation of natural resources, they also began the seizure of land, spread disease that decimated Native American populations, and introduced nonnative species (*see also* 4–5), such as foreign cattle. European exploitation and mapping led as much to the destruction and disappearance of the virgin American continent and its peoples as to the creation of a New World.

—*Chris Woodford*

Further Reading
Carnes, Mark C., John Garraty, and Patrick Williams. *Mapping America's Past: A Historical Atlas.* New York: Henry Holt, 1996.
Lopez, Barry. *Arctic Dreams: Imagination and Desire in a Northern Landscape.* New York: Scribner's, 1986.
Meinig, D.W. *The Shaping of America: A Geographical Perspective.* New Haven, Conn.: Yale University Press, 1986.
Wilford, John Noble. *The Mapmakers.* New York: Alfred A. Knopf, 2000.

Commodification of Nature: Export of Resources to the Old World

European governments, in France and England particularly, believed that the North American continent would provide the resources needed to ensure and expand their power. Colonies could supply raw materials or semifinished goods that manufacturers in the mother country would process into finished goods for sale at home or trade abroad. European nations applied this economic policy, which became known as mercantilism, as they sought economic, political, and military power. Between 1492 and the late 1770s, mercantilism fueled the international rivalry for the exploitation of nature, particularly for fish, furs, and forest products on or near the North American continent.

Fish. During the first decade of the sixteenth century, fishermen from England, France, and Portugal worked the Grand Banks off Canada's eastern shore, and many processed their catches on Newfoundland. By 1578 English fishermen regularly trolled their nets for cod (*see also* 178–79), halibut, mackerel, and haddock over the Grand Banks. London merchants collected the fish and sold them in Spain or the Wine Islands of Madeira, the Azores, and the Canaries. Traders from New England (present-day New Hampshire and Maine) also sold the best grades of fish to the Roman Catholic regions of southern Europe, while they traded the poorer grades to Barbados to feed the slave population. The Treaty of Utrecht

(1713) transferred Acadia, present-day Nova Scotia, from France to England, and British fishermen began to use its coast to dry fish for sale in the West Indies. By 1750 some four hundred vessels employing six thousand men from Massachusetts took an annual catch, primarily cod, valued at a quarter million dollars. Whaling had also become an important industry by the mid-eighteenth century. By 1775, New England produced 30,000 barrels of whale oil annually, most of which merchants sent to Great Britain for lighting lamps, lubricating machines, making soap, and finishing leather.

Furs. The Europeans' exploitation of animals for furs (*see also* 32–33) began as an offshoot of their fishing expeditions for cod

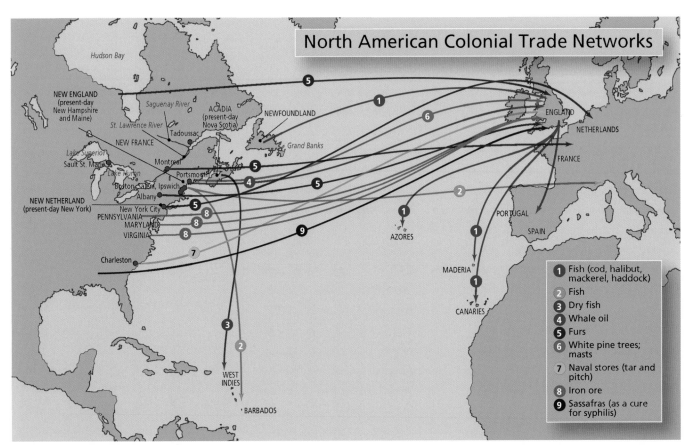

North American Colonial Trade Networks

1. Fish (cod, halibut, mackerel, haddock)
2. Fish
3. Dry fish
4. Whale oil
5. Furs
6. White pine trees; masts
7. Naval stores (tar and pitch)
8. Iron ore
9. Sassafras (as a cure for syphilis)

Fish, furs, and forest products, particularly naval stores, were major extractive industries that took advantage of the environment on the North American continent. British and American colonials traded these products to Europe and the Caribbean in an extensive network that supported their economies as well as the slave trade.

off Canada from the 1490s through the 1580s. In 1581 French merchants sent ships to the St. Lawrence River to trade with Native Americans for furs. By 1600, the French traded extensively for furs at their settlement of Tadoussac at the mouth of the Saguenay River on the St. Lawrence. In 1606, the Dutch entered the northeastern fur trade, and the economy of New Netherland (present-day New York) soon became dependent on this trade. The West India Company monopolized the fur trade, although considerable smuggling occurred within New England and Virginia for shipment to London. By the 1650s, the Dutch shipped more than 45,000 pelts annually from the Hudson Valley.

The British entered the fur trade soon after the Pilgrims arrived in 1620. Beginning in the 1630s, the Puritans controlled the fur trade until the beaver became extinct in southern New England late in the seventeenth century. By 1680, the British fur trade centered at Albany, New York, and the government actively worked to protect it from the French. French interests remained along the St. Lawrence River and at Sault St. Marie between Lake Superior and Lake Huron where Native Americans from many western nations met to trade. Montreal served as the French center for the fur trade. The British, however, controlled the fur trade of the Hudson Bay region. By the mid-seventeenth century the fur trade had become an international business with a complex system of management structures and supply chains.

Although the beaver population declined during the first decade of settlement in the English colonies, the fur trade remained important for the French, who penetrated far into Canada trading and trapping until the British drove them from New France in 1763. To the south, deerskins (*see also* 24) for the manufacture of gloves and other leather apparel replaced the beaver and

mink pelts in the international trade as those animal populations declined. During the 1760s the southeastern Native Americans killed more than 1 million deer annually for the fur trade. By the turn of the nineteenth century, British and American fur traders also began exploiting the sea otters along the Pacific Northwest Coast. British traders primarily sold those pelts in Macao, China, while American traders returned to Boston and New York City with their cargoes for use in domestic manufacture or shipment to Great Britain and France.

Timber. The New World was rich with more than just animal life; forests (*see also* 8–9) covered 90 percent of British North America and provided masts for the British navy and merchant marine as well as planking for shipbuilding. In 1651 British ships arrived in Boston to acquire masts for the Royal Navy, and the cutting of white pine trees became extensive in New England by 1665. The British government encouraged such use by paying a premium of £1 per ton on masts, yards, and bowsprits. In 1691, the Massachusetts Charter reserved all trees measuring 24 inches (0.6 meter) in diameter 3 feet (0.9 meter) from the ground for the British Crown.

The North American colonies also gave England an assured supply of timber products to keep its merchant marine and navy strong without relying on customary suppliers in the Baltic, especially Sweden, where international politics and changing alliances could interrupt or close off supply. In 1705

Further Reading

McCusker, John, and Russell Menard. *The Economy of British America, 1607–1789.* Chapel Hill: University of North Carolina Press, 1991.

Perkins, Edwin J. *The Economy of Colonial America.* 2nd ed. New York: Columbia University Press, 1988.

Phillips, Paul Chrisler, with J. W. Smurr. *The Fur Trade.* 2 vols. Norman: University of Oklahoma Press, 1961.

the British government offered a bounty to encourage the production of naval stores and, by 1718, 82,000 barrels of tar and pitch were exported from the colonies annually. The production of naval stores, especially tar and pitch, was centered in the Carolinas. Sawmills also produced large quantities of lumber and staves, the latter used for making barrels for the shipment of tobacco (*see also* 20–21), molasses, rum, and other products. By 1676 Charleston, South Carolina; Portsmouth, New Hampshire; and Boston, Salem, and Ipswich in Massachusetts were major shipbuilding towns.

Great Britain also exploited the North American forests for the smelting of iron ore (*see also* 72–73), which it needed for its army, navy, and industries. Because of the technology of the age, iron could be smelted only with wood charcoal; England had decimated its forests, thus the New World supply was crucial. Previously, England had re-lied on Sweden for iron ingots (blocks of metal) that it processed into various products, but the forests and iron ore deposits of the North American continent presented the opportunity to end English reliance on Swedish iron. American iron furnaces used the forests to fuel the smelters, and innumerable trees were felled for fuel. By 1775, Pennsylvania, Maryland, and Virginia produced approximately 21,000 tons of iron annually; the American colonies ranked third in world production behind Russia and Sweden.

The British, French, and Dutch exploited the North American continent for fish, furs, and forest products, but the fur-bearing animals suffered the brunt of this exploitation. Indeed, the greatest European damage to the North American environment was the decimation of the fur-bearing animal population in the northeastern and southeastern areas of the present-day United States and the sea otter population in the Pacific Northwest.

—*R. Douglas Hurt*

Pre-Contact: Indigenous Populations in the United States and Canada

Native Americans are descendants of Eurasian people who crossed the Bering Strait from present-day Siberia to western Alaska via a land bridge during the last Ice Age. The ancestors of Native Americans probably migrated to the North American continent between twelve thousand and sixty thousand years ago; by 9500 B.C., these bands of hunters had completed their migration. The ice-free corridor permitted movement from north-western Alaska to the Great Plains, and the ancestors of Native Americans moved south with relative ease. On the eve of European contact, an estimated fifty million Native Americans occupied the North American continent, from the Inuit (Eskimo) in the Arctic to a host of peoples in Mexico. Speaking as many as two thousand languages, a great number of complex Native American cultures had developed, inhabiting the desert Southwest, the humid East, the cool Pacific Northwest Coast, and the cold subarctic. Native Americans adapted to their environments and used the natural resources of their regions.

East and Great Lakes. The Algonquian-speaking cultural groups occupied the eastern seaboard from present-day Nova Scotia to North Carolina, while the

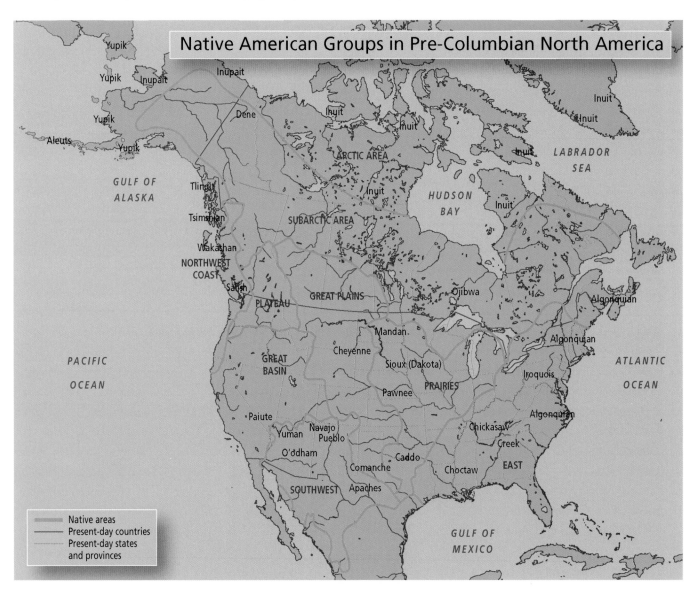

Native American Groups in Pre-Columbian North America

Major Native American cultural groups and lands at the time of European contact.
Source: Adapted from Alice B. Kehoe, *North American Indians: A Comprehensive Account* (Englewood Cliffs, N.J.: Prentice Hall, 1992), 104,161, 225, 288, 430, 481.

Iroquois claimed present-day central New York and lands into the Ohio Valley. The Muskogeans, including the Chickasaw, Choctaw, and Creek, occupied the region from present-day South Carolina and Florida westward across the lower South to the Mississippi River. These Native American groups lived in temporary villages and skillfully used the environment to meet their food needs by hunting, fishing, and raising crops, particularly corn (maize), beans, and squash.

In the region of the Upper Great Lakes, many tribes or cultural groups gathered wild rice, but the Ojibwa also sowed wild rice seed and weeded the crops. Wild rice was a different variety from the numerous varieties of domesticated African rice, which African slaves or their masters introduced to the Chesapeake region and Carolinas during the seventeenth century.

Prairies and Great Plains. When the Europeans arrived in the New World, several Native American cultural groups, including the Caddo, Pawnee, and Mandan, lived on the eastern fringes of the Great Plains because they could not easily traverse or hunt across that vast grassland without horses. These tribes also raised corn, beans, and squash as well as sunflowers and tobacco. During the eighteenth century, horses introduced by the Spanish made their way north from Mexico primarily by trade and capture, and the Sioux (Dakota), Cheyenne, and Comanche, among others, soon spread onto the Great Plains and created a new cultural identity based on buffalo hunting (*see also* 36–37) and the ownership of horses as a measure of wealth and prestige.

Southwest and Great Basin. In the Southwest, indigenous cultural groups, including the Pueblo, O'odham (Pima and Papago), and Yuman, as well as the Navajo who belonged to the complex Apache culture, lived by hunting, gathering, and raising a few crops along river floodplains. Southwestern natives who practiced

agriculture also raised cotton from the Rio Grande to the Hopi country in present-day Arizona. In the Great Basin of Nevada, Utah, and California, Native American bands, such as the Paiutes, lived by gathering seeds of sage, sunflower, and goosefoot (chenopod). They also dug camos (a meadow lily bulb) and wappato (a tuber), for drying and pounding into meal, and they harvested pinyon nuts as well as hunted antelope, rabbits, marmots, and occasionally a few bison and deer.

Northwest. Along the Pacific Northwest Coast, Native American cultural groups, from the Tlingit of southeastern Alaska and the Tsimshian of northern British Columbia to the Wakashan and Salish linguistic families in the south, fished, hunted, and gathered for subsistence. During the late eighteenth century, British and American traders seeking sea otter pelts found the natives to be willing participants in trade, and together they nearly brought the sea otter population to extinction while driving the fur trade (*see also* 32–33) inland for the exploitation of the beaver.

Subarctic and Arctic. To the north, the Inuit lived in the subarctic region from present-day Alaska to Baffin Island and Newfoundland. The Inuit divided into small bands linked by culture and language. In Alaska the northern Inuit are known as Inupait. Along the Arctic coast where the sea froze during the winter, the Inupait's ancestors hunted seals; during the summer they hunted caribou and fished in the Arctic Ocean. Along the Pacific Coast, the sea did not freeze and the Inuit, here known as the Yupik, hunted seals, sea lions, and whales from boats throughout the year. Yupik men also hunted caribou, moose, and fished for salmon, whitefish, cod, and pike. To the south, the Dene, an Athabascan-speaking people, occupied the region from southern Alaska to the Hudson Bay. The Dene adapted to the forested valleys and primarily depended on caribou for their food supply.

Further Reading

Dickason, Olive Patricia. *Canada's First Nations: A History of Founding Peoples from Earliest Times.* 3rd ed. New York: Oxford University Press, 2002.

Hoxie, Frederick E., ed. *Encyclopedia of North American Indians.* Boston: Houghton Mifflin, 1996.

Kehoe, Alice B. *North American Indians: A Comprehensive Account.* Englewood Cliffs, N.J.: Prentice Hall, 1992.

On the Alaskan Peninsula and Aleutian Islands, the Aleut took advantage of the Japanese Current that kept the water of the Pacific Ocean relatively warm and drew whales, which they hunted, to the area in the summer. The rocky islands provided breeding areas for sea lions, seals, walruses, and birds, which the Aleut also hunted; the absence of sea ice permitted fishing throughout the year. The Aleut harvested berries and kelp for their major plant food, and those who lived on the peninsula also hunted caribou and bear.

At the time of European contact, each Native American cultural group had adapted to its environment, using it for food, shelter, and articles for trade, but the arrival of Europeans would significantly disrupt the indigenous way of life. Native American populations were decimated by European-borne diseases to which they did not have immunity. As Native Americans adopted European plants and animals (*see also* 4–5), they began to use their environment differently, shifting from their earlier forms of subsistence. European demand for furs destroyed fur-bearing populations as Native Americans hunted and trapped them to exchange their hides for European goods. In time, many Native American groups would clash with or retreat from the European peoples (*see also* 24–25) who had vastly different views about the appropriate use of the environment and the use of the natural resources on the North American continent.

—*R. Douglas Hurt*

Spanish in Florida and the Southwest

I n the 1500s the Spanish founded settlements in the present-day U.S. Southwest and Florida. The additional lands enlarged the territorial jurisdiction of New Spain (present-day Mexico), established a defensive zone against rival European powers, and were a possible source of mineral wealth. The indigenous inhabitants of these lands were equally important to the Spanish Crown as potential converts to Roman Catholic Christianity, laborers, mates, tax-paying subjects, and military allies. To establish permanent settlements the Spaniards had to adapt to the environment by creating irrigation networks, devising land policies, and introducing crops and animals suitable to the Southwest's dry climate.

Early Exploration. Spaniards began visiting Florida and the Southwest in the early sixteenth century in search of mineral wealth and indigenous laborers. Explorers on an expedition to Florida in 1513 failed to find gold, but they did claim the land for the Spanish Crown and attempted to make slaves of Native Americans for shipment to Spain's Caribbean colonies. Alarmed by the establishment in Florida of a colony of French Huguenots in 1562, Spanish officials sent a military expedition to construct a series of presidios (forts) to guard the peninsula's coasts. Accompanying the soldiers were Franciscan missionaries who established Christian missions in northern Florida. Conflicts with Native Americans led the Spanish to abandon most of these settlements except St. Augustine, which is the oldest continuously inhabited European settlement in North America.

The exploration of the Gulf Coast and the Southwest by Spaniards was the unplanned result of an expedition to Florida in 1528 that lost its direction. The written account of a member of the lost party, featuring tales of large native civilizations and turing tales of large native civilizations and cities of gold in the vicinity of New Mexico, inspired future expeditions. The search for these fabled mines and a desire to convert Native Americans to Christianity eventually led to the establishment of Spanish settlements, Santa Fe and Albuquerque for example, among the Pueblo tribes of New Mexico in the early 1600s.

Settlement. In the seventeenth and eighteenth centuries, the Spanish spread throughout the Southwest as missionaries sought more Native American converts and as a defensive measure against other European powers that were colonizing North America. To claim more land for the Spanish Crown and additional souls for the Catholic church, Jesuit missionaries moved into southern Arizona in the 1690s to work among the Pima tribe. Threatened by French colonization along the Mississippi River and in Louisiana, Spanish officials also sent colonists to establish a series of presidios and Franciscan

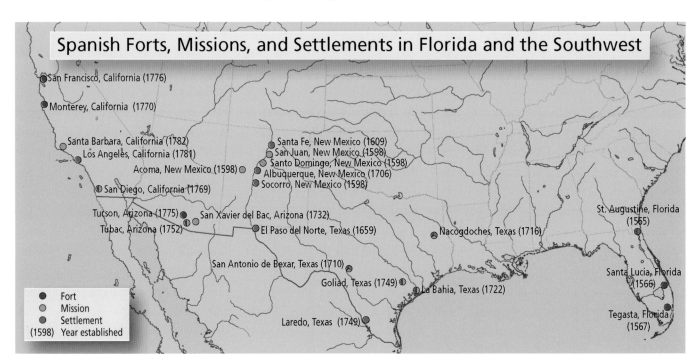

Spanish Forts, Missions, and Settlements in Florida and the Southwest

San Francisco, California (1776)
Monterey, California (1770)
Santa Barbara, California (1782)
Los Angeles, California (1781)
Acoma, New Mexico (1598)
San Diego, California (1769)
Tucson, Arizona (1775)
Tubac, Arizona (1752)
San Xavier del Bac, Arizona (1732)
Santa Fe, New Mexico (1609)
San Juan, New Mexico (1598)
Santo Domingo, New Mexico (1598)
Albuquerque, New Mexico (1706)
Socorro, New Mexico (1598)
El Paso del Norte, Texas (1659)
Nacogdoches, Texas (1716)
St. Augustine, Florida (1565)
San Antonio de Bexar, Texas (1710)
Goliad, Texas (1749)
La Bahia, Texas (1722)
Santa Lucia, Florida (1566)
Laredo, Texas (1749)
Tegasta, Florida (1567)

- Fort
- Mission
- Settlement
(1598) Year established

Spaniards expanded into Florida from the Caribbean and into the present-day southwestern United States from northern Mexico beginning in the early sixteenth century. The settlements included missions, presidios (forts), and towns.

Source: Adapted from Helen Hornbeck Tanner, ed., *The Settling of North America: The Atlas of the Great Migrations into North America from the Ice Age to the Present* (New York: Macmillan, 1995).

missions throughout Texas in the 1710s. The forts served to protect the missions from attacks by Native Americans and to guard against incursions by rival European powers. This defensive colonization led to the founding of San Antonio and Nacogdoches in Texas as well as Tubac and Tucson in Arizona. A rumored Russian invasion of the Pacific Northwest caused Spanish officials to establish a string of protective settlements in California, including four presidios, twenty-five missions, and several towns, among which were San Diego, Monterey, and Los Angeles.

The Southwest's arid climate limited the spread of the Spanish throughout the borderlands. Scarcity of water restricted the construction of Spanish settlements to areas along rivers where the colonists could build irrigation networks. The need for water led Spanish colonists in each settlement to build irrigation channels before constructing permanent homes. A special administrator in each town oversaw the irrigation system and distributed water rights among residents, each of whom had a responsibility to build and maintain the community's irrigation channels. The scarcity of water made allocations of water rights for grazing and irrigation equally as important as distributions of land, if not more so. Land grants to individuals and communities were typically larger in arid regions than in areas where animals could graze on lush vegetation. The tracts were usually long, rectangular parcels instead of square grants, with small segments bordering rivers to assure the greatest number of grantees with access to water.

The large distances between towns in the borderlands and population centers in central New Spain also limited the growth of settlements. Colonists throughout the Southwest had difficulty obtaining trade goods and military supplies because Spain's mercantile system required all trade to pass through official channels, which resulted in delays and scarcity. The restrictions on trade undercut the incentive to produce surpluses and forced Spanish communities to rely on trade with Native Americans, pay exorbitant prices for common goods, or engage in contraband trade with French or British colonists.

Colonists throughout the borderlands replicated the urban layouts familiar to them by organizing towns along Spanish models. Most towns were built near presidios and missions because civilians needed military protection and religious counsel. The center of each settlement was the main plaza, which was lined with government structures, church buildings, and shops. Surrounding the main square were residential streets laid out in a grid pattern, common pasture, municipal property, and private farmlands. Although the lack of building supplies and money for capital improvements often prevented colonists from achieving the ideal city design, the Spanish urban model influenced the layout of their most prominent towns at the end of the eighteenth century: St. Augustine, San Antonio, Santa Fe, and Los Angeles.

Natives. Faced with a labor shortage throughout the Southwest, the Spaniards competed with other European colonists for control over Native Americans. The friars gathered the indigenous peoples in missions and sought to convert them to Christianity. In addition to religious instruction, the missionaries educated Native Americans about Spanish society and language in an effort to transform them into loyal Spanish subjects. Newly converted Native Americans provided the labor to both feed the mission population and finance its operations by constructing the missions' buildings, harvesting crops, tending livestock, and processing raw materials into finished goods. Failing to find large mineral deposits, Spaniards focused on subsistence agriculture (including corn, wheat, and cotton) as well as sheep and cattle breeding. Civilians secured Native American workers through *encomiendas* (legal titles to their labor), *repartamientos* (rotary labor draft), or *rescate* (ransoms paid for Native American captives). The dearth of workers combined with Spanish soldiers' low pay prompted the soldiers to capture Native Americans and sell them into slavery.

Impact. As the first Europeans to settle the Southwest and Florida, Spanish colonists transformed the environment and culture of the regions. They introduced European crops, livestock, buildings, and tools as well as Spanish law, language, societal norms, and the Roman Catholic religion. Interactions with the region's indigenous peoples, in turn, changed the Spaniards. Spanish society altered as European colonists adopted indigenous crops, construction methods, and hunting techniques. Spanish culture also changed with the incorporation of indigenous religious, language, and dietary practices, and, perhaps most important, as a result of the increase in the number of children resulting from Spanish-Native American unions. Future communities would continue to see the legacy of the Spanish-Native American intermixture in the place names, building styles, food, and population of the Southwest and Florida.

—*Omar Valerio-Jiménez*

Further Reading

Hine, Robert V., and John Mack Faragher. *The American West: A New Interpretive History.* New Haven, Conn.: Yale University Press, 2000.

Hundley, Norris, Jr. *The Great Thirst: Californians and Water, 1770s–1990s.* Rev. ed. Berkeley: University of California Press, 2001.

Kessell, John L. *Spain in the Southwest: A Narrative History of Colonial New Mexico,* *Arizona, Texas, and California.* Norman: University of Oklahoma Press, 2002.

Weber, David J. *The Spanish Frontier in North America.* New Haven, Conn.: Yale University Press, 1992.

White, Richard. *"It's Your Misfortune and None of My Own": A History of the American West.* Norman: University of Oklahoma Press, 1991.

New England Agrarian Commonwealths

Early New England settlers in the 1620s brought with them not only seeds, livestock, and fruit trees (*see also* 4–5) but also a traditional pattern of open-field villages that would prove quite effective in their new environment. The original settlers, or proprietors, of a new town would typically each receive a house lot in the village center large enough for a house, garden, small orchard, outbuildings, and night pasture, as well as plots in common meadows for hay, fields for crops, and woodland for building materials, fuels, and fencing. They also had shared rights to and responsibilities for the remaining pasture, rough woods, and other lands in the town or commonwealth. Traditions of management and governance developed in these commonwealths would later influence the formation of the United States.

Settlement. These New England colonists benefited from several factors that greatly contributed to their success. Native populations had been significantly reduced by disease introduced by explorers during the previous century and almost all the settlements established before 1650 made use of sites previously cleared by Native Americans, either along the immediate coast or on the lower reaches of major rivers such as the Connecticut or Merrimack. In 1629, the king of England chartered the Massachusetts Bay Company, composed of Puritan investors, to establish and support a colony in New England. Rather than mandating management from England, this charter allowed for the creation of a general court in Boston to oversee colonial affairs. This general court set requirements and granted establishment rights to towns, but then left the governance to individual town boards and officials. Proprietors did not pay for their lots, but were expected to maintain

fencing and contribute in many other ways to the social and economic well-being of the town or commonwealth. Typically, the head of each household had a voice in town decisions. Finally, unlike the typical English system of tenant farmers, proprietors became freeholders (owners) of their lots and could transfer or sell their rights subject to agreement by town members.

As populations grew in the mid-seventeenth century, new towns were established farther inland, but still mostly along rivers on sites with natural wet meadows for hay. Pasture and woodlots covered the nearby hills. The Massachusetts Bay Charter provided for compensation for native lands and initial relations with native groups were generally peaceful. However, growing European populations led to increasing tensions that culminated in the uprising known as King Philip's War (1675–76). Upland settlement

increased after this war, but the protracted French and Indian wars, starting in the 1690s, made outlying villages subject to intermittent raids and slowed settlement expansion through the early decades of the eighteenth century. New towns largely filled gaps within settled areas. With the signing of the Treaty of Paris (1763), which ended these hostilities, settlements rapidly extended into what are now northwest Connecticut, the Massachusetts Berkshires, Vermont, New Hampshire, and southwestern Maine.

Unlike the early towns along the coast and rivers, which made use of marshes, meadows, and abandoned native fields, new upland towns were cleared from forest (*see also* 6–7) and here the best farmland was often found on broad, relatively level ridges of till deposited by the glaciers. The steeper, often swampy, narrow north-south valleys carved by the glaciers remained woodlots,

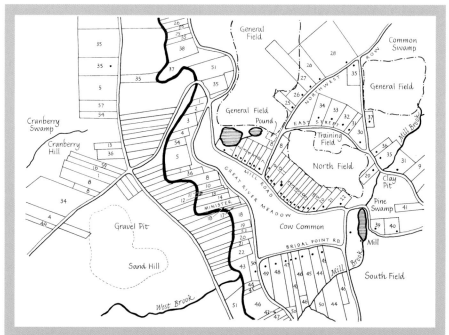

In this historical map (c. 1650) of the Sudbury Village Center in Massachusetts, numbers (1–51) indicate ownership and dots indicate house lots. Each proprietor received a house lot in the village center and other plots of land scattered throughout the town. The remaining land was held in common ownership.
Source: Reproduction from Sumner Chilton Powell, *Puritan Village: The Formation of a New England Town* (Middletown, Conn.: Wesleyan University Press, 1963), plate XIV.

Historical map (c. 1640) showing location of plots granted to John Goodnow in Sudbury, Massachusetts. Each proprietor received plots of meadow, field, and upland distributed throughout the town.
Source: Reproduction from Sumner Chilton Powell, *Puritan Village: The Formation of a New England Town* (Middletown, Conn.: Wesleyan University Press, 1963), plate XV.

supplying fuel and other wood for farms. Moreover, following the wars, land was often auctioned to pay war debts or granted to soldiers or their heirs in compensation for service. These changes signaled a gradual shift from the granting of free land to form communal villages toward a more materialistic structure based on commerce.

Agricultural Practices. The early commonwealths were based on self-sufficient agriculture. Animals grazed the upland pastures and were fed hay harvested from the salt marshes and meadows. Manure collected from the night pastures fertilized the fields and gardens growing grain and vegetables to feed farm families. Native corn proved a much more reliable crop than other grains and

was often fertilized with small herring, or alewives, which swam in great numbers up even small streams to spawn in headwater ponds. Orchards provided table fruit and, more important, hard cider, the favored drink throughout the region.

Soon agricultural patterns developed in certain regions, especially those near water transportation, specializing in particular crops for commerce, such as onions in coastal Rhode Island and cattle in coastal New Hampshire. Towns along the Connecticut River early on grew tobacco, a very valuable commercial crop. Farm animals provided meat, dairy products, and fiber as well as a mobile trade commodity. Local resources were also exploited as coastal towns in New Hampshire and

Maine exported lumber and wood for fuel, and other coastal communities developed commerce in dried and salted fish.

Trade. The English settlers in New England were familiar with a market economy and quickly established extensive trade relationships (*see also* 12–13). Fishing boats and merchant ships were provisioned from nearby towns, southern tobacco plantations (*see also* 20–21) were a market for foodstuffs, food and wood for fuel were shipped to growing towns all along the coast, lumber and wood products were sent to Europe and England, and animals, food, and other supplies went to the West Indies. All this trade also led to an active shipbuilding industry in coastal towns.

The independence, self-sufficiency, private ownership, common responsibility, and equal representation that typified these early commonwealths strongly influenced the founders of a new nation in 1776. These characteristics persist in the town meeting form of government still practiced today in many New England towns. The village pattern, with colonial houses clustered along streets surrounding an open common and fields beyond, although now often regrown to forest or recently developed, remains a defining feature of New England.

—*John F. O'Keefe*

Further Reading

Albers, Jan. *Hands on the Land: A History of the Vermont Landscape.* Cambridge, Mass.: MIT Press, 2000.

Cronon, William. *Changes in the Land: Indians, Colonists, and the Ecology of New England.* New York: Hill and Wang, 1983.

Powell, Sumner Chilton. *Puritan Village: The Formation of a New England Town.* Middletown, Conn.: Wesleyan University Press, 1963.

Russell, Howard S. *A Long, Deep Furrow: Three Centuries of Farming in New England.* Hanover, N.H.: University Press of New England, 1982.

Chesapeake Bay Region: Early Tobacco South

Tobacco and tobacco planters played a prominent role in the long history of the exploitation of both soils and humans in the American South. After the first permanent English settlement was established at Jamestown in 1607 in what would become the state of Virginia, colonists struggled to find a way to support themselves with soils and in a climate that were alien to them. Tobacco appeared to provide a solution but also created problems: depletion of soil fertility and increased soil erosion. Native Americans had cultivated tobacco in small amounts for medicinal purposes and as a social lubricant long before Europeans arrived. Although the English eventually settled upon a different variety for commercial purposes than that grown by Native Americans, they first learned about the weed from Native Americans.

Export. By the second decade of the Virginia colony, tobacco was well established as a valuable crop and the Jamestown settlers were exporting more than 60,000 pounds (22,400 kilograms) of tobacco a year. The English Navigation Acts of the 1660s designated tobacco as one of the protected and tariff-free "enumerated goods" that were funneled through English ports, thus making it a favored colonial export by the extensive English commercial empire (*see also* 12–13). By the end of the century, Virginia and, to a lesser extent, Maryland had prospered from the cultivation and sale of tobacco. The greatest proportion of exported American tobacco came from plantations along the shores of Chesapeake Bay and its tributaries. By 1775, tobacco represented 75 percent of Virginia's total exports—and 60 percent of the total colonial exports—to England. The first settlements were located on the long shoreline of the bay and on the extensive navigable waterways that fed into it; thus transport was relatively easy—ships that carried Virginia tobacco—to England could easily moor themselves on the shoreline of the plantations that grew tobacco.

Labor. Finding the workforce (*see also* 30–31) to grow this labor-intensive crop proved to be a greater challenge than figuring out how to grow tobacco. At first, the Virginia colonists relied on indentured servants from England. A high unemployment rate in England in the first half of the

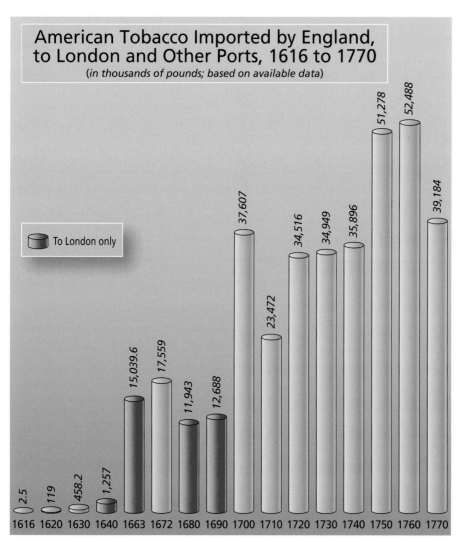

American Tobacco Imported by England, to London and Other Ports, 1616 to 1770
(in thousands of pounds; based on available data)

To London only

2.5 · 119 · 458.2 · 1,257 · 15,039.6 · 17,559 · 11,943 · 12,688 · 37,607 · 23,472 · 34,516 · 34,949 · 35,896 · 51,278 · 52,488 · 39,184

1616 1620 1630 1640 1663 1672 1680 1690 1700 1710 1720 1730 1740 1750 1760 1770

Tobacco production rose in enormous increments in the first fifty years after tobacco growing was embraced by farmers in Virginia in the seventeenth century. But the expansion into fresh lands and the embrace of slavery as a labor system, as well as the sustained commitment to tobacco culture by leading Chesapeake planters, contributed to continued—and significant—increases in production after 1670 and into the eighteenth century. Early planters kept track of their tobacco production by recording the number of units that they sold.
Source: Data from U.S. Bureau of the Census, *Historical Statistics of the United States, Colonial Times to 1970.* Bicentennial ed., Part 1. Series Z 441-448 and 457-459 (Washington, D.C.: Government Printing Office, 1975), 1190–1191.

seventeenth century produced a ready supply of poor laborers who were willing to work for four or five years in Virginia in return for passage to the colony. But these laborers had to be replaced often: the mortality rate was very high; when they ran away they could blend easily into other white populations in the colonies and were therefore usually irretrievable; and when their terms of indenture were up, they were free to leave. Tobacco growers then began using imported Africans as laborers. By the 1660s, the colony had established statutes that reflected the different status of Africans in the colony and the emergence of slavery as an institution. By the end of the century most of the planting, hoeing, harvesting, and curing of Virginia's profitable weed was done by African slaves. Tobacco and slavery became intertwined; by the end of the seventeenth century, both were deeply entrenched in Virginia.

Agricultural Practices. Tobacco created enormous revenues for a few, but this wealth rested upon the labor of countless slaves and the exploitation and eventual depletion of the soil. Soils in the southern colonies were generally poor. They tended to be clayey, with little organic content. A hot climate and heavy rainfall caused organic material on the soil's surface to decompose quickly, returning few nutrients to the soil. When planters cleared extensive tracts of forest to grow tobacco—a plant that requires much space

Seventeenth-century engraving of a Virginia tobacco farm. (© Bettmann/Corbis)

between the rows and consequently offers little protection to the soil from heavy rain—the soil was exposed to further leaching and erosion. Tobacco itself is a heavy "feeder" and quickly exhausted the scant nutrients in the soil in which it was grown. Furthermore, tobacco growers practiced monoculture, so the fields in which tobacco was grown received none of the benefits of crop rotation.

Virginia planters recognized that the yield of a tobacco crop was low, and tended to decline quickly on newly cultivated lands that even at the outset were not very fertile. But the complex equation of labor, market, and production costs kept them committed to tobacco until late in the colonial era. When land was cheap and labor expensive, clearing new land to farm was more economical than engaging in labor-intensive procedures for improving the soil or letting the land lie fallow for a year or two before returning it to production. Some planters had extensive plantations and could easily clear new fields on the land they already possessed; others moved to new tracts of

land, cleared yet more forests, and cultivated tobacco there. A few planters experimented with crop rotation and with adding marl and other materials to tobacco fields to retain or restore fertility, but these efforts were mainly eccentric experiments that were marginal to the mainstream of southern tobacco agriculture.

Virginia planters had the embarrassing honor, then, of producing the conditions for the first large-scale soil erosion in the New World. They also pioneered a process of "soil mining," which extracted fertility from the soil without replacing it, which became a tradition in southern tobacco and cotton agriculture until the mid-nineteenth century. Tobacco continued to be an important crop in the South after the Revolutionary War, but the largest portion of it would be raised in Tennessee, Kentucky, and North Carolina rather than Virginia. Tobacco was often a very profitable weed, but the wealth it yielded required the degradation of both human beings and the land.

—Mart A. Stewart

Further Reading

Breen, T. H. *Tobacco Culture: The Mentality of the Great Tidewater Planters on the Eve of the Revolution.* Princeton, N.J.: Princeton University Press, 1985.

Kirby, Jack Temple. *Poquosin: A Study of Rural Landscape and Society.* Chapel Hill: University of North Carolina Press, 1995.

Kulikoff, Allan. *Tobacco and Slaves: The Development of Southern Cultures in the Chesapeake, 1680–1800.* Chapel Hill: University of North Carolina Press, 1986.

The Seigneurial System in New France

European settlers in North America believed that land was a commodity that could be bought, rented, and sold. In New France, the colonial government imported the feudal system, which divided the rural population into seigneurs (landlords) and habitants (tenants) who shared the attributes of land ownership. From the beginning of large-scale French settlement until the mid-nineteenth century, the seigneurial system significantly influenced landholding patterns and social relations between settlers.

Land Grants. Initial grants of seigneuries (estates) were made to institutions like religious orders or to elite individuals, including nobles, officials, military officers, and bourgeois. But anyone could buy land from a seigneur. In Canada, the French Crown granted land to seigneurs in return for a pledge of *foi et hommage* (fidelity and homage); seigneurs, in turn, divided their lordships into a seigneurial domaine and habitant farms. Seigneurs could farm the domaine themselves or rent it to tenants. They were obliged, however, to grant *routres* (tenant farms) to habitants.

Habitants. Under this system, habitants were required to clear the land and establish farms. They owed the seigneurs annual payments of *cens et rentes. Cens* were a nominal fee that served as a token of subordination; *rentes* were a more substantial rent that could be paid in cash or produce. To grind their wheat, habitants used the seigneurial mill; for this service, they gave the seigneurs a fourteenth of the grain, a fee known as *banalities*. Habitants could sell their farms, in which case the seigneur received *lods et ventes,* a twelfth of the payment, from the buyer.

Settlement. Patterns of settlement in New France were dictated by geography and the preferences of habitant farmers rather than by the seigneurial system. In the seventeenth and eighteenth centuries, rivers formed the principal avenues of commerce and communication in Canada. The desirability of riverfront land led to the granting of seigneuries in the shape of long, narrow rectangles, located at right angles to the rivers. Seigneuries, in turn, were subdivided into long, narrow lots that gave each family access to the rivers. When riverfront land was filled up, seigneurs granted new rows of *rangs* (narrow farms) behind the river lots. This arrangement allowed families to live close to their neighbors, while avoiding concentration in villages where they would have been under the observation of seigneurs, clerics, and government officials. Pehr Kalm, a Swedish botanist who visited New France in the mid-eighteenth century, suggested that all of Canada

. . . could really be called a village, beginning at Montreal and ending at Quebec, which is at a distance of more than one hundred and eighty miles . . . The prospect is exceedingly beautiful when the river flows on for several miles in a straight line, because it then shortens the distances between the houses, and makes them form one continued village.

Agricultural Practices. R. C. Harris, a leading historian of the seigneurial system, has calculated that about 40 percent of the cleared arable land of a representative habitant farm would be planted with wheat. Farmers devoted about 15 percent to oats and barley—destined to serve as animal feed—peas, and a kitchen garden of onions, cabbage, lettuce, beans, carrots, cucumbers, red beets, radish, parsnips, thyme, and marjoram. The remainder of the land lay fallow, providing pasturage for horses, cattle, oxen, and pigs. "The sown fields," observed Kalm, "looked yellow at a distance and the fallow ones green." Much of this produce was paid to the seigneur in rent, to the clergy in tithes (taxes), and consumed by the habitant family. Surpluses could be sold in the towns or, in the eighteenth century, exported to Louisbourg in Acadia (Nova Scotia) or the French West Indies.

Decline. A feudal system that divided settlers into landlords and tenants might seem out of place in frontier America, but during the French colonial era the system worked reasonably well. However, following the opening of export markets in Louisbourg in 1720, and in Britain after the British conquest in 1760, seigneurs guarded their rights more rigorously and charged increasingly higher fees for land. Resentment among habitants about these changes contributed to the outbreak of armed risings in 1775 and 1776, concurrent with the American Revolution, and in 1837 and 1838 during the Lower Canadian Resistance. The seigneurial system was finally abolished in 1854, when habitants were permitted to buy their land from the seigneurs. The geographic impact of the seigneurial system, however, has persisted into the twenty-first century. Airline passengers flying over Québec will see the narrow *routres* of former seigneuries, still in use as working farms.

—*Peter MacLeod*

Further Reading
Dechêne, Louise. *Habitants and Merchants in Seventeenth Century Montreal.* Montreal: McGill-Queen's University Press, 1992.
Greer, Allan. *Peasant, Lord, and Merchant: Rural Society in Three Quebec Parishes, 1740–1840.* Toronto: University of Toronto Press, 1985.
Harris, Richard Colebrook. *The Seigneurial System in Early Canada: A Geographical Study.* Madison: University of Wisconsin Press, 1984.

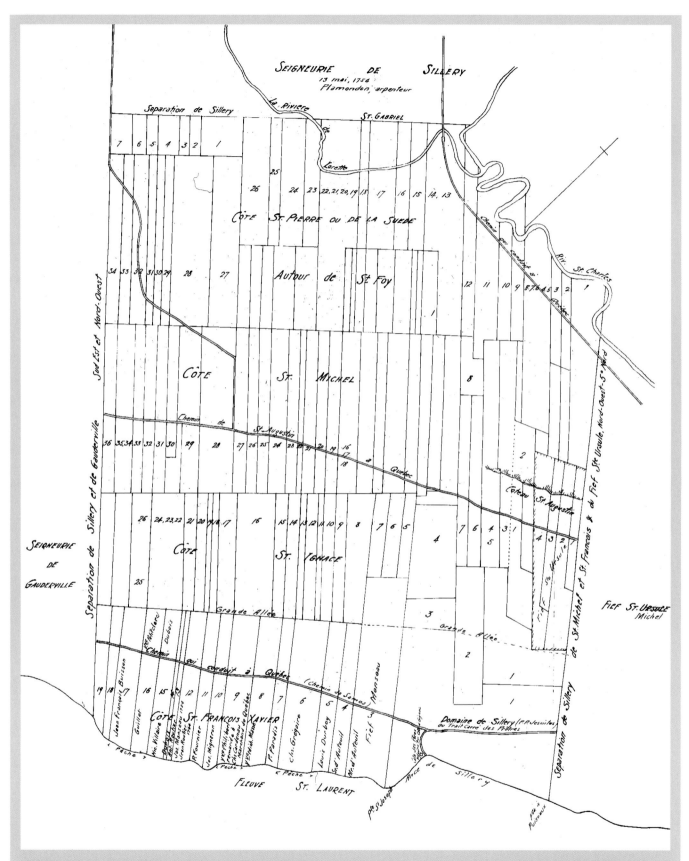

This historical map of the seigneurie of Sillery, produced by surveyor Ignace Plamondon in 1754, clearly shows the narrow rectangles of seigneuries and routres. Sillery, located along the St. Lawrence River near Québec City, was named after Noël Brulart de Sillery, a deeply religious Frenchman who was a knight of Malta and made a large donation to finance a Jesuit mission on the site. The mission later moved, and French settlers occupied the seigneurie. (National Archives of Canada, NMC-20261)

Relationship to the Land: Indigenous and European Views

North America's native people (*see also* 14–15) used the continent's vast resources to sustain themselves. Europeans, however, saw North America as a wilderness ripe for conquest and its resources as potential commodities for the world market (*see also* 12–13). As the European system of land use became pervasive along the Atlantic Coast, Native Americans and colonists alike had to adapt to dramatic changes in the natural environment.

Native Practices and Beliefs. Across much of pre-Columbian North America, Native Americans practiced shifting seasonal subsistence. In the north, natives relied on fish and wild plants during the warm months; in the fall and winter, they hunted beaver, deer, elk, moose, and caribou. Farther south, where the milder climate allowed for agriculture, Native Americans cultivated various foods, including corn, beans, and squash. Beans helped replace nitrogen taken out of the soil by corn; cornstalks, in turn, served as bean poles and the spreading leaves of squash plants helped limit erosion and keep down weeds. Because their diet changed as various foods became available, Native Americans valued a river, field, or patch of woods for what it could produce at a given season. The European belief that land should be used in perpetuity for a single purpose was a concept alien to Native American culture.

Native American societies were hierarchical and competitive, but they did not encourage unrestricted accumulation of land or material possessions. Instead, native culture emphasized concern for the communal good. On the Pacific Coast, such values were expressed in potlatch ceremonies, elaborate rituals of feasting and dancing during which tribal leaders distributed great stores of food and possessions to others in the community. Those who gave away the most possessions earned the greatest respect. Generosity and friendship, not material wealth, became the basis for status and an effective way of assuring allegiance and maintaining social order.

Native peoples believed that everything in nature had spiritual power. They practiced many rituals designed to ensure proper relationships between humans and the land's other inhabitants. Plains tribes, who depended on buffalo (*see also* 36–37) for food and other necessities, used elaborate dances, songs, and sacred stones to attract bison for slaughter. Before killing the animals, Plains hunters offered words of respect and apology, thanking the buffalo for allowing themselves to be killed.

Droughts, floods, early frosts, or other unseasonable weather might ruin crops and force pre-Columbian native peoples to rely more on game and wild foods. During such lean times, hunters occasionally pressured and reduced local animal populations. Where Native Americans farmed intensively, as on the floodplains of the Southeast, even complementary crops such as beans and corn eventually depleted soils and forced villages to relocate. Like humans everywhere, native

Wildlife as Commodity: White-Tailed Deer in the Southeast

When Europeans landed in North America, the continent was home to some forty million white-tailed deer. The animals were especially important to Native Americans of the Southeast who depended on venison for food and on deerskins for clothing. In addition, deer had a prominent place in southeastern cosmology. Upon taking one of the animals, hunters offered prayers asking for the deer's forgiveness.

To European settlers, though, deer were primarily a source of leather, a commodity much valued on the other side of the Atlantic. Buckskin breeches were especially popular among English aristocrats who wore the garments much like modern Americans wear jeans. Early explorers offered Native Americans metal utensils in exchange for the hides. By the 1700s, however, English traders used liquor to barter for deerskins. In a native culture unfamiliar with alcohol and addiction, liquor created its own infinite demand. Over the course of the eighteenth century, Native Americans also suffered devastating losses from Old World diseases and became increasingly dependent on tools, guns, and other items supplied by colonial merchants.

Forced to trade to survive, southeastern Native Americans killed deer in unprecedented numbers. Rituals became less important and native hunters often left skinned carcasses in the woods to rot. By 1715, one million deerskins had been shipped from Virginia and South Carolina; two million from South Carolina alone by 1740, another one million from Savannah, Georgia, by 1773. By 1800, many southeastern Native American cultures, including the Creek, Choctaw, and Cherokee, faced serious shortages of venison and deerskins.

Worried that deer might become extinct, colonial governments made it illegal to take deerskins during certain seasons. In 1772, Virginia outlawed all commercial hunting for four years. The white-tailed deer was no longer simply a commodity. It was also an endangered species.

peoples left their mark on the land. But, in keeping with their belief system, they did not consider themselves separate from or superior to the rest of the natural world.

European Practices and Views. In contrast, the Europeans who settled North America drew sharp distinctions between themselves and nature. They regarded unsettled regions as "wilderness," which to them meant "desert" or "wasteland." As a result, Europeans failed to realize that Native Americans depended on uncultivated lands, such as forests, for much of their food. Nor did colonists understand the division of labor within Native American society. Only Native American women, who tended the fields, appeared to engage in productive labor. Europeans viewed hunting and fishing—crucial subsistence activities performed by Native American men—as sport or diversion. Convinced that the native peoples did not make adequate use of the land, most colonists believed they had the right to tame the wilderness and make it productive.

Europeans came from a Christian culture that celebrated individual achievement and took literally the Genesis directive to exert dominion over the Earth. Some

Further Reading
Cronon, William. *Changes in the Land: Indians, Colonists, and the Ecology of New England.* New York: Hill and Wang, 1983.
Hughes, J. Donald. *North American Indian Ecology.* 2nd ed. El Paso: Texas Western Press, University of Texas El Paso, 1996.

Krech, Shepard, III. *The Ecological Indian: Myth and History.* New York: W.W. Norton, 1999.
Silver, Timothy. *A New Face on the Countryside: Indians, Colonists, and Slaves in South Atlantic Forests, 1500–1800.* Cambridge: Cambridge University Press, 1990.

English Protestants, including New England Puritans (*see also* 18–19), believed that civilizing the landscape was an important step toward personal salvation. Wilderness, they thought, was the dark domain of Satan. When English people cut trees and planted fields, the settlers battled the devil and engaged in the kind of hard work that could lead to worldly success and a place in God's eternal kingdom.

By the early sixteenth century, Europe was part of a world economy in which profit and material possessions defined one's status. Within that capitalist system, land became a symbol of wealth and agriculture a means of producing commodities for the market. Accordingly, colonial farming differed from Native American farming in important ways. Native peoples used their fields for subsistence, whereas European settlers grew cash crops such as tobacco (*see also*

20–21) and rice. Europeans usually fenced their plots and sowed them with a single crop, a practice known as monoculture, which frequently led to erosion and soil exhaustion. To obtain meat, Native Americans hunted game animals, whereas Europeans raised livestock, such as cattle and hogs, for food and export. Other resources, including fish, deerskins, beaver pelts, and timber also became staples in the transatlantic trade. Although they sometimes feared its wildness, Europeans viewed North America as a bountiful land that, once settled, would yield splendid rewards.

Impact of European Settlement. The European presence dramatically affected native peoples and the land they inhabited. Old World diseases, to which Native Americans lacked immunity, depopulated villages, sometimes by as much as 90 percent. Surviving Native Americans became increasingly enmeshed in the world economy and began to hunt animals for their fur and skin (*see also* 32–33) to supply the European market. Such trade led to the near extinction of deer, beaver, and other animals. With game in short supply, some of the remaining groups of Native Americans began keeping livestock both for subsistence and for sale to colonial merchants. Europeans, too, encountered unexpected difficulties. Local shortages of game, timber, and firewood prompted colonial authorities to pass legislation designed to limit hunting and curb commercial exploitation of forests (*see also* 8–9). In a world dominated by European values, both cultures faced scarcity in what had once been a land of plenty.

—*Timothy Silver*

In this 1591 engraving by Theodor de Bry, native men and women from present-day Florida cultivate a field and plant corn or beans. (From the collections of the Library of Congress)

CHAPTER TWO

Expansion and Conflict
(1770s–1850s)

"Among the lucky circumstances that favored the establishment and assured the maintenance of a democratic republic in the United States," wrote French aristocrat Alexis de Tocqueville in *Democracy in America* (1835), "the most important was the choice of the land itself in which the Americans live." But the presence of a well-wooded land was not enough, he declared in his famous treatise: "while their fathers gave them a love of equality and liberty . . . it was God who, by handing a limitless continent over to them, gave them the means of long remaining equal and free."

Expansion. Few in the United States or Canada who moved west in the late eighteenth and early nineteenth centuries to conquer this land would have disputed Tocqueville's claims. Both Canada and the United States believed that western expansion was given divine sanction, driven by democratic impulse, and framed around "Manifest Destiny." Many read with approval American poet William Cullen Bryant's 1824 praise of the vast wilderness, his Romantic assertion that "The groves were God's first temple." This did not inhibit human manipulation of the environment, as long as it was done in good faith: "Ere man learned/To hew the shaft, and lay the architrave/And spread the roof above them." Moving west and south, felling trees, and planting wheat, cotton, or corn was the Lord's work— whether the labor used was paid or slave.

Forests. When the European migrants first penetrated the dense forests, they were overwhelmed by the quantity and quality of the woods. The British and French navies immediately laid claim to the tallest and most true specimens—to be used as masts in their warships—but their claims were often ignored in the colonists' rush to convert forest into farmland. Colonists' lives revolved around clearing the land and subsequent consumption of wood. Cheap and readily available, wood was also the main source of fuel on the frontier and in the eastern cities. The innumerable chimneys that rose up to define these towns' low skylines revealed the reliance on wood for heating and cooking. The amount of land annually consumed was enormous: Philadelphia in the winter of 1826–27 burned 11 square miles (29 square kilometers) of forest.

Animals. Rapidly decimated, too, were the animals that had inhabited these forest ecosystems. Deer, bear, and panther were hunted for food and to diminish the number of competitors and predators that might threaten the survival of the herds of domesticated animals that grazed on lands in the United States and Canada. The most significant assault on local fauna, however, was that launched against the beaver and other fur-bearing animals in response to a booming European market for New World pelts and skin. Gathering large pools of capital, major organizations like the Hudson's Bay Company paid hundreds of Native Americans and white trappers to search distant watersheds for the valuable animals. At first, the trade was robust and beaver were plentiful. When European hat fashions changed in the mid-nineteenth century, pelt prices plummeted, and trapping virtually ceased. The same pattern would unfold later in the nineteenth century around a larger animal, the buffalo; as the bison robe trade grew quickly, the animal was hunted almost to extinction, and then the market collapsed.

Native Americans. The damage that resulted from the fur trade was not just environmental. By participating in a global commercial activity linked to a cash-and-barter economy, Native American tribes sealed their fates. Those living in the Great Lakes region and the Northern Plains, for example, entered into a new era in which their lives and livelihoods were tied to far-distant markets; as prices for beaver pelt or buffalo skins rose, they gained new forms of wealth and social status based on traditional skills. When profits disappeared because of the vagaries of European taste, Native Americans suffered greatly.

Native American cultures and living conditions were further affected by European land hunger and the resulting land policies in Canada and the United States. As white settlers pushed west along trails, rivers, and lakes seeking new sources of agricultural and mineral wealth, they battled with indigenous peoples. Local skirmishes, regional hostilities, and brutal massacres, when linked to an upsurge in white population in these contested territories, led the U.S. government to devise a new strategy to contain Native Americans. In the mid-nineteenth century, as westward migration pressed well past the Mississippi and into the Great Plains, the federal government conceived of a series of "reserves," later known as reservations, on which indigenous peoples would be forced to live. Usually compelled to accept disadvantageous terms in treaties with U.S. commissioners, and then relocated to areas poor in water and other resources, the Cherokee and Cree, the Sioux, Kiowa, and Apache tribes would become strangers in unfamiliar lands.

Social Experimentation. Only after the indigenous landscapes and peoples had been eliminated did North Americans experiment with the utopian fantasies that had so captivated them in the early nineteenth century. Drawing on European Romanticism and socialism, and on home-grown aspirations to build small-scale communitarian societies, a number of men and women, many of whom were known as transcendentalists, invested considerable energy and labor into the creation of places like Brook Farm in Massachusetts and the Oneida community in upstate New York. Although most of these social experiments in North America failed to endure, many of the residents were active in the most important reform initiatives of the pre–Civil War era, including campaigns to abolish slavery, improve nutrition, enact prohibition on alcohol, and advance women's rights. Like the Puritans of New England two centuries earlier, these well-meaning reformers sallied forth to make new heavens in the New World.

—*Char Miller*

An undated illustration by William H. Johnson depicting a covered wagon caravan on the Oregon Trail. (© Bettmann/Corbis)

Farming in Southern Ontario

Agriculture has been practiced for thousands of years in the area now known as Southern Ontario—the southernmost quarter of the province of Ontario, created during Canadian confederation in 1867 (the territory was previously the French colony of Canada from 1608 to 1763, and the British colony of Québec (1763–91), Upper Canada (1791–1841), and Canada West (1841–67). This islandlike territory—approximately the same size as the state of Oregon—is sometimes called the Great Lakes Peninsula because of its extensive shoreline on Lakes Huron, Erie, and Ontario. European settlement began at scattered French fur trading posts (*see also* 32–33) in the seventeenth century; by the 1730s, the French had established farms in the Detroit River area. Between the 1770s and 1850, farming would begin to change Southern Ontario's natural landscape by the concurrent processes of cutting and clearing the original—largely forested—vegetation, damming streams, and introducing exotic species of plants and animals, for example, wheat and cattle.

Forests. Most of the Great Lakes Peninsula was forested (*see also* 34–35). It was said a squirrel could travel its length or breadth without having the inconvenience of touching the solid ground. The clearing and deforestation of this large area was done slowly, following early farmers' need for open land for cultivation.

The forest was composed of both deciduous and coniferous trees, within which a range of species was present depending on local site conditions of temperature, moisture, and geology. In the more northerly, thin-soil, Canadian Shield–dominated area, needle-leaved coniferous trees like the eastern white pine were

widespread. In the peninsula's southwest, broad-leaved deciduous trees characterized a mixed forest with maple, beech, and basswood—typical of the lower Great Lakes basin. Settlers favored sites that included more temperate Carolinian species—butternut, chestnut, and black walnut. Generally speaking, farming grew harder north and east of the Great Lakes Peninsula—the growing season was shorter, soil depth shallower, and the surface topography was of a lesser agricultural quality.

Settlement. The French fur trade created scattered outposts, although in the far southwest of Ontario some farms had been

established before 1750. These posts were assumed by the British after the conquest of French Canada and were subsequently important in attracting Loyalist refugees from the thirteen colonies that would become the United States. The Loyalists, who sided with Britain during the American Revolution, moved to safe havens just north of the border with western Québec. The four areas settled by the Loyalists—who were mostly farmers—lay on the Canadian side of Lake Ontario and the St. Lawrence, Niagara, and Detroit Rivers; these lands were well suited for agriculture with good soil, sufficient rain and other sources of

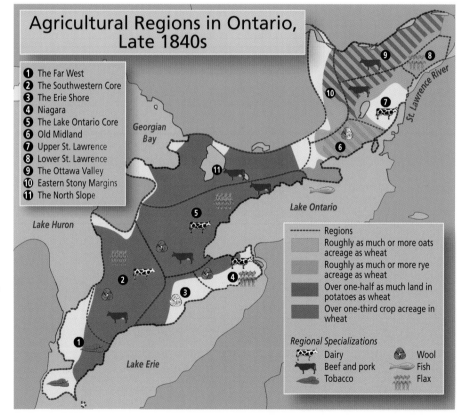

The eleven agricultural regions in Ontario were all south or southeast of the thin-soil Canadian Shield and ranged from the Far West region, which was the most favored climatically (yet least accessible to the main ocean export route of the St. Lawrence River) and could cultivate heat-loving tobacco, to relatively good farming regions near Lakes Erie and Ontario. North and east of Lake Ontario the climate allowed a shorter growing season, and, despite greater access to the main St. Lawrence River route, the range and kind of crops were reduced to mixed farming of cereals other than wheat, but including oats and rye, as well as considerable livestock production.

Source: Adapted from J. David Wood, *Making Ontario: Agricultural Colonization and Landscape Re-creation Before the Railway* (Montreal: McGill-Queen's University Press, 2000), 100. Courtesy of McGill-Queen's University Press.

water, and a growing season that permitted crops to mature. In 1791 Upper Canada was proclaimed a separate province—the first British inland colony—and intended as a haven for immigrants from both the British Isles as well as the new United States.

Agricultural impact on the landscape increased in tandem with the rate of immigration. Before 1820, Upper Canada's population was so small—some ninety-five thousand inhabitants—that its effect was minimal. Careless granting of land to attract settlers also lessened the overall effect of agriculture because many new owners did not occupy their land and merely awaited speculative gain in value. Much of the prime farmland remained uncultivated for many years, partly because the poorer immigrants tended to settle in the United States or in more remote parts of Canada, such as the backwoods of Upper Canada, where free land grants were still available. As a result, before about 1820, the forest was cleared in only a few, relatively local areas by early pioneers. These farmers felled trees and cultivated stump-filled, untidy-looking clearings; in so doing, they unknowingly were assuming the role of ecological revolutionaries who, according to historical geographer J. David Wood, began to change forever the "face of the earth" and "gained backbone for the settlement process."

By 1820 the agricultural settlement of the Great Lakes Peninsula was continuous in the more-accessible areas, which, accordingly, had experienced most environmental impact. Clearing the land consumed a large part of a settler's time and effort and replaced one vegetation component—mature trees—with another—forest-derived weeds. Such low-growing vegetation would be another obstacle to farmers. As farming became established, the more extensive areas of cleared land introduced new problems: an altered local climate, with greater freezing and snow drifting

Further Reading

Gerriets, Marilyn. "Agricultural Resources, Agricultural Production and Settlement at Confederation." *Acadiensis* 21, no. 2 (2002): 129–56.

Jones, Robert Leslie. *History of Agriculture in Ontario: 1613–1880.* Toronto: University of Toronto Press, 1946.

Kelly, Kenneth. "The Impact of Nineteenth Century Agricultural Settlement on the Land." In *Perspectives on Landscape and Settlement in Nineteenth Century Ontario,* edited by J. D. Wood. Toronto: McClelland and Stewart, 1975.

Reaman, G. E. *A History of Agriculture in Ontario.* Vol. 1. Toronto: Saunders, 1970.

Wood, J. David. *Making Ontario: Agricultural Colonization and Landscape Re-creation before the Railway.* Montreal: McGill-Queen's University Press, 2000.

during the winter and harsher drought during the summer. The wheat monoculture attracted insects and bacteria from earlier-developed New York state.

Agricultural Production. The farming system was essentially commercial with a short rotation of planting wheat, letting fields lie fallow, and then planting wheat again (wheat–fallow–wheat). By 1850, according to J. David Wood, eleven farming regions had emerged, all of which produced some wheat, but their specializations reflected local natural or commercial conditions. For example, livestock was important in the southern regions either as live exports to the United States or for products like milk, meat, and wool for nearby settlements and towns. Feed production—oats and rye for draft animals (used for plowing and pulling heavy loads) and potatoes for the humans—was particularly important in the easternmost regions near the lumbering districts. More localized specializations by 1850 included tobacco near Lake Erie, and flax (used for making linen) and lake fishing in eastern Lake Ontario. Wheat had become specialized by mid-century, with winter wheat emerging as the preferred commercial export crop grown in the established and climatically favored farming areas of the southwest and Lake Ontario region; spring wheat was grown in the more recently settled and generally less accessible northern areas.

The wheat–fallow–wheat rotation system and forest clearing persisted for a longer period of time away from waterways in more settled areas because these regions were

occupied later and had less access to diverse markets. Continuous growing of wheat exhausts soil; however, firm evidence for pre-1850 soil exhaustion is scanty and published opinions that soil exhaustion had occurred are often merely parroting news reports describing soil conditions from far older farming areas. A persistent impediment to early agriculture in Upper Canada—as in many other frontier areas—was the acute shortage of farm laborers, with the ratio of farmers to hired hands in 1848 being approximately ten to one.

An occasional mixed farm produced both vegetable and animal products; these farms were important as examples of "scientific farming" and as sources of higher-quality animals but were rare and usually not profitable. Concentrations of mixed farms occurred in southwestern Upper Canada, Wentworth County, York County around Yonge Street, the southwestern shoreline of Lake Simcoe, and in the Peterborough area.

By 1850, as Kenneth Kelly has noted, Upper Canada was in various stages of agricultural development and was characterized by a "mosaic of farmscapes" rather than a single continuous farming landscape. Numerous isolated farms of roughly similar size, form, and appearance—most engaged in growing commercial wheat—were scattered across a still largely forested territory. The greatest farming development and diversity of production was along the Great Lakes shoreline in the southern area of the province.

—*Alan G. Brunger*

Plantation Economy and Labor in the U.S. South

Plantations—large agricultural estates cultivated by bonded or slave labor under central direction—were closely tied to the agriculture and labor system that enabled them to flourish. In North America's British colonies of Virginia, the Carolinas, and Georgia, where plantation agriculture was initially established, enormous amounts of labor carved plantations out of forests and swamps. At first, indentured servants from Europe were used to transform the landscape. By the late seventeenth century, however, slavery was firmly established in Virginia and the Carolinas, and thereafter slaves provided the labor for shaping the environment to productive ends throughout the plantation South.

Although most farmers in the antebellum South did not own slaves, those who did dominated agricultural production. The most profitable crops—rice, tobacco (*see also* 20–21), sugar, and cotton (indigo, used as a dye, was important only before the American Revolution)—were cultivated on plantations by slaves. Planters who owned slaves also possessed power, not just to dominate other human beings and profit from their labor, but also over the difficult environment. Slavery and exploitation of the environment went hand in hand.

Agricultural Labor. All of the main plantation commodity crops, especially rice and sugar, demanded intense labor and, every few years, extensive tracts of unworked land. Rice plantations along the South Carolina and Georgia coasts yielded over 90 percent of American rice on the eve of the Civil War (*see also* 68–69). Sugar plantations along the lower Mississippi (the only part of the South with a growing season long enough for sugarcane to be grown with consistent success) earned sugar planters some of the highest profits in the South. But both crops required massive manipulation of the environment. Rice was grown in well-engineered landscapes of canals and drains that tapped the rise and fall of tidewater rivers to flood and drain the fields. Slaves had to dig out by hand the rice fields from freshwater swamps. Sugar plantations had a twice yearly need of heavy labor—when the rattoon (segments of harvested cane that were used to sprout new cane) was planted to make new crops in the spring, and when the relatively heavy cane had to be harvested and processed in the fall and early winter. Sugar processing required large quantities of firewood, which slaves cut from forests adjacent to the plantations.

Short-staple cotton (also known as short-strand cotton)—a more resilient crop—did not require as complete an adjustment of the environment as did rice, sugar, or the silky long-staple cotton grown on the sea islands of Georgia and South Carolina. It also could be grown wherever the growing season was long enough (about two hundred days between frosts), and by large plantations as well as by independent farmers. For instance, some of the South's cotton was grown by the three-quarters of southern whites who did not own slaves, though not in the same quantity. Short-staple cotton was also nonperishable and could be easily stored and shipped. But the difficulty of processing the cotton by hand made it a crop of such marginal profitability that some southerners believed plantation agriculture would never permanently take hold outside of the original plantation districts of the colonial South.

Invention of the Gin. Eli Whitney's invention of the cotton gin in 1793 and a rapidly expanding market for cotton among

A late-nineteenth-century Currier & Ives lithograph showing the daily activities of a cotton plantation on the Mississippi River. (From the collections of the Library of Congress)

British and, later, American textile manufacturers, made short-staple cotton the most important crop in the South and assured the expansion of the plantation system. Although slavery was not essential to the production of cotton, white southerners assumed that slavery was essential to the efficient production of large quantities of cotton. The invention of the cotton gin and the growth of cotton plantation culture also contributed to the expansion of slavery.

Cotton Production. The spread of row-crop monoculture expanded the plantation landscape within the region, and the "Cotton South" took shape. By the 1820s and 1830s, cotton production had spread west of the Appalachians to the rich prairie lands, alluvial river bottoms, and uplands throughout central Alabama and Mississippi. Southern rivers, especially the Mississippi, were essential to this growth, linking cotton ports on rivers to ocean ports in the South. By 1860, three-quarters of the area's cotton was moving on the South's river system through Mobile, Alabama; New Orleans, Louisiana; and the young Texas ports.

Production of cotton in the South increased from about 2 million pounds (0.7 million kilograms) in 1791 to over 1 billion pounds (0.4 billion kilograms) in 1860. By 1840, the plantations of the American South were producing more than 60 percent of the world's cotton, and throughout the period exports of cotton made up over half the earnings from U.S. exports. Capital generated by cotton earnings not only supported a large class of cotton producers in the South, but attracted foreign investment

The Cotton Gin

Eli Whitney's cotton gin was a machine for removing the seeds from the bolls (seed capsules) of short-strand (or short-staple) cotton. Before the invention of the gin in 1793, cleaning the seeds from the fiber in the mature blooms of the short-strand cotton plant was done by hand.

Short-strand cotton is especially protective of its seeds. Removing the seeds, a slow and labor-intensive process, created a labor bottleneck in the production of cotton. Because short-strand cotton also fetched a lower price per pound than the fine, silky, long-strand sea island cotton that was grown in small quantities in the Caribbean and on the islands off South Carolina and Georgia, its high production costs could not be sustained.

Whitney's invention of the gin transformed cotton production in the South. The gin had two shafts with wire teeth rotating in a wire box. The first rotating shaft separated the fiber from the seeds; the second lifted the fiber from the teeth of the first and deposited it outside the box. A person operating a simple Whitney gin could clean 50 times more cotton in a day than an individual separating the fiber by hand. Cotton gins contributed to the increase in both production and profits on cotton plantations.

In the years after the invention of the gin, cotton growers moved westward and began cultivating fresh lands in the present-day states of Alabama, Mississippi, Louisiana, Arkansas, and Texas. They took their slaves with them, establishing the institution of slavery at the same time that they enthroned cotton as king throughout the region. Although many factors contributed to the growth of slavery in the American South, the Whitney gin was important to this expansion because it cut production costs and enabled short-staple cotton to be grown profitably.

and contributed to the industrial growth of the North.

Following the Civil War, southerners remained committed to commodity-crop plantation agriculture, despite the abolishment of slavery and the destruction of the landscape. Southerners returned cotton production to its prewar levels after 1879 by implementing the sharecropping system, which locked laborers—usually African Americans—into a credit and debt arrangement with landowners and the public institutions that supported them. The South's commitment to cotton growing lasted until the 1930s and 1940s, when fertilizer, soil conservation efforts, and the mechanical cotton picker

contributed to the modernization of southern agriculture

Impact. Plantation agriculture profoundly altered some parts of the natural environment. On cultivated lands, the removal of ground cover and the dominant monoculture made soils vulnerable to erosion. When planters had their slaves plow instead of use a hoe to prepare the ground, soils eroded even more quickly. Row-crop agriculture that "skimmed" the land also destroyed soil fertility, created the conditions that contributed to flood and drought, and modified the southern landscape by changing relationships of ecosystems. Soils in the old cotton plantation districts of the South continue to show signs of depletion and erosion, and the residents of these regions—many of them descendents of slaves and sharecroppers—continue to be among the poorest in the United States.

—*Mart A. Stewart*

Further Reading

Cowdrey, Albert E. *This Land, This South: An Environmental History.* Rev. ed. Lexington: University Press of Kentucky, 1996.
Gray, Lewis Cecil. *History of Agriculture in the Southern United States to 1860.* 2 vols.

Washington, D.C.: Carnegie Institution of Washington, 1933.
Stewart, Mart A. *"What Nature Suffers to Groe": Life, Labor, and Landscape on the Georgia Coast, 1680–1920.* Athens: University of Georgia Press, 1996.

The Fur Trade

From roughly 1700 to 1850 the ceaseless quest for furs spurred constant exploration throughout North America that yielded geographic knowledge and improved maps of the continent (*see also* 10–11). Although primarily an economic enterprise, the fur trade also established the foundation for interactions between European newcomers and indigenous populations. Reaching from North America across the Atlantic to Europe and across the Pacific to China, the fur trade was a global business based upon the slaughter of millions of animals, including beaver, otter, muskrat, and later, bison (*see also* 36–37).

Fur Trading Companies. Organized in 1670, the Hudson's Bay Company (HBC) played a dominant role in Canada's fur trade. Prince Rupert of the Rhine, and later King Charles II of England, granted the HBC a royal charter to the territory whose rivers drained into the Hudson Bay. Between 1769 and 1868, the company would export for sale in London the skins, furs, and feathers of 4,708,702 beaver; 1,507,240 mink; 1,240,571 marten; 1,052,051 lynx; 891,091 fox; 467,549 wolf; 288,016 bear; 275,032 badger; 94,326 swan; 68,694 wolverine. The HBC would rule Canada's West until confederation in 1870. Its main Canadian competitor was the North West Company, founded by partners who traded south of the HBC's deeded lands. By 1820 the North West Company had merged with the HBC. From 1820 until 1850 U.S. firms competed against the Canadian giant, but none ever gained dominance over it. John Jacob Astor tried, becoming America's wealthiest fur trader and its first millionaire. His American Fur Company (1808–34) aggressively marketed furs in the United States, Europe, and Asia, and he came close to monopolizing the U.S. fur trade.

Trading Posts. In about 1827 John Astor and St. Louis merchant-capitalist Pierre Chouteau, Jr., established Fort Union (in present-day North Dakota), a large, elaborate, and profitable trading post, at the confluence of the Missouri and Yellowstone Rivers. By exchanging many kind of goods for hides, furs, and bison robes, Fort Union and its satellite posts dominated the Northern Plains fur trade from 1830 until 1865. Among Euro-Americans, the fur traders were the most knowledgeable about Native Americans. Relationships among Native American and Euro-American traders, trappers, and hunters varied, ranging from friendship and marriage to murder and warfare. Trading posts offered a neutral setting where Euro-Americans exchanged manufactured goods for products like skins, dried meat, and—on the western prairies—bison robes.

Trapping. Trappers known as "mountain men" exploited the Rocky Mountain fur trade between 1820 and 1840. Instead of establishing fixed posts where goods were bartered for furs and hides, in 1822 Missouri entrepreneurs William H. Ashley and Andrew Henry hired hunters and trappers and sent "brigades" west to trap beaver and to trade with Native Americans. Fur companies employed British and French Canadian, Métis (mixed-blood), or American trappers to trap beaver, mink, fox, wolf, and other animals. In the Rocky Mountain trade's heyday, competing companies employed about one thousand trappers and traders. Some eastern Native American nations joined "brigades," while most western Native American nations mainly hunted bison and other animals using guns or bow and arrow.

Beaver Trade. The beaver (*Castor canadensis*), North America's largest rodent,

Jedediah S. Smith

Jedediah ("Jed") S. Smith (1799–1831) was the greatest explorer and cartographer among the "mountain men." Unlike many fur trappers, Smith was literate and keenly interested in exploration. He became the first American to reach the Pacific Ocean by trekking southwestward from the Great Salt Lake to Mexican California via the Mojave Desert (1826–27). He helped to identify South Pass (in present-day Wyoming) as a suitable path for wagons to cross the Rocky Mountains; this route would soon become part of the Oregon Trail.

Smith's life was dramatic, but brief. At age thirty, he retired from the mountain trade and engaged in the Santa Fe trade, considered safer because much of the commerce was conducted among Anglo-Americans and Hispanic New Mexicans. In the spring of 1831, however, Comanche warriors killed Smith at a waterhole on the Santa Fe Trail.

Smith's spectacular career was little known until the mid-twentieth century, when fragments of his letters and journals came to light. In 1827, Smith wrote about his arduous journey across the Great Salt Lake Desert, during which he suffered from exhaustion and hunger. He describes some of his encounters with animals—antelope, bear, deer, and hares—which he tried to kill for meat. He also encountered native peoples, including some Pahnakkee at a lodge who brought "some pieces of Buffalo Robes" and informed Smith that "after a few days travel to the North East Buffalo were plenty." Once he had brought some of his men safely from California to the rendezvous near Great Salt Lake, Smith departed to relieve men still in California. He wrote: "My preparations being made I left . . . with eighteen men and such supplies as I needed. . . . I of course expected to find Beaver, which with us hunters is a primary object, but I was also led on by the love of novelty common to all, which is much increased by the pursuit of its gratification."

A mid-nineteenth-century lithograph of Native Americans exchanging goods at the Fort Union trading post. (From the collections of the Library of Congress)

was the trappers' main prey. Beaver by the million lived throughout North America. With their ability to fell trees, construct dams and lodges (beaver houses), and redirect watercourses, beavers created habitats by flooding land along rivers and streams. Their European cousin, *Castor fiber*, had suffered population decline from overhunting, but by the time European beavers ceased to be commercially viable, the European occupation of North America had begun, and the quest for beaver fur drove it westward. The beavers' luxurious underfur provided hatters with excellent material; a large adult beaver weighed up to 70 pounds (26 kilograms) and provided fur for about fifteen hats.

While the fur trade frontier surged westward from 1700 to 1850, beaver colonies suffered localized and severe, but temporary, population decline. Dams broke down, and habitat reduction affected wetlands and forests, as well as waterfowl and other creatures that used the beavers' riparian (riverside) and pond environments. No animals targeted by trappers for their fur became extinct, though overhunting drove Pacific Coast sea otter perilously close by 1830. In areas of minimal competition with American traders, the HBC curtailed beaver trapping, allowing populations to increase. High-intensity beaver trapping continued

until about 1840, when demand for fur felt declined. Beaver skin prices, which had reached $6 per pound in the late 1820s, fell to about 50¢ per pound by 1850. By the late nineteenth century, conservation and preservation programs in the United States and Canada (*see also* 110–115) helped beaver make an impressive resurgence. In part, this success reflected the animals' extraordinary ability to survive despite habitat degradation and the rapidly increasing human population that encroached on its habitat.

Bison Robe Trade. Between 1820 and 1870 the bison robe trade was as important as the beaver trade. Success in the robe trade required coordinated efforts of Native American men and women, as well as nonnative traders. Native American men hunted bison, while the women butchered them and tanned the hides, producing soft, warm robes. Native Americans traded thousands of robes each year at HBC and U.S. posts. Some scholars believe the high number of robes traded during this period explains the depletion of bison by the 1880s, while others argue that the robe trade operated on a sustained yield basis (where the annual harvest did not exceed the herds' rate of natural increase).

The traditional robe trade differed from hide hunters' activities of the 1870s and

1880s. The earlier trade relied on Native American hunters, robe tanners, and meat producers, and entailed cross-cultural diplomacy, while the later hide hunters' profits came from untanned bison hides that supplied leather for eastern factories. In addition, after the Civil War, the Texas cattle that were driven to railheads on the Northern Plains carried brucellosis, bovine tuberculosis, and anthrax that may have killed bison. By 1885 only a few hundred bison remained, but thereafter preservationists initiated successful efforts to protect this American symbol from extinction.

Today states and provinces allow hunting and trapping of beaver and other wildlife to control populations and to maintain environmentally healthy wetlands. But controversy involving fur-bearing animals and their environments continues. With practically no natural predators remaining, uncontrolled animal populations rapidly grow too large. While many isolated northern Canadian Native communities trap and hunt to generate income and to maintain their traditional culture, many believe that trapping—especially with steel leghold traps—is inhumane and should be banned. Reconciling the seemingly incompatible goals of traditional Native American communities, sport hunters, trappers, conservationists, and antifur activists presents a significant challenge for the future.

—*Barton H. Barbour*

Further Reading

Barbour, Barton H. *Fort Union and the Upper Missouri Fur Trade.* Norman: University of Oklahoma Press, 2001.

Flores, Dan. "Bison Ecology and Bison Diplomacy: The Southern Plains from 1800 to 1850." *Journal of American History* 78, no. 2 (September 1991): 465–85.

Lopez, Barry. *Arctic Dreams: Imagination and Desire in a Northern Landscape.* New York: Scribner's, 1986.

Morgan, Lewis H. *The American Beaver and His Works.* 1868. Reprint. New York: Dover, 1986.

Utley, Robert M. *A Life Wild and Perilous: Mountain Men and the Paths to the Pacific.* New York: Henry Holt, 1997.

Great Lakes Timber

The upper Great Lakes region also had forests of the species of soft, easily worked white pine found in New England (*see also* 8–9). It was all part of the same great forest that stretched across the northeastern United States and southern Canada. The opening of the Erie Canal in 1825 (*see also* 44–45) initiated settlement and development in the Ohio Valley and other western territories. As farmers cleared hardwood forests in the southern parts of Wisconsin, Minnesota, and Michigan for agriculture (*see also* 6–7), lumbermen began clearcutting the white pine in the central and northern parts of

these territories and in Canada, forever altering the landscape of the Old Northwest (the region northwest of the Ohio River). Farmers settling the prairies of Indiana, Illinois, Nebraska, Iowa, and, to a lesser extent, the Canadian Plains, encountered land with so few trees that they had to obtain wood from other areas. They looked to the Great Lakes region for wood to build homes, barns, and fences because of its proximity and huge supply of lumber.

Transport of Timber. This dependence on northern wood tied the economies of the Great Lakes and prairie regions together. The small town of Chicago was

transformed into a booming trade town. The upper Mississippi River and the Illinois–Michigan Canal, completed in 1848, provided the "highways" to move the rafts of logs and lumber in the era before railroads and trucks. The canal allowed Chicago wholesalers to sell Michigan and Canadian lumber to buyers in the prairie region—buyers who previously relied on timber shipped in from western New York, Pennsylvania, and eastern Canada (these logs were floated down the Ohio River and then up the Illinois River). With lumber accessible from nearby Chicago markets, the price fell by 50 percent, making the costs of

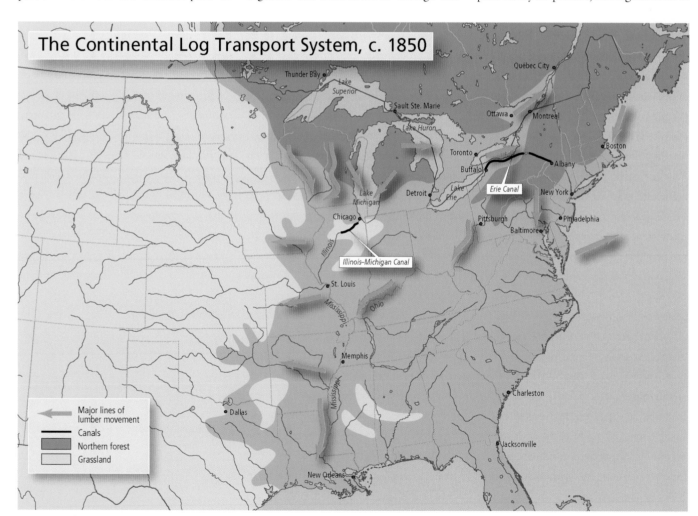

The opening of the Erie Canal and the Illinois–Michigan Canal in the Great Lakes region made small towns like Albany, Buffalo, Pittsburgh, Chicago, and St. Louis into major hubs in the emerging lumber transport and distribution system.

Source: Michael Williams, *Americans and Their Forests* (New York: Cambridge University Press, 1989), 177. Adapted with the permission of Cambridge University Press.

Lumbermen in Michigan transport a load of lumber through the snow during the nineteenth century. (From the collections of the Library of Congress)

shipping lumber to prairie settlements affordable. By 1856, Chicago had replaced Albany, New York, as the nation's leading wholesale lumber market.

Treaties. The lack of regular, reliable, and easy transport had been one impediment to opening the Midwest; another was the presence of Native Americans in these territories. Beginning in the 1830s, the government renegotiated treaties with the Chippewa, Winnebago, and Sioux; these new treaties took away these tribes' title to their lands.

Land Speculation. The removal of Native Americans (*see also* 46–47) from these regions began the first of many land speculation booms, and buying and selling land became a big business. Entrepreneurs easily assembled some of the first lumber empires. Starting in the 1860s, Frederick Weyerhaeuser, Orrin H. Ingram, and other timbermen made millions by buying forests in the Great Lakes region, cutting the timber, and supplying it to the prairie farmers. They would then sell the stripped

land to newly arriving farmers before they had to pay taxes on it.

Railroads. After the Civil War, the transcontinental railroad lines (*see also* 70–71), which had been granted land by the federal government, opened the western territories to additional settlement. They then sold the land granted to them for less than $1.25 an acre. The railroads also consumed great quantities of wood, using lumber for ties, bridges, and engine fuel. Although often called the "iron road," railroads could easily, as historian Sherry Hessler Olson has noted, be called "wooden roads." More wood than steel went into their construction, and railroads consumed as much as

one-quarter of each year's timber cut. An estimated 195,000 acres (78,900 hectares) of forested land (or about one-quarter the size of Rhode Island) was needed to supply the thirty-nine million crossties used by railroads in 1870, and the demand only increased as more lines were built and the older ones needed replacement ties.

Impact. The construction of rail lines meant more land was opened to settlement. As more farmers settled in the territories, the demand for wood increased, which in turn led to the cutting of more timber in the Great Lakes region. Soon the region's supply of white pine and jack pine started dwindling, just as it had in the East a few decades earlier.

When lumbermen moved west once again looking for more timber supplies, they left behind a devastated region. The debris accumulated during cutting provided fuel for fires that swept the Great Lakes region repeatedly from 1871 through 1910. The Great Peshtigo (Wisconsin) fire of 1871 killed fifteen hundred people and scorched 50 square miles (129 square kilometers), and fires in Michigan that same year consumed 2.5 million acres (1 million hectares). Stunted bush grew where vast forests once stood. Land too far north to support agriculture was converted to dairy land because it could grow only hay and grass. This damage caused Americans to reexamine and reevaluate the practices of both the lumber industry and federal government; in the closing decades of the nineteenth century, conservation (*see also* 112–13) became a public concern and a movement was born.

—James G. Lewis

Further Reading
Apsey, Mike, et al. *The Perpetual Forest: Using Lessons from the Past to Sustain Canada's Forests in the Future.* Vancouver, B.C.: FORCAST, 2000.
Cox, Thomas R., Robert S. Maxwell, Phillip Drennon Thomas, and Joseph J. Malone. *This Well-Wooded Land: Americans and Their Forests from Colonial Times to the Present.* Lincoln: University of Nebraska Press, 1985.

Keenleyside, Hugh L. "Forests of Canada." *Canadian Geographical Journal* 41 (July 1950): 2–15.
Olson, Sherry Hessler. *Depletion Myth: A History of Railroad Use of Timber.* Cambridge, Mass.: Harvard University Press, 1971.
Williams, Michael. *Americans and Their Forests: A Historical Geography.* Cambridge: Cambridge University Press, 1992.

Extermination of the Buffalo

The historic range of the North American bison (commonly known as buffalo) spanned the Great Slave Lake, in the present-day Northwest Territories of Canada, to northern Mexico. They were found from the foothills of the Rocky Mountains to the Atlantic shore. Scholars believe that the bison were concentrated on the Great Plains, where they numbered about thirty million, and migrated to eastern North America around the mid-1400s. Their eastern habitat consisted of present-day Kentucky, Ohio, Illinois, Indiana, Georgia, the Carolinas, and Mississippi. However, following the arrival of Anglo-Europeans in the sixteenth century, bison would become the object of slaughter and waste.

Eastern Bison. After European settlement of the New World, the eastern bison were hunted to extinction to provide food for two major groups: the military and settlers. During the eighteenth century, England and France provisioned their western armies and forts with salted bison meat supplied by market hunters employed by large trading firms. Although the distances and difficulties in transport (*see also* 44–45) often made these ventures unprofitable, the trade of bison meat was still destructive to the herds. Settlers also took advantage of the natural habits of the bison, shooting them as they gathered around salt licks. Hunters took only the preferred cuts: the tongue, hump roast, and ribs. The bison were exterminated from the eastern United States by the 1830s.

Hunting Practices of Natives. On the Great Plains, European hunters' practices differed considerably from those of Native Americans (*see also* 14–15). Native American hunters utilized most of the bison, while European hunters were interested only in the hide and select cuts of meat. Plains tribes' use of the bison was as varied as their many different cultures. They preserved bison meat by drying, while they stretched, scraped, and tanned the hides for clothing. They also used hides for shelter, food storage, and cooking. Sinew and ligaments served as thread and cords, while bones were fashioned into implements, including hoes and boat paddles.

The arrival of Europeans in the sixteenth century transformed Native Americans' subsistence patterns and their relationships with the bison. By the early 1800s Native Americans had become firmly entrenched in the fur trade, hunting and butchering the buffalo for their hides, which they tanned to produce soft robes (*see also* 32–33). European traders introduced tribes to manufactured goods, upon which they quickly became dependent. Native Americans expanded production and traded finished robes for manufactured goods at inflated prices. Accordingly, the bison population was significantly depleted.

Industrial Demands. Following the Civil War, hunting bison for their hides evolved from the robe trade. Hides were manufactured into the industrial belts that ran factory machines, which became more important as the United States continued to industrialize. A buffalo hunting team usually consisted of three men: The first was the shooter who would sit in a blind, downwind from the herd, armed with a .50 caliber Sharps rifle. The shooter would first kill the dominant cow. After the first shot, the kill was limited

An 1897 print from Muller Luchsinger and Company depicting a buffalo hunter shooting a buffalo in the West while two Native Americans ride alongside him with spears. (From the collections of the Library of Congress)

only by the amount of ammunition and the speed of the shooter's reload. The two other men were employed as skinners, who cut the hide from the bison. The carcass was abandoned to carrion eaters—crows, buzzards, coyotes, and wolves. Just as the popularity of the top hat of the previous century had decimated the beaver, the demands of American industry would contribute to the destruction of the bison.

Impact of the Railroads. The railroads (*see also* 70–71) provided easy access to bison herds for hide and sport hunters and made transporting the hides to the East much more economical. After the completion by the 1870s of the main railroad routes, such as the Northern Pacific, Union Pacific, and Central Pacific, freight rates fell dramatically. The construction of the tracks also created a barrier to the bison and concentrated them into smaller areas that allowed easier hunting. In 1884 a herd of seventy-five thousand bison was reported in eastern Montana. Within one year five thousand hide hunters had reduced their number to a few hundred. By the mid-1880s the bison was nearing extinction.

Diminished Buffalo Populations. The destruction of the bison did not alarm most inhabitants of the United States. Native Americans could be more easily controlled without the bison, while settlers could move onto western lands and plant crops without the fear of having their labor destroyed by migrating herds. Once the number of bison had been

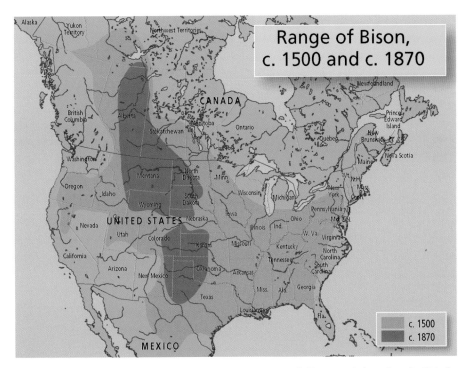

Range of Bison, c. 1500 and c. 1870

c. 1500
c. 1870

In about 1500, before Europeans arrived in North America, the range of the bison covered almost the entire United States and extended up into the Northwest Territories of Canada and down to northern Mexico. By about 1870, the robe trade, hide hunting, and the construction of the railroads reduced the bison's range to the western Great Plains, from Texas in the United States to Alberta in Canada.
Source: Adapted from Bryan Hodgson, "Buffalo: Back Home on the Range," National Geographic 186, no. 5 (November 1994), 70.

reduced to a few thousand, however, attitudes began to change. In the late nineteenth century, amid a growing conservation movement in the United States (*see also* 112–13), naturalists, zoologists, and others became concerned about the depletion of natural resources. In 1905 the American Bison Society was organized under the guidance of William Hornaday and other philanthropists, including Andrew Carnegie. Their mission was to save a sample of the bison and the species from extinction. However, they did not seek to restore the bison's former range because they wanted to

leave the West open for settlement (*see also* 52–53).

Of the estimated thirty million bison that inhabited the Great Plains in 1850, only about twenty-five hundred were left by 1900. The remaining wild herds, like those found in Yellowstone National Park, were still threatened by hunters. What was left of the other bison was found in eastern zoos where visitors viewed them as an oddity rather than the norm. Today bison are found throughout the United States and Canada, including Hawaii. The majority of these bison are located in semi-domesticated herds that are raised for meat production. A few wild herds still exist in Custer National Park in South Dakota and the Great Slave Lake Bison Preserve in the Northwest Territories of Canada. At the beginning of the twenty-first century the population of the North American bison is about 250,000 and continues to grow.

—*Matthew D. Taylor*

Further Reading
Danz, Harold P. *Of Bison and Man*. Niwot: University Press of Colorado, 1997.
Dary, David. *The Buffalo Book: The Full Saga of the American Animal*. Rev. ed. Athens: Swallow Press/Ohio University Press, 1989.
Isenberg, Andrew C. *The Destruction of the Bison: An Environmental History*,
1750–1920. Cambridge: Cambridge University Press, 2000.
McHugh, Tom. *The Time of the Buffalo*. New York: Alfred A. Knopf, 1972.
Roe, Frank Gilbert. *The North American Buffalo: A Critical Study of the Species in Its Wild State*. 2nd ed. Newton Abbot, England: David & Charles, 1972.

Public Land Policies: The U.S. Experience

The distribution of the U.S. public domain lands into private hands between about 1780 and 1935 was one of the major land reforms in world history. It replaced feudal, aristocratic, and royal concepts of ownership that dominated European nations in favor, it was said, of the independent freeholder. The opportunity to own a plot of land on which to grow one's own food, husband a few domestic animals, and house and feed a family was an American dream as powerful as political liberty. Widespread speculation, large landholdings, high prices, corporate exploitation, and special government exceptions for railroad development did undercut the reforms, but the promise was largely fulfilled during this century and a half.

The U.S. Constitution does not specifically mention land policies, but its "internal improvements" clause was intended to help facilitate geographic expansion. The Fourteenth Amendment, ratified in 1868, firmly restated the rights of private property

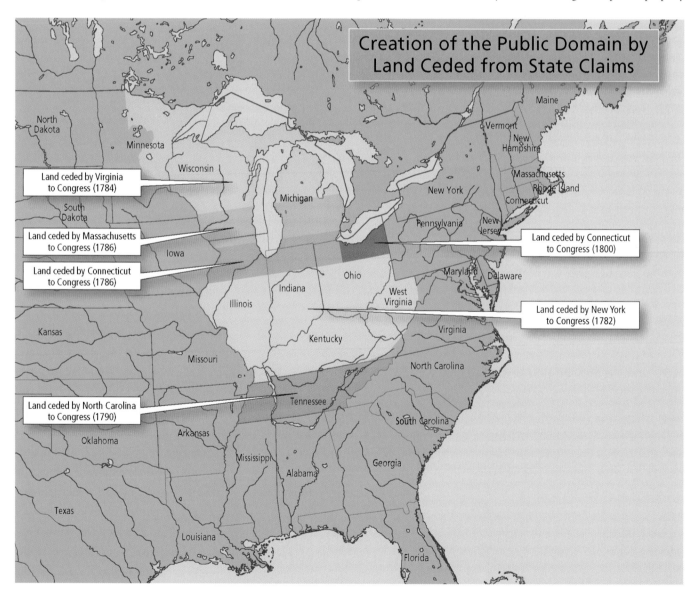

Creation of the Public Domain by Land Ceded from State Claims

Land ceded by Virginia to Congress (1784)

Land ceded by Massachusetts to Congress (1786)

Land ceded by Connecticut to Congress (1786)

Land ceded by North Carolina to Congress (1790)

Land ceded by Connecticut to Congress (1800)

Land ceded by New York to Congress (1782)

Public land ownership had often overlapped with competing states, private speculative empires, land warrants belonging to veterans, and land-grabbing settlers. The new public domain still included Native American nations, as well as British and Spanish claims, but it was secured between about 1780 and 1815 by legislative acts, diplomacy, and war.

Source: Adapted from John Opie, *Nature's Nation: An Environmental History of the United States* (Fort Worth, Tex.: Harcourt Brace College Publishers, 1998), 92. Courtesy of Wadsworth Publishing Company.

owners first affirmed in the Fourth Article. "Squatters" (preemptors) often rushed to claim the best parcels even before the land was surveyed and put up for sale. For much of U.S. history, settlers believed they could prosper on the famous "quarter section of 160 acres," but they often failed in the arid western plains. U.S. western expansion (*see also* 52–53) involved not only taming the land, but also dividing public land into private property that could be turned into profitable commodities or sold in the marketplace. No other force in U.S. history did more to encourage individual autonomy and a sense of control and dominion over the natural world.

Public Domain. The public domain came into existence when the original thirteen states, notably Virginia, ceded their western land claims to the central government between 1780 and 1802. In the sweeping Land Ordinance of 1785, the Confederation government turned the nation's landscape west of the current Pennsylvania–Ohio state line into a vast grid of townships and sections. According to the ordinance, government surveyors were to divide the western territory "into townships of six miles square, by lines running due north and south, and others crossing these at right angles." For the next 150 years, maps planned the direction of furrow, fence, and road, creating a vertical-horizontal rhythm in the land. Each township contained mile-square sections of 640 acres (259 hectares), which became a standardized, interchangeable commodity. The price of land was $1 an acre, unfortunately far too expensive for farmers who were fortunate to generate $100 a year. Land was free to many war veterans, who often sold their rights to speculators, and large purchasers often received steep discounts.

The Land Ordinance also applied to all future territories, which were to include the Northwest Territories, established in 1787, and the Louisiana Purchase, which in 1803 added 828,000 square miles (2,145,000 square kilometers) to the United States and doubled its public domain. Some previous holdings, such as the original thirteen colonies, preexisting French and Spanish land titles, and all of Texas, were exempt from the ordinance. Land rushes, speculation, little federal income, and open abuses led Congress to pass numerous revisions of the ordinance throughout the entire history of the public domain. As a result, prices changed, settlers were offered credit, minimum acreage diminished to 160 acres (65 hectares) or less, and regional land offices facilitated surveys and sales. Squatters received federal protection by congressional action in 1830 and 1841 because many Americans believed that they deserved proper land title after demonstrating initiative by searching out a tract of land, establishing its perimeters, and setting up and living in dwellings on the land. However, this subverted the "first survey, then sell" system.

Settlement. In the fifty years following the passage of the 1785 Land Ordinance, more than 4.5 million people poured into the vast public domain west of the Appalachians. However, the land was not "vacant," as stated in Secretary of Treasury Alexander Hamilton's complaint in 1791, but occupied by native peoples who were pushed aside by treaty, disease, deception, or force (*see also* 46–47). Overall, public domain legislation transferred 1.3 billion acres (0.5 billion hectares)—72 percent of the total—from public trust into private hands.

In 1862, President Abraham Lincoln signed the legendary Homestead Act, which donated 160 acres (65 hectares) to anyone who would settle on the land and work it for five years. But the threat of "starvin' to death" on the "gov't claim" in five years meant relatively few homestead applications—in the 1870s, the formation of three hundred thousand homesteads was outdistanced by the establishment of 1.3 million other new farms. In 1862, Lincoln also signed the generous Pacific Railroad Act that, with revisions, ceded 213 million acres (86 million hectares) in large corridors—120 miles (190 kilometers) wide in the western territories—across much of Minnesota, Iowa, Kansas, Nebraska, Alabama, and toward the Pacific coast in three wide lanes. Public land was traded for the spread of the railroads (*see also* 70–71), which would transform an ungovernable geography into a connected nation-state.

In the United States, public land policies shaped long-standing traditions about private property, eminent domain, urban zoning, economic development, industrial pollution, and wilderness protection (*see also* 146–47). A classic example is the Mining Law of 1872, which allowed private exploitation of "all valuable mineral deposits in lands belonging to the United States" at marginal cost. It is still in effect today. The transfer of the U.S. public domain into private hands came to an end in 1935, when the Taylor Grazing Act set aside about 142 million acres (57 million hectares) for grazing districts and President Franklin D. Roosevelt by executive order took the remaining public domain, more than 165 million acres (67 million hectares), off the market.

—*John Opie*

Further Reading

Gates, Paul W. *History of Public Land Law Development.* New York: Arno Press, 1979.

Opie, John. *The Law of the Land: 200 Years of American Farmland Policy.* Lincoln: University of Nebraska Press, 1994.

Price, Edward T. *Dividing the Land: Early American Beginnings of Our Private Property Mosaic.* Chicago: University of Chicago Press, 1995.

Robbins, Roy M. *Our Landed Heritage: The Public Domain, 1776–1970.* 2nd ed., Lincoln: University of Nebraska Press, 1976.

Crown Land Policies: The Canadian Experience

For the estimated half-million indigenous peoples of Canada's pre-Columbian era (*see also* 14–15), land—both as space and as a source of sustenance—was indistinguishable from life itself. Ecological equilibrium prevailed and land policy was not a cultural concept. Beginning in the sixteenth century, however, land in Canada (specifically, from the Great Lakes eastward to Newfoundland) took on a more defined meaning and became Crown land, a limitless warehouse under the authority of European monarchies.

Exploitation of Resources. Crown lands provided resources (*see also* 12–13)—

principally fish and fur—for Europeans little inclined to occupy what the French philosopher Voltaire called "a few acres of snow." In Newfoundland, which had no clear land policy, the fishing community simply settled on the shores, holding no title to the land. In French Canada (the St. Lawrence River valley and small areas along the Atlantic coastline) landlords, or seigneurs, served as the king's agents, managing France's Crown lands in trust, but also without clear title. This seigneurial system (*see also* 22–23) was a remnant of medieval European governance, and the few habitant farmers could, at best, achieve the status of tenant for life

on a continent where land ownership was to become the norm.

Far to the north flourished the Hudson's Bay Company, founded by royal charter in England in 1670 and given exclusive rights to trap fur-bearing animals from the lands draining into Hudson Bay (*see also* 32–33). This massive territory, still not fully mapped by the 1860s, remained British land. Some of the most important Crown lands were those that grew the timber (*see also* 42–43) used for ships' masts. Britain needed this resource to maintain its naval preeminence—commanding the seas and assuring its authority over the Canadian landmass. The timber stands of the Ottawa River valley and the Appalachian interior of New Brunswick and the Gaspé Peninsula were sometimes leased to timber companies but seldom sold. The Crown collected royalties on the timber, but investment in the land was minimal, and plunder was the norm. The indigenous peoples, for instance, nearly starved as game animals disappeared from Petit Nord, north of Lake Superior, in the 1820s.

British Land Policies. Firmly establishing British control of Canadian land took on new urgency with the American Revolution. The allegiance of some fifty thousand French people in Québec and of indigenous peoples scattered between the Great Lakes and the Maritime Provinces (Nova Scotia, Prince Edward Island, and New Brunswick) was far from assured. The Québec Act (1774), a British statute, consolidated French–Canadian loyalty by affirming French language, religion, and law. In addition, the seigneurial system was maintained; this system of land ownership, distribution, and use lasted until 1854, nearly a century after the end of French rule.

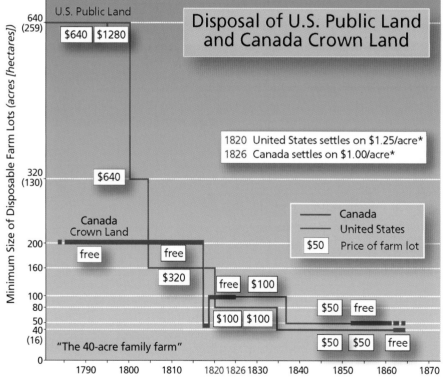

U.S. and Canadian values are given in comparable dollar figures.
Following the American Revolution, the trans-Appalachian West opened for farming settlement. Ontario, a part of British Crown land, and Ohio, a U.S. possession, demonstrated two different approaches to land allotment. Whereas the United States used the revenue from land sales to pay war debts, the British gave away Canadian land to establish a permanent British community. From the late 1700s through the middle of the nineteenth century, the United States gradually lowered the price of land, while the British raised the price. Both reduced the minimum acreage required, gradually reaching the 40-acre (16-hectare) farm, a standard plot of land for farming before mechanization became the norm in about the middle of the nineteenth century.

L A N D   U S E   M A N A G E M E N T

In a particularly audacious clause, Britain claimed land westward through the heartland of what was to become the United States—to the confluence of the Mississippi and Ohio Rivers in present-day Illinois. Treaties marking the surrender of New France (1763), the end of the American Revolution (1783), and the end of the War of 1812 with the United States (1814) all redrew Canadian boundaries, finally setting the international boundary between present-day Canada and the United States through the Great Lakes region. These treaties did not explicitly address land policy, and Crown ownership was presumed.

Loyalist grants mark the real beginning of the transfer of Canada's public lands into private hands. Following the American Revolution, nearly eighty thousand United Empire Loyalists fled north to Canada, some to the Atlantic region but most to Ontario. In recognition of their support for Britain, the Crown granted them land. High-ranking officers received as much as 7,000 acres (2,800 hectares), ordinary civilians maybe 50 (20 hectares), and a band of Iroquois Loyalists over 10,000 (4,000 hectares).

Disposal of Crown Lands. By the early nineteenth century the land itself was clearly becoming recognized as a valuable resource, not just somewhere to trap beaver or cut pine. Writing in 1798, English economist Thomas Malthus had predicted widespread famine as the suddenly accelerating growth of world population threatened to outstrip its food supply. Selling Crown lands for agricultural purposes, particularly in Ontario (*see also* 28–29), seemed to offer a solution to this predicted catastrophe. Commercial farming introduced land title, inheritance laws, and a permanent society—these lands had become real estate.

Anticipating such commodification, the Crown had withheld nearly one-third of the lots for its own revenue, scattering them throughout the rectangular survey grid in

Further Reading
Gates, Lillian F. *Land Policies of Upper Canada*. Toronto: University of Toronto Press, 1968.
Harris, Cole. *The Seigneurial System in Early Canada*. Madison: University of Wisconsin Press, 1984.
Historical Atlas of Canada. 3 vols. Toronto, University of Toronto Press, 1987, 1990–93.
McIlwraith, Thomas F. "British North America, 1763–1867." In *North America: the Historical Geography of a Changing Continent*, edited by Thomas F. McIlwraith and Edward K. Muller. New York: Rowman and Littlefield Publishers, 2001.
Ray, Arthur J. *I Have Lived Here since the World Began: An Illustrated History of Canada's Native People*. Toronto: Key Porter Books, 1996.
Wynn, Graeme. *Timber Colony: A Historical Geography of Early Nineteenth Century New Brunswick*. Toronto: University of Toronto Press, 1981.

hopes that they might rise in value as farmers worked the surrounding lands. Immigration was too slow and settlement too thinly spread for this plan to be lucrative, however, and by 1830 most reserved lots were thrown in with the general pool of lands for public sale. Ontario farming acreage thus developed by filling in gaps, quite in contrast with the frontier wave model frequently used to describe settlement expansion in the United States.

Changes to the Land. Disposal of Crown lands unleashed a frenzy of unplanned and harmful changes to the land by the new owners, who were intoxicated with the possibilities of using their private property as they wished. Pioneer farmers made fields by clearcutting forests; millers built dams that obstructed fish migration; townspeople left runoff to silt up harbors; railroad engineers altered the topography with cuts and fills; careless importers introduced English sparrows. All desired to engage in a commercial economy; these desires would be reinforced by new legislation. Britain's Corn (i.e., grain) Laws (1815–46) and Timber Acts (1810–49) established preferential tariffs that encouraged the exploitation of colonial resources and further privatization of public lands. During the nineteenth century, the management of Crown lands was gradually transferred from Britain to Canada; only then did administrators begin to recognize the impact that their actions—for example, clearing the forests—would have on both public and private space.

New Landholding Patterns. By the middle of the nineteenth century Crown lands had shrunk to include only territory that did not interest Europeans. In eastern Canada this included principally the Precambrian Shield—hundreds of square miles of black spruce and muskeg stretching from north of Lake Huron to the prairie grasslands—and boreal forest. Much of it was circumscribed space, treaty reserves where First Nations peoples (*see also* 48–49) supposedly could retain traditional lifestyles. Bounded territory was not part of traditional culture, but First Nations in modern Canada have clearly embraced the concept of land as a commodity, and ownership of their reserves became an important issue in the twentieth century.

The policy of selling Crown land into private hands was well established by the time of Canada's Confederation in 1867. A flourishing real estate market had spread beyond the farmlands to the industrial towns. Individuals seeking better lives moved easily from rural Québec into industrial cities in New England or from Ontario into the agricultural Midwest of the United States. Canada could offer its inhabitants land only from the Precambrian Shield, which remained Crown land and was transferred in stages from British to Canadian jurisdiction. Not until the late 1890s would the Canadian prairies again arouse interest as private landholdings and initiate another wave of disposal of Crown land.

—*Thomas F. McIlwraith*

The Age of Wood

The central place of wood in everyday life and the dependence upon it in the eighteenth and nineteenth centuries made that era the "Age of Wood." Wood was the predominant material used in early settlers' homes—from the furniture resting on wood floors inside clapboard or log cabin homes with wood shingle roofs to the fuel in the hearth. Tools, utensils, and storage containers like barrels and boxes were also made of wood. In addition, wood was used in the manufacture of wagons, ships, and carriages, and in iron smelting and paper production. The growing international demand for American and Canadian wood in the late eighteenth and nineteenth centuries left the eastern seaboard nearly stripped of its forests.

U.S. Timber Industry. In the early days of the American republic, shipbuilding was a vital industry that required a continual supply of timber. Recognizing the importance of retaining live oak trees for the navy and merchant fleet, in 1799 the federal government provided $200,000 for the purchase and protection of live oak, which was found only in the South. Although the navy patrolled the coasts to prevent theft by inhabitants and explored local waterways for more sources of timber, the protection proved inadequate. However, the live oak industry was only a small segment of the timber industry in the South. The huge stands of quality southern pine suitable for domestic uses led to the establishment of large commercial lumbering operations in the South. In areas too poor for cotton farming (*see also* 30–31), settlers often worked in the lumber industry. By the 1830s, naval stores (the collective name of masts, turpentine, pitch tar, and resin) had become almost as big an industry as cotton.

Whether working in the North or South, lumbermen had a profound impact on the land. Land stripped of trees left soil vulnerable to erosion; this soil, once swept into rivers and streams, left some smaller waterways unnavigable or with too little flow to run mills powered by water. Some streams filled in completely. Wood scraps and sawdust left behind by loggers could easily catch fire from human carelessness or during lightning storms. Devastating fires in New Hampshire in 1761 and 1762 destroyed so much standing timber that lumbermen had to move to Maine for work.

The New Hampshire fires proved beneficial for Maine because they eliminated a major regional source (and thus a competitor) of the highly coveted white pine, the wood of choice for furniture and construction because of its lightness, softness, and durability. Blessed with rivers suited for transporting logs, Maine's loggers readily delivered their harvests of white pine to Boston and other eastern port cities. By 1820, Maine had become the leading state for lumber production, competing directly with Canada's New Brunswick in exporting to the British colonies in the Caribbean. The fierce competition for white pine along the ill-defined border with Canada in the northern part of the state led, in 1839, to armed conflict between New Brunswick and Maine lumbermen in what became known as the Aroostook War. A treaty delineating the international boundary and clarifying the American lumbermen's privileges on the St. John River was signed in 1842. Maine led other northern U.S. states in lumber production until 1859, when it lost its place as leader in lumber production to New York, Pennsylvania, and the states of the Great

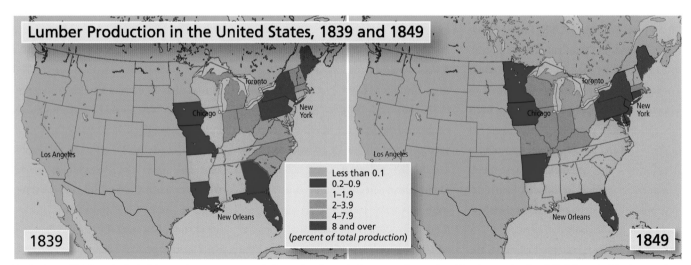

Lumber Production in the United States, 1839 and 1849

Less than 0.1
0.2–0.9
1–1.9
2–3.9
4–7.9
8 and over
(percent of total production)

1839

1849

Production, aided by technological innovations, grew to meet the increasing demand of an expanding nation. Note how production shifted from the Northeast and Mid-Atlantic regions in 1839 to the upper Midwest by 1849.

Source: Michael Williams, *Americans and Their Forests* (New York: Cambridge University Press, 1989), 162. Underlying data from H. B. Steer, *Lumber Production in the United States, 1799–1946* (Washington, D.C.: U.S. Dept. of Agriculture, 1948). Adapted with the permission of Cambridge University Press.

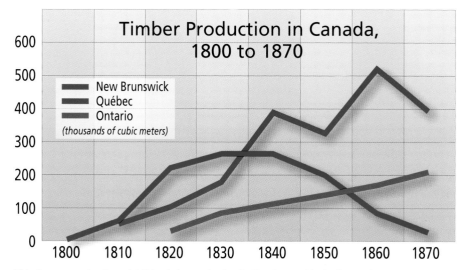

Timber Production in Canada, 1800 to 1870

New Brunswick
Québec
Ontario
(thousands of cubic meters)

This chart traces the rise and fall in timber production in New Brunswick, Québec, and Ontario.
Source: Adapted from Les Reed, *Two Centuries of Softwood Lumber War Between Canada and the United States: A Chronicle of Trade Barriers Viewed in the Context of Saw Timber Depletion* (Montreal: The Free Trade Lumber Council, May 2001), 23.

Lakes region (*see also* 34–35) and the Pacific Northwest (*see also* 60–61).

Canada's Timber Industry. The Aroostook War was just one way in which war and military needs shaped the Canadian timber industry. Prior to 1763, Canada had formal colonial ties with both France and Britain; the British and French Royal Navies relied heavily upon their colonies' forests to provide naval stores. The best trees in "the king's woods" of Canada were reserved for the navies under the "broad arrow" law—it was illegal for settlers to cut trees marked with the "broad arrow" symbol. After Britain took control of Québec in 1763, it tried to regulate the timber trade by granting licenses to cut timber, but Québec's settlers ignored the law. So much timber was cut along the St. Lawrence River and its tributaries that soil from runoff clogged the rivers. The royal government then levied a charge on shipping to pay for navigational improvements in the waterways.

At the height of the Napoleonic Wars (1806–10), Britain was cut off from its traditional sources of lumber in Russia and the Baltic states. By 1811, Britain was more dependent than ever on Canadian lumber. To guarantee supply, Britain placed a tariff on

non-colonial lumber so high that only Canada could afford to sell in Britain. U.S. demand for construction materials in western New York and Ohio and in the rapidly growing urban and industrial markets of New England and New York exceeded what the New England and Appalachian forests could supply. As a result, Ontario and Québec increased production in the 1820s and 1830s to meet the combined British and American demand. When Britain dropped the protective tariff in 1849, Canada reoriented its lumber trade toward the United States to compensate for the loss of trade with Britain.

In 1859, Angus Logan perfected his process for the manufacture of wood pulp and of paper from pulp, thus dramatically changing the role of timber in the Canadian economy. Soda pulp and sulphite mills, which used a chemical process to remove the lignin in wood, quickly popped up in eastern Canada to manufacture pulp for newspapers and magazines. The mills used softwoods, including the widely available spruce and balsam fir, because hardwood fibers were too short to make paper of adequate strength. The British, American, and domestic paper markets were close to insatiable in their demands, thus establishing

and assuring the wood industry's economic importance to Canada.

The use of wood for pulp, consumer goods, and building and railroad construction offset the decline of wood used for fuel in iron and steel manufacturing and home heating in both Canada and the United States. As America's population rapidly increased after 1865, the demand for wood continued to climb until 1907. Domestic use in Canada did not begin to rise rapidly until Manitoba, Alberta, and Saskatchewan experienced large-scale settlement after 1898. The demands of the Industrial Revolution, combined with the massive influx of immigrants in the latter half of the nineteenth century (*see also* 78–79), had an astounding impact on the landscape, especially in the United States. Whereas roughly 100 million acres (40 million hectares) of its forest had been cleared for agriculture and consumption by 1850, an additional 190 million acres (77 million hectares) was cleared within the next sixty years—nearly twice what had been taken during the previous two hundred years. The "Age of Wood" might just as easily be called the "Age of Disappearing Woods."

—*James G. Lewis*

Further Reading
Apsey, Mike, et al. *The Perpetual Forest: Using Lessons from the Past to Sustain Canada's Forests in the Future.* Vancouver, B.C.: FORCAST, 2000.
Cox, Thomas R., Robert S. Maxwell, Phillip Drennon Thomas, and Joseph J. Malone. *This Well-Wooded Land: Americans and Their Forests from Colonial Times to the Present.* Lincoln: University of Nebraska Press, 1985.
Keenleyside, Hugh L. "Forests of Canada." *Canadian Geographical Journal* 41 (July 1950): 2–15.
Walker, Laurence C. *The Southern Forest: A Chronicle.* Austin: The University of Texas Press, 1991.
Williams, Michael. *Americans and Their Forests: A Historical Geography.* Cambridge: Cambridge University Press, 1992.
The State of Canada's Forests, 1996–1997: Learning from History. Ottawa: Her Majesty the Queen in Right of Canada, 1997.

The Transportation Revolution

For European explorers and settlers in North America before the nineteenth century, trade and travel could take weeks or months. Overseas travel between North America and Britain and Europe could consume three months. Early roads followed Native American or animal trails, and most travelers went by foot or rode a horse, mule, or in a farmer's wagon. Winter travel was often impossible, while rains in spring, summer, and autumn could make roads impassible quagmires. Travel by water was often the best option, despite frozen rivers, lakes, and seaports in the winter, and ungovernable conditions like currents and tides. Frontier settlers and rural farmers remained isolated from markets; in addition, poor communication channels severely hampered the development of any colonial or national unity.

Early Roads. In 1808, president Thomas Jefferson's Secretary of the Treasury Albert Gallatin interpreted the U.S. Constitution's phrase "internal improvements" to mean that the federal government could unite the nation with roads, canals, and harbors. One outcome was the National Road (now US 40), completed in the 1850s; this highway stretched from Baltimore, Maryland, to St. Louis, Missouri. Canada, with far fewer people in a more challenging geography, suffered from community isolation even more than the United States. Roads were often little more than dirt tracks and their condition worsened in the rain. The discovery of gold in British Columbia (*see also* 66–67) would later encourage the construction of the famous Cariboo Road; in 1864 that road ran from the Pacific coast to parts of inland Canada and included wooden bridges and narrow passages blasted from rock walls.

Water Travel. Early travel on rivers like the Hudson, Ohio, Mississippi, and Missouri, as well as on the Great Lakes, remained limited, relying on wind power and human and animal muscle. Communications and trade upstream were virtually impossible. Boatmen who floated their goods in two weeks from Pittsburgh down the Ohio and then the Mississippi to New Orleans had to return empty-handed by foot on the Natchez Trace—a trail used by Native Americans that originated in Mississippi and passed through Alabama and Tennessee. The successful marriage of the steam engine to a passenger boat by inventor and engineer Robert Fulton in 1807 transformed water travel. Soon hundreds of steamboats plied America's rivers; the greater safety offered resulted in increased travel on the Great Lakes, and entry into the western territories was facilitated. By 1825 a trip upstream from New Orleans to New York City took only twenty-four days by way of inland rivers and canals. On the Atlantic, American whaling and clipper sailing ships that had once been the envy of the world would be surpassed by large and speedy steamships.

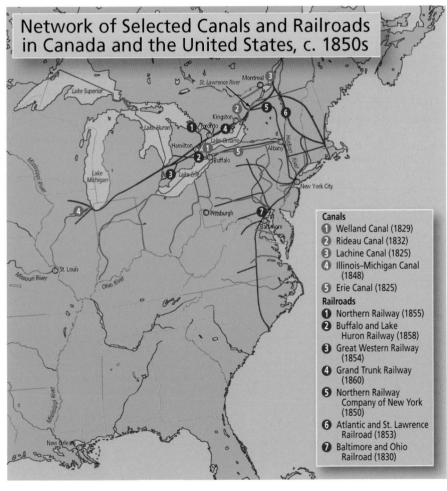

Network of Selected Canals and Railroads in Canada and the United States, c. 1850s

Canals
1. Welland Canal (1829)
2. Rideau Canal (1832)
3. Lachine Canal (1825)
4. Illinois–Michigan Canal (1848)
5. Erie Canal (1825)

Railroads
1. Northern Railway (1855)
2. Buffalo and Lake Huron Railway (1858)
3. Great Western Railway (1854)
4. Grand Trunk Railway (1860)
5. Northern Railway Company of New York (1850)
6. Atlantic and St. Lawrence Railroad (1853)
7. Baltimore and Ohio Railroad (1830)

Note: The years included in the legend box indicate when a canal or railroad was completed.
By the 1850s, the United States had built a nationwide transportation infrastructure. Public roads, canals, and railroads connected towns and cities, linking rivers, lakes, and the Atlantic coastline. Canada's development of new transportation routes, specifically railroads, would significantly expand after the 1850s.
Sources: Adapted from Donald Gordon Grady Kerr, A Historical Atlas of Canada. 2nd ed. (Don Mills, Ontario: Nelson, 1966), 48, 49, 65; and WGBH Educational Foundation, A Biography of America: The Industrial Revolution. 2000. <http://www.learner.org/biographyofamerica/prog07/feature/>.

With new innovations contributing to efficient water travel, the United States began to construct new water routes between important regions. The hugely successful Erie Canal, built between 1817 and 1825 across 363 miles (584 kilometers) of New York state from Albany to Buffalo, used public and private funds to connect the commercial East with the agricultural Great Lakes region. Travel that had taken twenty days between Albany and Buffalo now required only eight days via the canal, and goods could be shipped at a fifth of their earlier cost. In 1827 the U.S. Congress commissioned the Illinois–Michigan Canal to connect the Great Lakes with the Mississippi River. By 1840, Americans enjoyed the benefits of 3,300 miles (5,310 kilometers) of canals. Canal construction was costly, but operating costs were quite low. Equally important, such engineering marvels helped to unite the people and economies of various regions, contributing to national and personal prosperity.

In Canada, freshwater connections through major rivers and the Great Lakes offered the first commercial travel links, helping to shape the country's population centers. The Lachine Canal, built between 1821 and 1825, bypassed the St. Lawrence River rapids upstream from Montreal. Montreal in Québec and Kingston in Ontario were also linked by the Rideau Canal, constructed between 1826 and 1832. The first Welland Canal opened in 1829 to connect Lake Ontario to Lake Erie. Further plans for an extensive canal system, especially for the Maritime Provinces (Prince Edward Island, Nova Scotia, and New Brunswick), would be superseded by the emerging railroads.

Overland Trails. Neither canals nor rivers helped North Americans to traverse the semiarid plains or the arid West. Pioneers struggled across the inhospitable Plains, through mountain passes, and across waterless deserts, often traveling in Conestoga

Further Reading
Harris, R. Cole, and John Warkentin. *Canada Before Confederation: A Study in Historical Geography.* New York: Oxford University Press, 1974.
Jackson, W. Turrentine. *Wagon Roads West: A Study of Federal Road Surveys and Construction in the Trans-Mississippi West,* 1846–1869. New Haven, Conn.: Yale University Press, 1964.
Jakle, John H. *Images of the Ohio Valley: A Historical Geography of Travel, 1740 to 1860.* New York: Oxford University Press, 1977.
Winther, Oscar Osburn. *The Transportation Frontier: Trans-Mississippi West, 1865–1890.* Albuquerque: University of New Mexico, 1974.

wagons (named after the Pennsylvania region of their origin) pulled by horses or oxen, on horseback, or even pulling carts by hand. On a good day they covered 20 miles (32 kilometers). Although dreams of gold drew the first speculators to the West in 1849, the greatest number of pioneers were farmers seeking rich soil and plentiful rain in California, the Oregon country, and the Canadian Plains. In 1852, for example, ten thousand people struck out for Oregon and fifty thousand for California. In one of the great voluntary migrations of people, farmers and speculators struggled across 2,000 miles (3,200 kilometers) along the famous Oregon Trail, the California Trail, and the Mormon Trek (*see also* 52–53).

Railroads. Nothing would knit North America together like the railroad. From its start as a curious toy-like steam engine followed by little open cars on the Baltimore and Ohio Railroad (the line's first 13-mile [21-kilometer] track was completed in 1830), the railroads bound together an otherwise impossibly expansive continent. The rails were not constrained by impediments of geography and the limits of waterways could be ignored. As one construction boss put it, "Where a mule can go, I can make a locomotive go." Railroad lines combined engineering miracles with the labor of thousands of workers. Travel by rail was three times faster than that by horse and wagon, while the costs of travel and shipping declined. Climate and seasons were no longer crucial considerations. Passenger or freight cars could be added or subtracted depending on commerce, and the aptly named "Iron Horse" never tired.

By the 1850s in Canada, rail lines connected Toronto, Hamilton, and Montreal to the northeastern and midwestern United States. By the 1870s, the Intercolonial Railway linked the Maritime Provinces to Québec and Ontario. Most famous were the Great Western Railway, completed in 1854, and the Grand Trunk Railway, completed in 1860. Both sought to open western Canada's hinterland and garner commerce from the United States.

By moving goods, wealth, and people, the grid of rails became the dominant infrastructure of the United States and Canada. The entire continent had become compacted and standardized with the building of a uniform rail gauge network and the creation of four standard time zones across North America. The railroads also created new demands for iron, steel, coal, and manufacturing of locomotives, railcars, and steel rails (*see also* 64–65 *and* 72–73). By 1860, the United States had laid an unprecedented network of 26,000 miles (41,800 kilometers) of track, mostly in the northeastern and midwestern states. (During the Civil War, the southern Confederacy was severely hampered by limited railroad connections.) Many believe that the first transcontinental railroad connection in 1869 (*see also* 70–71)—3,317 miles (5,338 kilometers) between New York and San Francisco, built at record speed—was the supreme technological achievement of the United States in the nineteenth century. By the 1880s, Canada also had a transcontinental rail system.

—*John Opie*

Native Americans: Reservations and Relocations in the United States

English colonizers established the first reservations for Native Americans during the seventeenth century; Native Americans were required to move from lands that the colonizers wanted for white settlement. In 1638, Connecticut established the first of several reservations on the pretense that special areas were needed to protect small, Christianized tribes from white encroachment. This reservation consisted of 1,200 acres (500 hectares) for the Quinnipiac tribe. After the creation of the United States, the national government established reservations by treaty, executive order, or congressional decree. The government sent traders and missionaries to those reserves to show Native Americans how to live, farm, and work in an effort to destroy native culture and promote assimilation into white society.

Between the American Revolution and 1850, a growing imbalance of economic, political, and military power characterized Native American and white relations. After the War of Independence (1776–83), Congress attempted to treat Native Americans, many of whom had supported Great Britain, as conquered peoples. The national government made treaties with various tribes, arbitrarily drew boundaries, and refused to offer compensation for lands that the Native Americans were forced to cede. This government did not recognize Native Americans' rights of possession to the lands on which they lived, hunted, and farmed. Native Americans, who did not consider themselves conquered peoples, did not acquiesce to the official ignoring of their rights. Nevertheless, Native Americans continued to lose their lands to settlers despite

promises by government officials to protect the newly defined Native American lands from encroachment by whites.

Acquisition of Lands. By 1786, the policies of the government in relation to Native Americans had failed. Native Americans north and south of the Ohio River resisted the implementation of treaties that required them to cede substantial portions of their lands. Confronted with the prospect of a war that it could not afford, Congress changed its method for the acquisition of Native American lands. In 1787, Congress turned from coercion to a policy of conciliation and purchase. This policy, acknowledged in the Northwest

Ordinance of 1787, promised that the government would not take Native American lands without the consent of those living on it. Instead, the national government would negotiate cession treaties that included compensation for the acquisition of Native American lands. This policy, however, assumed that various Native American groups would willingly negotiate and sell their lands. The Intercourse Act of 1790 attempted to make the cession treaty process a workable policy by prohibiting individuals and states from purchasing Native American lands; only the federal government could do so by treaty. The practical result of this act

By about 1860 the removal of the eastern Native Americans, including the Five Civilized Tribes, to reservation lands had been completed. This forced exodus was marked by the suffering of tribes like the Cherokee on the "Trail of Tears" during the 1830s. At the same time, Native Americans of the Far West came under U.S. jurisdiction. With the exception of removals such as the Long Walk of the Navajo in the early 1860s, most of the western Native American nations would not be forced onto reservations until after the Civil War.

Source: Adapted from Mark C. Carnes, *Mapping America's Past: A Historical Atlas* (New York: Henry Holt, 1996), 132–33.

was the recognition of the right of Native American title to land by possession.

Warfare. White settlers, however, frequently ignored federal law and squatted on lands that Native Americans refused to cede. Warfare broke out north of the Ohio River between Native Americans and white settlers and the federal government during the early 1790s. After General Anthony Wayne defeated the northern nations, including the Shawnee, Miami, and Delaware, at the Battle of Fallen Timbers in 1794, the government imposed the Greenville Treaty of 1795, which resulted in the further loss of Native American lands north of the Ohio River.

Removal. Early in the nineteenth century, President Thomas Jefferson suggested solving the "Indian problem"—that is, Native American resistance to the forced selling of their lands to whites—by moving the tribes west of the Mississippi River. Jefferson believed that Native Americans could be taught to farm and rely on agriculture for subsistence, which would help them eventually to acculturate to white society. After the War of 1812 Jefferson's idea for removal gained new supporters, including Andrew Jackson. Although the federal government continued to recognize Native Americans' right of possession, it actively worked to acquire Native American lands by cession treaties and to relocate the eastern tribes west of the Mississippi River.

During the 1820s the demands for removal increased. Some whites who wanted Native American lands favored removal if Native Americans received fair compensation for their lands, while others cared little about fairness and merely sought removal of Native Americans where their presence prevented expansion of white settlement. By 1825 most of the Native Americans in the Old Northwest (which would become the states of Illinois, Indiana, Michigan,

Ohio, and Wisconsin) had been moved west of the Mississippi and placed on tribal reserves (relatively small tracts of land) under their own jurisdiction. Whites also sought control of Native American lands south of the Ohio River. In 1830, during the presidency of Andrew Jackson, Congress passed the Indian Removal Act, which required most tribes to move beyond the Mississippi River. Not all tribes peacefully accepted removal, but the federal government crushed this resistance in the Black Hawk War (1832), the Creek War (1835–36), and the Second Seminole War (1835–42). Between 1831 and 1839, most of the Choctaw, Chickasaw, Creek, Seminole, and Cherokee, collectively known as the Five Civilized Tribes, exchanged their lands east of the Mississippi River for lands to the west, between Missouri and Arkansas and the 100th meridian, an area called Indian Territory.

The Choctaw were the first tribe to be relocated under the Indian Removal Act. They began leaving their homeland in present-day Mississippi in October 1831 and experienced incredible hardship. The Creek and Chickasaw followed, but the Cherokee moved west from Georgia only after the army and state militia forced them from their homes. Approximately fourteen thousand Cherokee emigrated and perhaps as many as four thousand died from dysentery and starvation. The particularly brutal removal of the Cherokee has led the term "Trail of Tears" to be associated with them, symbolizing the removal process and Native American–white relations of the era. In the 1830s and 1840s, the federal government also negotiated the removal of most of the remaining northern tribes, including the Potawatomie, Miami, Sauk and Fox, and Wyandot. The removal of most of the Seminole from Florida would not occur until 1859.

Further Reading

Hagan, William T. *The American Indian.* Rev. ed. Chicago: University of Chicago Press, 1993.

Hurt, R. Douglas. *The Indian Frontier, 1763–1846.* Albuquerque: University of New Mexico Press, 2002.

Prucha, Francis Paul. *The Great Father: The United States Government and the American Indians.* 2 vols. Lincoln: University of Nebraska Press, 1995.

During the 1840s, white settlers who made their way west on the overland trails (*see also* 52–53) encroached on Native American lands, and many whites ultimately settled on lands that Native Americans claimed in the Pacific Northwest. The U.S. victory in 1848 over Mexico in the Mexican War brought additional Native American peoples (who were located in present-day New Mexico, Arizona, and California) under the authority of the United States. However, those tribes and the nomadic Native Americans of the Great Plains remained beyond the control of the federal government until after the Civil War.

Reservations. In 1850, Commissioner of Indian Affairs Luke Lea proposed a system of reservations that would place all tribes on reserves where they could be controlled, educated, Christianized, and taught to farm. These reservations would be permanent, limited areas where Native Americans would live in fixed homes, eventually own their land, and have systematic support from the federal government. The removal of all Native American tribes to reservations would not be achieved until after the Civil War. The expulsion of the Native Americans from their lands east of the Mississippi River and their removal to reservations enabled white settlers to use the environment for agriculture on an unprecedented scale while depriving the Native American people of the lands that they used for hunting, fishing, and farming (*see also* 154–55).

—*R. Douglas Hurt*

Canada's First Nations

Between 1763 and 1876 access to wildlife resources by First Nations—the modern term used to refer to Canada's indigenous peoples—was affected by treaties, settlement, and government policy in Canada. This involvement was prompted by increasing numbers of settlers and farmers occupying First Nations land. British settlers, who believed strongly in the concept of private property, did not want First Nations peoples "trespassing" on their land to gain access to or use traditional resources. Treaties—the legal means through which land became available for settlement—necessitated a legal definition of *Indian*. This term was used by Europeans for First Nations and today constitutes a legal definition under federal legislation. Those not defined as Indians existed outside of the treaty system. This group included Métis (those of mixed First Nations and European heritage); non-status Indians (those who had lost their status and special rights); and non-treaty Indians (those who qualified as status Indians, but had not yet signed a treaty). British and Canadian officials did not consider Métis and non-status Indians to possess any extraordinary rights to wildlife resources or land. Non-treaty Indians possessed full rights to their land until they entered into treaties with the Canadian government, at which point they found themselves subject to conservation laws and other federal and provincial laws.

Early Treaties. The British treaty system grew out of Pontiac's Rebellion in the Ohio Valley in 1763 (in present-day Ohio in the United States). Pontiac, an Ottawa chief, organized and led a confederacy of tribes against British settlers occupying First Nations land either without permission or via questionable treaties. Pontiac's followers were concerned more with the actual loss of territory than with restricted access to wildlife. Although unsuccessful, Pontiac's Rebellion convinced the British government that a formal treaty process was needed to both recognize First Nations ownership of land and provide the British with the legal means to acquire land from indigenous groups. This Royal Proclamation of 1763 forbade any private citizen from purchasing land from "the several Nations or Tribes of Indians" within the British colonies. Only the British Crown could obtain land through treaty, and then sell it to settlers.

Britain's recognition of First Nations land ownership continued in the remaining British colonies after the American Revolution (1776–83). As Loyalists fled to the colony of Upper Canada (created in 1791, and today constituting what is southern and central Ontario), Britain entered into formal treaties with the Ojibwa who lived in the area. Early treaties were concerned primarily with acquiring land for settlement; the colonial governments of British North America (Canada) did not consider wildlife to be economically important enough to restrict anyone's use of or access to it. None of these treaties, therefore, explicitly recognized First Nations access to wildlife; however, the abundance of natural resources, combined with a small settler population, served to minimize conflict between settlers and members of the First Nations over access during the early settlement of Upper Canada.

By the 1830s the official policy of the British Indian Department switched from courting First Nations as military allies for war with the United States (an increasingly remote possibility) to trying to "civilize" and Christianize them. At the same time, increased settlement was also limiting First

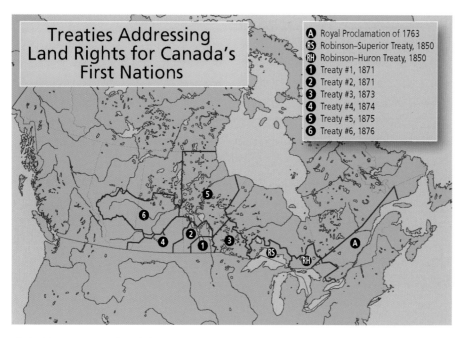

Treaties Addressing Land Rights for Canada's First Nations

- **A** Royal Proclamation of 1763
- **RS** Robinson–Superior Treaty, 1850
- **RH** Robinson–Huron Treaty, 1850
- **1** Treaty #1, 1871
- **2** Treaty #2, 1871
- **3** Treaty #3, 1873
- **4** Treaty #4, 1874
- **5** Treaty #5, 1875
- **6** Treaty #6, 1876

The British government, through the Royal Proclamation of 1763, established a formal treaty system with Canada's First Nations. The Robinson–Huron and Robinson–Superior Treaties of 1850 recognized First Nations hunting and fishing rights, while six Numbered Treaties—created between 1871 and 1876—protected First Nations wildlife rights as long as they did not interfere with government conservation laws.
Sources: Adapted from Olive Patricia Dickason, *Canada's First Nations: A History of Founding Peoples from Earliest Times* (Don Mills, Ont.: Oxford University Press, 2002), 254; and Carl Waldman, *Atlas of the North American Indian* (New York: Facts On File, 1985), 212.

Further Reading

Dickason, Olive Patricia. *Canada's First Nations: A History of Founding Peoples from Earliest Times.* 3rd ed. Don Mills, Ont.: Oxford University Press, 2002.

Krech, Shepard, III. *The Ecological Indian: Myth and History.* New York: W. W. Norton, 1999.

Rogers, Edward S., and Donald B. Smith, eds. *Aboriginal Ontario: Historical Perspectives on the First Nations.* Toronto: Dundurn Press, 1994.

Smith, Donald B. "The Dispossession of the Mississauga Indians: A Missing Chapter in the Early History of Upper Canada." *Ontario History* 73, no. 2 (1981): 61–87.

Nations access to wildlife. Reduced First Nations opportunities to hunt, therefore, actually complemented Canada's new Indian policy. The government—making no effort to protect First Nations access to resources—attempted to facilitate the assimilation of indigenous groups by encouraging them to abandon hunting, adopt farming, and permanently relocate to reserves.

Northern Treaties. In northern lands unsuitable for farming, the government allowed First Nations to hunt and fish without interference, as the government was more interested in timber and mineral resources like copper and iron. The Robinson–Huron and Robinson–Superior Treaties of 1850 (which cover part of the lands north of Lake Huron and Lake Superior—a remote part of Upper Canada at the time) were the first treaties to recognize explicitly First Nations hunting and fishing rights in exchange for Crown access to other natural resources. Crown negotiator William Robinson promised the Ojibwa who signed the treaties that they and their descendants would retain their right to hunt, trap, and fish.

New Restrictions. Whereas early laws restricting access to natural resources exempted First Nations, new pressures led to the application of wildlife conservation laws (*see also* 96–97) to indigenous groups during the last half of the nineteenth century. Commercial pressure, for example, caused the government to restrict Ojibwa and Iroquois fishing on the Great Lakes even though Upper Canada's 1857 Fisheries Act provided exemptions for both tribes. Settlers also increasingly refused to allow First Nations peoples access to traditional hunting

and fishing grounds if they were located on their property.

In 1851 the government of Canada passed An Act for the Better Protection of the Lands and Property of the Indians in Lower Canada (present-day southern Québec) to further refine the legal definition of *Indian*. According to the act, to be an Indian one had to belong to a recognized tribe; be married to an Indian and living with his tribe; have been adopted in infancy by a tribe and living with them; or be living with a different tribe but still have one Indian parent. Those not defined legally as Indian were treated as ordinary subjects of the Crown and were required to obey all laws, including restrictions on hunting and fishing, as they applied to all other inhabitants of Canada.

Impact of Confederation. In 1860, Britain transferred control of First Nation affairs to the Province of Canada. After Canada's Confederation in 1867, constitutional responsibility for First Nations peoples was given to the federal government in Ottawa rather than being vested in the provinces. A federal Department of Indian Affairs was established, and further legislation that legally defined *Indian* was passed. In 1869, An Act for the Gradual Enfranchisement of Indians defined an Indian specifically as "no person of less than one-fourth Indian blood." With the Indian Act of 1876, which consolidated decades of Indian legislation into a single act, the defining characteristics of Indian status became 25 percent "Indian blood" and band membership. Band membership meant that one was a treaty Indian (as bands, which were located on reserves, were created through

the treaty process), and that your name was on a "band list." Non-treaty and non-status Indians lacked band membership. The 1876 Indian Act explicitly excluded Métis.

Following confederation, settlers moved farther west into what would become northern Ontario, Manitoba, Saskatchewan, and Alberta, which necessitated new treaties to prevent tension between indigenous groups and settlers. Between 1871 and 1876, six Numbered Treaties (numbered sequentially starting with one) were signed with the Ojibwa, Cree, Assiniboine, and Chipewyan peoples. Reflecting the reality that settlement inevitably restricted First Nations hunting opportunities, each numbered treaty noted that First Nations wildlife rights were protected insofar as they did not conflict with government conservation laws. Historical evidence, however, reveals that this proviso was not explained to the First Nations that signed the treaties.

Under Canada's constitution, wildlife remained under provincial control (unless located in a territory, in which case the federal government regulated it). Severe restrictions were not placed on wildlife resources until the 1890s. By this point tourism in conjunction with an increasing network of provincial and federal parks (*see also* 112–13) made wildlife a valuable resource, and both levels of government enforced regulations regardless of treaties with First Nations. Conflict over resource use continues: Métis in Manitoba and Ontario have filed suits arguing that they have a right to hunt and fish as an aboriginal people. Non-status Indians, including the Golden Lake Algonquian of Ontario, are seeking government recognition of their claims to a land and resource base. Treaty and status Indians have fared best in Canada, winning a number of victories in the Supreme Court of Canada to have their treaty hunting rights respected by all levels of government.

—David Calverley

The Return to Nature: Transcendentalism and Utopian Communities

In the mid-nineteenth century, American transcendentalism (1836–60), which considered nature and wilderness to be the source of truth about the individual and society, flourished. In Canada and the United States, transcendentalism became associated with back-to-the-land and utopian social movements—social experiments that attempted to create harmonious and ordered communities. The weak central governments in Canada and the United States largely ignored these social experiments, thus creating an atmosphere of tolerance.

Transcendentalism. The literary work of American transcendentalists reflected the shift toward experimentation and a greater appreciation of nature. American philosopher Ralph Waldo Emerson wrote his seminal book of essays, *Nature* (1836), describing the mystical unity of man and nature. Although the first edition of five hundred took thirteen years to sell out, Emerson's work would have a significant effect on groups like the Quakers, Shakers, and Owenites. In 1845 and 1846, American writer Henry David Thoreau lived at Walden Pond near Concord, Massachusetts, testing Emerson's principles, including rejection of materialism and close observation of nature. Thoreau recorded the results in a journal of personal discovery about the effects of the wild, seasons, solitude, and self-sufficiency, publishing them in *A Week on the Concord and Merrimack Rivers* (1849), *The Maine Woods* (1864), and *Excursions* (1864).

Utopian Communities. Concurrent with Thoreau's solitary experiment at Walden Pond, others were attempting to establish ideal communities in Canada and the United States. Most of these communities agreed at least in part with the transcendental precept that a return to nature was essential to the revitalization of human beings. This might mean simple access to wild places or a bucolic setting for the experimental community; by choosing to live in or near wilderness, participants had the opportunity to develop a genuine relationship with nature. Many members of these communities were dissatisfied with political corruption, crime, religious intolerance, the noise and pollution of the cities, and the abstract creeds of Protestant denominations. By participating in an experimental community, they hoped to discard all that was false in society and discover the original and genuine based on individual experience in the presence of nature.

One of the driving forces behind these experiments was religion, and charismatic leaders with theological backgrounds often held communities together; for example, John Humphrey Noyes at Oneida Creek, New York (Oneida Community, est. 1848), George Ripley at West Roxbury, Massachusetts (Brook Farm, est. 1841), and Amos Bronson Alcott in Worcester County, Massachusetts (Fruitlands, est. 1843). The Oneida Community, for instance, began as a Bible study group and became interested in free love practices and a return to the principles of the primitive Christian church. Fruitlands began as an extension of Alcott's family, but eventually broke up over the attempt of several members to introduce a Shaker-like celibacy based on the Bible.

Because many communes were associated with influential leadership, they often collapsed after the death or absence of a specific leader. Social engineering (managing and planning the immediate social contract between people) seemed to fare better. The Amana Society, which originally settled near Buffalo in New York state, lasted from 1843 to 1932 because the enterprise prospered through the marketing of agricultural

Children from the Oneida community in New York state dance in the upper sitting room during children's hour. (© Bettmann/Corbis)

products like wheat, corn, and vegetables. As the colony grew in economic strength, however, its spiritual center seemed to dissipate in favor of trade as religious meetings gave way to economic planning sessions. The Oneida Community outlasted the tumultuous career of Noyes because of social engineering: After the society came to an end in 1880, it continued as a flatware manufacturer, the Oneida Company, Ltd., well into the twentieth century.

In addition to social experiments based on religion and social engineering, a number of other theories were influential in the United States and Canada during the early nineteenth century. Brook Farm and Fruitlands enjoyed short ecstatic lives that tested theories of labor and spirituality. Fruitlands, for example, experimented with an innovative division of labor based on personal preferences, individualized spiritual pursuits (worship respecting all idiosyncrasies), dietary changes (essentially vegan), and, above all, the chance to create a singular and authentic self in conjunction with experience in nature. Fruitlands promoted the idea that the spirit abiding in each person would unify the group, with organizing and operational principles revealed by this coming together. Accordingly, the community abandoned plans, rules, mission statements, and other overarching guidelines because they believed that true commitment to idealism would ensure correct behavior and viable social organization.

Further Reading

Berry, Brian J. *America's Utopian Experiments: Communal Havens from Long-Wave Crises.* Hanover, N.H.: University Press of New England, 1992.

Fogarty, Robert S. *Dictionary of American Communal and Utopian History.* Westport, Conn.: Greenwood Press, 1980.

Nordhoff, Charles. *The Communistic Societies of the United States: From Personal Visit and Observation.* 1875. Reprint, New York: Dover Publications, 1966.

Brook Farm

Brook Farm, established at West Roxbury, Massachusetts, in 1841, consisted of two hundred acres of farmland. Founded by George Ripley, it is the most well known of any of the North American social experiments. Transcendentalist leader Ralph Waldo Emerson visited and lectured at Brook Farm, but was not a member of the community.

Brook Farm was influenced by teacher and social reformer Albert Brisbane, who in 1840 introduced the ideas of the great European socialist, Charles Fourier, to Concord, Massachusetts. Fourier proposed the Phalanx, a name he invented for the unit of a social structure (almost like a small town), as the ideal community (best if rural in setting) that should be built around a central building or Phalanstery. According to Fourier, the building should be massive with "colonades, domes, and peristyles," and should include a reception hall, workshops, playrooms for children, music rooms, dining rooms, meeting rooms, and a library. In 1843 Brook Farm became a Fourierist Phalanx.

The leaders of Brook Farm maintained that all labor was sacred when done in the common interest and all labor was therefore worth the same wage per hour. Household, land, and board were kept in common and no single member owned any of the means of production. The members of the community preferred linen for clothing and bedding because its source in the flax plant incurred none of the moral ambiguity of other fabrics, such as cotton, which was produced by slaves, or wool, which robbed sheep of natural protection. Education served as the center of activity around the farm, whether in field, barn, or house, and was often experientially based, with children leaving the classroom to take nature walks and personally examine the natural world.

In 1846 a great fire destroyed the central Phalanstery, and the community went bankrupt and dissolved, its members returning to their previous lives. However, the influence of the Brook Farm social experiment persisted. Henry David Thoreau, John Muir, John Burroughs, and other late-nineteenth-century nature writers often reflected on ideas derived from Brook Farm, such as the recognition that nature is fragile and requires stewardship, and the belief that contact with nature best reveals one's humanity. The experiences and ideas generated by the commune influenced important thinking for the rest of the nineteenth century and well into the next.

Canada and the United States shared experimental colonies across their border. When Noyes was driven from the Oneida Community in 1870 by local citizens because he was an adulterer, he sought refuge in Niagara Falls, Canada, where he lived outside the communal structure. When the Hutterites, a religious group founded in Switzerland after the Reformation in the sixteenth century, alarmed local populations and local law enforcement with their expansionist land purchases and pacifist outlook, they moved into Saskatchewan in central Canada where they raised wheat.

Influence on Later Movements. Directly or indirectly, these nineteenth-century experiments led to twentieth-century environmental movements: conservation, preservation, and various back-to-the-earth movements (*see also* 110–115). Later in the twentieth century, American environmentalist Aldo Leopold (*see also* 124–25) wrote *A Sand County Almanac* (1949) and brought the concern for the natural world into focus with his land ethic that laid out the human responsibility to return forests and grasslands to health and to give back to the land what has been taken. Today, the environmental movements (*see also* 162–65) and environmental protection at all government levels in the United States and Canada owe much to nineteenth-century utopian communities and transcendentalism.

—*Michael H. Strelow*

Manifest Destiny and the Politics of U.S. Western Expansion

During the eighteenth and nineteenth centuries, many believed that expansion of the United States was divinely ordained: It was God's will for the United States to stretch from the Atlantic Ocean to the Pacific Ocean. Known as Manifest Destiny, this apparently simple tenet was used to justify westward expansion of the United States. It masked, however, a wider set of political, economic, and social motives for expanding the nation and much darker undercurrents, including the wholesale environmental transformation of the continent and the decimation of the Native American population (*see also* 46–47).

Roots of Manifest Destiny. The expression "Manifest Destiny" was coined by journalist and diplomat John O'Sullivan in the July–August 1845 issue of *United States Magazine and Democratic Review.* Commenting on the annexation of Texas, he wrote of a "manifest destiny to overspread the continent allotted by Providence for the free development of our multiplying millions." In an earlier article, O'Sullivan had argued that the expansion of America brought an opportunity to create an ideal civilization that would not repeat the religious wars of Europe and the rapacious barbarism of its monarchies.

Manifest Destiny embodied a broad set of ideas. In religious terms, it crystallized an ideal that had inspired early communities; Alexander Whitaker, a Virginia minister, had clearly been speaking of Manifest Destiny in 1613, for example, when he preached: "God hath opened this passage unto us and led us by the hand unto this work." In politics, Manifest Destiny offered a response to territorial disputes. As a philosophy, it borrowed elements of conservative thought, for example, the importance of individualism, the power of nationalism, and the idea of social Darwinism—that societies and their people behave in self-serving ways to ensure

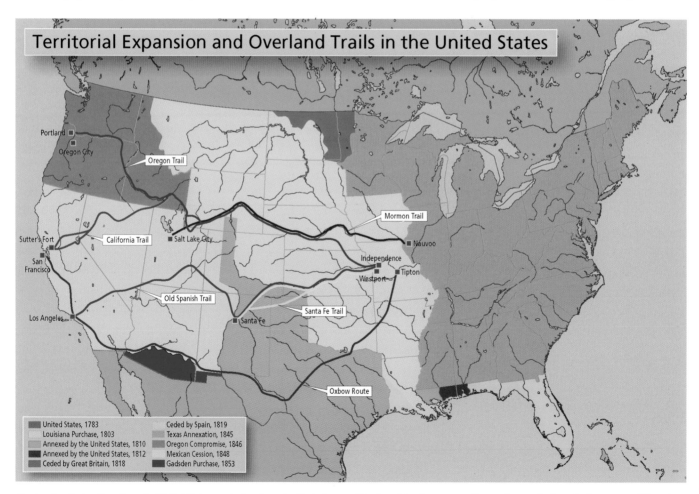

Territorial Expansion and Overland Trails in the United States

Portland
Oregon City
Oregon Trail
Sutter's Fort
California Trail
Salt Lake City
San Francisco
Old Spanish Trail
Los Angeles
Santa Fe
Santa Fe Trail
Mormon Trail
Nauvoo
Independence
Westport
Tipton
Oxbow Route

United States, 1783
Louisiana Purchase, 1803
Annexed by the United States, 1810
Annexed by the United States, 1812
Ceded by Great Britain, 1818
Ceded by Spain, 1819
Texas Annexation, 1845
Oregon Compromise, 1846
Mexican Cession, 1848
Gadsden Purchase, 1853

During the nineteenth century, the United States acquired vast new territories by a combination of purchase, annexation, and surrender from foreign powers, while settlers made their way to the frontier along wagon trails to the West. Many people saw the conquest of the continent as God's divine plan—the Manifest Destiny of Americans.

the "survival of the fittest" (*see also* 82–83). Finally, Manifest Destiny captured the romanticism that became increasingly important in North American art and writing (*see also* 86–87) during the nineteenth century. One of the most famous paintings of this period, Emmanuel Leutze's *Westward the Course of Empire* (1861), shows wagon trains of expectant pioneers waving excitedly toward the West.

Causes of Western Expansion. A divine mandate may have been claimed for the United States, but western expansion proceeded for a host of other reasons. The economic imperative to expand agricultural lands and to take advantage of mineral-rich areas like California (*see also* 66–67) was strong. More people were needed to work these areas and the U.S. population grew rapidly (almost fivefold between 1800 and 1850), making the acquisition of frontier lands inevitable. Technology also played a role. Agricultural innovations (*see also* 56–57) like the Deere plow and McCormick reaper made working ever-larger acreage possible. Transportation advances (*see also* 44–45), including the construction of canals in the early 1800s and railroads throughout the nineteenth century, created national markets for goods, while long-distance communications like the telegraph developed by Samuel Morse in 1837 and mass-circulation newspapers (made possible by the invention of the fast rotary press in 1846) held the nation together. New legislation cloaked the doctrine of Manifest Destiny in respectability. The Land Act of 1796 allowed 640-acre (260-hectare) lots of virgin territory to be sold to speculators; the Preemption Act of 1841 allowed squatters to purchase their own territories; and the Homestead Act of 1862 provided settlers with free farms.

Some historians contend that the spirit of Manifest Destiny runs through every period of U.S. history, but it is most closely associated with the nineteenth century when the nation was expanding westward at its fastest rate. By the early 1800s, settlers had crossed the Appalachian Mountains; during the 1820s, they reached the Mississippi River. A decade later, the frontier had pushed into Iowa, Arkansas, and the eastern parts of Texas. By the 1840s, pioneers were crossing the Great Plains to the West.

Territorial Conflicts. The rapid acceleration of western expansion during the nineteenth century inevitably brought conflict with other nations. Indeed, territorial rivalry between the United States, Britain, and Mexico provided much of the political motivation for western expansion; the notion of Manifest Destiny could be used by the United States to help solve these disputes in its own favor. In 1818, U.S. forces under General (and future president) Andrew Jackson pushed south into Florida, forcing the Spanish to relinquish that territory and, in the Adams–Onís Treaty of 1819, to cede all territories north of California, effectively opening up the West to future annexation. In 1823, President James Monroe warned Europeans not to interfere in the politics of the Western Hemisphere; this so-called Monroe Doctrine was firmly grounded in the rhetoric of Manifest Destiny. The election in 1828 and 1832 of Andrew Jackson, known as "Old Hickory," put into office a president who favored common people—western farmers and settlers—over powerful East Coast interests.

As settlers moved farther and farther west, they made the territorial claims of other nations increasingly untenable. The 1844 election of James Polk (sometimes known as "Young Hickory") to the presidency on an unapologetically expansionist ticket marked the true arrival of Manifest Destiny with key disputes over Oregon, Texas, and Mexico. About five thousand settlers had occupied Oregon by the 1840s, thus obliging the British government to cede

Further Reading

Cherry, Conrad, ed. *God's New Israel: Religious Interpretations of American Destiny.* Englewood Cliffs, N.J.: Prentice-Hall, 1971.

Haynes, Sam. *James K. Polk and the Expansionist Impulse.* 2nd ed. New York: Longman, 2002.

McLynn, Frank. *Wagons West: The Epic Story of America's Overland Trails.* London: Jonathan Cape, 2002.

Ward, Geoffrey. *The West: An Illustrated History.* Boston: Little, Brown, 1996.

all parts of the territory south of the 49th parallel to the United States in 1846. When some of the twenty thousand settlers in Texas protested Mexican rule in 1835, annexation of Texas (which occurred in 1845) became inevitable. Additional territories, from Texas to the Pacific Ocean, were added following the Mexican War (1846–48). Finally, in the 1853 Gadsden Purchase, the United States bought from Mexico the southern part of present-day Arizona and New Mexico and thus acquired all its present territories with the exception of Alaska and Hawaii.

Consequences. This optimistic, nationalistic, and defiant philosophy had a darker side. Agricultural expansion brought the decimation of forests and wilderness areas; urbanization (which increased by 92 percent in the 1840s alone) meant a dramatic increase in the use of natural resources; canals and water-powered factories led to the diversion and death of rivers, dams disrupted the free movement of fish species including salmon; and railroads contributed to the demise of the bison (*see also* 36–37). Nowhere was the sinister side of Manifest Destiny more evident than in the plight of the Native American population, uprooted and pushed across the nation virtually to extinction. Arguably, Manifest Destiny was no worse than the imperialist policies of nations like Britain, yet in its darker deeds it was a far cry from the ideal civilization proposed by O'Sullivan.

—*Chris Woodford*

CHAPTER THREE

Landscape of Industrialization
(1850s–1920s)

The railroad, Henry David Thoreau believed, was a harbinger of tremendous change. "When I hear the iron horse make the hills echo with his snort like thunder, shaking the earth with his feet, and breathing fire and smoke from his nostrils," he wrote in *Walden* (1854), "it seems as if the earth had got a race now worthy to inhabit it."

Was this railroad a good thing? Thoreau doubted that it was. Although he was grateful for the rail line along which he walked more easily from his home in Concord, Massachusetts, to his sanctuary on Walden Pond, and although he enjoyed the company of birds that sang from their perches created by the rail corridor through the forest, Thoreau worried about the railroad's larger social and environmental consequences. The rapid spread of the tracks throughout his beloved New England hastened commercial development and increased the tempo of human life. Driven ever faster by the railroad's energy, becoming like this steam machine, his fellow citizens were poised to triumph over nature.

Impact of the Railroads. Thoreau was right in his observation that the railroad was altering the settled eastern regions of the United States and Canada; he was also correct in his sense that the railroad would contribute greatly to the conquest of western territories in Canada and the United States. Beginning in the mid-nineteenth century, investors poured immense amounts of capital into the construction of a web of rail networks linking cities to agricultural hinterlands. These investments had an especially sustained impact in the United States. Regional economic orientations became more entrenched: slave labor and cotton production dominated southern life, while in the West, homesteaders plowed the prairie,

ranchers ran herds of sheep, goat, and cattle, and miners hustled into the mountains to strike it rich. The northeastern states became increasingly industrialized. These economic emphases had serious political ramifications, not least of which was the increasing and accelerated tensions that eventually exploded into the Civil War in the United States in 1861. Yet the very dependence on the railroad that Thoreau had once decried, enabled the northern states to launch an ultimately successful invasion of the Confederacy, moving troops, war matériel, and food quickly and effectively to the South.

Timber Production and Renewal. Following the Civil War, transcontinental rail lines were laid in the United States; in 1869, the newly reunited nation celebrated the completion of its first east–west link; in 1885, Canada completed an Atlantic-to-Pacific route. As migrants rolled west, commodities flowed east, timber chief among them. The U.S. and Canadian appetite for wood seemed as limitless as the western forests. Well-financed corporations supported the lumber industry through greater mechanization; the industry grew as the cutting and hauling of logs intensified, and rail and ocean transport carried wood across the continent and to new Asian and South American markets. By the late nineteenth century, American lumber production had become centered in the Pacific Northwest, and within fifty years British Columbia would play the same prominent role in Canadian timber production.

This rapid increase in logging sparked worries over a "timber famine," and as the woods were cleared, prices rose. These environmental and economic pressures would force resource developers to adopt more conservative approaches to logging. By the early twentieth century, for instance, the first tree farms had been established, an acknowledgment that intensively harvesting and then abandoning forests was no longer profitable.

Industrialization of Agriculture. Like their contemporaries in timber production, farmers also took advantage of new mechanical devices. Beginning in the 1870s, farmers in western Canada and the United States purchased more efficient plows, and later tractors, to till more land and reduce human energy and effort; with these machines, production soared, food prices dropped, and the number of laborers and animals needed to harvest and market crops decreased sharply. The effect on both nations' economies was profound, as agriculture no longer dominated; in 1850, more than one-half of the United States was involved in farming; by 1930 only 25 percent of the population was so occupied.

Migration to the Cities. Freed from the soil, hundreds of thousands of men and women joined with millions of new immigrants to seek work in the burgeoning cities of Chicago, Illinois; Toronto, Ontario; and New York City. This urbanized labor force entered factories and sweatshops, providing one essential—labor—to the Industrial Revolution. Their presence in such great numbers also forced the reconstruction of the built environment. In response to chaotic growth and dangerous epidemics, a new infrastructure of streets and trolleys, water pipelines and sewage systems was hastily and incompletely assembled; much-needed fire departments and police protection were also established. Other social problems persisted in these vast metropolises: The invention of the elevator and spread of mass transit permitted new residential patterns to be established. These new living patterns were tightly segregated along racial, ethnic, and economic lines; high-density slums and low-density garden suburbs, like the pall of smoke that befouled the air, became the markers of an urban–industrial landscape.

Romanticism and Reform. The speed with which western forests had been converted into wood products and the speed with which North American cities had become polluted sinkholes caused an anguished

The Canadian Pacific Railway—Canada's first transcontinental railroad—cutting through Wapta Canyon in British Columbia in the early twentieth century. (From the collections of the Library of Congress)

rethinking of the Industrial Era. Painters and writers in Canada and the United States, men and women who drew on a shared faith in European Romanticism, challenged assumptions that humans could consume nature's bounty without restraint. In conveying the West's startling and beautiful landscapes, for instance, these artists and critics demanded that their contemporaries approach the landscape with greater wonder and reverence, even with a sense of awe. Similarly, the so-called City Beautiful movement, which reached its height at the start of the twentieth century, called for dramatic changes in the crowded and fetid conditions in which millions of immigrants lived. Landscape architect Frederick Law Olmsted, like boosters in the American Park and Outdoor Art Association and the Ottawa Improvements Commission, mapped out large urban parks as "breathing spaces" for the poor and downtrodden. Those in the City Beautiful movement sketched plans for monumental plazas and municipal centers as ceremonial spaces; sections of the capital cities of Ottawa and Washington, D.C., were reconfigured as bold statements of civic and national pride. All of these proposals, whether realized or not, reflected the era's deep anxieties about how best to address the massive impact of urbanization and industrialization.

—*Char Miller*

Agricultural Innovations and Technology

The second half of the nineteenth century began a period of transition from the world of human-powered agriculture to the highly mechanized agricultural world of today. Improved farming machinery combined with the horses and, later, tractors that pulled them brought in nothing less than a revolution in productivity. Coupled with increased demand for food crops and other farm produce from a burgeoning population, this fundamentally changed both the nature of agriculture and the environment of North America.

Humans had used agricultural machines for millennia. Plows pulled by oxen, for example, were used in Palestine in about 1000 B.C. and had been improved by successive innovations. What actually transformed agricultural technology was the Industrial Revolution, which began in North America around the middle of the nineteenth century. The Industrial Revolution brought new materials (such as cast iron and steel), new forms of power (first steam, later gasoline and diesel), and new attitudes and techniques (widespread mechanization and mass production) to society.

Deere Plow. Nothing illustrates the change of thinking quite so well as John Deere's development of the self-cleaning steel plow. A blacksmith by trade, Deere had moved from his native Vermont in the 1830s to join early settlers in Illinois. The heavy and fertile midwestern soil proved much harder to plow than the sandy soil of New England; farmers would have to stop every few feet to scrape the sticky humus from the plow blade, making plowing, already a slow and laborious process, even more arduous. In 1837, Deere developed a plow made of highly polished and carefully shaped steel that cleaned away the soil automatically. By 1848, he had opened a factory at Moline, Illinois, where he was soon mass-producing more than one thousand plows a year. However efficient, the Deere plow was costly. Other innovators, including James Oliver of Indiana, jumped into the field. Oliver would develop a lower-cost iron plow called the "sod buster" in 1868.

McCormick Reaper. The steel plow was not the only agricultural innovation of this period. In 1831, Virginia-based inventor Cyrus Hall McCormick had developed the first successful reaping machine, one of the forerunners of the modern combine harvester, which was widely adopted throughout North America and Europe. By 1847, McCormick had opened a factory in Chicago to mass-produce his invention and, in the years that followed, he continued to refine

An undated illustrated cover of the McCormick Harvesting Machine Company's catalog. (© Bettmann/Corbis)

and improve it. The first McCormick reaper did little more than cut the stalks of wheat, which then had to be gathered by hand. Successive improvements included a board at the back of the reaper so that the stalks could be pushed more easily into piles by the operator, the addition of rakes called "sails" that removed the stalks mechanically, and, in the 1870s, extra machinery that would bind the grain stalks into sheaves automatically.

Agricultural Productivity. Innovations like the Deere plow and McCormick reaper, which were designed to be drawn by horses, improved farm productivity dramatically. In 1850, about seventy-five to ninety hours were needed to plant and harvest 2.5 acres (1 hectare) of corn using hand-propelled implements and other manual methods. By 1890, the same amount of corn could be produced in only thirty-five to forty hours using the latest mechanized plows, harrows, and planters, while 5 acres (2 hectares) of wheat could be produced in just forty to fifty hours using horse-powered machines. By the beginning of the twentieth century, farm machinery and implements were largely powered by horses and mules, not humans.

Animal power and efficient mass-produced implements doubled productivity, but even greater productivity gains became possible with the arrival of tractors (machines that convert the rotational power of an engine into tractive, or pulling, power). Steam-powered traction engines were available as early as the 1850s and could plow an area

The Fordson Model F

U.S. industrialist Henry Ford is best remembered for making automobiles popular through the mass production of his best-selling 1908 Model T Ford. The son of a farmer, Ford proved to be no less important a figure in the history of agricultural technology.

After using car parts to develop a prototype "automobile plow" in 1907 (the word "tractor" had only just been coined), Ford set up an independent company, the Henry Ford & Son Corporation, to manufacture the world's first mass-produced tractor in 1917. Based on the assembly of mass-produced components instead of a single large chassis, the Fordson Model F was much cheaper to produce than its rivals. It was also smaller and more attractive to farmers who could not afford large machines. About 750,000 Fordsons were sold, capturing three-quarters of the U.S. market, before Ford changed the design a decade later. The biggest orders initially came from Britain, where the government wanted to encourage the use of machinery to compensate for the manpower it had lost during World War I.

Weighing about 1.2 tons, the Fordson was both sturdy and lightweight. It had a four-cylinder, twenty-horsepower engine that could produce ten horsepower of traction. It had many drawbacks, however: Being light, it could easily tip over backward and its traction was often poor. Yet it was significantly cheaper than rival machines. Refinement of mass-production techniques allowed Ford to reduce the price from $750 in 1918 to just $395 in 1922, putting many rivals out of business.

Further Reading

Beemer, Rod, and Chester Peterson. *Inside John Deere: A Factory History.* Osceola, Wis.: Motorbooks International, 1999.

Hurt, R. Douglas. *Agricultural Technology in the Twentieth Century.* Manhattan, Kan.: Sunflower University Press, 1991

———. *American Farm Tools from Hand-Power to Steam-Power.* Manhattan, Kan.: Sunflower University Press, 1982.

Leffingwell, Randy. *Ford Farm Tractors.* Osceola, Wis.: Motorbooks International, 1998.

around 10 times as quickly as a horse; however, they were cumbersome and costly, their boilers frequently exploded, and, because of their immense weight, they tended to compact the soil and reduce its fertility.

Tractors. Modern gasoline-driven tractors appeared near the end of the nineteenth century. The first such machine is thought to have been built in 1889 by the Charter Gas Engine Company of Sterling, Illinois, using a gasoline engine attached to the chassis (framework) of a steam traction engine. Other models soon appeared from manufacturers like John Froelich, later taken over by the Deere Company, and the Dissinger brothers of Wrightsville, Pennsylvania. By the early 1900s, tractors had become both bigger (with more powerful engines, they could plow larger areas more quickly) and smaller (thus becoming more affordable to the small farmer). Other variations included "motor plows" (with small engines and a seat for the driver) and tractors with tracks (pioneered in the early 1900s by Daniel Best and Benjamin Holt, who later bought out Best and formed the modern Caterpillar Company in 1910).

Meanwhile, the best-selling early tractor was Henry Ford's 1917 Model F Fordson.

Farmers began using the new technology immediately. By 1918, tractors were estimated to have replaced some 1.5 million horses and 250,000 farm laborers. During the 1920s, the number of farmers using tractors is estimated to have increased at least fivefold. By 1929, around three-quarters of the wheat on the Great Plains was being harvested by mechanical combines. As farms became more mechanized, they became larger and more efficient. During the 1850s, some 60 percent of the population was employed in agriculture; by 1900, the figure had fallen to 37 percent, and by 1930, it was just 25 percent. More land was being turned over to agriculture, but the number of farms began a long and steady decline. By drastically reducing the need for human labor at a time when industrialization was encouraging urban expansion (*see also* 78–79), agricultural innovations and technology were key in the transformation of the agrarian society of yesterday into the urban society of today.

—*Chris Woodford*

The Frontier: Cattle Ranching

Spanish explorers first brought cattle and horses to North America, arriving in Florida in 1521 and in New Mexico in 1598. These hardy creole cattle were descended from Andalucian fighting bulls and would become the Longhorns of Texas, the Southwest, and West. With their thick, heavy hides, these cattle provided an important export for Spanish ranchers in what is today Texas, California, and the American Southwest (*see also* 16–17). Their tough, stringy meat could be dried for local consumption or export.

During the seventeenth century, British settlers brought other breeds including Shorthorn and Jersey cattle. In the colonial and early national periods, cattle grazed on mixed farms that also raised other livestock and grew crops. Most farms numbered their cattle in the dozens; few farms held more than a few hundred head. The multipurpose English Shorthorn cattle grazed along the eastern seaboard of the colonial United States and produced meat, milk, tallow, and hides, the last two important for export to Great Britain.

Western Cattle. Prior to the midnineteenth century, Native Americans and bison (*see also* 36–37), not cowboys and cattle, populated the frontier west of the Mississippi River. During the 1840s, a few livestock traders along western trails began to exchange stock with settlers bound for Oregon or California. These pioneering "road ranchers"—for example, Richard Grant at Fort Hall, Idaho—learned that cattle could survive northwestern winters on the open range. The 1850 Census counted 11,394,000 beef cattle in the United States, with most still located in the eastern states of New York, Ohio, Georgia, Virginia, and Pennsylvania. As Americans moved westward (*see also* 52–53), however,

so did the nation's cattle population. By 1860, Texas held more cattle than any state, with nearly three million of the nation's seventeen million head. The Lone Star State would remain the nation's premier cattle producer for decades.

After recovering from losses experienced during the Civil War (*see also* 68–69),

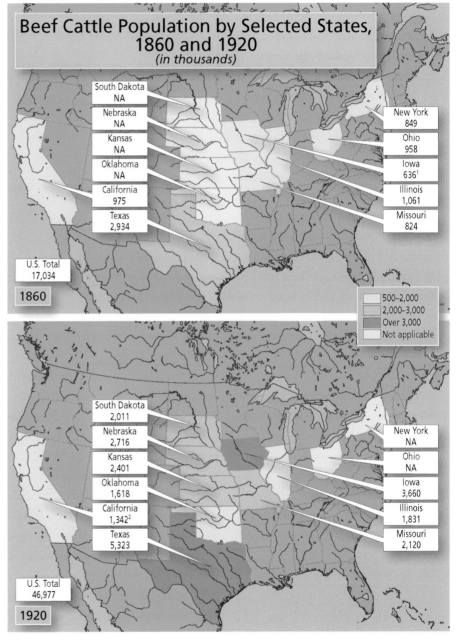

Beef Cattle Population by Selected States, 1860 and 1920
(in thousands)

1860

South Dakota NA
Nebraska NA
Kansas NA
Oklahoma NA
California 975
Texas 2,934

U.S. Total 17,034

New York 849
Ohio 958
Iowa 636[1]
Illinois 1,061
Missouri 824

500–2,000
2,000–3,000
Over 3,000
Not applicable

1920

South Dakota 2,011
Nebraska 2,716
Kansas 2,401
Oklahoma 1,618
California 1,342[2]
Texas 5,323

U.S. Total 46,977

New York NA
Ohio NA
Iowa 3,660
Illinois 1,831
Missouri 2,120

[1] *Figure reflects 1870 data.*
[2] *Figure reflects 1910 data.*
NA: *Not applicable. The state either did not exist at this point or was not a top producer.*
Like its human population, the cattle population of the United States moved quickly westward during the latter half of the nineteenth century. The Great Plains states from Texas northward and the agricultural states of the Midwest became the centers for beef cattle production. Today, these states still have more land devoted to ranching than other sections of the country.
Source: Data from Edward Everett Dale, *The Range Cattle Industry: Ranching on the Great Plains from 1865 to 1925* (Norman: University of Oklahoma Press, 1960).

the cattle frontier of the American West would explode during the 1870s, giving rise to one of the great economic boom periods in American history. In 1865, cows in Texas fetched only $4 to $5 a head (left untended during the war, great herds, numbering in the millions, roamed the open range). At the same time, burgeoning eastern cities created a huge demand for beef, so packinghouses would pay $40 to $50 a head. Seeing great profits to be made, cattlemen in frontier regions hired cowboys to drive the animals northward to the nearest railroad stations in Missouri, Kansas, and other states. The great beef bonanza of the American West had begun.

The first major trail drive north from Texas was organized in 1866, as cowboys drove thousands of cattle to the railroad station in Sedalia, Missouri. Trail crews faced many hazards, including swollen rivers, alkali deserts, stampedes, injuries, and, occasionally, hostile Native Americans or farmers. The following year, the Union Pacific Railroad (*see also* 70–71) reached Abilene, Kansas. That same year, the Chisholm Trail opened, running about 1,000 miles (1,600 kilometers) from south Texas to Abilene. Other trails, such as the Western, connected to Dodge City, Kansas, and other cow towns throughout the West. With established trails, drovers could move large herds more quickly, cheaply, and safely to northern ranges in Montana, Wyoming, and the Dakotas.

According to Census counts, in 1870 Texas again ranked number one in cattle, followed by three Midwest states, Illinois, Ohio, and Missouri. Cowboys herded cattle even farther north from Texas and other southern ranges, following new routes like the Bozeman Trail. With plentiful open grazing lands, ranches quickly sprang up in what are now the states of Colorado, North and South Dakota, Montana, and Wyoming. Investors from the East as well as Europe made huge profits during the heady days of open-range

Further Reading

Dale, Edward Everett. *The Range Cattle Industry: Ranching on the Great Plains from 1865 to 1925.* Norman: University of Oklahoma Press, 1960.

Dary, David. *Cowboy Culture: A Saga of Five Centuries.* Lawrence: University Press of Kansas, 1989.

Slatta, Richard W. *Cowboys of the Americas.* New Haven, Conn.: Yale University Press, 1994.

Starrs, Paul F. *Let the Cowboy Ride: Cattle Ranching in the American West.* Baltimore, Md.: Johns Hopkins University Press, 1998.

cattle ranching. In 1850, America processed just $12 million in red meats; by 1920 the figure would reach $4.2 billion.

Decline of the Cattle Boom. During the mid-1880s, however, the great western cattle boom went bust. Driven by greed, cattlemen overstocked the western ranges and cattle prices plummeted. Extremely harsh winters from 1885 through 1887 killed millions of cattle. An estimated three-quarters of northern range cattle perished. Cowboy artist Charlie Russell's famous 1886 painting, *Waiting for a Chinook (Last of the 5,000),* starkly commemorated the great "die up." In most of the West, massive roundups and long trail drives passed quickly from history into mythology. Railroads and fencing now crisscrossed what had been the open range, reducing the demand for cowboy labor, ending the great trail drives, and cuttings costs. Railroads also gave ranchers economical access to more markets in the East, so they improved their cattle breeds and beef quality to satisfy these new demands. Fencing facilitated hybrid breeding by permitting ranchers to separate bulls from cows (heifers), so that, unlike on the open range, breeding could be monitored and controlled.

Development of Ranches. Cattle, however, remained a major part of the western landscape. Ranches of all sizes developed, from small family operations to sprawling multinational corporations. By the end of the nineteenth century, Richard King had accumulated some 1.27 million

acres (0.5 million hectares) in his south Texas ranch. He employed three hundred vaqueros (Mexican-American cowboys) who worked sixty-five thousand cattle and ten thousand horses. John Chisum's appropriately named "Rancho Grande" straddled the border between west Texas and New Mexico. In a single season, Chisum's cowboys branded eighteen thousand calves. In Nebraska and Wyoming, the Swan Land and Cattle Company owned or controlled 600,000 acres (243,000 hectares).

In 1900, more than six million head of cattle pastured in Texas; the states of Kansas, Iowa, Oklahoma, and Nebraska were in line behind Texas in number of cattle. In 1900, seven of the top-ten cattle-raising states were located west of the Mississippi. Cattle grazed virtually for free on public domain grasses. The nation's total head of cattle jumped from thirty-three million in 1910 to nearly forty-seven million a decade later, mostly concentrated on the Great Plains and in the Midwest.

Challenges to the Industry. The "Golden Age" of ranching established western ranchers as a powerful political lobby that, nevertheless, faced powerful market and political forces. In recent decades, cattle ranchers have responded to changing market demand with leaner beef. Ranching also faces challenges from rising land values as the open spaces of the West become increasingly populated.

Ranchers also have been attacked by environmentalists, who charge that the overgrazing of cattle and sheep degrades habitat, promotes soil erosion, and damages water quality. Today less than 10 percent remains of the tallgrass prairie that once covered 142 million acres (57 million hectares) in fourteen states. The Nature Conservancy, the National Park Service, and other groups are working to preserve grasslands in Oklahoma, Kansas, and Illinois. In such areas, bison, not cattle, graze on the native grasses.

—*Richard W. Slatta*

Harvesting the Pacific Northwest Forests

By the 1880s, most of the commercial forest stands of the Canadian and United States East and the Great Lakes region (*see also 34–35*) had been cleared. The lumber industry then turned to Washington, Oregon, northern California, and Canada's British Columbia. The lumber companies first had to overcome technical problems, including inadequate equipment for handling the larger trees, and transportation and logistical problems, including shipping lumber to markets 1,000 miles (1,600 kilometers) distant, before they could succeed. Solving these and other problems led to an unprecedented increase in timber production.

Impact of Railroads. The transcontinental railroads (*see also 70–71*) reached the West Coast in 1869, contributing to rapid

Softwood Lumber Production on the U.S. Pacific Coast, by State, 1869 to 1950

Softwood lumber production jumped at the start of the twentieth century in the United States as a result of improved technology, lower shipping costs, and the arrival of eastern money to fund the operations. Source: Adapted from Les Reed, Two Centuries of Softwood Lumber War Between Canada and the United States: A Chronicle of Trade Barriers Viewed in the Context of Saw Timber Depletion (Montreal: Free Trade Lumber Council, May 2001), 21, 34.

population growth and greater immigration to the Pacific Northwest. The arrival of settlers meant a rise in demand for wood to build new homes and cities. (Oregon saw its population more than double between 1890 and 1910 to nearly 673,000.) The high cost of shipping timber to the East by rail made the sale of wood more profitable at regional markets such as southern California; lumber barons also found shipping wood overseas to South America, China, New Zealand, and Australia to be a profitable enterprise. When the Great Northern Railroad sharply slashed its freight rates in 1893, shipping lumber to the Midwest became affordable.

The completion of the Canadian Pacific Railway in 1886 initially increased timber production in British Columbia as settlers poured into the interior region. They found the land unsuitable for agriculture, however, and lumber production suffered, along with the rest of the country, through a lengthy economic depression in the 1890s. Only with the arrival of significant numbers of settlers on the Canadian prairies after 1898 did timber production increase along the western Canadian coast. From 1901 to 1913, 65 to 75 percent of British Columbia's lumber production was shipped east, 5 to 17 percent was exported, and the rest was used in the province. British Columbia was responsible for one-quarter of Canada's total softwood lumber production in 1910, with most of it used within Canada itself. The opening of the Panama Canal in 1914 meant that sawmills in British Columbia could ship their cedar, Sitka spruce, and Douglas fir to the eastern seaboard and Europe, which helped revive the province's export business. However, British Columbia would not dominate

Canadian softwood lumber production until after World War II.

Impact of Technology. In addition to railroads opening the region's forests to development and exploitation, new saw technologies contributed to the increase in production. Steam-driven circular saws and later band saws enabled lumberjacks to cut more timber at faster speeds. In the 1870s double and even triple saws replaced circular saws, which could not cut more than half their diameter. A decade later the band saw replaced these earlier saws; its one continuous loop of blade could cut through an entire log.

When lumberjacks started using the ax and crosscut saw in combination, the time needed to fell a tree dropped by nearly four-fifths. In the mid-1880s, the introduction of a steam donkey engine that used steel cables to drag, or skid, fallen timber allowed lumbermen to remove larger logs more quickly and thereby increase production. Donkey engines, though, meant clearcutting the forests, and their use destroyed new growth and left behind logging or "stump deserts" and massive amounts of debris. When operating among piles of slash and debris, steam engines would sometimes generate sparks that could start fires. One fire in 1902 killed thirty-five people, consumed 600,000 to 700,000 acres (243,000 to 283,000 hectares) in Washington and Oregon, and caused $13 million of damage.

Peak Harvesting. In the American Pacific Northwest, timber production increased in the 1880s fourfold, to 2.6 billion board feet (6,000 billion cubic centimeters). Not until 1900, however, did a western state appear in the top ten producers. By 1910, however, Washington and

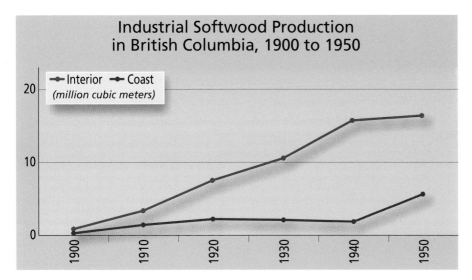

Industrial Softwood Production in British Columbia, 1900 to 1950

In Canada's British Columbia, demand did not increase until during and after World War II; by 1950, British Columbia was responsible for half of Canada's softwood lumber production.
Source: Adapted from Les Reed, Two Centuries of Softwood Lumber War Between Canada and the United States: A Chronicle of Trade Barriers Viewed in the Context of Saw Timber Depletion (Montreal: Free Trade Lumber Council, May 2001), 21, 34.

most land unsuitable for agriculture. Consequently, the lumber companies had difficulty selling their cleared land to farmers—a strategy that had earlier been so successful. The cutover land remained uncultivated and, in the absence of devastating fires, could grow another timber crop in twenty to thirty years. Most lumber companies, however, did not want to wait that long. The companies faced a difficult decision: Pay taxes on uncultivated land; let the state or federal government take it over; or hold on to the land and replant it.

With prodding from the U.S. federal government, Weyerhaeuser made the unusual decision to embrace conservation measures to stabilize timber prices. Although replanting was more expensive than buying mature timberlands, Weyerhaeuser, with the cooperation of the U.S. Forest Service (*see also* 92–93), created the first industrial tree farm in 1914. By the 1930s the company had fully adopted policies of selective cutting and replanting to ensure future supplies of timber. The introduction of newer technologies, such as gasoline-powered chainsaws and caterpillar tractors, in the 1920s and 1930s enabled lumbermen to selectively cut trees and leave behind seedling trees to reforest the areas. By implementing these practices and also cooperative fire suppression, timber companies were, in fact, practicing sustained-yield forestry. As a result, their Pacific holdings were ready for harvesting once again by the 1940s.

—James G. Lewis

Oregon ranked first and third, respectively, among all states in timber production. (Washington, Oregon, and California combined were producing five times as much lumber as British Columbia in 1900.)

By 1920, lumbermen had harvested most of the easily accessible timber along the coast and began to develop the interior regions (the area east of the Cascade Mountain range). The difficult terrain required huge amounts of capital to buy land and harvest trees. As few individuals could afford such outlay, resources of large companies like Weyerhaeuser Timber Company and International Paper were needed. Weyerhaeuser, for example, used profits from lumbering in the Great Lakes region to buy 900,000 acres (360,000 hectares) from the Northern Pacific Railway Company in Washington. At one point it held 1.9 million acres (0.8 million hectares) of land in the Pacific Northwest. In addition, only large companies could afford the expensive machinery needed to open up the interior regions to development. Where the slopes were too steep for railroads to be built in the Cascade Mountains and Sierra Nevadas, for example, lumbermen constructed massive

and complex water flume systems to send lumber down water slides. The flumes linked the sawmills in the upper elevations to the planing mills below, where the lumber was cut for final sale and shipping.

Depletion and Rejuvenation. Developing the interior regions would provide only a temporary solution to the overharvesting of the Pacific Northwest forests. Once these forests were gone, there was nowhere else to go. As historian Harold K. Steen observed, in the Pacific Northwest, "the lumbermen's westward migration ended. The blue Pacific Ocean, not another ridge of green forests, now met their gaze." Additionally, unlike the fertile and tillable lands of the Great Lakes, the South, and the East, the Pacific Northwest's poor soils, steep slopes, and continuous rainfall made

Further Reading

Apsey, Mike, et al. *The Perpetual Forest: Using Lessons from the Past to Sustain Canada's Forests in the Future.* Vancouver, B.C.: FORCAST, 2000.

Cox, Thomas R. *Mills and Markets: A History of the Pacific Coast Lumber Industry to 1900.* Seattle: University of Washington Press, 1974.

Cox, Thomas R., Robert S. Maxwell, Phillip Drennon Thomas, and Joseph J. Malone.

This Well-Wooded Land: Americans and Their Forests from Colonial Times to the Present. Lincoln: University of Nebraska Press, 1985.

Steen, Harold K. *The U.S. Forest Service: A History.* Seattle: University of Washington Press, 1976.

Williams, Michael. *Americans and Their Forests: A Historical Geography.* Cambridge: Cambridge University Press, 1992.

Rebirth of American Forests

Fearful of a drastic nationwide timber shortage in the 1870s, organizations like the American Forestry Association looked to the federal government to protect, restore, or even create forests in the United States. Congress in the 1860s and 1870s, however, was more interested in settling and developing public lands west of the Mississippi River than in protecting them. Despite taking some steps to introduce forestry management, most congressional efforts focused on forest protection. Congress did not seriously fund and promote active recovery of American forests until after the catastrophic fires of 1910.

Tree Planting Efforts. Trying to please settlers and forest advocates alike, Congress passed the Timber Culture Act (1873); this act promoted both tree planting and western settlement. When settlers pushed onto the Great Plains between the Mississippi River and the Rockies, they found a land so dry and treeless that nineteenth-century geographers called it the Great American Desert. But the scientific theory of the day, supported by Joseph Henry of the Smithsonian Institution and other prominent scientists, held that planting trees would help promote rainfall, and thus could turn the so-called desert into a Garden of Eden. Nebraska in particular led efforts to develop forests as a way to attract settlers and increase prosperity. In 1872, the state established the tree-planting holiday Arbor Day. Immediately popular in Nebraska (by 1922, Nebraskans had planted nearly 700,000 acres [280,000 hectares] of trees), Kansas and Tennessee declared Arbor Days in 1875, and Minnesota followed in 1876. By 1907, Arbor Day was observed by all U.S. states and in many foreign countries.

Arbor Day had two unexpected consequences. Although the widespread tree planting efforts did not bring increased rainfall to the Great Plains as had been hoped, the new trees did provide shelter. The "belts" of trees protected houses and crops from wind, stopped snowdrifts on highways and railroads, and provided shade for houses and animals in the summer. These shelterbelts also provided settlers with trees that could be cut for fuel and fencing material. Additionally, although Arbor Day focused attention only on tree planting, not forestry or forest management, it did increase public awareness of the value of trees and forests. The celebration made people more receptive to later efforts to protect forests.

Forest Management. Those efforts were slow in coming, though. Despite the appointment of Franklin B. Hough as first federal forestry agent in 1876 and the establishment of the Division of Forestry within the Department of Agriculture

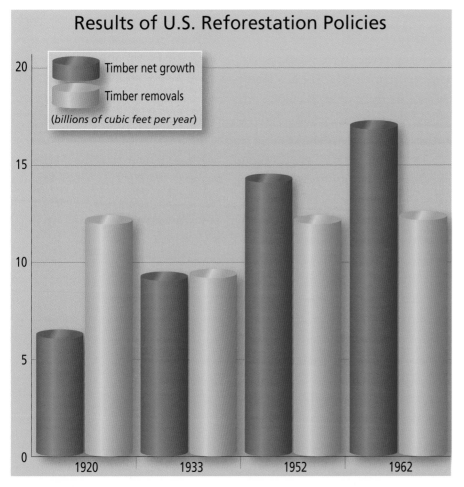

Results of U.S. Reforestation Policies

Timber net growth

Timber removals

(billions of cubic feet per year)

20

15

10

5

0

1920   1933   1952   1962

The abandonment of underproductive farmlands east of the Mississippi River, which began in the nineteenth century, initiated the recovery of the region's forests, while the establishment of federal forestry management policies and the creation of eastern national forests in the early twentieth century fueled the dramatic increase in the amount of forested land. As a result of these initiatives, by 1952 the annual growth of timber would exceed the annual timber harvest from U.S. national forests.

Source: Adapted from Douglas W. MacCleery, *American Forests: A History of Resiliency and Recovery* (Durham, N.C.: Forest History Society, 1993), 47. Underlying data from Waddell, Karen L., Daniel D. Oswald, and Douglas S. Powell, *Forest Statistics of the United States, 1987.* Resource Bulletin PNW-RB-168 (Portland, Ore.: U.S. Department of Agriculture, Pacific Northwest Research Station, 1989). Courtesy of Forest History Society.

shortly thereafter, the federal government in the 1870s still favored selling the public land as quickly as possible rather than conserving forests. For instance, Carl Schurz, secretary of interior (1877–81) for President Rutherford B. Hayes, tried to enforce existing legislation that outlawed forest destruction and timber theft, but could not overcome a corrupt federal bureaucracy and apathetic public.

The Timber Culture Act allowed for nearly twenty more years of clearcutting and mineral exploitation until a growing public outcry for action led Congress to repeal the act. Congress then passed the Forest Reserve Act of 1891, which gave the president the authority to set aside, and thus protect from development, public land in the West. More than 40 million acres (16 million hectares) in the northern Rocky Mountains had been protected by 1897, when Congress passed the Forest Management Act of 1897. That act placed the national forests under active forestry management by the Department of Interior for the first time. In the East, with no national forests to administer, the Department of Agriculture's Division of Forestry worked with private landowners and state agencies to design management plans for their forests.

Forest Recovery. During the next decade, the conservation movement (*see also* 110–11) encouraged more federal action to aid the recovery of the nation's forests. Congress established the U.S. Forest Service (*see also* 92–93) in 1905 within the Department of Agriculture and transferred the national forests over from the Department of Interior.

The Forest Service promoted fire suppression and selective cutting of timber as the cornerstones of its management policy for national forests. The policy encouraged forest preservation and regeneration in the West, but had a limited effect because only

Further Reading
Pyne, Stephen J. *Year of the Fires: The Story of the Great Fires of 1910*. New York: Viking, 2001.
Robbins, William G. *American Forestry: A History of National, State, and Private Cooperation*. Lincoln: University of Nebraska Press, 1985.
Steen, Harold K. *The U.S. Forest Service: A History*. Seattle: University of Washington Press, 1976.
Williams, Michael. *Americans and Their Forests: A Historical Geography*. Cambridge: Cambridge University Press, 1992.

a small amount of land was under the control of the Forest Service. Selective cutting required leaving behind some trees for seeding (the number left varied depending on species and location). Along with fire suppression, selective cutting enabled forests to regenerate naturally. To further aid rebirth, the Forest Service had initiated a tree-planting program in 1899 similar to its management plan program. The landowner had to supply workers and seeds or trees, and the agency would provide a strategy. By 1904, the Forest Service had developed 334 plans that provided schedules for over 13,000 acres (5,300 hectares) to speed regeneration.

Eastern Forests. As early as 1892, forest advocates had been promoting the creation of national forests in the East as a way to regenerate the forests of Appalachia. National lumber production reached its highest levels ever in 1907, but demand remained consistent. More and more timber companies joined forest advocates in finding new sources of timber, and backed the idea of supporting eastern national forests. The horrific fires of 1910 that engulfed over 5 million acres (2 million hectares) of national forest in Idaho, Washington, and Montana in one month and between 40 and 50 million acres (16 and 20 million hectares) nationwide provided the biggest incentive to the federal government to provide funds for reestablishing eastern forests. The fires led directly to passage of the Weeks Act in 1911, which authorized the federal government to purchase land to create new national forests. Within the first two

years, more than 700,000 acres (280,000 hectares) had been added to the national forest system in the East; within fifty years, nearly 20 million acres (8 million hectares) had been added, almost all in the East. The Weeks Law also provided federal matching funds for fire protection; it also encouraged federal and state governments and lumber companies to replant cleared lands and to protect public areas from disease and infestation.

In addition to active management of the land, changes in American society and culture also contributed to the rebirth of American forests. When people in the East abandoned farms to either resettle in the West or move to cities to find work, farmland not claimed for other purposes would frequently revert to forest. This process began as early as 1840 in New England, spreading to New York, Pennsylvania, and New Jersey by 1880, and then to Ohio, Indiana, and West Virginia after 1910. In the upper South, old cotton and tobacco fields reverted to pine forest as major crop production shifted to the coastal plains of Texas and Alabama and the new, irrigated areas farther west. This left millions of acres of land available for reforestation, either naturally or through active replanting. As a result of both federal legislation and land abandonment, the amount of forested land in the eastern and southern United States has steadily increased since 1900. Forty years after implementing the Weeks Law, the amount of annual growth outpaced timber removal, and American forests started to recover.

—*James G. Lewis*

Exploitation of Raw Materials for Industry

During the vast industrial expansion in North America in the late nineteenth century, the demand for raw materials grew and intensified. Copper from Michigan, lead from Wisconsin, coal from Pennsylvania, and eventually iron from Minnesota had fueled earlier developments in the United States. However, the greater demands of industry required new sources of raw materials. The western states and territories, which were opening as a result of precious metal (gold and silver) mining (*see also* 66–67), also possessed nonprecious metals like lead, copper, coal, and iron that would be exploited by industries during the late nineteenth and early twentieth centuries.

Unlike gold and silver, these less glamorous base metals never caught the public's attention. Some of these metals were by-products of gold and silver mining, for example, at Rossland, British Columbia. Lead production, a by-product of silver mining, increased in Comstock, Nevada, and Leadville, Colorado, as the great western districts (sites of mines) were at their peak of mining activity in the 1870s.

Copper. The great copper districts of newly settled areas in Montana, Utah, and Arizona eclipsed earlier mining centers in Michigan and elsewhere. These new mines began production in the 1880s, a time when new inventions, the telephone, telegraph, electrical products, and other household goods, created huge demand for copper. The metal was shipped throughout the country to industrial centers and beyond to world markets. By 1900, Butte, Montana, was famous throughout the world as a center of copper production, and mining towns in Utah and Arizona raced to challenge its supremacy. These three states, joined later by Alaska, came to dominate world copper production. For a while, western production created a world surplus, with Montana, for instance, jumping from 5,000 tons in 1882 to a record 176,000 tons by 1916.

With the completion of the Union Pacific Railroad—the first transcontinental line (*see also* 70–71)—in the United States in 1869, the era of the "iron horse" had begun. The railroad made shipping copper to the East economically feasible, while enabling eastern industry to send finished products (for example, boilers, wire, and train parts) west. Railroads soon connected all the major mining districts to markets throughout the country, reducing isolation, lowering the cost of living, and providing year-round, faster transportation. In Canada, new transportation routes (*see also* 42–43 *and* 70–71) developed less rapidly; the trans-Canadian railroad, reaching from Montreal to Vancouver, would not be completed until 1885.

Coal. The development of the railroad also affected other mining industries, including coal mining in Wyoming, Colorado, and Utah. The Union Pacific Railroad, in fact, opened the Wyoming coal market on its route across the continent. The railroad company built lines through several of the territory's abundant coal fields, which provided the first major economic development for Wyoming (the state produced 208,000 tons of coal in 1878). Likewise, major development of Colorado's coalfields awaited the arrival of the Denver and Rio Grande Railroad in the 1870s. By 1879, production of coal in that state reached 327,000 tons. Trailing only slightly behind came Utah, and together the three states furnished coal for the Rocky Mountain region and, to the east, the Great Plains.

Steel. The opening of western coal resources in the 1870s benefited communities in the Rocky Mountain region and allowed the region's industrial development, specifically steel production (*see also* 72–73).

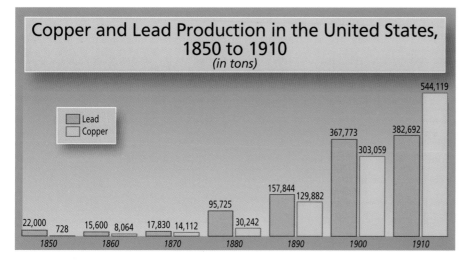

Copper and Lead Production in the United States, 1850 to 1910
(in tons)

Lead production, which was a by-product of silver mining, jumped after the Comstock and Leadville booms of the 1870s. The growth in copper production reflected the rise of the great Montana, Utah, and Arizona districts starting in the 1880s. As the demands of industry increased, lead and copper mines opened and production rose steadily at the end of the nineteenth century.
Source: Sam H. Schurr, *Historical Statistics of Minerals in the United States* (Washington, D.C.: Resources for the Future, 1960).

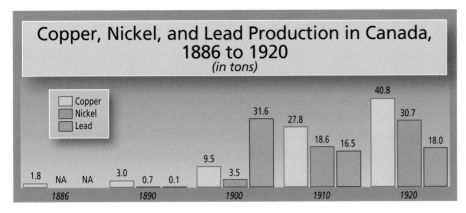

Copper, Nickel, and Lead Production in Canada, 1886 to 1920
(in tons)

NA: Not available.

Canada's mining industry trailed that of the United States during the nineteenth century. By the beginning of the twentieth century, however, mining of natural resources like copper and nickel began to increase and become important to Canada's economy.

Source: Statistics Canada. Historical Statistics of Canada. 5 Nov. 2002. <http://www.statcan.ca/english/freepub/11-516-XIE/sectionp/sectionp.htm#Metallic>. Underlying data from Statistics Canada, *Canadian Mineral Statistics, 1886–1956; Mining Events 1604–1956* (Ottawa: Statistics Canada, 1957). Used with the permission of Statistics Canada.

Pueblo, Colorado, for instance, thought of itself as the "Pittsburgh of the West." Raw materials like iron and coal came from nearby mines in Colorado and Wyoming, allowing Pueblo's steel mills to produce crucial items, including the rails that permitted railroads to expand and tap new mining towns and districts. Steel production created more business, jobs, and profits. The Denver and Rio Grande Railroad and the Colorado lines built in the 1880s profited from Pueblo's mills, which helped every district and town the railroads reached.

Smelting Industry. The smelting (reducing ore to gold and silver) industry benefited greatly from railroad and coal development. Coal, transformed into coke by heating to burn off impurities, provided the high temperatures needed in the smelting process; the railroads made possible the easier and cheaper transportation of fuel and ore to the major smelter sites like Denver, Colorado, and Salt Lake City, Utah. One of the major results of this concentration was the takeover of the smelters after 1900 by the gigantic and monopolistic American Smelting and Refining Company. As in the rest of the United States, the West witnessed the arrival of the trust, or business monopoly. The Anaconda, Phelps Dodge, and

Kennecott companies soon dominated the great Montana, Arizona, and Utah copper districts, and, to a lesser degree, other large companies gained control of many major precious metal mines. The railroad companies initially dominated the coalfields, but the 1906 Hepburn Act prohibited them from transporting the coal that they produced and forced the railroads to divest themselves of their coal interests. The Rockefeller family, for instance, soon gained control of many of Colorado's major coal mines as the railroads sold out.

Other Resources. Lead, copper, coal, and iron dominated the period of industrial expansion, but other raw materials would soon be discovered and exploited for various purposes. Carnotite and pitchblende, initially used for medical purposes, were mined on a small scale by the early 1900s in Colorado. Not until World War II did the mining of uranium, which was used for military purposes, take on major significance. Small oil deposits, particularly in Colorado, also served local needs for fuel and lighting. However, the oil industry (*see also* 104–05) would not reach its height until the automobile boom following World War I.

Like the United States, Canada also possessed enormous natural resources. However,

transportation difficulties, lack of operating capital, and competition from cheaper U.S. imports of copper and iron kept its mining industry lagging behind the United States. Ontario, with nickel, copper, and gold, would become the chief mineral-producing province in the early twentieth century.

Environmental Impact. Each of these mining "rushes" and consequent developments affected the environment. The roasting and smelting copper produced smoke with heavy metals in it; this smoke covered Butte and Anaconda, Montana, causing crops to wither and die and animals in the region to decline and die. Residents of Butte became concerned about the effect of the thick smoke on their own health. The farmers and ranchers of Butte sued the miners; twenty years of litigation ensued before a resolution was reached. The smelters were moved out of Butte, while at Anaconda taller smokestacks and other devices reduced local pollution. Smelter smoke in Denver and Salt Lake City also aroused the ire of residents, but no significant action was taken to curb it. For the most part, however, westerners of the era appreciated the jobs and economic benefits from mining and related industries more than they worried about short- or long-range environmental problems.

—Duane A. Smith

Further Reading

Hyde, Charles K. *Copper for America: The United States Copper Industry from Colonial Times to the 1990s.* Tucson: University of Arizona Press, 1998.

Malone, Michael P. *The Battle for Butte: Mining and Politics on the Northern Frontier, 1864–1906.* Helena: Montana Historical Society Press, 1995.

Mouat, Jeremy. *Roaring Days: Rossland's Mines and the History of British Columbia.* Vancouver: University of British Columbia Press, 1995.

Scamehorn, Lee. *Mill and Mine: The CF&I in the Twentieth Century.* Lincoln: University of Nebraska Press, 1992.

Taniguchi, Nancy J. *Necessary Fraud: Progressive Reform and Utah Coal.* Norman: University of Oklahoma Press, 1996.

Gold and Silver Mining in the West

In late 1848, Americans heard that gold had been found at Sutter's mill in California. The next spring a worldwide rush of people headed to this "promised land." Most of these individuals were novices with no experience of mining. Fortunately, they sought placer gold, free gold found in streams or ancient streambeds, an easy and inexpensive form of mining. Over the next sixty years, prospectors would search and miners would dig across the West, first for gold and then for silver. However, what began as a simple process became more complex with industrialization and the introduction of new technologies.

U.S. Gold Mining. The first miners who arrived in 1849, thereafter known as "forty-niners," used pans to separate gold from the sand and gravel. Gold, being a heavy metal, settled to the bottom as the miners swirled water around the pans. This time-consuming, arduous process did little to fulfill their dreams of quick wealth. Within less than a year, the miners changed methods, switching to the use of rockers, a cradle-like device that allowed more gravel to be washed faster. Soon the sluice box

replaced the cradle. These long, inclined troughs contained riffles, or bars, across the bottom to trap gold, as water swept the gold-bearing material down the sluice. To legally assert their interests, miners staked claims, with definite boundaries, to the land.

By the early 1850s, mining was no longer the "poor man's diggings." Miners, to have enough land to work, combined their claims. They either had to find partners or hire other miners to work for them. This kind of expansion and change in processes required money and the acquisition of new skills. As a result of this transformation, the mining industry began to exhibit the same patterns of industrialization that were affecting the rest of North America.

To work even faster, hydraulic mining was introduced by the mid-1850s. Hoses shot water, under tremendous pressure, against gold-bearing ground, washing gravel, mud, and rocks down long sluices into nearby valleys. This resulted in an environmental disaster that pitted California's valley farmers, whose land was threatened by the mess, against mountain miners. Eventually, in 1884, U.S. Circuit Court

Judge Lorenzo Sawyer would permanently prohibit mining companies from hydraulic mining that damaged property in valleys.

By the mid-1850s, miners also had started digging deep into the Earth to follow veins of gold. Called hard rock, or deep mining, this technique demanded skills in timbering, dewatering a mine, blasting, and separating the gold from the rock. Grass Valley and Nevada City in California became the centers of hard rock mining. Fortunately for the miners, this gold proved easy to separate from the gangue, or waste rock. After crushing the rock in mills, they mixed in mercury, which has an affinity for gold, and the miners literally picked the gold out. This gold amalgam was then heated, and the mercury boiled off.

U.S. Silver Mining. Mining entered a new phase in 1859 with the discovery of Nevada's famous Comstock silver deposits. Miners raced eastward over the mountains and staked claims, only to find themselves in an unfamiliar environment. Silver does not separate as easily or cheaply as gold, and smelting methods to separate the silver from copper, zinc, and lead had to be developed. The Washoe Pan Process was eventually developed in 1862. This method basically involved crushing, heating, and introducing chemicals into the gangue that separated the silver.

Nevada's Comstock mines proved deeper, less stable, and hotter than California's. The profits acquired from silver, however, allowed owners to develop the methods to overcome such problems. Hoists (lifting and lowering cages) allowed men, materials, and ore to be moved up and down, into and out of mines. Such mining used great amounts of timber to support the unmined rock and thus prevent cave-ins. Power drills enabled miners to work faster,

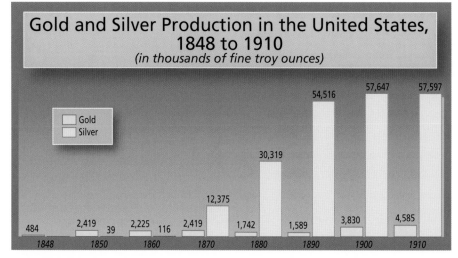

The discovery of gold in 1848 led to a dramatic increase in gold production by 1850. Likewise, the sudden spurt of silver production in the 1860s and 1870s reflects the success of the Comstock and Leadville mines.
Source: Sam H. Schurr, *Historical Statistics of Minerals in the United States* (Washington, D.C.: Resources for the Future, 1960).

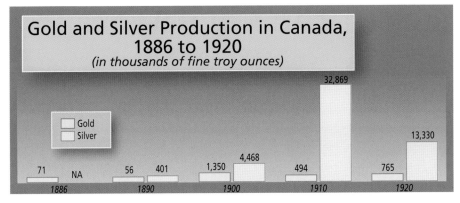

Gold and Silver Production in Canada, 1886 to 1920
(in thousands of fine troy ounces)

32,869

13,330

Gold
Silver

4,468

71   NA   56   401   1,350   494   765

1886   1890   1900   1910   1920

NA: Not available.
The Klondike gold rush led to an increase in Canada's production of gold, demonstrated here by the rise in production in 1900. Silver production would also rise at the beginning of the twentieth century.
Source: Statistics Canada. Historical Statistics of Canada. 5 Nov. 2002. <http://www.statcan.ca/english/freepub/11-516-XIE/sectionp/sectionp.htm#Metallic>. Underlying data from Statistics Canada. *Canadian Mineral Statistics, 1886–1956; Mining Events, 1604–1956* (Ottawa: Statistics Canada, 1957). Used with the permission of Statistics Canada.

but the rock dust thrown off by the drills led to health problems like respiratory diseases. Innovations like electricity, giant powder (dynamite) to blast the rock, and large pumps to remove water from the mines all displayed their worth on the Comstock. These mines and smelters produced smoke and acidic water, but these were generally ignored in the rush for riches.

In 1859, the Pikes Peak gold rush brought the hopeful to Colorado. By the end of the 1860s, miners had reached the future U.S. states of Idaho, Utah, Montana, Wyoming, New Mexico, and Arizona, as well as many other locations in Nevada. This vast area became an "urban West," as mining gave birth to communities like Leadville, Colorado; Park City, Utah; and Wallace, Idaho. The residents of these new towns polluted streams and scarred the land like the miners. They carved roads into hillsides and cut down trees to construct buildings; sewage ran down streams, and smoke hovered in mountain valleys.

Many districts (mine sites) offered new natural obstacles to miners: different geology, high elevation, complex mineralization making separation of the various ores difficult, and lack of transportation. When the first transcontinental railroad (*see also* 70–71) was finished in 1869, every

district wanted a railroad, but the railroad companies built lines only through sites promising great profit. The mining experience of California and Nevada was replicated elsewhere, particularly in smelting, although adaptations had to be made as miners encountered complex ores. The mining boom would come to an end in western Nevada in 1901–02.

Canadian Mining. Canada's first major gold rush occurred approximately fifty years earlier in British Columbia, after native peoples found gold in a tributary of the Fraser River. In 1860, miners involved in the Fraser River gold rush would discover gold in Cariboo, British Columbia; this discovery would draw almost ten thousand people to the nearby boomtown of Barkerville. Rossland, British Columbia, also joined the mining excitement after gold was found in 1887 on Red Mountain. In the Yukon Territory, gold was found near the Klondike River in 1896. When news of the discovery spread around the world the following year, more than one hundred thousand people traveled to the Yukon with hopes of striking it rich. However, the Klondike gold rush ended quickly; by 1899 most of the inhabitants of Dawson, a shantytown that quickly expanded during the height of the

rush, had left the area to return home or seek gold elsewhere.

Industrialization. By the turn of the nineteenth century, mining in the United States and Canada had become a completely industrialized business. Mining engineers now operated the mines, with electricity and equipment like power drills once unimaginable. Corporations owned the mines, and profits were spread far beyond the mountains and deserts of the West to the East and Europe. To compete in this new world, miners joined unions, and, as elsewhere, industrial strife resulted.

Environmental Consequences. For sixty years, mining had opened, developed, settled, and promoted the North American West. At the same time, this legendary era left behind problems for future generations, including environmental degradation. Polluted streams, eroded hillsides, acidic water draining from mines, scattered debris, and roads cutting across fragile mountain valleys remained for later communities to address and solve. For instance, the historic mining town of Leadville, Colorado, was declared a Superfund site (*see also* 152–53) in 1983 to help clean up mining wastes that were polluting the land and the nearby Arkansas River. In Leadville, mill tailings (waste products of ore mining) and mine dumps are still being removed or stabilized, streams cleaned up, and acidic mine drainage neutralized.

—*Duane A. Smith*

Further Reading
Francaviglia, Richard. *Hard Places: Reading the Landscape of America's Historic Mining Districts.* Iowa City: University of Iowa Press, 1991.
Mouat, Jeremy. *Roaring Days: Rossland's Mines and the History of British Columbia.* Vancouver: University of British Columbia Press, 1995.
Paul, Rodman W. *Mining Frontiers of the Far West, 1848–1880.* Rev. ed. Albuquerque: University of New Mexico Press, 2001.
Smith, Duane A. *Mining America: The Industry and the Environment, 1800–1980.* Niwot: University Press of Colorado, 1993.

The Impact of the Civil War

The Civil War, the deadliest and most destructive military conflict in the history of the United States, fundamentally altered the nation's social and economic structures. Between 1861 and 1865, war ravaged the nation, damaging both the natural and built environments. The Civil War not only brought immediate destruction to the areas where armies collided, it also had wide-reaching effects that caused long-term changes in the ways Americans interacted with the natural world.

Roots of Conflict. The causes of the war were complex and varied, but at root the conflict stemmed from the spread of slavery. For decades before actual fighting began, Americans had been embroiled in a debate over how the nation's resources and vast lands would be used and developed. The United States was still basically a rural nation. Many in the North hoped to settle the West with independent yeoman farmers dedicated to the tenets of "free labor" and "free soil." But northern states were beginning to industrialize and made increasing demands on the South to supply the raw materials (*see also* 64–65) essential to their factories and textile mills. To meet that demand, southerners pushed to expand their lucrative plantation system (*see also* 30–31), extending the cultivation of cash crops like cotton that were harvested by the labor of enslaved African Americans. By the mid-nineteenth century, the South and the North seemed to be on divergent though mutually beneficial trajectories, with the North moving more rapidly toward industrialization and the South toward greater dependence on "King Cotton." Thus, when eleven southern states seceded

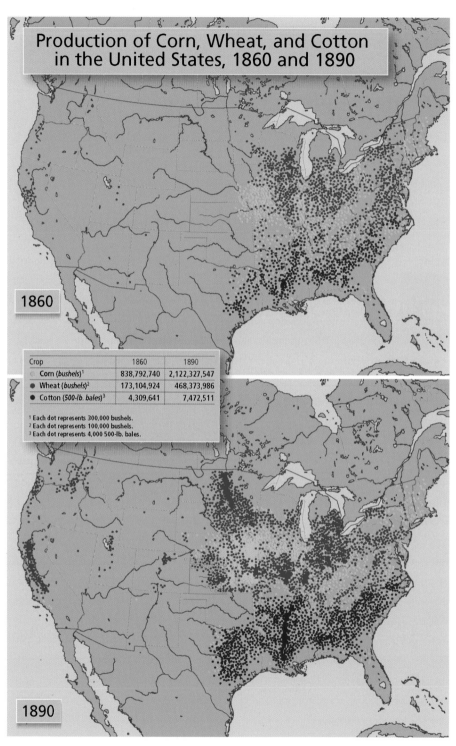

Production of Corn, Wheat, and Cotton in the United States, 1860 and 1890

1860

Crop	1860	1890
Corn (*bushels*)[1]	838,792,740	2,122,327,547
Wheat (*bushels*)[2]	173,104,924	468,373,986
Cotton (*500-lb. bales*)[3]	4,309,641	7,472,511

[1] Each dot represents 300,000 bushels.
[2] Each dot represents 100,000 bushels.
[3] Each dot represents 4,000 500-lb. bales.

1890

The Civil War precipitated long-term changes in U.S. agricultural practices. The wartime trends in the North toward mechanization, commercialization, and increased production levels of corn and wheat helped the Union win the war, while postwar migration and geographic expansion of commercial grain farming helped fuel the region's industrial and economic growth. In the South, cotton continued to be the primary cash crop in 1890 as it was in 1860. With the end of slavery and the development of the sharecropping system, cotton cultivation spread rapidly after the war as farmers moved westward in search of lands that were still fertile.

Source: Adapted from L. Clifford and Elizabeth H. Lord, *Historical Atlas of the United States.* Rev. ed. (New York: Henry Holt, 1953), 68–70, 142, 143, 145.

from the Union in 1861, precipitating armed conflict, each side had a different set of resources available for waging war.

War Mobilization. The process of mobilizing humans and resources for war had a significant impact on American agricultural practices. Not only did the onset of war require larger output from farms and factories to feed and equip millions of soldiers, it also demanded quicker and more efficient production. Enlistments in the armed forces caused a shortage of farm labor in the North, so farmers turned to mechanization to sow and harvest their crops (*see also* 56–57). To meet the demands of the vast Union armies, northern farmers stopped rotating crops and increased the amount of land planted with grains such as corn and wheat by nearly 2.7 million acres (1.1 million hectares) in the middle years of the war alone. The wartime increase in production levels and the new reliance on mechanized farming techniques fostered closer connections between rural and urban communities and ushered in the large-scale commercial farming that would come to characterize agricultural practices in the United States.

Humans, too, were mobilized in massive numbers; over three million men (and approximately four hundred women who disguised themselves as men) fought in the U.S. Civil War. Approximately 620,000 soldiers and unknown thousands of civilians died during the war, most of them from disease or malnutrition. Americans fought 10,455 battles and incurred 1,094,453 total casualties, including those who died, those who were wounded, and those missing-in-action. The Union forces lost more than 110,000 soldiers in battle and 224,580 to disease, while the Confederacy suffered approximately 94,000 battle deaths and 164,000 deaths from disease or malnutrition. The federal government established

the Sanitary Commission to combat the widespread problem of disease among the troops; this commission would continue its public health efforts after the war.

Animals also died in great numbers during the war. In the final months of the war, nearly five hundred horses were lost each day to gun or cannon fire, starvation, disease, or overwork. The mule population experienced similar losses. Cattle (*see also* 58–59) and hogs suffered even higher mortality rates, with the southern hog population almost completely decimated by the end of the war. These losses put greater demands on livestock herds in the West, further undermining the already overexploited ecosystem of the Great Plains.

Cotton. The war caused a great number of changes, but one practice that remained largely the same, in scale if not in kind, was the cultivation of cotton in the South. The Thirteenth Amendment freed four million African Americans from slavery, but it did not liberate them from the cotton industry. While many African Americans moved north or west to find new opportunities, the majority remained in the South and became tenant farmers. They and their white counterparts had to plant ever more cotton to pay their rents. Cotton quickly depletes soil's nutrients, so farmers increasingly relied on manufactured fertilizers, burdening themselves with even greater debt, and necessitating the planting of more acres in cotton. Thus, subsistence farming in both the North and the South became less prevalent, and commercial farming became the norm.

Destruction. In addition to the effects of mobilization, the military conflict itself altered the nation's landscape. Union General William Tecumseh Sherman cut a swath of destruction 60 miles (97 kilometers) wide through the heart of Georgia during his March to the

Further Reading

McPherson, James M. *Battle Cry of Freedom: The Civil War Era*. New York: Ballantine Books, 1989.

Kirby, Jack Temple. "The American Civil War: An Environmental View." July 2001. <http://www.nhc.rtp.nc.us:8080/tserve/nattrans/ntuseland/essays/amcwar.htm>.

Otto, John Solomon. *Southern Agriculture during the Civil War Era, 1860–1880*. Westport, Conn.: Greenwood, 1994.

Paludan, Phillip Shaw. "A People's Contest": *The Union & Civil War, 1861—1865*. 2nd ed., with a new preface. Lawrence: University Press of Kansas, 1996.

Steinberg, Theodore. "The Great Food Fight." In *Down to Earth: Nature's Role in American History*. New York: Oxford University Press, 2002.

Sea in 1864. The Confederates, too, were destructive, burning the town of Chambersburg, Pennsylvania, after its residents refused to pay a ransom. During the war both armies dug trenches and rifle pits to shield their soldiers from enemy fire, foraged in the forests and in fields for food for themselves and their animals, and dismantled fences, houses, and other buildings for fortifications and firewood. Cannon and rifle fire splintered large stands of trees and explosive mines gouged out large craters in the earth. Fires, intentional and otherwise, were common and destroyed cities, towns, forests, and farms; when added to the discharge of gunpowder from millions of guns and thousands of cannon, the smoke pollution near battle sites was substantial. The physical scars on the landscape caused by battle are largely invisible today; however, the National Park Service manages twenty battlefield preserves that memorialize the Civil War. Nearly 60,000 acres (24,000 hectares) of land have been removed from production, have become, ironically, sanctuaries for birds, animals, and plants, and are popular tourist destinations.

—Lisa M. Brady

Transcontinental Railroads

Few technological innovations have had as much environmental impact on North America as the transcontinental railroads built in the nineteenth century. The railroads that united the East and West Coasts of North America fueled the Industrial Revolution, led to territorial expansion and new settlements, revolutionized economic trade and markets, and hastened the transformation of a largely rural nation into a largely urban one.

Early Developments. The United States' first railroad (*see also* 44–45), the 13-mile (21-kilometer) Baltimore and Ohio Railroad, carried traffic from 1830 onward, with cars initially pulled by horses. Railroads

expanded rapidly thereafter, first in northeastern and Midatlantic states, with more than 9,000 miles (14,500 kilometers) of track laid by 1850, compared with just 32 miles (52 kilometers) in 1830. Railroad tracks were soon reaching toward the Midwest and beyond; but steam locomotives, the first imported from Britain in 1829, made possible the construction of truly transcontinental railroads.

U.S. Railroads. The Pacific Railroad Act of 1862, which authorized and funded the construction of the Union Pacific Railroad, gave the United States its first transcontinental railroad. On May 10, 1869, the Union Pacific line, inching westward from Nebraska, met the Central Pacific

Railroad, inching east from Sacramento, at Promontory Point in Utah. Later transcontinental railroads included the Great Northern, Northern Pacific, Southern Pacific, and the Atchison, Topeka, and Santa Fe. By 1860, all major northern cities were connected by the rail network. Some cities were especially well connected; Chicago, for example, had no fewer than eleven railroad lines radiating from it. The transcontinental network in the United States was effectively finished in 1910 with the completion of the Western Pacific line to Oakland, California.

The golden age of railroads lasted from the 1860s to the 1920s; by 1860, some 30,000 miles (48,000 kilometers) of track had

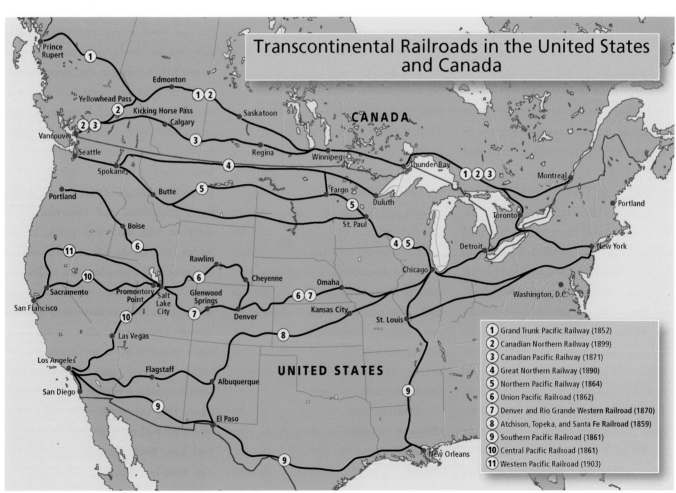

Transcontinental Railroads in the United States and Canada

1. Grand Trunk Pacific Railway (1852)
2. Canadian Northern Railway (1899)
3. Canadian Pacific Railway (1871)
4. Great Northern Railway (1890)
5. Northern Pacific Railway (1864)
6. Union Pacific Railroad (1862)
7. Denver and Rio Grande Western Railroad (1870)
8. Atchison, Topeka, and Santa Fe Railroad (1859)
9. Southern Pacific Railroad (1861)
10. Central Pacific Railroad (1861)
11. Western Pacific Railroad (1903)

Note: The years included in the legend box indicate when a railroad was authorized.
During the course of the nineteenth century, many railroads were constructed between the Atlantic and Pacific coasts of North America.
Source: Adapted from O. S. Nock, *World Atlas of Railways.* (New York: Bonanza Books, 1983), 104.

Workers celebrate the completion of the first transcontinental railroad at Promontory Point, Utah, in 1869.
(© Bettmann/Corbis)

been laid across the United States—more than three times the total in 1850. The network grew to 350,000 miles (563,000 kilometers) in 1910, finally reaching its peak in 1930, by which time nearly 430,000 miles (692,000 kilometers) of track had been laid. Such construction required huge investment. By 1880, an estimated $5 billion had been invested; by 1920, that figure had quadrupled.

Canadian Railroads. British army engineers constructed Canada's first railroad in Québec City in the 1820s; a number of major railroad construction projects soon followed. Completed in 1852, the Atlantic and St. Lawrence Railroad (known as the St. Lawrence and Atlantic Railroad in Québec) became the first cross-border line, running between Portland, Maine, and Montreal. It was subsequently taken over by the Grand Trunk Railway, which had been incorporated in 1852 to construct a line between Montreal and Toronto. The Grand Trunk Railway went on to dominate the rail network in eastern Canada. British Columbia's entry into the Canadian confederation in 1871 was secured by promises to link the province to the Canadian rail network. The Canadian Pacific Railway Company completed that task in 1885 when it finished the line between Montreal and Vancouver, effectively

creating a Canadian transcontinental railroad. In 1886 the inaugural transcontinental train made the journey from the Atlantic coast to the Pacific coast in 139 hours. A second transcontinental line, the Canadian Northern Railway, was built over a period of twenty years, from its incorporation in 1899, into a 10,000-mile (16,000-kilometer) network linking Montreal and Vancouver.

Built between 1905 and 1914, Canada's third transcontinental line, the Grand Trunk Pacific Railway, ran 3,543 miles (5,702 kilometers) across the country westward from Winnipeg, Manitoba, to the port of Prince Rupert on the Pacific coast in British Columbia. When the development of so many large projects financially imperiled their promoters, the Canadian government was forced to nationalize the country's railroads and form the Canadian National Railway Company in 1918 in an attempt to make a more efficient and profitable network.

Impact. The effects of transcontinental railroads were dramatic. In the 1830s, three weeks were needed to travel by boat from New York City to Chicago. Twenty years later, the same journey could be made by rail in less than two days. Transcontinental railroads slashed the cost of transporting freight in the United States from two cents per ton

per mile in 1865 to 75¢ per ton per mile in 1900, transforming local and regional markets for food, agricultural machinery, and other goods into national markets and making mass production and mass consumption inevitable. Railroads also spurred the growth of a massive iron and steel industry (*see also* 72–73), while the steam locomotives that hauled freight on them needed huge amounts of coal (*see also* 64–65 *and* 102–03). The railroads, their companies alone employing about two million people by 1920, were truly the engines of the Industrial Revolution.

The environmental cost was not small. Railroads opened up huge new tracts of land all the way to the Pacific Ocean. New settlements quickly sprang up around the railroads, for the railroad companies themselves sold land and encouraged settlements to secure long-term traffic. Those settlements had environmental impacts. In the Midwest, prairies were plowed and forests felled to raise grain. In the Great Plains, the coming of the railroads led to the decimation of bison herds (*see also* 36–37)—initially hunted to feed railroad workers—and the virtual collapse of Native American cultures. Nothing illustrates the impact of the transcontinental railroads more vividly than the creation, on November 18, 1883, of four North American time zones so train timetables could be standardized; in effect, this caused all commercial and much of personal life to revolve around the railroads.

—*Chris Woodford*

Further Reading

Ambrose, Stephen. *Nothing Like It in the World: The Men Who Built the Transcontinental Railroad 1863–1869.* New York: Simon & Schuster, 2000.

McDonnell, Greg. *The History of Canadian Railroads.* London: Footnote Productions/New Burlington Books, 1985.

Stover, John. *American Railroads.* 2nd ed. Chicago: University of Chicago Press, 1997.

Stover, John, and Mark Carnes. *The Routledge Historical Atlas of the American Railroads.* New York: Routledge, 1999.

Iron and Steel Production

As a result of colonial mercantilist policies in North America, the center of iron and steel production had remained in England. During the Revolutionary War, Americans realized that they were woefully short of iron forges and metal fabrication factories not only for rifles and cannons, bullets and cannonballs, but also for farm tools and simple items like nails and hinges. Even in the early nineteenth century, metal production in North America remained limited. But by the late nineteenth century, with rising demand for metal goods and the development of new technologies, the United States would become the world's leading producer of steel.

Iron. North Americans had prided themselves on their "Age of Wood" (*see also* 42–43) through the first half of the nineteenth century, which transformed a seemingly limitless forest into fences, houses, piers, and even underground water pipes, road surfaces, and wooden locks for canals. Iron production was dirty, hard, and dangerous work, requiring the extraction of iron ore from the bogs and rocks of the "iron belt" that ran through Vermont, Massachusetts, New York, and New Jersey. In Canada, the early Forges Saint-Maurice,

near Trois-Rivières in Québec, began producing iron bars from bog iron ore and charcoal in the eighteenth century, and the Marmora Ironworks near Peterborough in Ontario would begin production in the early nineteenth century. Local forges and blacksmith shops produced shovels, hammers, axes, scythes, barrel hoops, and rifle barrels. To meet increasing demand for iron, in 1810, when domestic production of iron was only 918 tons, the United States had to import 11,000 tons of iron from Russia, Sweden, and England. Demand continued to rise with a growing population, improvements in grates and furnaces, better industrial techniques, and especially the production of steel railroad rails and railroad steam locomotives (*see also* 44–45 *and* 70–71).

Steel. In the 1870s and 1880s, Englishman Henry Bessemer and Scotsman Andrew Carnegie contributed to innovation in the steel industry. Steel is tougher and stronger than iron but for centuries was used only in expensive tools and swords because it was difficult to produce in large amounts. The Bessemer blast furnace, which sent a blast of superheated air through a combination of iron ore, limestone, and coke, solved problems

encountered in producing large quantities of steel: soon 2.5 tons could be produced in twenty minutes. Carnegie, who lived in and operated out of Pittsburgh, Pennsylvania, built a vertically integrated industrial operation that controlled every aspect of the steel-making process, from digging the iron ore to selling finished steel rails to the railroads. He joined with banker J. P. Morgan to form the U.S. Steel Corporation, which controlled more than 60 percent of the nation's steel production in the early twentieth century. Iron ore from Minnesota was transported to Pittsburgh; coal mined in West Virginia (*see also* 102–03) was shipped to Pittsburgh and roasted into coke; limestone quarried in Ohio was sent to Pittsburgh. Technological innovations in the United States allowed one American converter to do the work of five British or European units. Further innovations, notably, more effective open hearth production, would end the remarkable Bessemer process era by 1910.

Industrialist Abram Hewitt praised the new iron age in 1892: "I look upon the invention of Mr. Bessemer as almost the greatest invention of the ages. . . . Those who have studied its effects on transportation, the cheapening of food, the lowering of rents, the obliteration of aristocratic privilege will readily comprehend what I mean." Steel production also contributed to the development and introduction of John Deere's innovative steel-tipped plows and Cyrus McCormick's reaper (*see also* 56–57), which increased agricultural productivity and led to more abundant and inexpensive food. Despite the industrial slums (*see also* 82–83) and severe pollution in the steel cities of Pittsburgh, Youngstown and Cleveland in Ohio, Birmingham in Alabama, and Gary and

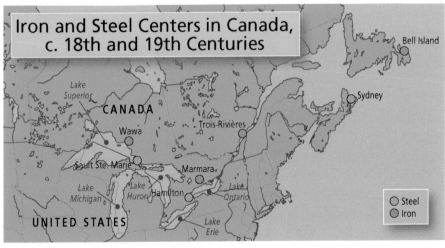

Iron and Steel Centers in Canada, c. 18th and 19th Centuries

Source: Adapted from Donald Gordon Grady Kerr, *A Historical Atlas of Canada.* 2nd ed. (Don Mills, Ontario: Nelson, 1966), 100.

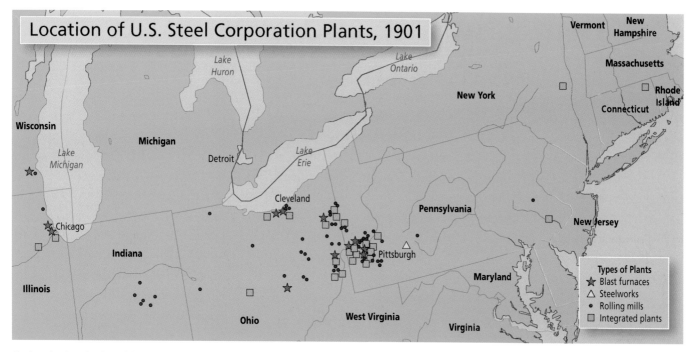

Location of U.S. Steel Corporation Plants, 1901

Types of Plants
☆ Blast furnaces
△ Steelworks
• Rolling mills
□ Integrated plants

Steel production, dominated by the U.S. Steel Corporation, defined industrialization in the United States in the late nineteenth and early twentieth centuries. The regions surrounding cities like Pittsburgh and Cleveland, where many of the steel plants and mills were located, would become the core of the nation's "Rustbelt" when the steel industry declined after World War II.
Source: Adapted from Kenneth Warren, The American Steel Industry: 1850–1970 (Oxford: Clarendon Press, 1973), fig. 17.

Hammond in Indiana, most Americans agreed with both Carnegie and Hewitt that cheap steel improved their standard of living by permitting the production of low-priced goods of high quality. Cheap steel offered, it was said, a "democracy of consumption" through mass production—Henry Ford's Model T automobile (*see also* 57) that sold in 1909 for $950 would fall to $290 by 1924. The auto industry would become steel's largest customer.

In Canada, steel production did not begin until the 1880s. In Ontario, steel-making was concentrated in Sault Ste. Marie (between Lakes Superior and Huron), with the Algoma Steel Company dominating production, and in Hamilton (southwest of Toronto). In Nova Scotia, the town of Sydney on Cape Breton Island became a major center of steel production after the construction of a steel mill in 1901.

By 1900 the United States had surpassed the formidable steel industries of Britain and Germany to lead the world in steel production. The United States, along with Canada, enjoyed major natural resources of iron ore, coal, and limestone that could be exploited for industrial uses (*see also* 64–65). In contrast to the United States, Canadian steel production would not be impressive until World War II. The mass production of steel for the railroads, bridges and buildings, machine tools, the automobile industry, and household appliances opened the door for today's consumer society.

Environmental Impact. The steel industry contributed not only to an industrial revolution and a consumer society, but also to unhealthy smog-ridden cities (*see also* 106–07) and disappearing natural resources. For instance, steel cities like Pittsburgh and Cleveland became virtual "company towns" whose workers and their families were exposed to heavy air and water pollution (*see also* 74–75). Thus, the stage was set for a major confrontation in the latter half of the twentieth century between environmentalism that condemned industrial pollution and waste, and consumerism that continuously sought more goods (*see also* 162–63). The Clean Air and Clean Water Acts, passed by the U.S. Congress in the 1970s, as well as Superfund hazardous waste regulations (*see also* 152–53), forced the cleanup of America's northeastern "Rustbelt" cities. By the 1970s and 1980s, however, cheaper steel from Japan and Europe caused the collapse of the U.S. steel industry because of high labor costs and the overconsumption of steel's raw materials in the United States.

—*John Opie*

Further Reading
Giedion, Siegfried. *Mechanization Takes Command.* New York: Norton, 1969.
Licht, Walter. *Industrializing America: The Nineteenth Century.* Baltimore, Md.: Johns Hopkins University Press, 1995.

Wall, Joseph Frazier. *Andrew Carnegie.* Pittsburgh: University of Pittsburgh Press, 1989.
Heron, Craig. *Working in Steel, The Early Years in Canada, 1883–1935.* Toronto: McClelland and Stewart, 1988.

Water Supply and Wastewater Disposal in the United States

Water is essential for human life. Urban areas make the heaviest demands on this limited resource. Throughout U.S. history, cities required water for domestic needs such as drinking and washing, industrial purposes, street cleaning, and fire fighting. Until the second half of the nineteenth century, most American urbanites depended on local sources such as wells, ponds, streams, and rainwater cisterns for household water supplies. Water consumption per capita averaged between 3 and 5 gallons (11 and 19 liters) a day. Local supplies, however, ultimately proved inadequate for the needs of growing cities (*see also* 78–79), as wells and ponds became polluted and

groundwater levels receded. The desire of city dwellers for copious supplies of cleaner water for household and industrial use, concerns over public health threats from polluted water and filthy streets, and the lack of sufficient water to control fires led to a search for new sources.

Early Water Systems. In 1801, Philadelphia, motivated by a severe yellow fever epidemic and believing that such epidemics were caused by poor water supplies and unsanitary conditions, became the first large city to construct a municipal waterworks, drawing from the Schuylkill River. Other cities followed, with Cincinnati and Pittsburgh installing water systems that in the 1820s drew

from nearby rivers; New York began receiving water from the Croton Reservoir in 1841, and Boston from the Cochituate Reservoir in 1848. By 1880, 598 U.S. cities had water systems, with large cities usually possessing publicly owned waterworks and smaller cities using privately owned systems. The inadequacies of many private systems in supplying water for fires or the needs of new neighborhoods, however, resulted in a trend toward public ownership.

As running water became available in the home and emphasis on sanitation and cleanliness became greater, more and more households adopted water-using appliances such as sinks, showers, and flush toilets.

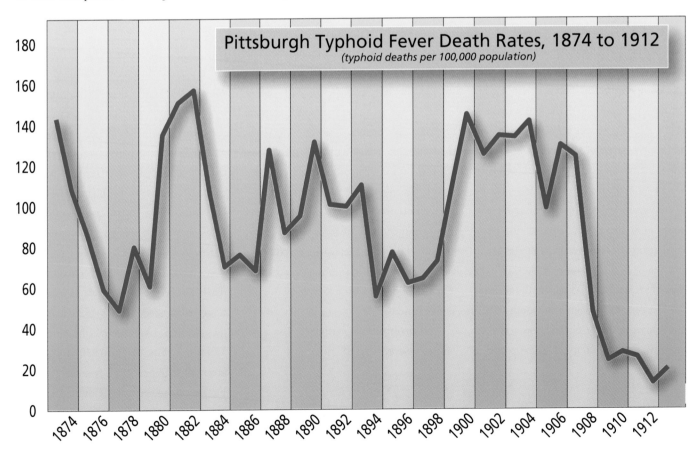

Pittsburgh Typhoid Fever Death Rates, 1874 to 1912
(typhoid deaths per 100,000 population)

Pittsburgh had the highest typhoid death rates in the nation before it began filtering its water in 1907.

Source: Adapted from Erwin Eugene Lanpher, *City of Pittsburgh, Pennsylvania: Its Water Works* (1930; reprint, LaCrosse, Wis.: Brookhaven Press, 1999).

Urban consumption of water increased significantly. Chicago, for example, increased from 33 gallons (125 liters) per capita per day in 1856 to 144 (545 liters) in 1882 and Detroit grew from 55 gallons (208 liters) per capita per day in 1856 to 149 (564 liters) in 1882.

Sewerage Systems. Although many cities had installed waterworks by about 1875, few of them constructed sewer systems to remove wastewater. In most homes with running water, wastewater was initially diverted into cesspools or sewers for storm water. These connections created many problems; most serious from a public health perspective was the spread of feces-polluted wastewater. Believing that filthy conditions accelerated the spread of contagious disease, public health officials viewed overflowing cesspools with flush toilet connections as a threat to human health. After failing to solve the problem with so-called odorless excavators (vacuum pumps) to pump out cesspools, engineers and sanitarians increasingly argued for the construction of centralized sewer systems as the most efficient means to collect and dispose of wastewater.

In the late nineteenth and early twentieth centuries, American cities embarked on massive installation of waste removal (or sewerage) systems. Between 1890 and 1909, sewers in U.S. cities with populations more than twenty-five thousand increased from 6,005 miles (9,664 kilometers) to 24,972 (40,189 kilometers). In the United States, sewers served over 70 percent of the residents in cities with populations more than fifty thousand. Larger cities, faced with the necessity of removing storm water and household wastes, constructed combined sewers (human and storm wastes in the same pipe). Smaller cities utilized sanitary sewers, removing household wastes but allowing storm water to run off on streets or in surface channels.

Water Pollution. Regardless of the type of sewer, most cities disposed of their untreated sewage in neighboring waterways. The disposal of untreated sewage in streams and lakes from which downstream cities drew their water caused large increases in mortality and morbidity from typhoid fever and other infectious waterborne diseases. Cities like Pittsburgh, Cincinnati, Philadelphia, and Chicago, all of which drew their water supplies from water bodies into which they or upstream cities discharged raw sewage, had frequent epidemics of typhoid fever. Pittsburgh, for instance, had the highest death rate from typhoid fever in the United States from 1881 to 1906, an average of over one hundred deaths per year per one hundred thousand population.

In the 1890s, public health researchers, following the new germ theory, identified a relationship between sewage, drinking water, and disease. However, because downstream users usually experienced the epidemics, upstream cities continued for many years to build sewerage systems and to dispose of untreated wastes in adjacent waterways.

Regulation. Sanitarians and Progressive Era reformers pushed for laws and institutions to deal with the threats to health from urban sewage-disposal practices.

Further Reading

McCarthy, Michael P. *Typhoid and the Politics of Public Health in Nineteenth-Century Philadelphia.* Philadelphia: American Philosophical Society, 1987.
Melosi, Martin V. *The Sanitary City: Urban Infrastructure in America from Colonial Times to the Present.* Baltimore, Md.: Johns Hopkins University Press, 2000.
Nesson, Fern L. *Great Waters: A History of Boston's Water Supply.* Hanover, N.H.: University Press of New England, 1983.
Shapiro-Shapin, Carolyn G. "Filtering the City's Image: Progressivism, Local Control, and the St. Louis Water Supply, 1890–1906." *Bulletin of the History of Medicine* 54 (July 1999): 397–412.

States created boards of health (beginning with Massachusetts in 1869) and passed legislation to protect water quality by limiting sewage disposal in streams. By 1905, thirty-six states had legislation protecting drinking water from new sources of pollution, although in many cases existing sources were allowed to continue disposing of their untreated wastes in streams. Cities also moved to protect their water supplies by drawing them from a distant and protected watershed or by filtering their water. Many inland cities installed mechanical or sand filters after 1897, resulting in sharp declines in morbidity and mortality rates from typhoid fever and other diseases.

Water filtration, however, did not remove the sewage from the rivers and lakes, and some health authorities argued that cities should both filter their water and treat their sewage to protect both their own water supply and that of downstream cities. (Sewage treatment at this time essentially meant removing much but not all of the human waste from sewage before it was disposed in a waterway.) Few cities, however, followed these recommendations because they saw little reason to spend large amounts of money to protect the water supplies of communities downstream. Rather they maintained that those cities should filter their own water to protect the public health and that sewage purification should be utilized only to prevent obvious nuisances. By 1920, therefore, only a few cities treated their sewage and most discharged their sewage untreated into nearby bodies of water. Drinking water supplies of downstream or neighboring cities, however, were largely protected by filtration and chlorination. Not until about World War II had even half the cities in the United States begun to treat their sewage to protect stream ecology.

—*Joel A. Tarr*

Water Supply and Pollution in Canada

In 1850 most Canadians, whether they lived in cities or on farms, drew their domestic water supply from private, shallow wells. They dumped sanitary waste into pit privies or directly into rivers and streams—often adjacent to the wells or water intake pipes that supplied their drinking water (*see also* 190–91). Most communities did not provide municipal water and sewerage services until the late nineteenth century; even then, those services were generally poorly designed and reached very few in the community. Unsurprisingly, waterborne illnesses, cholera and typhoid in particular, plagued urban centers like Halifax in Nova Scotia, Québec City and Montreal in Québec, and Kingston and Toronto in Ontario throughout the late nineteenth century. Improvement in water services and professionalization of the sanitary engineering and public health fields in the twentieth century helped to reduce cases of waterborne illnesses. Ontario, in particular, serves as a good example of this transition from inadequate water and sewerage services to reliable and safe water supplies for most urban Canadians.

Population Increase. Urban growth in Ontario concentrated in the Great Lakes basin, which proved to be an ideal location for industrial development because of the region's steady supply of agricultural products to support urban laborers and easy access via water to the northern and western hinterlands with their vast natural resources. Like other communities across Canada, most Great Lakes municipalities drew their water supply from surface waters and released their untreated organic waste into the same body of water, although generally downstream. By the turn of the century, however, increasing population density in the basin meant growing infection and mortality from waterborne diseases, especially typhoid fever.

Spread of Disease. Municipal water supplies contaminated by the feces of people carrying cholera and typhoid proved to be the primary cause for the spread of disease in the late nineteenth century. Although the medical community recognized the source of contagion, most people considered sewage-fouled rivers and lakes in the vicinity of human settlement to be inevitable. Local politicians were reluctant to spend on relatively expensive sewage treatment facilities, when these systems appeared to be of greater benefit to downstream communities than their own. Provincial efforts to improve sanitation were hampered by an inadequate legal and regulatory framework, which resulted in an inability to impose uniformly safe standards on all communities.

Regulation. Concern about the growth of waterborne disease in Ontario and efforts to control the spread of disease resulted in a struggle between the provincial Board of Health and local communities in the late nineteenth century. The provincial Board of Health could order a community to adopt remedial water or sewerage works but had little influence over the design or

An 1875 Canadian Illustrated News *cartoon depicting the figure of Death riding through the streets of Montreal with the spirits of "Cholera," "Fever," and "Small Pox." (National Library of Canada/C-62719)*

Further Reading

Hagopian, John. "The Political Geography of Water Provision in Paris, Ontario, 1882–1924." *Urban History Review* 22 (November 1994): 32–51.

MacDougall, Heather. "Public Health and the 'Sanitary Idea' in Toronto 1866–1888." In *Essays in the History of Canadian Medicine,* edited by Wendy Mitchinson and Janice Dicken McGinnis. Toronto: McClelland and Stewart, 1988.

Read, Jennifer. "'A Sort of Destiny': The Multi-jurisdictional Response to Sewage Pollution in the Great Lakes, 1900–1930." *Scientia Canadensis* 22-23 (1998–1999): 103–129.

Tarr, Joel A., James McCurley, and Terry F. Yosie. "The Development and Impact of Urban Wastewater Technology: Changing Concepts of Water Quality Control, 1850–1930." In *Pollution and Reform in American Cities 1870—1930,* edited by Martin Melosi. Austin: University of Texas Press, 1980.

operation of these systems. A community was free to construct whatever it chose and to manage the infrastructure as it saw fit. In practice, communities often built inadequate facilities, delayed construction, or failed to manage them appropriately when they were completed. Legislation would transform the Board of Health from a part-time volunteer institution with little authority in the 1880s to a centralized, professional organization staffed by trained public health professionals in the 1920s.

In 1912, the Ontario legislature passed the Public Health Act, which created a public health program that gave the Board of Health authority to address decades of inadequate water systems. The act forbade municipalities from building water or sewerage infrastructure without the approval of the central board. Accordingly, planned construction had to be adequate for the size of the community. The Board of Health was also empowered to force communities to manage completed work properly.

The 1912 legislation divided the province into seven health districts. Prior to the passage of the Public Health Act, local medical officers of health had been part-time, general practitioners from the community, subject to local pressures to maintain the best image of the city possible. The legislation enabled the Board of Health to appoint full-time public health professionals as district health officers. These district officers investigated incidences and causes of disease and were able to order appropriate remedial measures for the community.

Water Treatment. One of the most effective remedial measures for compromised municipal water supplies available to district health officers was to order a community to install hypochlorite treatment. Some public health officials worried that continuous chemical treatment of drinking water set a dangerous precedent as it treated the water consumed by a community rather than the waste that was fouling their water. For others, especially municipal officials, hypochlorite treatment was attractive because funds spent benefited the community that elected the officials by protecting the community's health and welfare.

By 1915, most communities across Ontario had adopted hypochlorite treatment and the incidence of waterborne illnesses had dropped dramatically. Unfortunately, while the health of Ontarians improved, the condition of the province's rivers and streams steadily declined. By the mid-twentieth century, the minimally treated organic human waste released from municipalities was joined by chemical waste from the growing industrial and manufacturing enterprises in the Great Lakes basin. This pollution damaged the health and habitat of fish, aquatic birds, and other animals, and reduced the natural beauty of the province's rivers and streams.

As urban centers grew across Canada in the early twentieth century (*see also* 78–79), hypochlorite treatment of municipal water supplies proved to be the technology most readily adopted. By 1930, most urban Canadians were served by a safe and reliable water supply, managed by educated and technically proficient professionals and subject only to occasional compromises by flooding or infrastructure problems.

—*Jennifer Read*

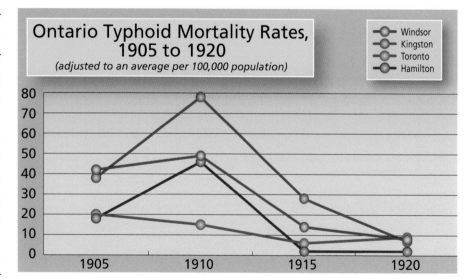

The typhoid mortality rates for select Ontario communities, as reported by medical officers of health, declined sharply after 1910 when most communities with municipal water systems across the province had adopted hypochlorite treatment. Public health officials considered a mortality rate of 24 or above to indicate a compromised water system. Residual typhoid outbreaks were generally traced to contaminated milk after 1915.
Source: Adapted from Table One: Typhoid Death Rates, Jennifer Read, "'A Sort of Destiny': The Multi-jurisdictional Response to Sewage Pollution in the Great Lakes, 1900-1930," *Scientia Canadensis* 22-23 (1998–1999), 108.

Urbanization: Population Shifts and Migration Patterns

Between 1850 and 1920, the United States and Canada were transformed from rural nations to urban nations, with the result that residents, old and new, of the growing cities faced new challenges associated with urban living. Although both nations had vital urban cultures throughout their histories, most of the population lived in the countryside until 1850. The shift to urban living over the next seven decades was the result of several influences and would transform the use of land, water, and resources in North America.

Industrial Growth. Cities grew in population as individuals moved to urban areas for work in the quickly expanding industries of both Canada and the United States. Production of commodities ranging from packed meat to automobiles grew exponentially in the late nineteenth and early twentieth centuries, and demand for labor in the urban factories was high.

Immigration. Individuals came to the cities from rural areas of North America and from abroad. Between 1820 and 1880, the majority of immigrants to the United States and Canada were from northern Europe. During those six decades, more than 85 percent of the thirty-three million people who immigrated to the United States came from Germany, Scandinavia, or the United Kingdom. During the forty years following 1880, economic and political unrest in eastern, central, and southern Europe led millions from those regions to immigrate to North America. Smaller numbers of migrants from Mexico and East Asia joined the wave of immigration, with an average of about six million people arriving in the United States in each decade between 1880 and 1920. More than eight million immigrants entered the United States between 1900 and 1909. Canada saw a similar rise in immigration, welcoming slightly more than three hundred thousand migrants between

1890 and 1899 and 1.4 million immigrants between 1900 and 1909. Not all the immigrants stayed—Italians often worked in North American cities for a few months or years, then returned to Italy once they had earned enough money to purchase land—but urban populations grew rapidly.

Migration to Cities. World War I caused industrial production in cities to rise as factories geared up to supply needed arms, uniforms, and other equipment. Promises of well-paying jobs in northern cities lured African-American and white sharecroppers from agricultural work in the rural South. African-American newspapers in the United States like the *Chicago Defender* and *Pittsburgh Courier* ran editorials and published ads from northern labor agents encouraging southern readers to leave the poverty and racial discrimination of the rural South and to come and take advantage of opportunities in northern cities. Approximately five hundred

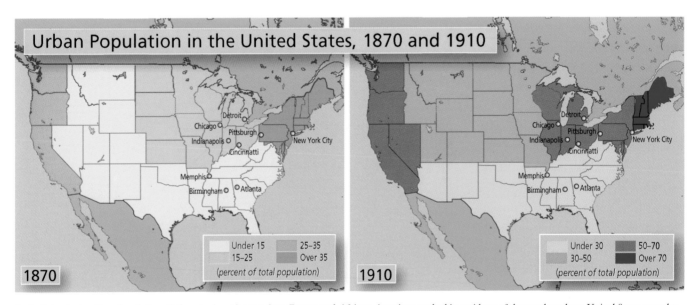

In the late nineteenth and early twentieth centuries, migrants from Europe and African-American and white residents of the rural southern United States moved to cities in the industrialized urban Northeast, Midwest, and to a lesser extent, the western United States. Those regions were primarily urban by 1910.

Source: Adapted from David Ward, *Cities and Immigrants: A Geography of Change in Nineteenth-Century America* (New York: Oxford University Press, 1971), 30, 42. Used by permission of Oxford University Press, Inc.

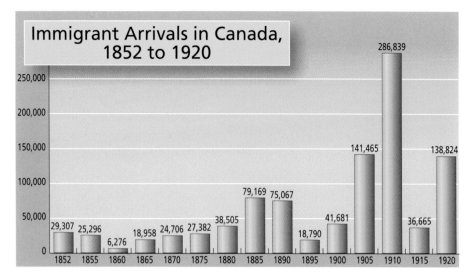

Immigrant Arrivals in Canada, 1852 to 1920

Year	Arrivals
1852	29,307
1855	25,296
1860	6,276
1865	18,958
1870	24,706
1875	27,382
1880	38,505
1885	79,169
1890	75,067
1895	18,790
1900	41,681
1905	141,465
1910	286,839
1915	36,665
1920	138,824

Canada's population grew in large part because of immigration between 1852 and 1920. In just the first decade of the twentieth century, about 1.4 million migrants arrived in Canada, many of them seeking work in the nation's largest cities. Toronto and Montreal, which saw their populations more than double between 1890 and 1910, annexed surrounding suburbs to accommodate the new residents.
Source: Statistics Canada. Historical Statistics of Canada. <http://www.statcan.ca/english/freepub/11-516-XIE/sectiona/sectiona.htm#Immigration>. Underlying data from Department of Manpower and Immigration, 1976 Immigration Statistics. Table 2. (Ottawa: Statistics Canada, 1977), 4. Used with the permission of Statistics Canada.

thousand African-American southerners moved to northern cities between 1916 and 1919. Many of these migrants moved north gradually, initially to southern cities like Birmingham, Alabama; Memphis, Tennessee; and Atlanta, Georgia; then to Cincinnati, Ohio, and Indianapolis, Indiana; and finally to Chicago, Illinois; Pittsburgh, Pennsylvania; and Detroit, Michigan. Rural Canadians often moved to small towns prior to settling in Toronto, Ontario; Montreal, Québec; and Vancouver, British Columbia. This pattern, known as chain migration, occurred throughout North America.

Life in the Cities. New urban residents found several kinds of housing. Tenements—crowded apartment buildings with few amenities—were common housing stock in poor neighborhoods (*see also* 82–83). Apartment buildings made efficient use of space to house large numbers of people in very dense areas (for example, Manhattan and Brooklyn in New York City) where space was at a premium. Where land was affordable, some migrants purchased small tracts and used pattern books

and affordable construction materials to build their own houses. The balloon-frame home construction method allowed a couple of people to quickly nail a frame together and put up a house in a matter of days; prospective home owners could build new houses without relying on professional architects or builders. Toronto, Chicago, Pittsburgh, Montreal, and Detroit saw many new neighborhoods emerge as immigrant communities built their own housing.

Cities expanded outward as urban services (*see also* 80–81) like streetcars, sewers, and firefighting operations moved beyond the central business district to growing residential neighborhoods. Many urban areas annexed surrounding suburbs in the late nineteenth century. Chicago added most of its current south side, annexing 133 square miles (345 square kilometers) in 1889. In 1898, Brooklyn (then the fourth-largest city in the United States) became a borough of New York City and Toronto annexed many of its suburbs between 1906 and 1912, including North Toronto. Montreal annexed several

neighboring towns between 1883 and 1905, including Hochelaga and Villeray.

Increased population density and industrial activity made cities dirty and dangerous. Working-class residents in the inner cities were exposed to smoke (*see also* 106–07) from factories and coal-burning stoves in houses; used water polluted by human waste and industrial waste; and lived near mounds of garbage. Rising consumption led to crises in the collection of garbage and in supplying clean water (*see also* 74–77) to urban residents. Cities built public works systems including waterworks, sewers, incinerators, and dumps to address these crises. Such infrastructure was expensive to build and maintain and thus increased taxes on urban residents.

Rise of Suburbs. Middle- and upper-class residents in Canada and the United States increasingly sought to live on the edges of the city, where they could commute to work on streetcars, subways, and subsequently in their own automobiles, and live in quiet, clean neighborhoods. In 1920, the rate of growth of suburbs surpassed that of cities for the first time. This trend would intensify after World War II, leading to loss of population in many cities as residents moved to the surrounding suburbs (*see also* 160–61).

—*Carl Zimring*

Further Reading

Bodnar, John. *The Transplanted: A History of Immigrants in Urban America.* Bloomington: Indiana University Press, 1985.

Fligstein, Neil. *Going North, Migration of Blacks and Whites from the South, 1900–1950.* New York: Academic Press, 1981.

Jackson, Kenneth T. *Crabgrass Frontier: The Suburbanization of the United States.* New York: Oxford University Press, 1987.

Trotter, Joe William, Jr., ed. *The Great Migration in Historical Perspective: New Dimensions of Race, Class, and Gender.* Bloomington: Indiana University Press, 1991.

Ward, David. *Cities and Immigrants: A Geography of Change in Nineteenth-Century America.* New York: Oxford University Press, 1971.

The Built Environment in the City

Before the 1850s, the built environment of many North American cities, Boston and Montreal, for example, displayed patterns of preindustrial town planning and primitive infrastructure. These "walking cities" displayed buildings seldom taller than three stories, open sewers and often polluted well water, and crowded, muddy streets. At mid-century, armed with new technology and new techniques, engineers exploded the older limits of the urban form: They stretched cities outward with connective rail networks, bridges, and paved boulevards; they plunged beneath the surface of the metropolis to create networks of water delivery, waste disposal, and human transport (subways); and they built endlessly upward.

Bridges. Monumental bridges symbolized this emerging landscape of material and technical innovation. Railroad companies (*see also* 44–45 *and* 70–71) like the Erie Rail Road built steel bridges, replacing older iron and wooden bridges. This early period of steel bridge building included the construction of the Eads Bridge in St. Louis, Missouri, the Glasgow Bridge in Glasgow, Missouri, and the Brooklyn Bridge in New York City. Between 1869 and 1883, Scottish-born American engineer John Roebling and his son, Colonel Washington Roebling, introduced steel cables to support the Brooklyn Bridge's span. Engineers like American Charles Conrad Schneider, who is credited with inventing the now common, counterbalanced cantilever bridge with arms supporting a suspended span, built scores of utilitarian railroad bridges by the turn of the century, including many for the Canadian Pacific Railway Company.

Mass Transit. By the 1860s, Montreal, New York, and Philadelphia each had privately owned systems of horse-drawn railways that crisscrossed downtown centers, moving people from home to workplace. As cities grew in size, faster trains, more lines, and increased service became necessary. These demands, combined with speculative building in cities like New York and Los Angeles, were to produce a series of mass transit innovations from horse-drawn railcars to electric trolleys by century's end. By 1902, trolleys, powered by overhead electric wires, dominated city streets and accounted for 94 percent of street railway mileage in the United States.

The crowded streets required dedicated rights-of-way for these trolleys. An early effort to address the problem of crowded and dangerous streets in cities like Chicago and New York was to build elevated tracks, nicknamed "els," that transported trains above the traffic. Beginning with Boston in 1898, metal cylinders were used to tunnel beneath city streets to build subways that would hide noisy and unsightly trains. William Barclay Parsons designed the first New York City subway, which opened in 1904. Parsons's method of digging trenches for the tunnels, and then covering them over, became a popular construction method of subways.

Infrastructure Improvements. A new infrastructure of water pipes, sewer systems (*see also* 74–77), and power lines

Urban Wildlife

Although cities are habitats managed for humans, they are home to a variety of wildlife that live in close proximity to humans. Rodents, birds, insects, and many other creatures, thrive in the often unintentionally hospitable environments that people create.

The vertical rise of nineteenth-century cities and ample supply of human refuse and feed from urban stables allowed the common North American street pigeon to flourish in cities like New York and Boston, where it roosted in the windowsills of clifflike buildings. Similarly, rodents such as gray squirrels (*Sciurus*) were and are a familiar feature of the urban landscape, scampering through the trees and grasses of urban parks.

Rats and cockroaches continue to be familiar to the urban landscape, though not as welcome. Despite repeated attempts to eradicate brown rats (*Rattus norvegicus*) during the late nineteenth and early twentieth centuries, rats thrived in city sewers and damp basements. Cockroaches (especially the *Blattella germanica* and *Periplanata Americana*) have also plagued North American cities, multiplying in urban dwellings.

While municipal authorities have long worked to keep pests at bay, over the course of the nineteenth century wildlife enthusiasts intentionally imported bird species including starlings (*Starnus vulgaris,* introduced in the 1890s). Such animals brought song, grace, and increasingly, indignation to cities. Starlings in particular have multiplied in North American cities over the last hundred years, collecting en masse in trees and public areas where they defecate on cars, drive away native bird species, and create a noisy nuisance.

As urban sprawl redefines the city's form, especially in the western United States, relations between people and wildlife have become increasingly strained. Although not as densely populated as traditional vertical cities, advancing sprawl continues to transform animal habitats. In some American cities, Seattle, for example, environmentalists seek to repair the urban fabric by "day-lighting"—uncovering streams to bring back habitat for migrating salmon. But new roads, clearings for development, and exotic landscaping continue to drive wild creatures from their homes or attract animals to the varied, grassy terrains of golf courses, playing fields and playgrounds, and backyards.

The span of the Brooklyn Bridge in New York City, supported by steel cables. (© Alan Schein Photography/Corbis)

innovators, but electricity was still a luxury concentrated in downtown business districts. The cost of electricity soon fell as consumption by homeowners and factories increased. By the twentieth century, electrical engineers had developed more comprehensive citywide systems of distribution that were based on large-scale generating stations powered by steam or water that were connected to a network of substations around cities and in outlying neighborhoods.

Along with sewer, water, and electric services, middle-class neighborhoods defined their property values and exclusivity with paved streets and roads. In the 1870s, the Public Works Department in New York City laid macadamized pavement (crushed rock) over the existing dirt streets to attract the middle class to new neighborhoods. Washington, D.C., had experimented with coal tar pavements by the end of the century. As movements for municipal improvements gained momentum in the 1890s, many cities and fashionable suburbs replaced wooden plank sidewalks and dirt streets with concrete. By 1900, 200 miles (320 kilometers) of these roads had been built in the United States.

Increasingly the metropolis concentrated people, technology, and services into the familiar clump of buildings and concrete. With better steel and the perfection of the speed elevator in 1887, which used steel cables, downtown buildings grew progressively taller. In the twentieth century cities would continue both their vertical ascent and outward sprawl.

—*Jeffrey C. Sanders*

followed the subterranean direction of city services and expanding trolley lines. Reformers made clean water and sewer systems central to their sanitation and public health crusades near the end of the century, but municipal and private networks spread unevenly, with early services available to the middle class living on the edges of expanding cities. Real estate developers provided the luxury of indoor running water, a necessity for modern middle-class households with indoor plumbing. By the end of the nineteenth century, concern about fire and public health had led to public ownership and financing for waterworks, mains, reservoirs, pumping stations, and trunk sewers in cities. In 1850 only eighty-four waterworks existed in American cities; by 1880 there were 599.

Underground wastewater networks developed slowly in comparison, with many cities continuing to use open sewers, cesspools, and low-lying swampy areas as wastewater collection areas. After 1870, however, larger American cities, including Brooklyn, Chicago, and Boston, had built underground sewer lines: combined systems that included pipes for storm water overflow,

to prevent frequent flooding, and pipes for household wastewater and effluent (liquid waste products from factories and packing houses). By the 1920s North American cities used comprehensive systems of water and waste disposal developed with and supported by public money.

Electric lines, which made trolley expansion in the 1890s possible, also developed slowly as the private firms that distributed power first provided services to the wealthy and middle class in order to accumulate capital to build more infrastructure. Power lines followed trolley lines into new and established neighborhoods, replacing gas with electric lights on main streets. By the 1890s, cities like Chicago had distribution networks and marketing plans developed by

Further Reading

Burrows, Edwin G., and Mike Wallace. *Gotham: A History of New York City to 1898*. New York: Oxford University Press, 1999.

Kostof, Spiro. *A History of Architecture: Settings and Rituals*. New York: Oxford University Press, 1995.

Lewis, Robert Davis. *Manufacturing Montreal: The Making of an Industrial Landscape, 1850 to 1930*. Baltimore, Md.: Johns Hopkins University Press, 2000.

Melosi, Martin V. *The Sanitary City: Urban Infrastructure in America from Colonial Times to the Present*. Baltimore, Md.: Johns Hopkins University Press, 2000.

Plowden, David. *Bridges: The Spans of North America*. New York: Norton, 2002.

Tarr, Joel A., and Gabriel Dupuy, eds. *Technology and the Rise of the Networked City in Europe and America*. Philadelphia: Temple University Press, 1988.

Social Darwinism and "Survival of the Fittest" in the United States

Although industrialization and urbanization (*see also* 78–79) brought prosperity to the United States, they also led to industrial pollution, the exploitation of workers, and a dramatically uneven distribution of wealth. By the middle of the nineteenth century, the social and economic changes brought about by the growth of industry and cities forced Americans to reexamine social policy. The problems associated with industrialization and urbanization would lead to the development of a philosophy called social Darwinism, which was inspired by the theories of biological evolution proposed by Charles Darwin. In works like *Origin of Species* (1859) and *The Descent of Man* (1871), Darwin set forth his theories about how new species are formed and how other species become extinct. Although scholars disagree over the extent to which Darwin believed his theories could be applied to human societies, philosophers and economists of the nineteenth and early twentieth centuries used these biological theories to explain economic, racial, and gender inequities in U.S. society.

The nineteenth-century British philosopher Herbert Spencer is considered to be the father of social Darwinism. He is credited with coining "survival of the fittest," although Darwin used the phrase himself in a later edition of *Origin*. Spencer enjoyed immense popularity and was influential in the spread of social Darwinism to many parts of the world. For Spencer, society was evolving toward increasing individualism; accordingly, he saw state intervention in social life as an inhibitor of the natural progression of societal evolution. Spencer believed the evolution of some societies had progressed beyond that of others, and he arranged societies in a hierarchy of progress with Anglo societies at the top.

Distribution of Wealth. William Graham Sumner was the prime advocate of Spencer's ideas in the United States. A professor of political economy at Yale from 1872 to 1909, Sumner also argued against state welfare and for individualism and a laissez-faire economy (one driven by free-market forces rather than by government intervention). He believed that human beings compete for limited resources, that only the best can reach the top, and that the survival and reproduction of weaker competitors served only to degrade the entire human species.

While reformers sought to eliminate poor worker conditions and redistribute wealth more equally, Spencer, Sumner, and others saw such inequalities as indicators that society was operating within the

Canadian Social Darwinism

Although the ideology of social Darwinists developed in Canada to a lesser degree than in Britain and the United States, the Social Gospel movement found a following among Canadian reformers and was especially strong among middle-class Methodists and Presbyterians. The movement began in western cities, including Winnipeg in Manitoba and Regina in Saskatchewan, as a response to the massive immigration (*see also* 78–79) of the 1890s and early twentieth century. This influx of people exacerbated the problems of the quickly growing industrial cities. Rapid industrialization and urbanization had brought about more pollution, slum conditions, and poorly planned cities, as well as boom-and-bust economic cycles and a severe gap between the upper-class and industrial workers.

The Social Gospel movement campaigned against urban problems, including alcohol abuse and the exploitation of immigrants. But the movement was not entirely united about how to implement a program of reform. Some reformers sought to bring about change through education, others worked to replace laissez-faire economics with state intervention, and still others established settlement houses that offered shelter and food to those in need. James Shaver Woodsworth (1874–1942) was one of the most prominent ministers of the Social Gospel movement. Not only did Woodsworth work to improve the conditions of urban immigrants living in the slums of cities like Winnipeg, he also inspired many of his fellow reformers to embrace his politics of democratic socialism.

The movement did not remain solely a middle-class phenomenon. It also appealed to labor and agricultural leaders and played a vital role in trade unionization and the writing and passage of labor laws like the Ontario Workman's Compensation Act (1914), which gave financial compensation to workers injured on the job. Perhaps the most significant contribution of the Social Gospel movement to Canadian history was as the foundation for the socialist Co-operative Commonwealth Federation (CCF) established during the Great Depression of the 1930s. The CCF consisted of labor forces, progressives, and socialists who wanted to create a political mechanism whose main goal was to improve, through economic reform, the conditions of those affected by the depression. Many of the leaders of the Social Gospel movement also played a vital role in the establishment of the CCF, including Woodsworth, who was elected as the first president of the CCF.

Tenement housing in New York City, c. 1889. (From the collections of the Library of Congress)

dictates of natural evolution. For example, in late-nineteenth-century New York, the slums and tenements crammed the poor and mostly immigrant populations into dark, crowded, and refuse-laden neighborhoods with inadequate ventilation, sewerage, and water systems (*see also* 74–75). At the same time, New York's wealthy built extravagant homes and filled them with expensive, imported objects. Social Darwinists like Sumner and Spencer interpreted these contrasting stations of life as natural expressions of the "survival of the fittest."

Racial and Gender Inequities. Social Darwinism was used to explain the superiority of Aryans (those of northern European ancestry [Nordics] and Indo-Europeans) over other races and to justify empire building in the United States in the late nineteenth and early twentieth centuries, when continued settlement in U.S. western territories (*see also* 52–53) was encouraged. The United States also cast its territorial net into the Pacific and the Caribbean. Social Darwinists relied on their belief in the evolutionary superiority of men as an argument against women's suffrage and contraception. Social Darwinists, and much of American

society in the late nineteenth century, feared that if women taxed their mental capacities, the female reproductive system would be compromised.

Conspicuous Consumption. Despite the influence of the theories of social Darwinists, many reformers rejected fundamentals of the ideology but maintained some social Darwinist ideas in their own, more inclusive brand of social policy. Thorstein Veblen, an American economist, challenged the idea that the human experience was a struggle over limited resources. Veblen criticized the consumption ethic of middle-class and upper-class America in *The Theory of the Leisure Class* (1899). In his criticism of the elaborate dress, expensive housing, and leisure activities of the rich, Veblen coined the term *conspicuous consumption*. He called for a more holistic economic approach in which laissez-faire profit-mindedness was replaced by an economy and social policy carefully planned by social experts.

Social Gospel Movement. Following Veblen's lead, other reformers rejected some tenets of conservative social Darwinism while retaining other elements. For instance, the Social Gospel movement sought to use Christian morality as a tool against the drastically uneven distribution of wealth and poor working conditions produced by capitalism and industrialism. The most well-known leader of the movement was Walter Rauschenbusch, who was catapulted to fame with his publication of *Christianity and the Social Crisis* (1907). Rauschenbusch's heaven or "Kingdom of God" was not a distant afterlife, but could be found in the connectedness of humanity itself. While the Social Gospel movement rejected Darwinian natural selection, it subscribed to an evolutionary idea that morality had developed, or evolved, to dominate the baser, more animal aspects of human nature. Unlike the earlier conservative social

Darwinists like Sumner, Rauschenbusch saw potential in a socialist economy and rejected the laissez-faire capitalism that allowed for the success of a few at the expense of the masses.

Although the influence of social Darwinist thought waned throughout the twentieth century, elements of this ideology remained. As a response to a flood of immigrants (*see also* 78–79), including Italians and Slovakians, who arrived at the beginning of the twentieth century, eugenics (selective breeding of humans for biological superiority) became an increasingly popular concept among middle-class and upper-class white Americans. The idea that immigrants not of English origin were biologically and socially inferior, or less evolved, than Anglo Americans, clearly had its roots in social Darwinism. Social Darwinism reveals the power that "science" can have over social thought, and the ease with which scientific reasoning can be appropriated to justify unequal relations of power and environmental injustice (*see also* 192–93). Although social Darwinism no longer enjoys a strong following, the problems caused by limited resources in the contemporary world often lead more-powerful nations to use similar justifications to exploit the labor and resources of others.

—*Sarah Payne*

Further Reading

Allen, Richard. *The Social Passion: Religion and Social Reform in Canada, 1914–28.* Toronto: University of Toronto Press, 1973.

Degler, Carl N. *In Search of Human Nature: The Decline and Revival of Darwinism in American Social Thought.* New York: Oxford University Press, 1991.

Hawkins, Mike. *Social Darwinism in European and American Thought, 1860–1945.* Cambridge: Cambridge University Press, 1997.

Hofstadter, Richard. *Social Darwinism in American Thought 1860–1915.* Rev. ed. Boston: Beacon Press, 1955.

City Beautiful Movement

The City Beautiful movement originated from a climate of reform in the late nineteenth century. Known as the Progressive Era, this period saw an emerging professional class addressing the social and environmental ills of Gilded Age cities. At the movement's height between 1900 and 1910, a variety of citizen and professional organizations joined together in a systematic effort to plan, manage, and, most of all, beautify the industrial-era city. This City Beautiful movement channeled diverse reform energies and class anxieties into an urban revival that left a lasting imprint on North American cities after the turn of the century. The physical legacy of this movement endures in the neoclassical civic centers, parks and boulevards, and heroic statuary that abound in cities including Washington, D.C., Denver, San Francisco, and Ottawa.

Urban Reform. By 1870, waves of immigration (*see also* 78–79) had crowded ill-equipped North American cities. Between 1850 and 1900, New York City's population alone grew from 515,547 to 3,437,202.

Anxious about this growing urban mass of humanity, some of the middle class fled the cities, but others applied their energies to solving urban problems and bolstering what they saw as an imperiled civil order. One strain of reform—from which the City Beautiful movement would grow—focused specifically on the physical environment of cities (*see also* 80–81), including sewerage systems, housing, and sanitation.

As early as the 1840s and 1850s, the urban park movement (*see also* 98–99) in cities like Boston and its suburbs set aside undeveloped land as picturesque pleasure grounds. Landscape architect Frederick Law Olmsted, who began work on New York's Central Park in 1858, was the most influential exponent of plans for urban parks that emphasized a mixture of beauty and utility. Olmsted was never officially a part of the City Beautiful movement—although his sons and their Olmsted Brothers firm would be. In contrast to other environmental reformers, Olmsted was less sanguine about redeeming cities or their inhabitants, but he believed that his

parks served as a restorative respite for urban dwellers. Other park advocates, such as Boston's Josiah Quincy and Chicago's William Kent, followed the lead of Settlement House activist Jane Addams. Placing playgrounds, parks, and swimming pools in poor neighborhoods in the 1890s, they hoped to channel youthful energies away from vice and toward organized sports and other activities considered to be character-building. The growing City Beautiful movement brought together Olmsted's plans and the moral intervention approach of Kent and Quincy.

Rise of the Movement. In the late 1880s and 1890s numerous national and local associations in the United States and Canada, including the American Park and Outdoor Art Association (1887) and the Ottawa Improvements Commission (1898), lobbied city officials to improve waterworks and sewers and to beautify the city with parkways, ornate lampposts, and fountains. Created by Richard M. Hunt in 1893, the New York Municipal Arts Society began to articulate a comprehensive planning vision of the City Beautiful movement that combined Olmsted's ideas with the vogue for neoclassical or Greco-Roman design elements such as Corinthian columns, triangular pediments, and grand boulevards. Other, similar societies like the National Municipal League (1894) and the American Society of Municipal Improvements (1894) exemplified the evolving philosophy, which combined improvement of urban infrastructure, beautification, and professional planning.

The City Beautiful movement borrowed heavily from European examples. It looked to the city plan and monuments of Paris. The École des Beaux Arts design academy in Paris, which stressed order, dignity, and harmony, provided the movement's familiar architectural elements: the civic

The Palace of Mechanic Arts at the World's Columbian Exposition in Chicago, Illinois. (From the collections of the Library of Congress)

center and plaza (or mall) scheme, neo-classical public buildings, and ornate public memorials. Advocates of the movement thought that such urban forms could inspire civic virtue and elevate the American city.

Columbian Exposition. The term City Beautiful was coined in 1899 by George Kriehn, but as a unified plan it first appeared at the World's Columbian Exposition in Chicago in 1892. Architect and fair director Daniel H. Burnham brought together Olmsted, the sculptor Augustus Saint-Gaudens, and the architecture firm McKim, Mead, and White to design the fairgrounds on the marshy lands of Jackson Park. The result was the "White City," a persuasive advertisement for City Beautiful planning that combined Beaux Arts structures and Olmsted's naturalized landscapes, in a clean, well-run, urban utopia. During an economic depression, and on the heels of the Haymarket Affair—the labor riots, bombing, and subsequent trials in 1886 that shook Chicago—the Columbian Exposition constructed a powerful symbol of democratic stability and middle-class hegemony.

Other Beautification Plans. The City Beautiful movement reached its apex after the turn of the century. In 1901, Burnham and others from the Chicago team created the McMillan Plan, the Senate Park Commission's redesign of Washington, D.C., which employed the same Beaux Arts and Olmstedian principles; this combination

Further Reading

Boyer, Paul. *Urban Masses and Moral Order in America, 1820–1920.* Cambridge, Mass.: Harvard University Press, 1978.

Gordon, David L. A. "From Noblesse Oblige to Nationalism: Elite Involvement in Planning Canada's Capital." *Journal of Urban History* 28 (November 2001): 3–34.

Scott, Mel. *American City Planning Since 1890.* Berkeley: University of California Press, 1971.

Wilson, William H. *The City Beautiful Movement.* Baltimore, Md.: Johns Hopkins University Press, 1989.

The McMillan Plan of 1901

The McMillan Plan of 1901 in Washington, D.C., was the first full expression of the City Beautiful movement planning philosophy following the overwhelmingly popular World's Columbian Exposition in Chicago. The U.S. capital had been partly based upon city planner Pierre L'Enfant's comprehensive neoclassical city plan, but his 1791 design was never fully realized. At the turn of the century, members of the American Institute for Architects pressured politicians for the completion of L'Enfant's original design to honor the city's centennial. The plan was named for Senator James McMillan, who created the Senate Park Commission in 1901. The resulting plan went well beyond L'Enfant's design, creating the familiar look of present-day Washington, D.C.

McMillan hired architect Daniel H. Burnham to create the plan, along with landscape architect Frederick Law Olmsted, Jr., architect Charles F. McKim, and sculptor Augustus Saint-Gaudens. Because Congress controlled the district, Washington, D.C., offered an urban climate free of the usual democratic and economic hurdles of city planning. In accordance with City Beautiful planning ideas, Burnham chose to reorganize the city plan around a monumental core of Beaux Arts–style buildings following European neoclassical examples and L'Enfant's original vision for the city. Burnham set neoclassical federal buildings for the Supreme Court and Congress around Capitol Square and convinced the Pennsylvania Railroad president Alexander J. Cassatt to move the existing station from the base of the Capitol, where its tracks cut across the Mall, to the new Burnham-designed Union Station facing Capitol Square.

When unveiled to the public at the city's Corcoran Gallery in 1902, the plan showcased power and political legitimacy for the federal government at a tumultuous time in American history: The United States had just witnessed William McKinley's assassination and was also poised for overseas expansion. The four-decade effort produced the familiar landmarks of the Mall, the Lincoln and Jefferson Memorials, Union Station, and the Memorial Bridge across the Potomac River to Arlington Cemetery, as well as a park system that stretched beyond the monumental core.

was repeated in cities throughout the United States and Canada. Also in 1901, chief City Beautiful exponent Charles Mulford Robinson published his best-selling book *The Improvement of Towns and Cities,* which further popularized the movement. Soon, cities large and small, from Los Angeles to Santa Fe, New Mexico, wanted a comprehensive City Beautiful plan. Not all plans came to fruition. Robinson's 1907 proposal for boulevards, parkways, and beautification of the Los Angeles River never materialized, nor did Seattle's civic center plan. But similar to the McMillan Plan, the Ottawa–Hull commission (1915) in Canada's capital, led by Beaux Arts–influenced planner and Burnham associate Edward H. Bennett, eventually remade the municipal plaza in City Beautiful style.

After 1909, the City Beautiful movement was increasingly criticized for its overblown style and extravagance. At the same time, the mix of lay and professional collaboration diminished as city bureaucracies and specialization came to dominate urban planning. By World War I, the movement and the Progressive Era zeal that helped propel it had waned. Today in the United States and Canada, grassroots and professional organizations similar to City Beautiful, including the U.S. group Congress on New Urbanism, seek to address urban revitalization and sustainable community, while coalitions like the New Mexico–based Southwest Organizing Project combine social justice and urban environmental concerns in a continued effort to perfect the city.

—*Jeffrey C. Sanders*

Romanticism of Nature: American and Canadian Writers and Artists

During the nineteenth century, popular attitudes to nature owed much to the work of artists and writers. While some depicted nature with painstaking realism, most sought to dramatize the wildness, mystery, and exoticism of newly discovered lands. Romanticism, as this approach was known, brought a new appreciation of nature and inspired the ideals both of early conservation pioneers and modern environmentalists.

Romanticism was a broadly defined movement in the arts that flourished in Europe during the late eighteenth and early nineteenth centuries. Where earlier movements, such as Classicism, had been dignified by restraint, uninhibited Romanticism produced art and literature suffused with passion and mysticism, celebrating the freedom of wild nature in a rejection of the ever-advancing Industrial Revolution. In the United States and Canada, Romanticism created a new national identity based on dramatic depictions of wilderness, with paintings that looked like the Garden of Eden and writings that emphasized a deep spiritual connection between humans and nature.

American Artists. The most notable Romantic artists in the United States belonged to the Hudson River school (1820–80). Central among them, English-born artist Thomas Cole specialized in arcadian landscapes that depicted a spiritual calm in wilderness areas along the Hudson River and in the Catskill Mountains of New York state. Other members of the school included Asher Brown Durand and Thomas Doughty. A later generation of Hudson River artists, notably Frederick Church, recorded the unspoiled wonder of the continent in more detailed and realistic works. One of Church's best-known landscapes is a vast image of Niagara (1857), the falls depicted as a boiling sea tumbling through a rainbow into the bowels of the Earth. German-born Albert Bierstadt traveled with surveying expeditions, capturing a sense of Manifest Destiny (*see also* 52–53)—the pioneers' God-given imperative to conquer new territory—in huge, detailed paintings of wild places like the Rocky Mountains and Yosemite in the western United States.

Romantic visions of nature were not always utopian; Romanticism frequently contained darker undercurrents—a wistful nostalgia for something important that had been forever lost or a dreadful foreboding that it soon would be. The changing portrayals of Native Americans by artists like Charles Bird King, George Catlin, and Karl Bodmer have been seen as a metaphor for the conquest of nature: Early-nineteenth-century depictions of "noble savages" were replaced by images of Native Americans fighting white explorers and settlers or subduing their women, which eventually gave way to poignant portrayals of the decline of Native American cultures. Some captured decline in other ways. Bierstadt's 1889 canvas *The Last of the Buffalo* inaccurately depicted the animal's demise (*see also* 36–37) at the hands of rapacious Native Americans, rather than white hunters. Some years earlier, in a series of five paintings called *The Course of Empire*, Thomas Cole had hinted that the progress of civilization, through the conquest of nature, might prove to be a misguided and doomed endeavor.

American Writers. Romantic ideals were prominent in nineteenth-century literature as well as art. Henry David Thoreau famously returned to the simplicity of "life in the woods" in his 1854 book *Walden;* his celebration of wilderness and support for

The Legacy of John James Audubon

Perhaps the best known of all American nature painters, John James Audubon also left the most enduring legacy. Born in Haiti in 1785, he pursued an unsuccessful business career in the United States until the age of 34, when he became a full-time artist. Between 1827 and 1838, he produced his magnum opus, a set of four beautifully illustrated volumes, *The Birds of America,* based on huge oil paintings of all 435 species of North American birds then known. The equivalent of modern-day nature documentaries, Audubon's illustrations transformed perceptions of wildlife by depicting birds realistically in their natural habitats.

During his lifetime, Audubon warned of the perils facing nature and argued strongly for conservation. In 1886, some years after Audubon's death, *Forest and Stream* magazine editor George Bird Grinnell sought support from his readers for the formation of a bird preservation group that he named the Audubon Society. In the first three months alone, 38,000 people joined, but the society was later disbanded. During the 1890s, however, independent Audubon Societies were formed in states across the country. In 1905, they joined forces to form what is now known as the National Audubon Society, a conservation organization that seeks to protect the environment through a mixture of advocacy, education, and research.

Further Reading

Bergon, Frank, ed. *The Wilderness Reader*. Reno: University of Nevada Press, 1994.

Graham, Frank. *The Audubon Ark: A History of the National Audubon Society*. New York: Alfred A. Knopf, 1990.

Grey Owl. *Tales of an Empty Cabin*. London: L. Dickson, 1936.

Lyon, Thomas J., ed. *This Incomparable Land: A Guide to American Nature Writing*.

Minneapolis, Minn.: Milkweed Editions, 2001.

Hughes, Robert. *American Visions: The Epic History of Art in America*. New York: Alfred A. Knopf, 1997.

Smith, Donald B. *From the Land of the Shadows: The Making of Grey Owl*. Seattle: University of Washington Press, 1999.

Thoreau, Henry David. *Walden*. 1854. Reprint, New York: Modern Library, 2000.

civil disobedience have underpinned the philosophy of modern radical environmentalists. Thoreau's friend and contemporary, essayist and poet Ralph Waldo Emerson, also found a spiritual home in nature ("In the woods, we return to reason and faith. There I feel that nothing can befall me in life—no disgrace, no calamity . . . which nature cannot repair . . . all mean egotism vanishes . . . I am nothing; I see all; the currents of the Universal Being circulate through me; I am part or particle of God." [*Nature*, 1836]). Emerson and Thoreau were key exponents of transcendentalism (*see also* 50–51), a philosophy that valued spiritual insights over rational and empirical ideas. Walt Whitman's poems also stressed a spiritual feature of Romantic thought, the oneness of people and nature ("Give me solitude, give me Nature, give me again O Nature your primal sanities!" [*Leaves of Grass*, 1855]), while for the reclusive Emily Dickinson, careful observations of nature often provided useful metaphors for emotional complexities.

Canadian Artists. Canadian art also celebrated wild nature. The romance of nature proved a popular theme for artists including Québec-born Joseph Légaré, the first Canadian to paint wilderness landscapes in oils. Cornelius Krieghoff's rural snow scenes were fashionable with collectors in Europe. With the sun shining and smoke billowing from the chimney of a log cabin, Krieghoff's *Winter Landscape, Laval* (1862) depicts the simple attractions of a cozy life in the wilderness. The Hudson River school's blend of realism and romance found parallels with Canadian landscape artists including Otto Jacobi, John Fraser, Lucius O'Brien, and Robert Whale. Paul Kane painted Native Americans in Canada much as George Catlin and Albert Bierstadt had done south of the border. Some Canadian art was unique and separate from that of U.S. artists, however; an early-twentieth-century movement of artists called the Group of Seven produced vibrant, post-Impressionist canvases taking the lakes, forests, and mountains of Ontario as their inspiration.

Canadian Writers. Romanticism was equally evident in Canadian literature. Finding a spiritual home in nature has always been a major theme for Canadian poets, including Charles Sangster ("Oh, that my heart/Were calm and peaceful as these dreamy groves!" "The Three Voices," c. 1916) and Robert W. Service ("Cling with my love to nature/As a child to the mother-knee." "In the Forest," c. 1860). British-born Archibald Belaney went one better than Thoreau, not simply retreating to a log cabin, but also fraudulently reinventing himself as the Native American wildlife writer, "Grey Owl." Belaney, who devoted his life to calling for the preservation of wilderness in books including *Tales of an Empty Cabin* (1936), has since been portrayed as a pioneering environmentalist.

Arguably, the Romantic writers and artists invented the environment—fragile nature that can, by choice, be either consumed or destroyed. If nature had previously been something purely to plunder, the Romantics demonstrated that wilderness was something to appreciate and preserve for its own sake. Their work inspired the founding of conservation organizations including the National Audubon Society, named for wildlife artist John James Audubon, while the principles they cherished—the drama of wilderness, the spiritual unity of people and nature, and the need to preserve the natural world—would become the bedrock of modern environmentalism.

—Chris Woodford

John Fraser's 1873 September Afternoon, Eastern Townships. *(National Gallery of Canada, Ottawa)*

CHAPTER FOUR

The Conservation Era
(1880s–1920s)

By the late nineteenth century, North Americans had concluded that their natural resources were more limited than they realized. Earlier assumptions of infinite supplies of lumber, coal, or water were disproved by incontrovertible evidence from western states and provinces—the once-innumerable bison were gone, formerly thick forests had been turned into a sea of stumps, and rich mines were exhausted. Citizens began to reconsider their economic behavior, one consequence of which was the gradual acceptance in both countries of the need to act more prudently. The American Forest Congress, founded to promote forest conservation, held an important meeting in Cincinnati, Ohio, in 1882; Canadian delegates to that meeting urged their U.S. counterparts to join them for a similar gathering later that year in Montreal. Out of these paired conferences came the impetus for greater activism on behalf of conservation.

Conservation in Canada. In Canada, new national parks were planned, with the magnificent Banff Park established in the Rocky Mountains in 1882; Algonquin, a provincial park located in Ontario, was set aside a decade later. More significant still was the creation in 1909 of the Commission of Conservation, the first national authority formed to assess and advocate regulation of natural resources, town planning, and wildlife preservation. Although provincial governments often enacted stricter regulations than the national body, a situation that escalated when the federal commission was dissolved in 1921, cross-border environmental issues remained the purview of the national government. A glittering example of the success of high-level Canadian and U.S. cooperation on conservation has been the International Joint Commission, which has adjudicated the Boundary Waters Treaty since 1909.

Conservation in the United States. The United States has never formed a national committee like the one Canada briefly enjoyed, but the conservation movement in the United States, and the regulatory environment it spawned, was generally defined at the national level. American conservationists recognized that the federal government was key to controlling the resource-rich public domain in the West. Their strategy was evident with the establishment of the first national park at Yellowstone, Wyoming, in the 1870s and the first forest reserves, which received legislative sanction in 1891.

When committed conservationist Theodore Roosevelt became president in 1901, the idea of federal regulation of resources gained a powerful advocate. During his tenure, his Administration created 150 national forests, and a new agency, the U.S. Forest Service, to regulate their use. It also established five new national parks, eighteen national monuments, and a host of wildlife sanctuaries.

Preservation Initiatives. Men and women on both sides of the border embraced conservationism and helped sustain and reinforce the establishment of urban park systems throughout North America. Frederick Law Olmsted, Frederick Todd, and others designed an array of new urban landscapes for recreation and solitude in New York City, Seattle, Washington; and Portland, Oregon, in the United States and in Winnipeg, Manitoba; Edmonton, Alberta; and Montreal, Québec, in Canada. Wildlife preservation efforts in Canada and the United States were also boosted as a consequence of the emerging conservation ethos.

But for all the widespread acceptance of its tenets, conservation did not go far enough to protect wilderness. Henry David Thoreau's earlier brief on behalf of wildness in *Walden* (1855) was revived in the writings of John Muir and others who called themselves preservationists; their

A reproduction of Thomas Moran's 1874 Yellowstone National Park, *showing a lake in America's first national park. (From the collections of the Library of Congress)*

ambition was to protect nature from human destruction. Although preservationists did not stop the construction of a reservoir that flooded California's Hetch Hetchy Valley in Yosemite National Park in the early twentieth century, environmentalists and the organizations they founded have continued to assert, as did Thoreau, that to preserve wilderness is to sustain the human spirit.

Water in the American West. Other conflicts over resources abounded. In the American West, white settlers and Native Americans went to court over water, as in the landmark 1908 *Winters* v. *U.S.* Supreme Court decision. A complex legal struggle over stream flow and rights of appropriation, as well as irrigation and reclamation in the semiarid and arid western prairies, has ever since shaped the development of rural economies and urban development.

New Fuels, Old Problems. Complicating the prospect of conserving natural resources was the discovery of seemingly infinite supplies of coal and petroleum. Driven by the Industrial Revolution's appetite for fuel, these competing extraction industries took huge risks to reap large profits. Mines were blasted ever deeper to haul out millions of tons of coal. Oil producers drilled for and pumped up what came to be known as "black gold" and did so as quickly as possible before moving on to new fields.

Although essential to the expansion of the industrial economy, these industries devastated lives, land, and water. The work environment in each was dirty and dangerous, and the resultant environmental pollution was overwhelming. In coal-producing regions, acid runoff from mines ruined thousands of miles of streams, rivers, and groundwater supplies. When oil became a standard source of fuel for domestic and industrial consumption, and gasoline powered the new automobiles, these uses created an array of widespread environmental problems that compromised public health, befouled the air, and sullied potable water. The industrialization of North America had left nothing unscathed, such that by the early twentieth century, Canada and the United States shared a good deal more than an east–west border of about 5,500 miles (8,900 kilometers).

—*Char Miller*

Irrigation and Farming in the United States and Canada

Supplying water to crops by irrigation is an ancient practice in areas where rainfall is insufficient for successful agriculture. Between 300 and 900 A.D. the Hohokam people of what is now Arizona built networks of canals on the Gila and Salt Rivers. Early Euro-American settlers in the U.S. and Canadian West created small, local irrigation works, while Mormon settlers created more substantial works covering over 16,000 acres (6,400 hectares) in Utah by 1850. By the late nineteenth century, truly massive irrigation works, made possible by the development of industrial technology, began to appear. A typical project featured a storage dam, which created a reservoir to store water for later use. Water released from the dam was steered by diversion dams into a system of canals, flumes (large pipes), and, sometimes, pumps to move water to agricultural land where it was distributed to individual farms via ditches, canals, or pipes. Irrigation made possible the opening of the arid lands of the West to settlement and development.

Supporters promised that irrigation would "reclaim" or "improve" western lands, which they portrayed as simply waiting for water to become fruitful. Irrigation engineers were understood to be working with nature, laying the groundwork for idyllic and natural, yet modern and prosperous communities. By opening up new farmlands and making water supply controlled and predictable, irrigation offered the ordinary man the chance to escape the factory and become an independent farmer, thus bettering himself, his family, and society in general. Finally, irrigation would contribute to national prosperity, turning the arid western regions of the United States and Canada into sources of cash crops, both to supply the tables of the eastern, industrial

cities with grain products and fruits and to provide commodities for overseas trade.

Canadian Projects. The largest Canadian project was built in southern Alberta. Under the authority of federal legislation, the Canadian Pacific Railway constructed the Bow River Scheme between 1904 and 1914. The project included the Bassano Dam across the Bow, and it irrigated over 600,000 acres (24,000 hectares) of arid prairie lands.

In British Columbia irrigation works were built from 1890 to 1914 by private development companies, primarily in the Okanagan valley, part of the dry interior plateau of the province. Irrigable land in the Okanagan was usually located atop low cliffs bordering Okanagan Lake; such geography made difficult the use of lake water for irrigation. The private development companies instead built dams and reservoirs on mountain

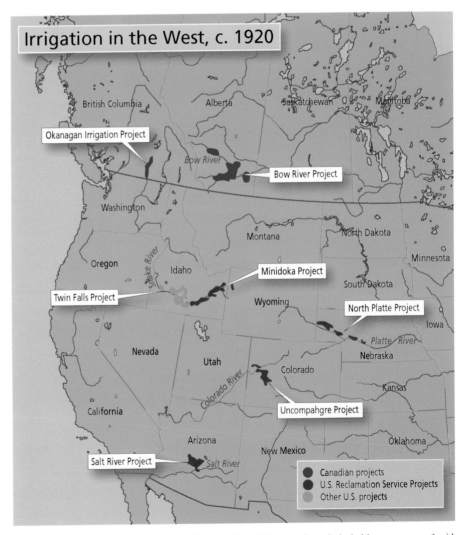

Irrigation in the West, c. 1920

Before 1920, most irrigation projects were built in the United States as Canada lacked large expanses of arid lands. Although significant areas of the United States continued to be watered by local or private irrigation projects, the largest single projects were carried out by the federal Reclamation Service.

Sources: Adapted from Clifford L. Lord and Elizabeth H. Lord, *Historical Atlas of the United States.* Rev. ed. (New York: Henry Holt, 1955), 172, plate 268; and Leonard M. Cantor, *A World Geography of Irrigation* (London: Oliver and Boyd, 1967), 219.

streams and conveyed water to farms via wooden flumes. The flumes and the companies themselves would not outlast World War I. In the postwar era, the provincial government reorganized the formerly private irrigation companies into local authorities known as irrigation districts that were controlled by the growers. Provincial governments also embarked on a project, the South Okanagan Irrigation Project, that employed more modern construction techniques including zinc flumes and concrete dams and canals.

U.S. Projects. At the end of the nineteenth century, irrigation in the American West resembled these Canadian projects—often relatively small and local, developed by private capital and state and local governments. By 1889, 3,631,000 acres (1,469,000 hectares) of western lands was irrigated, half of this acreage by Mormon irrigators. By the 1880s, however, local capital investment had clearly reached its limits. As irrigation was supposed to support independent yeoman farmers, inviting corporations to develop large irrigation projects was unthinkable.

Involving the federal government seemed to be the only answer. Under the Carey Act (1894), Congress offered 1 million acres (0.4 million hectares) of land to any state that would, in partnership with private industry, develop it. In Idaho, such ventures as the 200,000-acre (80,000-hectare) Twin Falls Project were built under the Carey Act. Outside Idaho, however, the act failed to develop much land. In 1902 Congress agreed to a more direct approach, passing the Reclamation (Newlands) Act, which created the federally controlled Reclamation Service (later the Bureau of Reclamation). The service was designed to be self-financing—initial monies for the Reclamation Fund would come from the sale of western lands and would be replenished to cover the costs of constructing new irrigation works by taxing farmers who used irrigation water. As irrigation was intended to benefit the ordinary farmer, farm sizes were to be kept small enough—160 acres (65 hectares)—for one family to work.

Within five years the Reclamation Service had started work on twenty-one projects across the West, including the Salt River Project in Arizona, Colorado's Uncompahgre Project, the North Platte Project in Wyoming and Nebraska, and the Minidoka Project in Idaho. Reclamation Service projects typically featured gigantic dams of stone and mortar and miles of canals that irrigated thousands of acres. The service's Roosevelt Dam on the Salt River was the world's highest in 1911 at 280 feet (90 meters). By 1916 the service had broken its own record with the Arrowrock Dam, towering 349 feet (106 meters) above Idaho's Boise River valley. By 1920, the service had irrigated 2,205,420 acres (892,500 hectares).

Obstacles. Despite the goals of the federal government, it became apparent very quickly that the service would not be self-financing and its primary business would not be developing new lands for individual farmers. The majority of land in the Salt River Project, for instance, was already owned and worked by farmers before the Reclamation Service arrived. At the same time, the predicted flood of settlers to the West, who would have helped pay for the irrigation projects through land sales, did not occur.

To ensure political support, the service tried to give all states an irrigation project, but projects needed to go to those states where significant amounts of land had been sold. As a result, states like Oregon and Washington, which had little need for irrigation, received as much attention as the arid states most in need of irrigation projects. Additionally, the service tended to bow to the wishes of its engineers, who were more interested in building impressive structures than in developing fertile land for farmers. Expenses rose as projects were built in areas with poor soils or insufficient drainage or without nearby markets. Farmers

Further Reading

Eagle, John A. *The Canadian Pacific Railway and the Development of Western Canada, 1896–1914.* Montreal & Kingston: McGill-Queen's University Press, 1989.

Fiege, Mark. *Irrigated Eden: The Making of an Agricultural Landscape in the American West.* Seattle & London: University of Washington Press, 1999.

Koroscil, Paul M. "Boosterism and the Settlement Process in the Okanagan Valley, British Columbia, 1890–1914." *Canadian Papers in Rural History* 5 (1986): 73–102.

Reisner, Marc. *Cadillac Desert: The American West and Its Disappearing Water.* New York: Penguin Books, 1993.

Worster, Donald. *Rivers of Empire: Water, Aridity and the Growth of the American West.* New York: Oxford University Press, 1985.

were given little help with or instruction in irrigated farming, leading to overwatering or the silting up of irrigation ditches. Collecting enough assessments from farmers to replenish the Reclamation Fund proved to be difficult. Despite a $20 million loan from the U.S. government and the extension of repayment terms from ten to twenty years, by 1922 only 10 percent of the fund had been repaid.

Future of Irrigation. By about the 1920s, irrigation was showing that it would not create a self-financing paradise for the individual farmer, though the idea would persist in both Canada and the United States through the decade. However, irrigation was still useful as a key component of national development in both countries. In Canada, the 1935 Prairie Farm Rehabilitation Act would underwrite irrigation projects as part of the federal government's attempts to help commercial prairie agriculture recover from the ecological and economic devastation of the Great Depression. In the United States, the irrigation projects of the conservation era laid the groundwork for truly massive projects like the Hoover and Grand Coulee Dams (*see also* 128–29), that would turn formerly free-flowing rivers like the Colorado into managed waterways to create factory farms and hydroelectricity.

—*James Murton*

Forest Management: United States Forest Service

In the mid-1800s, the United States Department of Interior, which controlled all federal public land, was more concerned with developing the land than with protecting it. But some American scientists were troubled by the rapid destruction of forests caused by lumbering. In 1873, the American Association for the Advancement of Science, led by Franklin B. Hough, a New York physician and statistician, petitioned Congress to intervene, informing Congress that destroying American forests might have a long-term national economic impact if the federal government did not stop wholesale clearcutting. In 1876, Congress appointed Hough as a forestry agent in the Department of Agriculture, and in 1881, Congress created the U.S. Division of Forestry within the Department of Agriculture to conduct scientific research on trees and forests and how they protect waterways from soil erosion. The decision reflected a growing awareness of the importance of forests and watersheds that would eventually lead to the establishment of the United States Forest Service in 1905.

Early Forest Management. In 1886, Bernhard Fernow, a forester born and trained in Germany, became chief of the U.S. Division of Forestry. Fernow's able leadership placed the agency on a solid scientific foundation; in addition, he furthered the cause of forestry through his publications and lectures. Fernow advocated that the federal government establish and maintain a forestry management program on public lands to ensure a perpetual supply of timber and protect watersheds. Adequate forest cover would preserve watersheds by preventing excessive runoff and soil erosion. He also offered specific recommendations for the structure of a forestry agency.

In 1891, with Fernow's encouragement, Congress passed the Forest Reserve Act, which authorized the president to set aside public land as federal forest reserves and place them under the control of the Department of Interior's General Land Office (GLO). The decision to give control to the GLO actually signified the desire of Congress to continue developing land, not protect it. Although the act did not give the U.S. Division of Forestry control over the nation's forests, Fernow continued to push to have more land reserved from exploitation. By 1897, further research on forest destruction led Congress to pass the Forest Management Act of 1897, which Fernow helped draft. The law authorized the supervised cutting and sale of timber and the protection of forests from fires, with the GLO placed in charge of the work. The Division of Forestry served as technical adviser on forestry to the GLO for the next eight years.

Gifford Pinchot replaced Fernow as chief in June 1898 and had an immediate

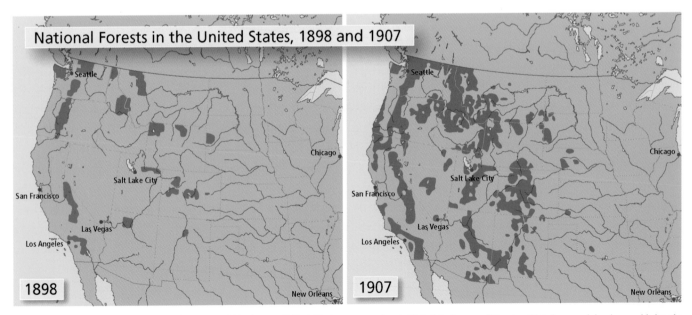

National Forests in the United States, 1898 and 1907

1898

1907

Map A: The national forests of the United States in 1898, the year Gifford Pinchot was appointed chief of the Bureau of Forestry. Note how much land was added to the U.S. forest system by 1907 (Map B), when Congress passed legislation preventing President Theodore Roosevelt from adding additional land to western national forests.
Source: Michael Williams, *Americans and Their Forests,* (New York: Cambridge University Press, 1989), 408. Adapted with the permission of Cambridge University Press.

impact. The energetic Pinchot considered government service an opportunity (and his moral duty) to help his fellow citizens. He rapidly expanded the forestry division, struck a deal with Secretary of Interior Ethan A. Hitchcock and private timber firms to undertake cooperative forestry management on the forest reserves and reforestation programs on private lands, and further expanded the division's research efforts.

United States Forest Service. After many years of lobbying by Pinchot, Congress, at the request of President Theodore Roosevelt, transferred 63 million acres (25 million hectares) of forest reserves to Pinchot's agency in 1905 and renamed the agency the United States Forest Service. In 1907, Congress renamed the reserves "national forests." In addition to timber management, foresters issued land use permits for grazing sheep and cattle and for mineral extraction, fought forest fires, and continued the agency's original research mission. Roosevelt added nearly 132 million acres (53 million hectares) by 1909, all of it west of the Mississippi River.

Pinchot's missionary zeal and high-handed attitude brought him into conflict with those who did not share his beliefs. In January 1910, in what has become known as the Ballinger–Pinchot Controversy, President William Howard Taft fired Pinchot for criticizing Secretary of Interior Richard Ballinger, disobeying orders, and meddling in Department of Interior business. His dismissal greatly weakened the Forest Service's political standing on Capitol Hill, and its opponents moved quickly to challenge its policies. Henry Graves, Pinchot's long-time friend and former assistant, had the difficult task of guiding the Forest Service out of the political storm into which Pinchot had steered it.

Graves's reserved ways stood in contrast to Pinchot's strident style, but this probably helped save the service from its congressional opponents. Some members of Congress wanted to transfer the national forests back to the Interior Department, or slash the Forest Service budget. In addition to preventing the transfer or even dismemberment of the Forest Service, in 1915 Graves also established the Branch of Research within the Forest Service but as a division separate from the administrative department. Researchers were thus relieved of the day-to-day administration of the national forests.

Graves was less successful in keeping the recreational lands in the national forests under the supervision of the Forest Service. In the 1910s, the populace increasingly sought to open the forests to recreational use or to preserve pristine areas; however, they wanted a new agency to handle areas like the Grand Canyon or Yosemite Park. Because of the Forest Service's mission to develop forests and its support of building a dam in Yosemite Park in 1914, its critics did not believe that it was the most appropriate agency to handle the preservation of land. In 1916, over the objections of Graves, Congress created the National Park Service to oversee most of the recreational lands and national monuments once managed by the Forest Service.

New Forest Policies. The establishment of the Park Service limited the role of the Forest Service; however, two events in the 1910s dramatically expanded its work. In the wake of the worst fire season on record in 1910, during which more than 5 million acres (2 million hectares) of national forest land in Idaho, Montana, and Washington burned in one month, the Forest Service shifted its focus. Congress passed the Weeks Act (1911), which provided money to promote cooperative fire protection between federal and state governments, and made systematic fire suppression a national policy. The Weeks Act also provided money to purchase land in the eastern United States to add to the national forest system for watershed protection in that region. For the first time, the federal government was no longer disposing of land, but purchasing it. By 1920, more than 2 million acres (800,000 hectares) had been purchased.

With the outbreak of World War I, the huge military demand for wood for fuel led to a closer cooperation between the government and private timber companies to cut more timber on public lands. Graves's successor, William Greeley (1920–28), supported the idea of closer cooperation and won a lengthy legislative and philosophical battle in 1924 with the passage of the Clark–McNary Act. This law created a partnership between federal, state, and private interests in promoting fire suppression and for other actions, such as acquiring more land for the national forest system, but did not, as opponents feared, impose federal regulation of forestry activity on private land. This policy, which left private landowners regulating themselves, has been a central tenet of the Forest Service ever since.

—James G. Lewis

Further Reading
Clary, David A. *Timber and the Forest Service.* Lawrence: University Press of Kansas, 1986.
Cox, Thomas R., Robert S. Maxwell, Phillip Drennon Thomas, and Joseph J. Malone. *This Well-Wooded Land: Americans and Their Forests from Colonial Times to the Present.* Lincoln: University of Nebraska Press, 1985.
Nelles, H. V. *The Politics of Development: Forests, Mines & Hydro-electric Power in Ontario, 1849–1941.* Hamden, Conn.: Archon Books, 1974.
Robbins, William G. *American Forestry: A History of National, State, and Private Cooperation.* Lincoln: University of Nebraska Press, 1985.
Steen, Harold K. *The U.S. Forest Service: A History.* Seattle: University of Washington Press, 1977.
Williams, Michael. *Americans and Their Forests: A Historical Geography.* Cambridge: Cambridge University Press, 1992.

Forest Management in Canada

The provinces of Canada have always held power and control over the land. The British North America Act of 1867, which established Canada as an independent nation, ensured that the provincial governments retained jurisdiction over resources and revenues from the land while the federal government controlled land in the western and northern territories. Consequently, the provinces have usually pioneered land management initiatives, including those involving the nation's forests (*see also 42–43, 60–61, and 126–27*).

Ontario. After an Ontario delegation attended the American Forestry Congress meeting in Montreal in 1882, Ontario's government created the position of clerk of forestry in the Department of Agriculture and the Arts in 1883. Placing the office in the Agriculture branch, however, revealed that the Ontario government favored more traditional forestry practices—woodlot management and reforestation of abandoned farmlands—rather than the scientific management practices and long-term planning that treated forests as a renewable resource.

Much to the frustration of conservationists, Ontario placed its provincial forest reserves, the first created in the country, under the control of political appointees instead of foresters. Influenced by the powerful Ontario Lumbermen's Association, which feared that the costs of forest management would cut into profits, the provincial government had made exploitation the cornerstone of its timber policy by 1905. Lumber companies left the land overcut and degraded, and lumbering activities were left to office clerks, rather than foresters, to monitor and control.

Québec. In contrast to Ontario, by 1904 Québec embraced conservation and worked to assure future timber supplies. The competition for land between settlers and lumbermen in northern Québec had forced the provincial government to take control of all forest activities. Between 1904 and 1908, its government set aside 106,075,829 acres (42,927,364 hectares) for forest reserves. The forest reserves were not "banked" areas of timber waiting to be cut in the future, but were lands on which lumber companies operated under government supervision.

Such supervision helped settle conflicts over land use by separating agricultural lands from timberlands.

To regulate lumbering practices, in 1909 Québec established the first provincial forestry service. The Québec Forestry Service slowly implemented scientific management while gaining the cooperation and confidence of the timber industry. Larger timber companies responded to regulation by developing working plans for cutting and regeneration. By 1917, Québec had abandoned the forest reserve system because the close regulation of lumbering activity no longer justified maintaining the reserves.

Federal Forest Management. Federal action lagged behind that of the eastern provinces. The federal government established the Timber, Mineral and Grazing Lands Office within the Department of Interior in 1873 to issue licenses for harvesting timber, but it did not regulate the actual harvests. In 1884, the federal government created forest reserves in the Canadian Rocky Mountains, but the government's lack of further efforts demonstrated indifference

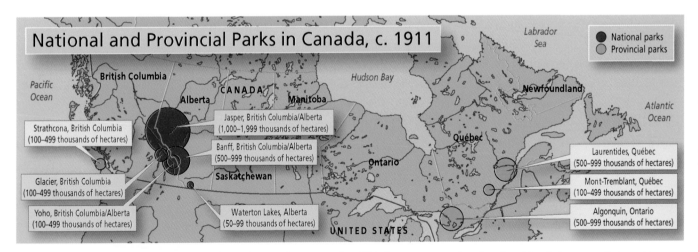

The parks established prior to 1911 precluded settlement in extensive areas and established game preserves, but also allowed for timber companies to continue cutting on the land. When tourists gained access to these logging areas, their horror turned to activism, leading to the establishment of the Canadian Forestry Association to encourage conservation and the hiring of professional foresters in various jurisdictions. The Dominion Forest Reserves and National Parks Act of 1911 separated park administration from forest reserve administration by establishing a separate Parks Branch to run the national parks. Provincial parks were also established during this period to protect the forests, as well as fish and wildlife.
Source: Adapted from Geoffrey Matthews, *Historical Atlas of Canada.* Vol. 3 (Toronto: University of Toronto Press, 1987–83), plate 35.

toward forest management. Continued widespread abuse of the federal licensing system finally led to an Order of Council, or executive order, in 1899.

The Order of Council split responsibilities for forest management between an agency and a subagency, emulating Ontario's divided system. The chief clerk of the Timber and Grazing Branch was responsible for the leasing of federal land for timber production. His subordinate, the chief inspector of the Timber and Forestry office, oversaw the protection and management of federal forests (mostly in the western territories), including all fire fighting, by scientifically trained foresters. Thus, the office that managed federal forests answered to the political appointees who controlled the land leases. This arrangement remained even after the Timber and Forestry office became independent and was renamed the Forestry Branch in 1901. (Nearly seventy years later, after several more name changes, including to the Dominion Forest Service in 1923, it would be renamed the Canadian Forest Service.) This division of responsibilities left the new forestry service largely restricted to managing its forest reserves, which became extensive in acreage but excluded all commercial timberland under lease.

Elihu Stewart, appointed chief inspector of timber and forestry in 1899, hoped to duplicate the success of Gifford Pinchot, the chief forester of the United States (*see also* 92–93), and of U.S. conservationists (*see also* 110–11). Stewart quickly assembled a staff and focused its work primarily on conservation, fire protection, and forest propagation. Most of the work was in the western provinces until the subagency took control of the land in 1930. To help with tree planting on the prairies, Stewart opened the first forest nursery at Indian Head in Saskatchewan in 1902.

Stewart's term coincided with a strong conservation movement in Canada (*see also* 112–13). Stewart had helped create the Canadian Forestry Association in 1900, an organization of politicians, lumbermen, and public figures that supported conservation measures. The federal government hosted Canada's first forest congress in 1906 to help raise awareness of the importance of forestry. The Dominion Forest Reserves Act was passed that same year, placing 3,459,400 acres (1,400,000 hectares) of prairie forest under scientific management by the federal government. The first forestry schools opened in 1907 at the University of Toronto, and two more had opened by 1910.

Succeeding Stewart in 1907, Robert H. Campbell expanded the scientific emphasis of the forestry branch. He established an economics division to gather statistical data on forests and forest products, and oversaw the opening of two forest products laboratories, which conducted tests on wood strength and durability, among other tasks. The Dominion Forest Reserves and National Parks Act of 1911 created a separate Dominion Parks Branch and also enlarged the forest reserves from 3,212,300 to 16,555,700 acres (1,300,000 to 6,699,900 hectares), but left the three agencies—Timber and Grazing, Forestry, and the Parks Service—with conflicting agendas for federal forest management. Nonetheless, Campbell guided the organization through the difficult years of World War I, working closely with the defense department. After the war and a bad fire season in 1919, the Forestry Branch stepped up its fire protection work by deploying aerial fire patrols in Alberta and British Columbia and launching a public information campaign. Poor health led to Campbell's resignation in 1924.

British Columbia. Learning from the mistakes of the other forestry services, British Columbia's provincial legislature avoided a battle for the consolidation of powers that had left the federal forest service and the Ontario service without complete control of forestry activities. The Forest Act of 1912 gave the new British Columbia Forest Branch jurisdiction over all matters relating to forestry, including revenue collection, fire protection and suppression, logging, reforestation, trade regulation in timber lands and logs, and the ability to enforce statutes. The act had the unexpected benefit of improving resource management and natural regeneration, and helped make British Columbia a leader in Canadian forestry. Harvey MacMillan served as chief forester in British Columbia from 1912 to 1916, successfully guiding the province through its difficult early years during World War I.

The Canadian Forest Service's subordinate position to provincial forest services has remained relatively unchanged. This arrangement has left the provinces in charge of the majority of commercial forest land. Whereas British Columbia and Québec implemented scientific management programs that promoted regeneration of trees, the provincial Ontario and federal Canadian governments enacted short-sighted practices with little thought given to conservation. Both levels of government later had to alter policies to protect the viability of the lumber industry (*see also* 126–27).

—*James G. Lewis*

Further Reading

Apsey, Mike, et al. *The Perpetual Forest: Using Lessons from the Past to Sustain Canada's Forests in the Future*. Vancouver, B.C.: FORCAST, 2000.

Drushka, Ken, and Bob Burt. "The Canadian Forest Service: Catalyst for the Forest Sector." *Forest History Today* (Spring-Fall 2001): 19–28.

Gillis, R. Peter, and Thomas R. Roach. *Lost Initiatives: Canada's Forest Industries, Forest Policy and Forest Conservation*. New York: Greenwood Press, 1986.

Rodgers, Andrew, III. *Bernhard Eduard Fernow: A Story of North American Forestry*. New York: Hafner Publishing Company, 1968.

The State of Canada's Forests, 1996–1997: Learning from History. Ottawa: Her Majesty the Queen in Right of Canada, 1997.

The Beginning of Wildlife Preservation in Canada

In the mid-nineteenth century, most Canadians believed that the country's natural resources were unlimited. Engaged in commercial agriculture and early industry, Canadians were cutting down forests, engaging in commercial and sport fishing, and killing animals for food, to protect crops and herds, and for sport. A significant reduction of certain animal populations in the late nineteenth century prompted preservationist activity at the local, provincial, and federal levels.

Divided jurisdiction partly contributed to the federal government's limited concern for wildlife. The Dominion of Canada, comprising formerly distinct British colonies, was established in 1867 by the British North America Act; the statute did not address the new government's role in regulating wildlife. (Fisheries, however, were federally regulated until 1898 when the courts declared a provincial role.) Wildlife, like other natural resources, was assumed to be under provincial jurisdiction. Accordingly, the eastern provinces (Ontario, Québec, Nova Scotia, New Brunswick, Prince Edward Island) and British Columbia assumed responsibility for "game" (*see also* 124–25) by regulating the number of animals killed, whether for sport or profit. The federal government retained the power to manage natural resources within the Northwest Territories, a vast frontier acquired in 1869 that spanned parts of modern Manitoba, Alberta, Saskatchewan, and the far north. This huge, undeveloped region reinforced the myth of unlimited natural wealth.

During the 1880s, the federal government increased its role in wildlife preservation. Widespread European settlement in the prairie West was only just beginning, prompted by Conservative prime minister John A. Macdonald's "National Policy" and his "doctrine of usefulness." Scenery, timber, minerals, and wildlife would be conserved for human use and profit. Although wildlife preservation was not yet a priority, park administrators later used the original legislation to protect some species—mountain sheep, elk, and deer among them—to further encourage tourism in the 1890s.

Provincial Action. Preservation emerged more forcefully at local and provincial levels. In the wake of widespread human settlement, habitat loss and indiscriminate slaughter had dramatically reduced some animal populations. Bison (*see also* 36–37) were almost wiped out by 1885, for example, and many species of birds (such as the passenger pigeon) were headed for extinction. Focused on halting this decline, a broad-based conservation movement sprang into action in the late nineteenth century. Local natural history societies, city-based scientists, and outdoor enthusiasts lobbied provincial politicians to conserve wildlife, not only for recreation and tourism, but also for moral and aesthetic reasons. In response, provincial governments formed commissions of inquiry, instituted closed seasons (during which no hunting was permitted), and established a patchwork of publicly owned game reserves and parks with enforcement officers and supporting bureaucracies.

Conflicts. The commonly used term "game" signaled important social conflicts. Hunting and angling had long been a part of British North America. Many, like some First Nations—native peoples of Canada (*see also* 48–49)—hunted and fished for subsistence, using their knowledge of the local environment. But such activity was increasingly challenged by middle- and upper-class sportsmen who hunted wild game as a temporary

Undated photo of members of the Great Lakes Ornithological Club outside their clubhouse in Point Pelee National Park. (Parks Canada, Point Pelee National Park and the National Museums of Canada)

James Bernard Harkin

James Bernard Harkin was Canada's first dominion parks commissioner (1911–36). His philosophical approach to conservation combined utility (economics) and aesthetics (morals). To obtain funding from development-minded federal legislators, he emphasized the tourism potential of scenery and wildlife protection. But Harkin also advocated nature preservation for physical and spiritual rejuvenation, and promoted national parks as sanctuaries where wildlife could live undisturbed.

Harkin was one of a small number of federal civil servants "working for wildlife" in Canada. Without scientific training, he was influenced by contacts in Canada and the United States. Like many administrators of his era, Harkin saw no contradiction in killing predators such as wolves, coyotes, foxes, cougars, eagles, and hawks, which, to his mind, threatened the deer, beaver, sheep, fish, or songbirds favored by park visitors. Nevertheless, Harkin contributed enormously to wildlife preservation. He lobbied to expand the parks system and to implement protective policies, and supported establishment of bird sanctuaries. A driving force behind the Migratory Bird Treaty (1916) and a national conference on wildlife protection (1919), Harkin promoted cooperation between Canada, the United States, and the provinces. He also encouraged the growth of a public, preservationist constituency for national parks, organized in 1923 as the Canadian National Parks Association. Harkin's most important contribution was to persuade elected officials that the protection and management of wildlife was an important responsibility of the federal government; without this recognition, many wildlife populations would have surely declined or become extinct.

relief from the stresses of living in cities and coping with industrial conditions. These hunters criticized subsistence hunters for failing to embrace the sporting ethic of "fair chase," which allegedly limited the kill. In the early twentieth century, sport hunters convinced provincial governments to take inventories of animals; to restock, import, or relocate game species; and to kill unwanted predators, such as cougars and wolves. Unfortunately, provincial game reserves and regulations often disrupted the livelihood of less politically powerful people (both native and nonnative), whose ability to hunt for food was now restricted.

Federal Action. At the federal level, dedicated civil servants augmented and supported surging local and regional initiatives. Influenced by U.S. and provincial contacts, this group convinced the federal government to assume a stronger role in wildlife preservation. Federal officials improved wildlife protection in national parks and forest reserves; they created parks to preserve

herds of plains bison (1908), pronghorn antelope (1915), and wood buffalo (1922); they established a scientific advisory board on wildlife protection (1916); and they set aside bird sanctuaries, including Point Pelee National Park (1918) in Ontario.

The Migratory Bird Treaty with the United States (1916) was their crowning achievement. This treaty enabled the federal government to impose closed seasons for hundreds of species of birds. The treaty, however, did not offer blanket protection. It neither addressed nor curbed pollution and habitat loss; it failed to protect hawks, owls, and eagles; and its negative impact on local and regional subsistence economies, especially in the Maritime Provinces (New Brunswick, Nova Scotia, and Prince Edward Island) and the North, made it controversial. For instance, Yukon and East Coast officials objected that the open season for migratory birds (set to favor the sport hunters of southern and central Canada) rendered unlawful their own traditional hunting season. (After

Newfoundland joined Canada in 1949, its rural citizens mounted a successful protest against federal regulations that suddenly prohibited fishermen from shooting birds for food.) The treaty was, nonetheless, a significant achievement and set a precedent for future successful and effective environmental negotiations between Canada and the United States.

By 1920, successive Canadian governments had taken several crucial steps to preserve wildlife. Their initiatives created a solid foundation for subsequent efforts by government officials and later environmentalists. However, the record was mixed. Early policies saved some wildlife species, such as moose, but undermined others, especially wolves. Moreover, the treatment of human populations was not evenhanded. State-sponsored wildlife preservation often best served the interests of middle- and upper-class Canadians, but took advantage of less powerful groups like the First Nations and nonnative rural residents. In the mid-twentieth century, wildlife preservation would become dominated by "scientific environmentalism," which based wildlife and other environmental policies on systematic ecological studies by professionally trained biologists working in government departments.

—*George Warecki*

Further Reading
Altmeyer, George. "Three Ideas of Nature in Canada, 1893–1914." *Journal of Canadian Studies* 11 (August 1976): 21–36.
Foster, Janet. *Working For Wildlife: The Beginning of Preservation in Canada.* 2nd ed. Toronto: University of Toronto Press, 1998.
Loo, Tina. "Making a Modern Wilderness: Conserving Wildlife in Twentieth-Century Canada." *Canadian Historical Review* 82 (March 2001): 92–121.
MacEachern, Alan. "Rationality and Rationalization in Canadian National Parks Predator Policy." In *Consuming Canada: Readings in Environmental History,* edited by Chad and Pam Gaffield. Toronto: Copp Clark, 1995.

Urban Parks and Landscape Architecture in the United States and Canada

ndustrialization forever changed the landscape of North American cities, creating the need for public parks as a refuge from the jumble and stress of the urban-industrial environment (*see also* 80–81). For Frederick Law Olmsted, the public park became "a countervailing force to improve the urban environment." Building on Olmsted's legacy, succeeding landscape architects designed parks for an ever-widening range of functions. Each park became part of a greater system that ranged from small inner-city spaces to expansive tracts located well beyond the suburban periphery. Large pleasure grounds of naturalistic design vied with the formalism of multipurpose parks to meet the changing recreational needs of the new industrial society.

Establishment of Urban Parks. Urban parks are public or "democratic" spaces designed for the use of all social groups. Parks are breathing spaces—what the senior Olmsted and others called the "lungs of the city"—where all residents, whether rich or poor, native-born or immigrant, might stroll, drive, or sit to enjoy the open air and view soul-replenishing scenery. States and provinces in the reform-minded Progressive Era passed legislation that facilitated the making of parks by municipal governments. Town and city councils or a parks board and its commissioners (sometimes elected, sometimes appointed) took on this important responsibility.

Finding funds to buy land and develop parks was always a problem. Philanthropic individuals in U.S. and Canadian cities sometimes donated land and even the capital to buy or improve park sites. In late-nineteenth-century Canada, large military reserves in urban areas were transformed, for example, into Halifax's Point Pleasant Park in Nova Scotia in 1866 (with the military retaining the right to use the park for defense purposes) and Vancouver's Stanley Park in British Columbia in 1888. More commonly, municipal taxes were levied upon homeowners to develop and maintain park systems.

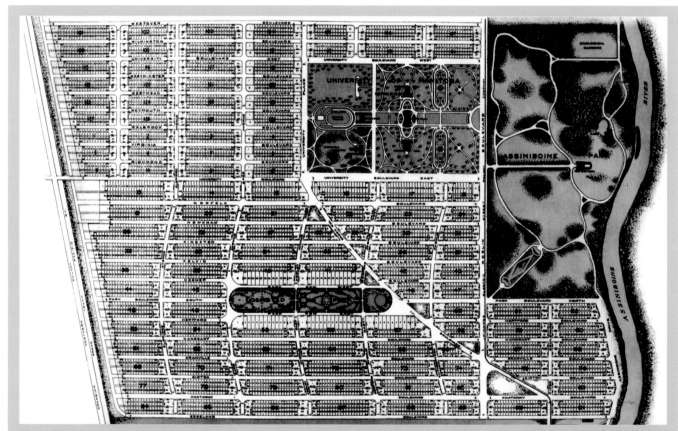

This historical map (c. 1910) of the Tuxedo Park area of Winnipeg, Manitoba, records the work of several famous landscape architects. Assiniboine Park was designed by Frederick Todd in 1904–05. The subdivision plan was created in 1906 by Rickson Outhet who trained in the office of Olmsted Brothers. The campus of the University of Manitoba (1909–10) and Olmsted Park (1910) are the work of their mentor, John Charles Olmsted. (Map collection of the Provincial Archives of Manitoba, N6337)

Most of today's park systems in U.S. and Canadian cities were formed between 1880 and 1920. Following the mid-nineteenth-century examples of New York City and Philadelphia, Pennsylvania, in the early 1880s Massachusetts state legislators enabled Boston officials to create the series of parks, including Franklin Park, that became known as the Emerald Necklace. Of naturalistic inspiration and form, the Necklace was designed by Frederick Law Olmsted with the help of his stepson, John Charles Olmsted. In the early 1890s, an Olmsted associate, Charles Eliot, planned a metropolitan system of parks on Boston's outskirts to permanently conserve natural landscapes. These were to be managed by the Trustees of Public Reservations, an organization created to preserve open space, but Boston's park system would actually be managed by the Metropolitan Park Commission (renamed the Metropolitan District Commission in 1919).

Spread of U.S. Urban Parks. As settlement spread westward across the United States (*see also* 52–53), the urban park movement gained widespread acceptance in the nation's regional centers. In Chicago, Illinois; St. Louis and Kansas City, Missouri; Milwaukee, Wisconsin; and Minneapolis–St. Paul, Minnesota, for example, parks of varying size and purpose were shaped by the landscape architects William Le Baron Jenny, George Kessler, Horace Cleveland, Warren Manning, and members of the Olmsted firm. The park movement spread to the southern United States and stretched to the Pacific Coast. In 1903, John Olmsted drew up the plans for the Seattle and Portland park systems, still celebrated a century later.

U.S. Landscape Design. The creation of a park's overall plan—that is, its landscape architecture—took place within a larger debate about park use and architectural design. By 1899, landscape architects were organized professionally in the United States

Further Reading

Birnbaum, Charles, and Robin Karson, eds. *Pioneers of American Landscape Design*. New York: McGraw-Hill, 2001.

Cranz, Galen. *The Politics of Park Design: A History of Urban Parks in America*. Cambridge, Mass.: MIT Press, 1982.

McFarland, E. "The Beginning of Municipal Park Systems." In *Recreational Land Use: Perspectives on Its Evolution in Canada*, edited by Geoff Wall and John S. Marsh. Ottawa: Carleton University Press, 1982.

Newton, Norman T. *Design on the Land: The Development of Landscape Architecture*. Cambridge, Mass.: Harvard University Press, 1971.

Wright, J. R. *The Public Park Movement, 1860–1914.* Vol. 2 of *Urban Parks in Ontario*. Toronto: Ministry of Tourism and Recreation, 1984.

Zaitzevsky, Cynthia. *Frederick Law Olmsted and the Boston Park System*. Cambridge, Mass.: Harvard University Press, 1982.

and by 1900 could study for the field at Harvard University. Students were introduced to two major and competing design strategies: the naturalistic or pastoral and picturesque so favored by Frederick Law Olmsted; and the classical formality of the Beaux Arts championed by City Beautiful proponents (*see also* 84–85). In time, a certain eclecticism became fashionable, if not theoretically acceptable, particularly in large urban parks that combined "rooms" of pastoral beauty for receptive recreational viewing with highly structured, rectangular spaces set aside for activities like running, cricket, or baseball. Where recreational needs combined with the reform-minded playground movement, for example, in Chicago, the layout of small parks became distinctly formal in design, organized with a clear spatial geometry.

Development of Parks in Canada. In Canada, park development followed a similar path. In 1877, the senior Olmsted had designed Montreal's Mount Royal Park in Québec along pastoral and picturesque lines to complement the site's natural beauty. Many Ontario towns and cities, supported by provincial legislation in the 1880s, joined the park movement. For instance, Toronto's pastoral High Park took shape on the city's western edge at this time.

Elsewhere, Frederick Todd, an American trained in the Olmsted office but a resident of Montreal since 1900, designed or envisioned many individual

parks and entire park systems across Canada—in Winnipeg, Manitoba; Regina, Saskatchewan; and Edmonton, Alberta; as well as in many Québec towns and a number of Ontario cities including Ottawa. Todd's Assiniboine Park in Winnipeg is noteworthy for combining naturalistic and formal landscape elements. The park's axial entryway is reminiscent of both the Mall in New York City's Central Park and the Greeting of Boston's Franklin Park. Once inside the park, curving roads wind through pastoral settings, revealing picturesque prairie and river valley landscapes.

By the close of the 1920s, parks had become important features of virtually every North American town and city. Parks of different sizes and for various uses were developed throughout urban space, making them accessible to almost everyone in the expanding industrial city. Parks were equal in importance to schools and other community facilities when planning new neighborhoods. At more widely spaced locations, which were sometimes joined by specially designed parkways, large regional parks attracted visitors from across an entire metropolitan area. As John Charles Olmsted remarked in 1910, parks offered relief from "strain due to the excessive artificiality of urban living." Urban parks ensured that people could walk within a natural setting, view beautiful scenery, or find a place for organized recreation.

—Larry McCann

Winters v. *U.S.* and the Development of the Doctrine of Reserved Water Rights

From the beginning of the "reservation era" in the mid-1800s in the United States (*see also* 46–47), Native American tribes struggled to maintain access to reliable supplies of water. Nonnative settlers cast a covetous eye on these sources of water, often resulting in long and bitter conflicts about Native American water rights. As settlements grew in the West (*see also* 52–53), the rights of Native Americans came under increasing pressure and lawsuits were brought. Ultimately, the U.S. Supreme Court ruled that Native Americans' right to water took precedence in its landmark 1908 *Winters* v. *U.S.* decision.

Reservations. In the nineteenth century the federal government established numerous reservations for Native Americans with the objective of forcing them to adopt the settled (non-nomadic), agricultural society favored by encroaching settlers. By 1889 more than two hundred reservations had been established; these covered approximately 116 million noncontiguous acres (47 million hectares), but the number of reservations changed constantly as new ones were created, existing ones were abolished, and some divided or consolidated. In 1867 the federal Bureau of Indian Affairs began a program of building irrigation projects on reservations to provide water for farms.

Western Settlement. Concurrently, white settlers moved westward in large numbers and began farming and ranching in many of the same valleys and plains where reservations were located. For example, in 1849 approximately one hundred thousand immigrants moved west. By 1890, the year the frontier was officially declared closed, eleven million people were living in the trans-Missouri West. They had established farms and begun building small water diversions (dams, weirs, and associated irrigation ditches).

Irrigation Projects. Because large irrigation projects (*see also* 90–91) were very expensive, settlers asked the federal government to construct these projects. Their request received a friendly hearing from Theodore Roosevelt, who became president in 1901. A firm believer in federally funded irrigation projects for the West, Roosevelt immediately began pushing Congress to create such a program. In 1902 Congress passed the Reclamation Act, which created a special fund for the "construction and maintenance of irrigation works for the storage, diversion, and development of water for the reclamation of arid and semiarid lands. . . ." A new government agency, the U.S. Reclamation Service, was created as part of the act to build these irrigation projects.

According to Roosevelt's message to Congress in 1907, this legislation would "put upon the land permanent home-makers, to use and develop it for themselves and for their children and children's children." However, many areas of the West did not have enough water to meet the needs of reservations and to build massive irrigation projects for incoming settlers; conflict between these competing users was inevitable. For example, in the later 1800s settlers in central Arizona began building irrigation projects upstream from the Pima tribe, drying up their agricultural lands—lands that the Pima had farmed for thousands of years.

Milk River Conflict. The federal government had promised far more than

Prior Appropriation Doctrine

The doctrine of federally reserved water rights, first enunciated in the *Winters* case in 1908, was in direct conflict with the prevailing water doctrine of the American West, known as the Prior Appropriation Doctrine. In the well-watered eastern United States, water laws were based on the assumption that water in the lakes and rivers was sufficient for all. But in the arid West, just a few users could easily dry up entire rivers. For example, the Milk River—the object of the *Winters* litigation—was often dried up by midsummer because of irrigation withdrawals. So Westerners developed a new water doctrine based on the phrase, "first in time, first in right." This doctrine required water to be diverted and used to obtain a water right. The first person to do so then held a water right superior to any subsequent claimant; the earliest water users had priority over everyone who filed for water rights after them. In times of shortage, the water users with priority held the right to take their entire appropriation of water, even if nothing was left for others.

In stark contrast, the reserved rights doctrine established in the *Winters* case was based on treaty rights and did not require a first diversion. The water would be reserved until the Native Americans had the means to divert the water and use it. The priority date was based on when the reservation was established, not when the inhabitants first diverted water. These contrasting water doctrines have been the source of thousands of court cases and political battles; they continue to be a major source of conflict in the ongoing water wars of the American West.

it could deliver; it promised reservation homelands for Native Americans—lands that would be worthless without water. The government had also lured thousands of settlers to the West with promises of free land and assistance in obtaining a dependable supply of water for irrigation. The inevitable conflict between settlers and Native Americans first erupted in Montana's Milk River Valley in 1905. The Milk River flows through sparse, rolling prairie that was once home to enormous herds of bison (*see also* 36–37). Taking advantage of the Homestead Act of 1862, which gave parcels of land to settlers if they promised to stay and work the land, emigrant farmers began to settle along the river. This river valley was also home to several reservations, including the Fort Belknap Reservation of the Gros Ventre and Assiniboine tribes. These tribes had signed a treaty in 1888 that established their reservation so they could become "self-supporting as a pastoral and agricultural people."

The Bureau of Indian Affairs began building an irrigation project for the Fort Belknap Reservation in 1903. At about the same time, the new settlers began building their own diversions upstream from the reservation. The late-summer flows of the Milk River were inadequate, however, to supply water for all these irrigation projects. At first the Native Americans appeared sure to lose another battle with their powerful white neighbors. Although the federal attorney for Montana, Carl Rasch, filed a lawsuit in 1905 to stop the diversions of water by the settlers, he was widely expected to lose; most observers believed that water development for the settlers would proceed quickly. The federal district court, however, ruled in favor of the Native Americans, the judge reasoning that "when the Indians made the treaty granting

Undated photo of the Milk River in Montana, near the Fort Belknap school, with low levels of water. The region sees little rain in the summer, and the river is the only dependable source of water, causing many of the farms in the area to quickly dry up. (Montana Historical Society, Helena)

rights to the United States, they reserved the right to the use of the waters of Milk River, at least to an extent reasonably necessary to irrigate their lands."

The settlers immediately appealed the decision, but lost again in 1905 in appellate court. Undeterred, they appealed to the U.S. Supreme Court, which agreed to hear *Winters* v. *U.S.* in 1908. The settlers were still confident of success as for more than one hundred years the United States had followed a policy of taking Native American resources and giving them to white settlers. The thinking of the time was that Native Americans would gradually be absorbed by the dominant society. The Supreme Court, however, ruled in favor of the Fort Belknap tribe, saying "it would be extreme to believe that within a year [of creating the reservation] Congress

destroyed the reservation and took from the Indians the consideration of their grant, leaving them a barren waste—took from them the means of continuing their old habits, yet did not leave them the power to change to new ones." Accordingly, Native Americans were considered to hold reserved water rights sufficient to meet the needs of their reservation.

The 1908 *Winters* decision was the first in a long series of cases that would challenge but ultimately affirm the reserved water rights of Native Americans. To this day Native Americans' reserved water rights are one of the most contentious issues in the West (*see also* 154–55). As populations of the western states grow ever larger, Native American tribes continue to face new challenges to their water rights.

—*Daniel McCool*

Further Reading

Burton, Lloyd. *American Indian Water Rights and the Limits of Law.* Lawrence: University Press of Kansas, 1991.

Hundley, Norris. "The Winters Decision and Indian Water Rights: A Mystery Reexamined." *Western Historical Quarterly* 13, no. 1 (Jan. 1982): 17–42.

McCool, Daniel. *Command of the Waters: Iron Triangles, Federal Water Development, and Indian Water.* 1987. Reprint, Tucson: University of Arizona Press, 1994.

Shurts, John. *Indian Reserved Water Rights: The Winters Doctrine in Its Social and Legal Context, 1880s–1930s.* Norman: University of Oklahoma Press, 2000.

Appalachian Coal Mining

Starting in 1740, coal became the world's premier fuel for more than two hundred years. Coal and its mining were essential to economic growth; coal held a strategic position in the global economy until displaced by petroleum in the 1950s. By 1904, the United States had emerged as the world's largest coal producer, with Appalachia its most productive region. Appalachia's coal deposits were rich and easily extracted. Coal mining has had a profound effect on the region, especially in terms of water pollution and changes to the landscape.

Coal Deposits. In the United States, coal deposits are of four primary types: anthracite, sub-bituminous, lignite, and bituminous. Although small anthracite deposits exist in New England, the nation's two primary anthracite fields are found in eastern Pennsylvania, stretching between Wayne and Dauphin counties. Both fields are unusually rich, with the coal located near the surface. Originally discovered in the 1790s, anthracite did not become commercially viable until 1810. Coal production in eastern Pennsylvania grew steadily from 5,000 tons between 1800 and 1809, to almost 76 million tons between 1850 and 1859. Sub-bituminous and lignite deposits are found primarily in the western United States. Although the West has large bituminous deposits, most bituminous coal is located in the East and Midwest and is divided into two major sections: the Central Competitive Field and the Appalachian Field.

Coalfields. The Central Competitive Field underlies parts of Arkansas, Illinois, Indiana, Iowa, Kansas, Michigan, Missouri, Ohio, and Pennsylvania. The Appalachian Field is found in West Virginia, Virginia, Maryland, Kentucky, Tennessee, and Alabama. These designations are somewhat artificial, as both Pennsylvania and Ohio are considered to be part of Appalachia.

Just what constitutes Appalachia is still uncertain. Scholar John C. Campbell wrote in 1919 that the region ended at West Virginia's northern border. The Appalachian Regional Commission (ARC) in the 1970s, however, defined the region as extending as far north as New York state, including Pennsylvania and eastern Ohio, and extending as far south as northwestern Georgia, central Alabama, and northeastern Mississippi.

The Central Competitive was the first of the two fields to open, becoming a major producer by 1859. Although Appalachian coal was plentiful, the deposits were located in areas considered to be too remote. After 1865, however, coal demand rose precipitously with the rise of the steel industry (*see also 72–73*) and the growth of the railroads (*see also 44–45 and 70–71*). Steel-makers used heat-distilled bituminous coal (coke) for fuel; railroad engines were powered by burning coal. Coal demand expanded dramatically around 1870 and continued to grow until 1920. This expansion coincided with the 1870 opening and continuing development of the Appalachian Field. Bituminous production prior to 1860 was comparable to that of anthracite, with anthracite having the edge. After 1870,

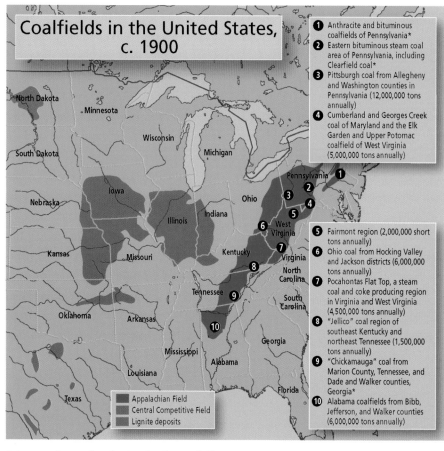

Coalfields in the United States, c. 1900

1. Anthracite and bituminous coalfields of Pennsylvania*
2. Eastern bituminous steam coal area of Pennsylvania, including Clearfield coal*
3. Pittsburgh coal from Allegheny and Washington counties in Pennsylvania (12,000,000 tons annually)
4. Cumberland and Georges Creek coal of Maryland and the Elk Garden and Upper Potomac coalfield of West Virginia (5,000,000 tons annually)
5. Fairmont region (2,000,000 short tons annually)
6. Ohio coal from Hocking Valley and Jackson districts (6,000,000 tons annually)
7. Pocahontas Flat Top, a steam coal and coke producing region in Virginia and West Virginia (4,500,000 tons annually)
8. "Jellico" coal region of southeast Kentucky and northeast Tennessee (1,500,000 tons annually)
9. "Chickamauga" coal from Marion County, Tennessee, and Dade and Walker counties, Georgia*
10. Alabama coalfields from Bibb, Jefferson, and Walker counties (6,000,000 tons annually)

Appalachian Field
Central Competitive Field
Lignite deposits

* Amount of annual production of coal unavailable.
Before 1870, anthracite fields in eastern Pennsylvania and bituminous coal from the Central Competitive Field in the Midwest dominated coal production. Production of coal expanded rapidly between 1870 and 1920 with the mining of bituminous coal from the Appalachian Field. Lignite deposits in the western United States, like those in South Dakota and Texas, also contributed to the emergence of the United States as a leading producer of coal.
Source: *Adapted from British Iron Trade Association,* American Industrial Conditions and Competition *(London: British Iron Trade Association, 1902), 13.*

however, bituminous production grew so rapidly that it eclipsed anthracite by the decade's end. By 1919, the United States was producing more coal than Germany and Great Britain combined.

Mining Techniques. Because of rapid growth and the relative ease of coal extraction, the U.S. coal industry between 1870 and 1920 was composed primarily of small producers. This promoted ruthless competition marked by low wages and dangerous working conditions. In addition, while efforts were made to increase productivity through mechanization, basic mining techniques remained essentially unchanged. Although some large-scale mining machinery would be added during the 1930s, mechanization would not begin in earnest until after 1950.

Starting in 1840, the two available extraction methods included Long Wall and Room and Pillar. Long Wall involved sinking a primary shaft at a coal deposit's edge and digging a tunnel to its end. After this, a coal-face (where the coal was actually mined) running the length of the deposit was established, thus creating a long wall, with the miners working their way back to the primary shaft. As the miners worked back, the ceiling or "overburden" in the mined section of the large room would be allowed to subside. Room and Pillar involved extracting the coal by creating a series of "rooms" connected by tunnels, with the overburden supported by coal pillars. Once workers mined a section of the deposit, they "pulled" the coal pillars and allowed the overburden to subside. This part of the process was extremely dangerous. Pressure on the pillars was immense and if they were not removed in just the right way, a cave-in could result.

Ironically, of these two methods, both coal operators and miners preferred the more dangerous Room and Pillar. Although Long Wall was safer and more efficient, miners felt

Further Reading
Baratz, Morton S. *The Union and the Coal Industry.* New Haven, Conn.: Yale University Press, 1955.
Campbell, John C. *The Southern Highlander and His Homeland.* 1921. Reprint, Spartanburg, S.C.: Reprint Co., 1973.
Dix, Keith. *What's a Coal Miner to Do? The Mechanization of Coal Mining.* Pittsburgh: University of Pittsburgh Press, 1988.
Majumdar, Shyamalk and E. Willard Miller, eds. *Pennsylvania Coal: Resources, Technology and Utilization.* Easton, Pa.: The Pennsylvania Academy of Science, 1983.

that it threatened their work autonomy. With Room and Pillar, miners could work at their own pace. Mine owners preferred Room and Pillar because it allowed a working coal-face to be established quickly.

Another constant danger to all coal miners was the interruption of the air supply and the presence of deadly gases, notably methane (fire damp) and carbon monoxide (white damp). Although several ventilation methods were used, a major breakthrough came with the invention of the Guibal fan, which was first demonstrated in 1854. Earlier designs had attempted to ventilate the shaft with forced air but none were successful because of a basic problem: Air has mass, therefore it has resistance. The Guibal design overcame this obstacle by pulling the stale air out of the mine, which created a partial vacuum, causing a column of fresh air to come in from the surface. The technology became central to all deep-shaft mining roughly by the 1880s.

Impact. Coal mining had a profound impact upon the environment in Appalachia. Lack of regulation of mining practices and the quick and individualistic growth of the industry adversely affected many of the region's ecological systems. In addition to slag piles (waste material from mines) dotting the landscape, acid drainage from mines into streams and lakes has become a major concern. Acid drainage occurs when sulfur-laden

minerals are exposed to air and water as a result of mining. With normal rainfall, sulfuric products are leached into the ground, making their way to the streams. (The process had been noted in the 1700s but did not become a matter of interest or concern until 1910.) Although active mines contribute to acid drainage, abandoned operations currently account for approximately 60 percent of all acid drainage. In fact, of the nearly 12,000 miles (19,000 kilometers) of streams in the United States ruined by acid drainage by 1970, almost 10,500 miles (17,000 kilometers), stretching from Pennsylvania to Alabama, were located in Appalachia. Bodies of water suffering such damage cannot provide wildlife habitat or serve other purposes such as swimming or providing drinking water (*see also* 190–91).

The introduction of large-scale mechanization after 1950 also resulted in serious ecological consequences for Appalachia. Mechanization spurred greater use of surface and strip mining, particularly mountaintop removal. Essentially, this process involves blasting a mountaintop with dynamite to remove its outer surface and expose the coal deposit. Once exposed, the coal is extracted by large machinery. Although such large operations allow for the removal of more coal with fewer miners, they also permanently scar the landscape with loss of forests and vegetation. Moreover, mountaintop removal operations can have a serious impact upon bodies of water, especially with "valley fill." Ground removed from the mountain is used to fill in valleys and thus covers streams, affecting water flow and creating an unstable ground surface. Controversy over these methods exists in Appalachia today. Aside from the ecological damage caused by these techniques, they provide relatively few jobs because the machines are very expensive and are thus designed to be operated by only one or two people.

—*Richard P. Mulcahy*

Petroleum and the Early Oil Industry

The modern petroleum industry began when entrepreneurs seeking a plentiful and inexpensive source of lamp oil extracted petroleum from hand-dug wells in Oil Springs, Ontario, in 1858, and from drilled wells in Titusville, Pennsylvania, in 1859. By the mid-1860s, western Pennsylvania was established as the center of a thriving oil industry, with producers extracting several million barrels of petroleum each year. Over the next three decades, the system for extracting, transporting, and refining petroleum developed into a major industry. A global market for kerosene and lubricating oils had emerged in 1890, with firms like Standard Oil (in the United States) and Royal Dutch (in the Netherlands) dominating that market.

In North America, Pennsylvania and the surrounding region remained the center of oil production until the end of the nineteenth century.

Changes in Oil Industry. At the turn of the twentieth century, the North American petroleum industry saw significant changes. First, the center of production shifted westward. In 1900, more than 90 percent of the 64 million barrels of petroleum extracted from deposits in the United States came from fields east of Illinois and north of Tennessee. By 1910, oil production had climbed to 210 million barrels per year, but eastern fields contributed only 34 million barrels, less than 20 percent of the total.

One harbinger of change came in 1901, when oil gushed out of an exploratory well at Spindletop near Beaumont, Texas. To reach profitable markets, several small companies began extracting crude oil at Spindletop and shipping it by steam-powered tankers to refineries on the East Coast. At the time, most oil moved from field to refinery through a network of buried pipelines controlled by Standard Oil, but none extended all the way to the Texas Gulf Coast. The new ocean route eliminated the need for long pipelines and bypassed the existing pipeline system. Although production at Spindletop soon declined, the field allowed several small companies—the forerunners of Gulf Oil, Texaco, and the Sun Company—to gain a foothold in the industry. Meanwhile, entrepreneurs in search of oil continued to discover new fields, making important discoveries in Oklahoma and California in the decade after oil was found at Spindletop.

Oil vs. Coal. The inexpensive and plentiful oil coming from Spindletop also encouraged the use of petroleum as an industrial fuel. Oil had many advantages over coal (*see also 64–65 and 102–03*): Oil did not have to be shoveled into a boiler, and a barrel of oil contained more energy than an equivalent volume of coal, reducing the space required for storage. Oil also produced less ash than coal.

However, petroleum had its disadvantages: It evaporated, emitted noxious vapors, and was prone to explosions. It also was generally a more expensive source of energy, typically several times more costly than an equivalent amount of coal. Although some industrial facilities, steamships, and railroads had used oil for fuel before Spindletop (especially in California where coal was expensive), use expanded significantly in the years after Spindletop. The oil-fired tankers carrying crude oil from Texas to the East Coast had also demonstrated the practicality of using heavy oil as a source of fuel. Many

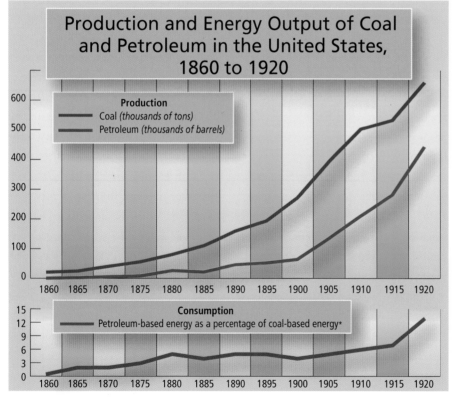

* *Assumes 7 barrels of petroleum to the ton and that petroleum has 1.5 times the energy content of oil. No adjustments have been made for exports and the manufacture of nonfuel products.*
Prior to the discovery of oil at Spindletop in Texas in 1901, the consumption of petroleum-based energy in the United States remained low in comparison to coal-based energy. However, the figures for the period 1905 to 1920 show the growing importance of oil as an energy source in the United States.
Source: *Sam H. Shurr, Historical Statistics of Minerals in the United States* (Washington, D.C.: Resources for the Future, 1960).

In 1901, oil was discovered at Spindletop near Beaumont, Texas. (© Bettmann/Corbis)

eight million motor vehicles were in operation. That year, to meet the demand for motor fuel, oil companies extracted 443 million barrels of crude oil from a network of widely distributed fields, most connected by pipeline to a system of increasingly sophisticated refineries. In all, refineries converted 28 percent (124 million barrels) of oil into motor fuels. Only 12 percent (54 million barrels) ended up as kerosene. Refiners sold the bulk of the remainder, which was generally unsuitable for use as a refined product, as industrial fuel (208 million barrels). Lubricating oils and other products (25 million barrels) rounded out the total.

Crude oil had become an integral component of the U.S. economy, supplying approximately 13 percent of the energy consumed in 1920. Natural gas (another component of petroleum) and water power each accounted for another several percent. Coal, though, remained the dominant source of energy, supplying about 75 percent of the total. Over the course of the twentieth century, dependence on each of these energy sources increased, with the relative importance of petroleum growing dramatically. By the start of the twenty-first century, oil consumption in the United States and Canada had risen to 7.4 billion barrels per year, representing approximately 39 percent of the energy consumed. Natural gas (26 percent), coal (24 percent), nuclear (9 percent), and hydropower (2 percent) supplied the balance.

—*Hugh S. Gorman*

firms, however, continued to use coal as its price remained competitive and the future availability of oil was uncertain.

From Kerosene to Gasoline. The electric lamp (invented in 1879) eventually weakened the market for kerosene, and oil companies began to work at meeting the growing demand for motor fuel. This shift from kerosene to gasoline as the industry's main product represented an even greater change than the geographic shift of production or the development of a market for industrial fuel. In the nineteenth century, refiners sold gasoline as a solvent and as a fuel for stoves and space heaters, but weak demand often forced companies to dispose of excess stock as a waste product. Most

small refiners simply ran the fluid into a pit and set it on fire. Experiments with horseless carriages in the 1890s generated additional demand for gasoline, raising the demand to about five million barrels per year. Significant change, however, did not come until 1909 when automobile manufacturer Henry Ford introduced the Model T. This popular and affordable car contributed to a steady rise in demand for gasoline. Ford's introduction of the assembly line for automobile manufacture in 1913 added to the number of cars on the road and further increased the demand for motor fuel.

By 1920, the shift from a kerosene- to a gasoline-based petroleum industry was complete. In the United States, approximately

Further Reading

Williamson, Harold F., and Arnold R. Daum. *The American Petroleum Industry: The Age of Illumination, 1859–1899.* Westport, Conn.: Greenwood Press, 1981.

Williamson, Harold F., Ralph L. Andreano, Arnold R. Daum, and Gilbert C. Klose. *The American Petroleum Industry: The Age of Energy, 1899–1959.* Evanston, Ill.: Northwestern University Press, 1963.

Yergin, Daniel. *The Prize: The Epic Quest for Oil, Money, and Power.* New York: Simon & Schuster, 1991.

Urban Smoke Pollution in the United States

Air pollution is a significant environmental concern and is closely linked to major health problems. Before the 1950s in the United States and Canada (*see also* 108–09), however, both reformers and engineers were primarily concerned with smoke pollution rather than other forms of air pollution, for example automobile emissions. Between 1880 and 1950, a number of American industrial cities, including Cincinnati, Ohio; Pittsburgh, Pennsylvania; and St. Louis, Missouri, suffered from heavy smoke pollution.

Coal. Increasing consumption of bituminous, or soft, coal (*see also* 64–65 *and* 102–03) was the primary cause of smoke pollution in North American urban areas. During the nineteenth century, coal supplanted wood as the chief fuel source for industry, railroad locomotives, and domestic heating. Anthracite coal, mined in eastern Pennsylvania, provided the critical fuel for the launching of America's industries in the early nineteenth century. Anthracite was a clean-burning coal, a sharp contrast with bituminous coal. Anthracite supplies began to run out in the late nineteenth century, and bituminous coal increasingly supplanted it as a preferred fuel in many American cities and industries. A further advantage of bituminous coal was that, unlike anthracite, it was found in numerous locations around the country; its more ready availability reduced production and transportation costs. In 1870 the United States consumed approximately 21 million tons of bituminous coal; by 1920 consumption had risen 2,500 percent to 508 million tons.

Bituminous coal, cheap and easily combustible, released many noxious by-products, for example, sulfur dioxide and soot; the burning of bituminous coal produced smoke of varying densities. Smoke affected the quality of urban life, reducing the hours and amount of sunlight, destroying vegetation, discoloring building facades, dirtying clothing, and causing respiratory and other health problems. Some Progressive reformers even claimed that the smoke contributed to crime by demoralizing the population. Many towns and cities had passed smoke control statutes as early as the first decades of the nineteenth century, but these ordinances were difficult to enforce. For most nineteenth-century urbanites, although smoke might be objectionable, it still symbolized the jobs and prosperity created by industry.

Early Reforms. More sustained attacks on urban smoke pollution began in the late nineteenth and early twentieth centuries. Women's groups often initiated these campaigns and they frequently formed part of Progressive municipal housekeeping campaigns that included other environmental improvements like clean water, better garbage collection, and

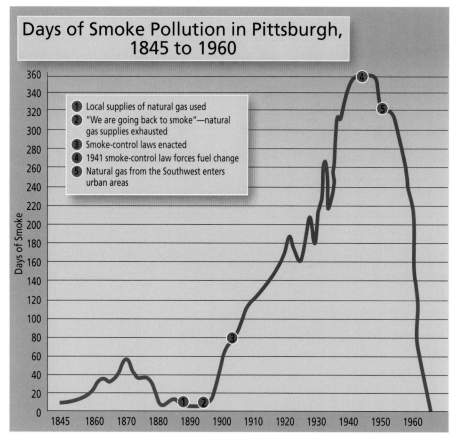

Days of Smoke Pollution in Pittsburgh, 1845 to 1960

① Local supplies of natural gas used
② "We are going back to smoke"—natural gas supplies exhausted
③ Smoke-control laws enacted
④ 1941 smoke-control law forces fuel change
⑤ Natural gas from the Southwest enters urban areas

Pittsburgh, a major industrial center, suffered from smoke pollution throughout the nineteenth century and much of the twentieth century. The number of days affected by significant smoke pollution reached a peak during the 1940s, with improvements beginning to occur around 1947 following the implementation of a smoke-control statute.

Source: Adapted from Cliff I. Davidson, "Air Pollution in Pittsburgh: A Historical Perspective," *APCA Journal* 29, no. 10 (October 1979), 1037.

improved street cleaning. Engineers were frequently part of antismoke crusades, arguing that smoke was a sign of incomplete and inefficient combustion and should be curtailed for the sake of efficiency. By World War I, seventy-five American cities had passed antismoke ordinances of varying degrees of restriction and enforceability. Driving these regulations was an attempt to reduce the nuisances caused by smoke as well as concern about possible negative effects on health. To a large extent, however, even though they initiated and supported vigorous smoke-control campaigns, reformers had only sporadic and short-lived success in reducing the smoke burden in cities like Chicago, Cincinnati, and Pittsburgh. In most cities that attempted to enforce strong sanctions, aggressive smoke regulators clashed with industry and railroad owners who believed that smoke control would prove costly to them.

Shifting Concerns. World War I diverted attention from smoke regulation; a wartime drive for production caused smoky conditions to increase in many cities. At the same time, the concerns of engineers, who knew smoke to be the result of inefficient combustion, focused on lost energy and resources. These concerns increasingly supplanted the broader arguments about health and cleanliness expressed by women's groups. Throughout the 1920s, cities paid limited attention to smoke problems, usually mounting public education campaigns rather than attempting to enforce strict regulations. The 1920s also witnessed a shift in the position of engineers on the cause of heavy smoke: Smoke from large industries and utilities was de-emphasized and domestic smoke became the prime concern. Home fires, argued the engineers, were particularly objectionable because they often produced heavy smoke that poured from low chimneys and hung

Further Reading
Dewey, Scott Hamilton. *Don't Breathe the Air: Air Pollution and U.S. Environmental Politics, 1945–1970.* College Station: Texas A&M University Press, 2000.
Stradling, David. *Smokestacks and Progressives: Environmentalists, Engineers, and Air Quality in America, 1881–1951.* Baltimore, Md.: Johns Hopkins University Press, 1999.

Tarr, Joel A. *The Search for the Ultimate Sink: Urban Pollution in Historical Perspective.* Akron, Ohio: University of Akron Press, 1996.
Tarr, Joel A., and Carl Zimring. "The Struggle for Smoke Control in St. Louis: Achievement and Emulation." In *Common Fields: An Environmental History of St. Louis,* edited by Andrew Hurley. St. Louis: Missouri Historical Society Press, 1997.

over cities. Regulating the coal-burning habits of homeowners, however, was politically very difficult and in the 1920s no city attempted to do so.

Smoke Regulations. The 1930s brought the Great Depression and coal consumption fell. Municipalities, however, again began to pay attention to the smoke problem. During this decade, the federal government played an important role, with the Works Progress Administration conducting a number of surveys in cities around the nation. The most critical antismoke campaigns took place in St. Louis and Pittsburgh, both heavy consumers of bituminous coal. In St. Louis, Raymond Tucker, a mechanical engineer who had been on the faculty of Washington University, played a key role when, in 1934, he was appointed personal secretary to the mayor with the mission "to clarify the air." Tucker argued that the solution to St. Louis's smoke problem was to require either the substitution of clean fuel for polluting bituminous coal or the use of mechanical coal feeders or stokers. After several years of conflict with the city council, during which St. Louis experienced dense smoke over the city, Tucker persuaded the council to approve ordinances requiring the use of clean fuel or stokers. Air quality greatly improved during the winter of 1940–41. In Pittsburgh, known as the smokiest city in the nation, observers noted St. Louis's success and in 1941 moved to copy and strengthen its successful ordinance. The war interrupted implementation of a similar ordinance in

Pittsburgh, but in 1947, after delays attributable to a shortage of clean fuel, Pittsburgh moved to enforce its smoke-control statute. The result was a large increase in the number of smoke-free days.

Although the regulations enacted in St. Louis and Pittsburgh were significant as moral and political statements, the market-driven substitution of cheap and clean natural gas for coal was the actual cause of the significant reduction in smoke pollution immediately after World War II. In both St. Louis and Pittsburgh, advocates of smoke control looked to treated coal (used as a replacement for bituminous but still based on bituminous) to solve the smoke problem as well as contribute to the creation of a new industry. Other clean fuels, including natural gas, were not available at competitive prices at the time the ordinances were enacted. The strategy of using treated coal, however, was never fully put to the test because natural gas was available in Pittsburgh and St. Louis after 1947. The advent of cheap and clean natural gas had not been foreseen but its entry made possible cleaner air over cities. In addition, another technological change—the conversion of the U.S. railroad fleet from steam to diesel electric locomotives—also played a significant role in reducing smoke pollution. By the 1950s, dense smoke had largely been eradicated from most American cities, but the larger problem of chemically based air pollution, the result of automobile exhaust, remained (*see also* 134–35).

—*Joel A. Tarr*

The Canadian Commission of Conservation: Urban Planning

In 1909, the United States, Canada, the British colony of Newfoundland, and Mexico signed the North American Declaration of Principles on Conservation. Shortly after returning from Washington, D.C., Canadian delegates created the Canadian Commission of Conservation. Between 1909 and 1921, this organization published more than two hundred reports, a blueprint for the sustainable use of soils, forests, water, air, minerals, fish, and wildlife and for the promotion of public health. The commission opposed the forestry practice of clearcutting, encouraged the use of organic fertilizers rather than chemical fertilizers in agriculture to build healthy soils, and promoted small hydroelectric dams rather than large ones that flooded thousands of acres. At its zenith, the advisory body had sixty-five employees. An important component of the commission's work was urban planning.

Urban Conditions. At the beginning of the twentieth century, living conditions in many of Canada's large cities could be described as hazardous, especially in the poorer neighborhoods. Clean drinking water was scarce and the air was often choked with smoke, dust, and industrial pollutants. Refuse and carcasses of dead animals littered the streets in the slums. Heavy rains or spring thaws caused sewage systems to overflow. Life expectancy for city dwellers in poor neighborhoods was short; infant mortality rates were comparable to those in some of today's poorest regions of the world; and epidemics of disease were frequent and deadly. For example, during World War I, for each Canadian soldier who perished in Europe, two civilians died from tuberculosis and influenza epidemics at home.

The commission took a broad and integrative approach to public health issues in urban areas, consistent with the tactics promoted by the Progressive Movement. Progressives believed that difficult social, economic, and environmental problems could be solved by relying on long-term planning, research, and public education, and by reducing waste and inefficiencies whenever possible. In addition, Progressives were not adverse to state intervention in the marketplace, including public ownership of strategic resources like hydroelectric facilities and municipal infrastructures, including waterworks, most of which were privately owned at the time.

The commission's first step in tackling these complex problems was to develop appropriate national standards for drinking water, sewage treatment, air quality, and waste management. As a second step, the commission offered assistance to provinces and municipalities to ensure that these standards were met. The commission helped provincial legislators in drafting effective urban planning laws and provided advice to city planners about optimal population densities and amenities like parks and recreation facilities (*see also* 84–85 *and* 98–99) that foster healthy living conditions.

Water. Water quality (*see also* 76–77) became a particularly significant focus. The commission challenged the popular notion that "the solution to pollution was dilution." Many epidemics could be traced to the poor quality of drinking water caused by the dumping of raw sewage into rivers and lakes. The commission insisted that all wastewater be treated prior to disposal. It proposed regular spot-checks of drinking and sewage water and recommended severe penalties when minimum standards were not met. Its employees conducted national inventories to find and popularize the most cost-effective sewage and drinking water treatment technologies and processes and organized national conferences to facilitate their implementation. The commission also worked to standardize plumbing and

Group picture taken in 1909 in Washington, D.C., of senior U.S., Canadian, and Mexican representatives who crafted the North American Declaration of Principles on Conservation. First row, from left to right: Henri S. Béland, Clifford Sifton, Sydney Fisher, Theodore Roosevelt, Romulo Escobar, Carlo Sellerier, Miguel A. de Quevedo; Second row: Robert E. Young, R. L. Bacon, Gifford Pinchot, Senator Cullum, J. R. Garfield, James Bryce, T. R. Shipp, P. C. Knox. (National Archives of Canada/C-16966)

North American Declaration of Principles on Conservation

U.S. president Theodore Roosevelt was aware that the natural environment and pollution did not respect national boundaries. Like many of his Progressive counterparts, he could not understand how the population and economic growth rates experienced at the turn of the nineteenth century in North America could be sustained without depleting the Earth's limited natural capital. Results from the 1908 national inventory of available natural resources undertaken by Henry Gannett of the U.S. Geological Survey confirmed the validity of Roosevelt's concerns. The report predicted that continuing "business as usual" would deplete most U.S. natural resources by the end of the twentieth century. At the end of his second term, Roosevelt was convinced that the conservation of natural resources was one of the most important issues facing world leaders. In February of 1909, during the last weeks of his presidency, he convened senior representatives from Mexico, Canada, the United States, and the British colony of Newfoundland to discuss the issue and draw a plan of action.

The 1909 Declaration of Principles stemming from the meeting was far ranging. It called for the protection of public health, the creation of vast forest reserves, the conservation of nonrenewable resources like minerals and coal, and the sustainable use of renewable resources like water, fish, wildlife, wood, and agricultural soils. Although Canadian delegates were successful in establishing the Commission on Conservation in Canada, the U.S. Congress voted against a similar commission for the United States. Gifford Pinchot, the head of the U.S. Forest Service, subsequently created the small, not-for-profit American Commission of Conservation that attempted, with limited success, to rally Americans to the cause of conservation. Mexico and Newfoundland did not implement any of the declaration's key recommendations.

waterworks equipment to reduce installation and maintenance costs.

Air. Air pollution was another important problem examined by the commission. In 1913, for example, when scientists from Pittsburgh, Pennsylvania, shared the results of their research on the air quality of their city (*see also* 106–07), members of the commission warned Canadian decision makers of the consequences of inaction by using the "smoke capital of the world" as an example. They recommended that filters be installed on all industrial smokestacks located in or near urban areas and successfully introduced affordable technology to capture even the most noxious substances. The commission promoted the establishment of new industries in areas located downwind of large urban centers, thus preventing polluted air from blowing to heavily populated areas. The commission also recommended that

cities ban the use of low-quality coal for home heating and asked that governments build dams and power lines to take advantage of clean heating opportunities offered by hydroelectricity.

Waste. Waste management was studied from a surprisingly broad perspective, even by today's standards. The commission recommended that all residential, commercial, and industrial waste be systematically collected by state agencies to reuse and recycle as much waste as possible. The commission ran a pilot "commodities market" for used newspapers, wood products, glass, and iron, as well as for a wide variety of industrial by-products, and helped match potential buyers and sellers. Members of the commission also recommended large-scale composting of organic matter to further reduce waste.

Impact of War and Recession. Between 1909 and 1914, the commission's

agenda of institutional reform and restraint in exploiting natural resources was enthusiastically endorsed by politicians, the business elite, and the informed public. The outbreak of World War I changed all that. Between 1914 and 1918, the commission's call for conservation (*see also* 110–13) was confronted with the nation's need to maximize wartime production or run the risk of defeat. The commission's agenda of sustainable development was put aside.

In 1921, Canada was in the midst of a severe recession. The government, looking for ways to reduce its huge postwar debt and eager to greatly increase economic output to foster growth, abolished the commission. Its employees found work in other federal departments and its archives were destroyed. The body had met many of its goals for urban planning: by 1921, most provinces had, or were in the process of adopting, laws, regulations, and standards based on the commission's recommendations, thereby improving the quality of life for millions of Canadians. However, World War I had also fundamentally altered the values and priorities of Canadians in their relationship to the environment. The preservation of nature and the conservation of natural resources for the benefit of future generations would be perceived as secondary to the reconstruction of the battered economy for the benefit of those who survived the Great War.

—Michel F. Girard

Further Reading

Cutright, Paul Russel. *Theodore Roosevelt: The Making of a Conservationist*. Urbana: University of Illinois Press, 1985.

Girard, Michel. "The Commission of Conservation as a Forerunner to the National Research Council, 1909–1921." *Scientia Canadensis* 15, no. 2 (1991): 19–40.

Kain, Roger, ed. *Planning for Conservation*. New York: St. Martin's Press, 1981.

Simpson, Michael. "Thomas Adams in Canada, 1914–1930." *Urban History Review.* 11, no. 2 (October 1982): 1–15.

The U.S. Conservation Movement

In the late 1800s, a handful of American scientists and government officials warned the U.S. Congress that, contrary to popular belief, America's natural resources appeared to be rapidly diminishing. These early conservationists pointed to George Perkins Marsh's book, *Man and Nature* (1864), citing his arguments that stripping the land of trees and overgrazing had caused many problems in eastern rivers like the Connecticut River. They feared that the destructive mining, lumbering, and farming practices in use west of the Mississippi River would repeat this pattern. Private citizen groups joined together with other early conservationists in petitioning Congress to either save or intelligently use America's natural resources before they were exhausted.

Early Conservation. Like preservationists (*see also* 114–15), who favored keeping the land "forever wild" because of its beauty and therapeutic powers, utilitarian conservationists favored preserving unique places like the Grand Canyon, but they also pointed out the economic value of natural resources. A forest, conservationists argued, had multiple uses, including timber cutting, grazing, and mining, but such activities needed to be regulated by qualified experts. This "gospel of efficiency," as historian Samuel P. Hays has named it, called for government scientists to employ technology, research, and rational planning to promote efficient use of natural resources and eliminate waste. By doing so, the government would "conserve" natural resources for use by future generations, and, in the words of government forester Gifford Pinchot, provide "for the greatest good to the greatest number for the longest time."

Beginning in 1876, conservationists and preservationists combined forces and pressed Congress for action. After many failed bills,

Congress passed the Forest Reserve Act in 1891. The law allowed the president to set aside forests for preservation; however, it did not provide for their protection or management. Congress responded to further public pressure by passing the Forest Management Act in 1897. Linking forests and water flow, this law brought together efforts to stop erosion and wasteful lumber practices, and supported efforts to ensure long-term timber supplies and protect domestic water supplies through efforts at flood control.

The conservation movement received a significant boost when Theodore Roosevelt became president in 1901. He supported both preservation and conservation and willingly challenged the developers who exploited the land for profit. In Gifford Pinchot, the chief of federal forestry from 1898 to 1910,

Roosevelt found the perfect leader and spokesman for the government's conservation efforts. Young, energetic, and articulate, Pinchot took up the cause with Roosevelt's backing. Roosevelt solicited Pinchot's advice on federal policies for water usage, grazing, and public land management.

Western Irrigation. The president made irrigation (*see also* 90–91), which would provide water to western states, the first step in his conservation program. In response to the president's message, Congress passed the Reclamation Act in 1902. The fees that settlers paid for public land in sixteen western states covered the costs of building the dams and irrigation canals needed to bring water to their land, thus creating a permanent revolving fund. Within the first five years of its existence,

George Perkins Marsh's *Man and Nature*

George Perkins Marsh's *Man and Nature* (1864) was the first book to question the destructive human impact on the environment. Advocating better management of America's natural resources through such practices as reforestation and erosion control, *Man and Nature* influenced early conservationists and helped transform U.S. government land management policies during the Progressive Era.

"Man has too long forgotten that the earth was given to him for usufruct alone, not for consumption, still less for profligate waste. Nature has provided against the absolute destruction of any of her elementary matter . . . But she has left it within the power of man irreparably to derange the combinations of inorganic matter and of organic life . . .

" . . . We have now felled forest enough everywhere, in many districts far too much. Let us restore this one element of material life to its normal proportions, and devise means for maintaining the permanence of its relation to the fields, the meadows, and the pastures, to the rain and the dews of heaven, to the springs and rivulets with which it waters the earth. The establishment of an approximately fixed ratio between the two most broadly characterized distinctions of rural surface—woodland and plough land—would involve a certain persistence of character in all the branches of industry, all the occupations and habits of life, which depend upon or are immediately connected with either, without implying a rigidity that should exclude flexibility of accommodation to the many changes of external circumstance which human wisdom can neither prevent nor foresee, and would thus help us to become, more emphatically, a well-ordered and stable commonwealth, and, not less conspicuously, a people of progress."

Source: Excerpted from George Perkins Marsh, *Man and Nature, or, Physical Geography as Modified by Human Action* (New York: C. Scribner, 1864).

President Theodore Roosevelt on Glacier Point at Yosemite Park, c. 1908. (© Corbis)

the Reclamation Service began twenty-one projects. The federal government supported and, ultimately, controlled large-scale irrigation projects that transformed the landscape, economy, and the social and political structures of much of the semiarid West. For example, Arizona, an early beneficiary of reclamation, saw its population more than triple between 1900 and 1930 to over 435,000.

Forest Management. After several years of failed attempts, in February 1905, Roosevelt and Pinchot convinced Congress to transfer the national forests from the Department of the Interior to the Department of Agriculture's forestry agency. The agricultural appropriations bill passed a month later changed the name of the Bureau of Forestry to the United States Forest Service (*see also* 92–93). Given control of millions of acres of forests, the Forest Service worked to ensure a continuous supply of lumber while trying to stabilize the lumber market.

Also in 1905, at Pinchot's urging, Roosevelt began removing millions of acres of public land from private development by placing them under federal control for scientific development. The federal government took on the responsibility not just of overseeing forestry and irrigation on public lands, but also of regulating cattle and sheep grazing, water power rights, and mineral extraction. Pinchot failed in his attempts to place the Forest Service in charge of all these activities, but the conservationists succeeded in their efforts to use science to better manage natural resources.

Conflicting Agendas. During Roosevelt's second administration (1905–09), the battle over land use divided the country into three factions—preservationists, conservationists, and developers. Preservationists like John Muir, who had supported Pinchot's earlier efforts to save forests from destruction, clashed with the government over the proposed dam in Hetch Hetchy Valley (*see also* 114) in Yosemite Park. When the federal government finally began construction in 1914, the national controversy had caused a permanent split between conservationists and preservationists.

Speaker of the House Joseph Cannon summed up the developers' side of the argument when he declared, "Not one cent for scenery!" Western political leaders opposed the Administration's charging for grazing privileges and the use of coal and water sites, and generally resented the federal government telling them how to handle what they considered to be their land. In 1907, western congressional leaders attached an amendment to the agricultural appropriations bill that prevented Roosevelt from setting aside more land for protection. An angry Congress also refused to fund the president's special commissions investigating conservation issues. Undaunted, Pinchot and Roosevelt continued to push their agenda in early 1909 at the end of Roosevelt's Administration.

Pinchot believed that Roosevelt's handpicked successor, President William Howard Taft, was not aggressive enough about conservation issues. After publicly criticizing Taft and Secretary of the Interior Richard Ballinger and meddling in Department of the Interior business, Pinchot was fired in 1910 for insubordination in what became known as the Ballinger–Pinchot Controversy. Pinchot's dismissal initially crippled the conservation movement, but he rallied his supporters and galvanized the movement during the resulting congressional hearings. The controversy angered Roosevelt and brought him back into the political arena to challenge Taft. Together Pinchot and Roosevelt created the Progressive "Bull Moose" Party in 1912 in hopes that Roosevelt might win back the White House and carry out their agenda. Roosevelt lost the election, but conservationists pressed on through private organizations like the National Conservation Association, and in their work for the various federal bureaus and agencies.

With the outbreak of World War I, the federal government set aside both conservation and preservation efforts to meet the resource demands of the war. The government did not take up conservation again until the 1930s. When it did, a second generation of conservation-minded scientists was fully committed to applying technology to resource management.

—*James G. Lewis*

Further Reading
Gould, Lewis. *The Presidency of Theodore Roosevelt*. Lawrence: University Press of Kansas, 1991.
Hays, Samuel P. *Conservation and the Gospel of Efficiency: The Progressive Conservation Movement, 1890–1920*. Cambridge, Mass.: Harvard University Press, 1959.
Miller, Char. *Gifford Pinchot and the Making of Modern Environmentalism*. Washington, D.C.: Island Press, 2001.
Pinchot, Gifford. *Breaking New Ground*. 1947. Reprint, Washington, D.C.: Island Press, 1998.
Reisner, Marc. *Cadillac Desert: The American West and Its Disappearing Water*. New York: Penguin Books, 1993.

The Conservation Movement in Canada

At the turn of the twentieth century, the new conservation movement in North America called for the planned and efficient use of natural resources to assure that they would be available for future generations. Historians have often assumed that concern about conservation was not as great in Canada as in the United States (*see also* 110–11), presumably because Canada still had an abundant supply of natural resources and therefore natural resources were less in need of protection. Although the conservation movement had less of a long-term influence in Canada, from roughly 1880 to 1920 its impact was as great as in the United States, if not greater.

In this era, North Americans increasingly began to worry that unregulated, wasteful use of nature would lead to a scarcity of resources. For citizens of the United States, the near-extinction of the buffalo (*see also* 36–37), the depletion of vast forests (*see also* 92–93), and the relentless push of settlers in the West (*see also* 52–53) supported these concerns. Canadians, whose natural resources were also at risk, were equally concerned. Canada had similar landforms, flora, and fauna, and Canadians developed similar ideas about the need to protect and preserve nature.

Forestry. The first Canadians to encourage conservation were independent foresters who believed that the nation's forest wealth was being wasted by the overcutting of small woodlot owners and a general carelessness that led to forest fires. A few, such as Ottawa lumber baron James Little and his forester son, William, attended the first American Forest Congress in 1882 in Cincinnati, Ohio, and invited organizers and attendees to meet again in Canada later that year. The Montreal Congress marked the birth of Canadian conservation: It introduced conservation concerns to the general public, led to the creation of forest reserves (*see also* 94–95) and tougher fire regulations, and gave the movement two leaders: William Little and Québec politician Henri Joly de Lotbinière. The movement grew, especially when foresters joined with other resource interests. For example, a coalition of Ontario sportsmen (seeking a continuous supply of moose, deer, duck, and other wildlife to hunt), watershed advocates (wanting to ensure that Ontario's agricultural land received sufficient water), and lumbermen (desiring parcels of land set aside for controlled forest use) contributed to the political process that established Algonquin Park on the Canadian Shield in 1893.

Wilderness Parks. Algonquin was a provincial park patterned after national parks being established in Canada's Rocky Mountains during this period, beginning with Banff in 1885—itself modeled after national parks in the United States (*see also* 114–15), such as Yosemite and Yellowstone. These wilderness parks are perhaps the greatest legacy of the Canadian conservation movement. (A distinct parks bureau, the Dominion Parks Branch, was established in 1911.) Provincial and Commonwealth governments approved of parks for the same economic reasons that supported the conservation movement in Canada: It was accepted that governments would make judicious use of the natural resources of parks. As a result, parks not only provided revenue from tourism, they also kept the land's wealth and resources under government control.

During this era, Canadians showed an increasing appreciation for nature. The parks were created, in great part, because

Algonquin Park visitors at the Highland Inn, Cache Lake, between 1908 and 1913. (Algonquin Park Museum Archives #2853/Mary Clare)

Creation of Banff National Park

In 1883, during construction of the Canadian Pacific Railway, workers Frank McCabe and William McCardell discovered hot mineral springs at Banff in the Rocky Mountains. They imagined opening a health spa similar to those popular in the United States and Europe. Rushing to beat out rival land speculators, they sought title to their claim from the Canadian government. The government agreed that Banff had great tourist potential—and so claimed the land for itself. Banff became Canada's first national park in 1885.

Canadian politicians drew their inspiration from parks created in the United States at Yosemite and Yellowstone in 1864 and 1872, respectively. In fact, the wording of the act that declared Banff to be "hereby reserved and set apart as a public park and pleasure ground for the benefit, advantage, and enjoyment of the people," followed the language of the Yellowstone Park Act. Parliamentary debates show that the government members had economic motives for establishing Banff: They saw it as opportunity to make otherwise inaccessible, mountainous terrain profitable by selling it to the public as scenery. Prime Minister John A. Macdonald argued that a park centered on the hot springs would "recuperate the patients and recoup the Treasury." But the politicians also understood that designating the area as a park would limit the use of its natural resources. Macdonald assured the House that Banff's timbers would be protected, and another member said, "If you intend to keep it as a park, you must shut out trade, traffic, and mining." Thus the establishment of Canada's first national park revealed both a desire for profit and an increasing respect for nature.

they provided a place for outdoor recreation (*see also* 138). Camping and canoeing became popular pastimes, especially for affluent Central Canadians; nature groups like Camp Temagami and the Canadian Alpine Club attracted the adventurous; and readers were hooked on the nature writings of Canadians Charles G. D. Roberts and Ernest Thompson Seton. Economically motivated conservationists were concerned that such "sentimentalism" would lead to large portions of land being taken out of use. However, they had little to fear in Canada, where those who simply appreciated nature did not actively organize to promote conservation and preservation.

Commission of Conservation. Conservationism became institutionalized in Canada to a greater degree than in the rest of North America. On the recommendation of a North American conservation congress hosted by U.S. president

Theodore Roosevelt in 1909, Prime Minister Wilfrid Laurier's government created a national conservation body, the Commission of Conservation (*see also* 108–09), to coordinate conservation within the federal government. (Neither Mexico nor the United States accomplished such coordination.) Although the commission held only advisory status, the nonpartisan, publicly funded group was expected to consider, investigate, and frame recommendations on all manner of conservation issues. Its committees— Fisheries, Game and Fur-Bearing Animals, Forests, Land, Minerals, Public Health, Waters and Waterpower, and Publicity

and Co-operative Organizations—reflected the growing range of interests among conservationists. The commission was involved in everything from rationalizing fish and game regulations with the United States (culminating in passage of the 1916 Migratory Birds Treaty), to town planning, to publishing hundreds of reports on the status of Canada's natural resources. However, in the economic boom following World War I, conservation was sometimes seen as standing in the way of unlimited development; prudent management of the nation's resources was now considered by some to be constrictive. As a result, the Commission of Conservation was dissolved in 1921; with that dissolution, the Canadian conservation movement came to an end.

Because the federal government in Canada had done more than its United States counterpart to accommodate—or, perhaps, coopt—public conservationist interests, no lobby groups equivalent to the Sierra Club in the United States formed to maintain the legacy of conservation after the general movement's demise. Nevertheless, between 1880 and 1920, the conservation movement significantly affected Canadian society by challenging the idea that the nation's natural wealth was boundless and eternal. The products of this conservation era—national parks, nature clubs, and wildlife treaties (*see also* 96–97)—remained; after long dormancy, Canadians would rally to a new form of environmentalism in the 1960s (*see also* 164–65).

—*Alan MacEachern*

Further Reading
Dorsey, Kurkpatrick. *The Dawn of Conservation Diplomacy: U.S.-Canadian Wildlife Protection Treaties in the Progressive Era.* Seattle: University of Washington Press, 1998.
Foster, Janet. *Working for Wildlife: The Beginning of Preservation in Canada.*
2nd ed. Toronto: University of Toronto Press, 1998.
Hewitt, Gordon C. *The Conservation of Wildlife in Canada.* New York: Scribner's Sons, 1921.
Lothian, W. F. *A Brief History of Canada's National Parks.* Ottawa: Environment Canada, Parks, 1987.

The Origin of the Preservation Movement in the United States

During the late 1800s and into the early 1900s, the idea and reality of conserving and preserving the nation's forests and natural wonders gained widespread public support in the United States. At first, the emerging conservation (*see also* 110–11) and preservation movements shared a common philosophy and goal: Certain public lands and natural resources were too valuable to be owned or controlled by private interests like the mining and timber industries. Rather, government should retain ownership of these lands and resources for the benefit of the public and to protect them from private claims and unregulated use. By 1900, the government had set aside 3.5 million acres (1.4 million hectares) in five national parks and about 50 million acres (20 million hectares) in forty forest reserves. Although the parks and forest reserves were protected from settlement or other private interests, the government could still decide, on a case-by-case basis, whether specific lands should be used for their resources or completely protected from development.

Disagreement over the management and use of these parks and forest reserves during this period led to a separation between the conservation and preservation movements. Conservationists believed in the scientific management and careful use of natural resources; preservationists believed in preserving portions of the forests and wild lands for their scenic and wilderness values. For example, conservationists were willing to allow regulated cattle and sheep grazing on public lands (rather than permitting unlimited free use, which was the practice of the day), whereas preservationists did not want to allow such grazing because it caused too much damage to the forests.

Influences. Contemporary scientific and literary ideas influenced the conservation and preservation movements. The idea that society had a responsibility to wisely use and restore natural resources was first made popular by George Perkins Marsh in his epic work, *Man and Nature* (1864). This popular book (*see also* 110) inspired both movements and helped educate the public about the harm caused by the destruction of forests and the abuse of the nation's natural resources. The preservation movement also was inspired by the leaders of American transcendentalism (*see also* 50–51), Ralph Waldo Emerson and Henry David Thoreau. The transcendentalists emphasized the spiritual rather than material values of wild nature and the need to protect forests and wild places for recreation and contemplation.

John Muir. The leading voice and public advocate for the preservation movement was John Muir. After making his home in California's Yosemite Valley and the high Sierra in 1869, Muir explored and studied the geology and flora of the region and

Hetch Hetchy Valley Dispute

The defining moment for the young conservation and preservation movements was the battle over the use of Yosemite's Hetch Hetchy Valley. This political fight reflected the conflicting ideas about the primary purpose of national parks and monuments nationwide.

In 1907, the city of San Francisco renewed its request to dam the Tuolumne River in the Hetch Hetchy Valley for a new source of water within Yosemite National Park. The Hetch Hetchy Valley was considered by many to be equal to Yosemite Valley in beauty and grandeur. Despite all the efforts of John Muir and the Sierra Club, which generated a huge national opposition to and public outcry against the dam, Congress approved the proposal to flood the valley in 1913. The flooding destroyed the valley's native environment and permanently changed its character.

The preservationists' losing battle to preserve Yosemite's Hetch Hetchy Valley was not merely a dispute over the use of the land; more broadly, it was a philosophical disagreement between the conservation and preservation movements best exemplified by Muir and Gifford Pinchot, who served as chief forester under President Theodore Roosevelt. Pinchot believed that all land and resources should be managed "for the greatest good to the greatest number for the longest time." In other words, he felt that natural resources should be efficiently developed for the present generation, and "not merely for the profit of a few." Although Muir agreed with Pinchot that the forests and wild lands should be developed for their material resources (water, timber, minerals, or electric power), he also believed that some portions of forests and wild lands should be preserved solely for their beauty and spiritual value. According to Muir, "specimen" places—"bits of pure wildness"—should be protected and remain undisturbed for future generations.

This philosophical divide—between conservation as development and preservation as sanctuary—remains to this day. The debate over whether to drill for oil in the Arctic National Wildlife Refuge was yet another chapter in this dispute. Preservationists saw the Refuge as one of the last remaining wild places on the North Slope of Alaska, while conservationists saw the proposed oil exploration as affecting only a small portion of the designated Refuge.

refined his new appreciation for the western wilderness. To Muir, mountain wilderness was a sacred place—to revere, not exploit. He recognized that people needed wilderness to escape the pressures of modern life and that mountains and forests are not only important sources of material resources but are also "fountains of life." Muir was angered by the unrestrained and unregulated logging, sheep grazing, and fires that were devastating the region around Yosemite Valley, the giant sequoia trees, and the beauty of the Sierra. He began to write against the destruction he was witnessing and urged the protection of these important areas.

National Parks. Partly as a result of Muir's writing and the advocacy of the emerging preservation movement, Congress began to establish parks well before the creation of the National Park Service in 1916. In 1872, Yellowstone was created in Wyoming with about 2.2 million acres (0.9 hectare) and, in 1890, Yosemite was created with about 1.5 million acres (0.6 million hectares) around the Sierra Valley. Sequoia and General Grant National Parks were also created in 1890 to protect the Sierra's sequoia trees.

The seemingly insoluble conflict between the demand to protect the nation's forests and local opposition to "locking up" natural resources made establishing new

Further Reading

Fox, Stephen. *John Muir and His Legacy: The American Conservation Movement.* Boston: Little, Brown, 1981.

Miller, Char. *Gifford Pinchot and the Making of Modern Environmentalism.* Washington, D.C.: Island Press, 2001.

Muir, John. *Our National Parks.* 1901. Reprint, San Francisco: Sierra Club Books, 1991.

Nash, Roderick. *Wilderness and the American Mind.* New Haven, Conn.: Yale University Press, 1982.

Runte, Alfred. *National Parks: The American Experience.* Lincoln: University of Nebraska Press, 1997.

Udall, Stewart. *The Quiet Crisis.* New York: Avon, 1970.

parks increasingly difficult for Congress. Accordingly, supporters of public protection for the parks and forests slipped a seemingly innocuous section into the Land Revision Act of 1891. Until its repeal in 1907, this act gave the president the authority to retain any forestland as a public reservation and allowed the president to lead national efforts to protect America's forests and wild lands. The creation of forest reserves under the Land Revision Act helped protect city water supplies, limit sheep grazing, and prevent valuable forests from being claimed by private timber companies, railroads, or land speculators. The lands reserved under this act from 1891 to 1907 now compose a large portion of the National Forest System and also some of America's most well-known national parks: Bryce Canyon in Utah, Crater Lake in Oregon, Grand Canyon in Arizona, Grand Teton in Wyoming, and Mount Rainier and Olympic in Washington, to name a few.

Sierra Club. To increase public support for the establishment and protection of these new parks and forest reserves, in 1892 Muir and some friends organized the Sierra Club, one of the nation's first environmental groups, to defend the mountain regions of the Pacific Coast. Since its founding, the Sierra Club has actively lobbied to protect national parks and monuments such as Yosemite, Dinosaur (*see also* 146), and the Grand Canyon from damming; national forests from indiscriminate logging and grazing; and, most recently, Alaska's Arctic National Wildlife Refuge (*see also* 184–85) from oil drilling.

Conflicting Views. Acrimony between the conservation and preservation movements continued, in part because the government, when creating the first national parks and forest reserves, did not clearly specify how they should be managed. With no clear consensus on how to carefully use natural resources and still preserve the beauty and wildness of national parks and

John Muir. (*From the collections of the Library of Congress*)

forests, public debate among members of Congress, government officials, and concerned citizens like Muir intensified. The passage of the Antiquities Act in 1906, which allowed the president to designate national monuments for "the proper care and management" of "historic landmarks, historic and prehistoric structures, and other objects of historic or scientific interest," brought the protection of land and its resources under the control of the government and ultimately led to the establishment of the National Park Service. The battle in the early twentieth century over the use and management of the Hetch Hetchy Valley in Yosemite National Park epitomized the divergent views of the conservation and preservation movements.

The visionary and tireless efforts of Muir and the early preservation movement laid the foundation for the wilderness and environmental movements to come. These early preservationists saw forests, not lumber; mountain meadows, not sheep pastures; wild rivers, not dams and reservoirs. They passionately believed that in "wildness lies the hope of the world . . ." and today their legacy can be found in the nation's monuments, forests, and national parks.

—*Ronald Eber*

The Boundary Waters Treaty of 1909:
An Expression of Progressivism

The purpose of the Boundary Waters Treaty of 1909 and the International Joint Commission (IJC) it established was to help resolve water-related disputes between Canada and the United States. Both the treaty and the IJC reflect the sensibilities and concerns of the first two decades of the twentieth century, known as the Progressive Era. Now approaching one hundred years of age, the commission and the treaty remain the primary instruments for managing shared water resources along the U.S.–Canada border.

Progressivism. The Progressive Era was a period of substantial social, industrial, and economic evolution in both Canada and the United States. Progressive reform was pervasive and included labor legislation intended to protect children and women from abusive work situations and antitrust legislation designed to ensure greater economic competition. The most fundamental development was the emergence of a range of new professions intended to manage the social, technical, and political problems of the day. Progressives believed that nonpartisan,

professionally trained experts, engineers, doctors, lawyers, and planners, for example, were best suited to manage society. Significant political reforms of the period placed technical experts in decision-making positions to reduce corruption and increase government efficiency.

Shared Water Management. The Boundary Waters Treaty of 1909 emerged out of this Progressive approach to resource management. When the treaty was being discussed and negotiated, the United States and Canada had many unresolved water-related issues. Most of these concerns fell into one of two categories: equitable allocation of water from rivers in the arid West that originated on one side of the border and flowed across the international boundary, (two such rivers were the St. Mary and Milk Rivers that began in Montana and flowed northeast into the Canadian provinces of Alberta and Saskatchewan); and equitable distribution of hydroelectric generating capacity in the Great Lakes basin, especially at Niagara Falls, located on the border, between Ontario and New York state.

In 1903, the two governments convened an International Waterways Commission to address the question of sharing water resources that crossed the boundary and equitably apportioning the hydroelectric potential at Niagara Falls. Although some members wished to treat each issue separately, the majority believed that a comprehensive approach that addressed current concerns and made provisions for the future was the best solution. The federal governments appointed two commissioners as negotiators: George Gibbons for Canada and George Clinton for the United States. The two men set out to draft an instrument that would guide nonpartisan, technical experts as they managed the shared water resources of Canada and the United States.

Boundary Waters Treaty. On January 11, 1909, Secretary of State Elihu Root and Britain's High Commissioner to the United States James Bryce, acting on behalf of Canada, signed the Treaty between the United Kingdom and the United States of America Relating to Boundary Waters and Questions Arising along the Boundary between Canada and the United States (known as the Boundary Waters Treaty of 1909). The treaty, which defined boundary waters as those waters along the international border, addressed issues relating to boundary waters as well as water (generally rivers) that crossed the boundary. With the exception of preexisting agreements, the treaty established that the governments would not allow any use, obstruction, or diversion that affected the "natural level or flow" of shared bodies of water without the approval of an appointed body of technical experts. The treaty addressed the apportionment of rivers flowing across the international boundary in

The Boundary Waters Treaty addressed the equitable distribution of the hydroelectric generating capacity of Niagara Falls, located on the U.S.–Canada border. (From the collections of the Library of Congress)

Article IV of the Boundary Waters Treaty

"It is further agreed that the waters herein defined as boundary waters and waters flowing across the boundary shall not be polluted on either side to the injury of health or property on the other."—*Article IV, Boundary Waters Treaty of 1909*

Arguably the most significant task the International Joint Commission (IJC) faces today is related to its work with pollution of and in boundary waters. Yet the basis for its authority for this work, the pollution clause in Article IV of the Boundary Waters Treaty of 1909, was added almost as an afterthought. The most pressing issues during treaty negotiations were the power generation potential at Niagara Falls and how to equitably distribute the flow of western streams for agricultural purposes.

Had pollution and human health been the main reasons for the treaty, the U.S. Senate likely would not have ratified it. When the Senate deliberated on the treaty in January 1909, several senators objected to the pollution clause in Article IV. They were concerned that the clause might be used to force large U.S. cities along the border, such as Detroit, Michigan, and Buffalo, New York, to assume expensive sewage disposal projects. The Canadian explanation that it would be enforced only in extreme cases mollified the senators. The U.S. Department of State hastened to add that the IJC would have no jurisdiction in this matter; rather, the U.S. and Canadian governments would impose the pollution clause themselves. Furthermore, a Department of State memo noted, Article IV would apply only to cases where pollution on one side of the border could be proved to have damaged health or property on the other side and the scientific evidence of the day made such proof very unlikely.

Ironically, in 1912 the IJC's first investigation was concerned with boundary water pollution. Furthermore, despite the earlier State Department assurances, the commission discovered that pollution released on one side of the international boundary was indeed affecting the health and property of people on the other side. Over the next fifty years the IJC investigated pollution several more times, culminating in the first Great Lakes Water Quality Agreement of 1972 (*see also* 166–67), which laid out a framework for eliminating current and preventing future pollution in those boundary waters.

roles for resolving border disputes. The process that the commission chose to carry out its investigative function best exemplifies the Progressive influence on the IJC. Under Article IX of the Boundary Waters Treaty, either the U.S. or Canadian government could ask the commission to examine any matter arising along the common border. The first such investigation, or reference, was to examine boundary waters pollution in 1912. Upon receipt of a request, the IJC assembled an international reference board (normally composed of equal numbers of Canadian and U.S. experts). Members of the study team did not represent their individual agencies but served in the "personal and professional" capacity. The international study team then collected the core data, assessed it, and made recommendations to the IJC. After receiving and reviewing the recommendations, the commission then asked for public input. The IJC then developed a set of recommendations for the two governments based upon the recommendations and public reaction. The IJC still carries out its business according to the pattern adopted during its first investigation into boundary waters pollution in 1912.

—Jennifer Read

the West and established how much of the Niagara River's flow could be diverted for hydroelectric power. The treaty also committed the two governments to avoid polluting waters on one side of the boundary to the "injury of health and property" on the other. Finally, the treaty established a hierarchy of uses for boundary waters—first, domestic and sanitary uses; then navigation; finally, power and irrigation—to help facilitate decision making.

The Progressive movement's influence on the Boundary Waters Treaty can be seen in the drafters' approach to managing shared water resources. The treaty established rules that could be applied to new situations as they arose. For instance, the negotiators hoped that by setting a hierarchy of uses for

waters, little room would be left for political machinations. Perhaps the most significant decision, however, was the establishment of the International Joint Commission (IJC).

International Joint Commission. The IJC consisted of six commissioners, three each appointed by the two federal governments. The first commissioners appointed in 1912 were engineers, lawyers, and technical experts. The IJC acted as a single body, reaching decisions by consensus and presenting joint reports to the two governments. Both characteristics are typical of Progressives' belief in the need for nonpartisan decision making and their faith in the ability of technical people to achieve that goal.

The Boundary Waters Treaty granted the IJC administrative, arbitral, and investigative

Further Reading

Chambers, John Whiteclay, II. *The Tyranny of Change: America in the Progressive Era, 1900–1917*. New Brunswick, N.J.: Rutgers University Press, 2000.

Hays, Samuel P. *Conservation and the Gospel of Efficiency: The Progressive Conservation Movement, 1890–1920*. 1959. Reprint, Pittsburgh: University of Pittsburgh Press, 1999.

Nelles, H. V., and Christopher Armstrong, "The Great Fight for Clean Government." *Urban History Review* 76 (1972): 50–66.

Read, Jennifer G. "'A Sort of Destiny': The Multi-jurisdictional Response to Sewage Pollution in the Great Lakes, 1900–1930." *Scientia Canadiensis* 51 (1999): 103–29.

Weaver, John C. "Order and Efficiency: Samuel Morely Wickett and the Urban Progressive Movement in Toronto, 1900–1915." *Ontario History* 69 (December 1977): 218–34.

CHAPTER FIVE

From the Depression to Atomic Power
(1930s–1960s)

n his much-acclaimed documentary, *The Plow That Broke the Plains* (1936), Pare Lorentz explored the interlocking causes of the 1930s Dust Bowl and its environmental costs. The film's opening voice-over focused the audience's attention on the land: "Four hundred million acres of windswept grass lands that spread up from the Texas panhandle to Canada—a high, treeless continent, without rivers, without streams . . . a country of high winds, and sun . . . and of little rain. . . . " As the title suggests, Lorentz laid the blame for the destruction on the sophisticated agricultural technology humans used to work the U.S. and Canadian Plains; at fault too was monoculture farming that leached nutrients out of the once-rich topsoil and inefficient plowing techniques that allowed wind and rain to sweep more soil away. Unable to grow crops amid swirling clouds of dust, farm families throughout the North American breadbasket were forced to abandon their homes in search of work in nearby cities or in distant states or provinces.

Lorentz did not just record this calamity, his film—which was underwritten by the U.S. Department of Agriculture (USDA)—also proposed a set of possible solutions, including the implementation of more conservation-oriented farming practices; the intervention of newly invigorated federal agencies to underwrite the reconstruction of agrarian communities and economies; and a reenergized citizenry committed to repairing a battered land. Out of despair would come hope.

Investment in the Land. The hope was not misplaced; New Deal programs and legislation in the United States focused on the restoration of the environment and the people dependent upon it. Decades of poor agricultural output had prompted the USDA to promote scientific research and investment in more powerful chemical fertilizers, activity that intensified after World War II. Hoping to forestall damaging floods that periodically ravaged western and midwestern river basins, the U.S. Department of the Interior spent millions of dollars constructing a network of monumental dams that controlled water flow and provided much-needed hydroelectric power along the Tennessee, Missouri, and Columbia Rivers.

Wildlife management also received a boost. Among those advocating greater attention to this area was ecologist Aldo Leopold. In the United States, his ideas influenced the Pittman–Robertson Act (1937), congressional legislation that turned the proceeds of a federal tax on the sale of ammunition and hunting weapons over to the states to restore wild lands and to restock fish and other declining populations of fauna. Canadians were just as alarmed as U.S. citizenry about the loss of habitat: In 1947 the Canadian federal government established the Dominion (now Canadian) Wildlife Service.

When confronted with unprecedented demand for Canadian wood during World War II, the provincial and federal governments initiated some of the first experiments in sustainable forestry. They hoped to ensure a steady supply of timber without destroying the forests. Not until the late 1970s, when British Columbia adopted a more ecological form of forest management, did sustainable forestry prove worthy of the name.

At the close of World War II, a larger, more prosperous middle class emerged. With greater leisure and more disposable income, they traveled to nearby lakes, streams, and parks; they loaded up their cars and went on extended tours of each nation's park systems. Those who had long advocated the preservation of wilderness now found that they had a larger audience who could put pressure on legislators to enact conservation-friendly legislation.

Consequences of Postwar Growth. Intertwined with these indisputable successes were a series of disturbing costs. The escalating expenses associated with the chemically derived recovery of North American agriculture contributed to the dominance of large agribusinesses, making small family farms relics of the past. As Rachel Carson discovered while writing *Silent Spring* (1962), modern agriculture's heavy reliance on fertilizers and pesticides was a kind of black thumb: Chemical fertilizers and pesticides degraded underground water supplies, polluted streams, and destroyed the reproductive capacities of certain animals. Other fauna were damaged with the erection of the massive dam and flood-control complexes in the U.S. West. These structures altered stream flow and temperature, which often caused die offs among indigenous fish populations and disrupted their migratory patterns.

The development of nuclear weapons and energy during the Cold War brought with them the possibility of consequences more dire even than ecosystem degradation and destruction. The United States and Canada poured billions of dollars into the establishment and spread of this industry.

Automobile traffic clogging a Philadelphia highway in the 1950s.
(© H. Armstrong Roberts/Corbis)

However, the 1952 partial meltdown of the Chalk River energy plant in Ottawa, Ontario, brought home the environmental threats of nuclear power and weaponry.

After the war, the environment in both Canada and the United States was faced with new problems. The economies of both countries were driven by consumer desires that constantly produced a new set of goods, easily purchased and as easily disposed. The advent of plastics and synthetics, for instance, lowered prices of furniture, toys, and other domestic products; as demand for these products skyrocketed, synthetic and plastic items contributed to greater economic development. Because these items were cheap—in all senses of the word—as they broke or fell out of fashion, they were simply discarded; by the late 1960s, many cities were in desperate need of new garbage dumps and landfills.

The automobile also clogged the urban environment. With the signing of the Trans-Canada Highway Act (1949) and the U.S. Federal-Aid Highway Act (1956), the two nations committed extraordinary funding to the construction of an automotive landscape. Freeways and toll routes increased the tempo of intra- and international commerce, accelerated industrial development, contributed to urban and suburban sprawl, and facilitated military defense plans. No sector of the United States was more affected by these alterations than the Sunbelt, a curve of states running from Virginia to California; its population soared in response to rapid economic expansion, growth that came with tremendous social ramifications and environmental costs.

While granting greater mobility to some, the new superhighways and expressways cut through and often isolated or destroyed poor neighborhoods, intensifying class and racial segregation; as they united disparate parts of Canada and the United States, and provided greater access to wild spaces, they also bulldozed through deserts, meadows, and wetlands. In helping to build the glittering, steel-and-glass skylines of Toronto and Vancouver, Houston and Los Angeles, the car also wrapped them in a smoggy haze. During this Atomic Age, North Americans were faced with a series of difficult choices.

—*Char Miller*

The Dust Bowl in the Great Plains

The "Dust Bowl" was the term coined for the nearly ten years of drought, dust storms, and high temperatures that the people of the Great Plains endured in the 1930s. Although all of the Great Plains experienced drought during that decade, the worst of the drought and dirt storms were concentrated in the Southern Plains, in an area including parts of Kansas, Oklahoma, Texas, New Mexico, and Colorado. This environmental crisis significantly affected the land and the people of the Southern Plains.

Causes. The Dust Bowl had a number of causes. The area is semiarid, receiving little rain—generally less than 20 inches (0.5 meter) yearly. The area's soils are light and easily blown by the high spring winds. During the 1930s, the area experienced extreme drought conditions, which were exacerbated by some of the highest summer temperatures on record. In southwestern Kansas, for example, rainfall for the decade averaged 20 percent below normal and, in some years, 50 percent below normal. In the summer of 1934, residents endured fifty days of temperatures at or above 100°F (38°C). The earth, normally dry, was baked and blown into a fine powder.

Drought and high temperatures alone were a recipe for disaster, but farming practices of the previous two decades made the situation considerably worse. During the 1910s and 1920s, farmers had plowed many acres of land previously left fallow or devoted to pasture for cattle. In 1890, only 5,762 farms and ranches were located in areas that would be affected by the Dust Bowl in Kansas, Colorado, and Texas. By 1910, this number had nearly doubled to 11,422. Most farmers developed their land without attention to conservation practices

like crop rotation and terracing and plowed to the very edges of their property in their eagerness to make a profit. Land that was already dry and sandy was no longer anchored by native grasses, making it particularly susceptible to wind erosion. This resulted in day after day of dirt storms, ranging from a simple haze of dirt in the air to rolling black storms that blotted out the Sun. During one particularly bad dust storm in 1935, geologists in Wichita, Kansas, estimated that 5 million tons of dust were suspended over the city. Breathing this fine dirt led to respiratory ailments, for example, dust pneumonia in humans, and caused the deaths of untold numbers of cattle and other livestock.

Impact. The costs were enormous, in human, economic, and environmental terms. During the Dust Bowl, thousands left the Great Plains. The population of Dust Bowl counties, on average, fell 25 percent, with 50 percent or more leaving in particularly hard-hit areas, including

Morton County, Kansas, and Baca County, Colorado. Those abandoning their farms most commonly made their way west to California, Oregon, and Washington. Those that remained endured a decade of hardships. Between the poor yields caused by the drought and the low prices paid for crops during the Great Depression, Dust Bowl farmers could not grow enough to meet the costs of production, let alone feed and clothe their families.

Conservation Initiatives. These farmers survived the decade because of the availability of New Deal farm programs like the Agricultural Adjustment Administration (AAA), established in 1933, and the Soil Conservation Service (SCS), established in 1935. The AAA paid farmers to restrict their production, and the SCS paid farmers to implement soil conservation on their farms. In 1936, for example, federal money allowed Dust Bowl farmers to apply conservation tillage to 4,469,270 acres (1,808,714 hectares) of land.

A farmer and his sons walk through a dust storm in Oklahoma. (From the collections of the Library of Congress)

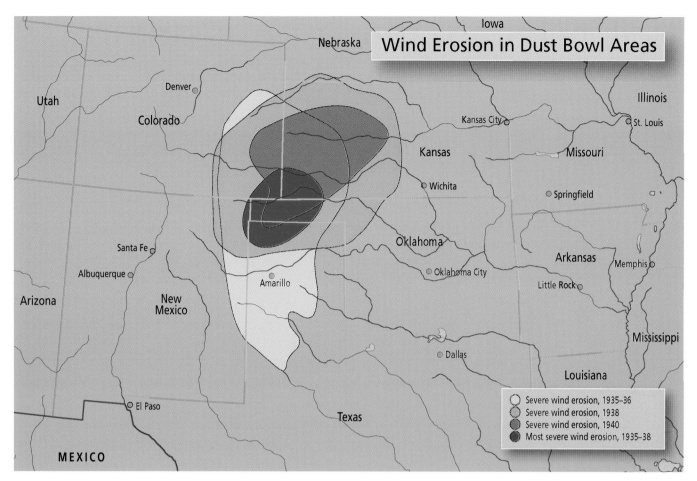

Although the exact boundaries of the Dust Bowl shifted from year to year, at least a portion of the Southern Plains remained subject to severe wind erosion throughout the decade.
Source: Adapted from Donald Worster, *Dust Bowl: The Southern Plains in the 1930s* (New York: Oxford University Press, 1982), 30. Used by permission of Oxford University Press, Inc.

Improved conservation practices initiated by New Deal programs, combined with increasing rainfall, helped to end the Dust Bowl by 1941. With the higher prices grain brought during World War II, the area returned to prosperity. Nevertheless, the Dust Bowl area still had soil susceptible to high winds and drought was always a

Further Reading

Hurt, R. Douglas. *The Dust Bowl: An Agricultural and Social History.* Chicago: Nelson-Hall, 1981.
Opie, John. *Ogallala: Water for a Dry Land.* 2nd ed. Lincoln: University of Nebraska Press, 2000.
Riney-Kehrberg, Pamela. *Rooted in Dust: Surviving Drought and Depression in Southwestern Kansas.* Lawrence: University Press of Kansas, 1994.
Worster, Donald. *Dust Bowl: The Southern Plains in the 1930s.* New York: Oxford University Press, 1982.

possibility. In the 1950s, rainfall was scant, and Dust Bowl conditions returned. Between 1952 and 1956, 12.9 million acres (5.2 million hectares) of land were blowing dust and had suffered damage from wind erosion. An even greater number of acres, 13.5 million (5.5 million hectares), had the potential to blow. Farmers and ranchers turned to the U. S. Department of Agriculture and Soil Conservation Service for help, and some began irrigating their lands as a means of mastering the drought. By the late 1950s, the crisis was over.

Reliance on Irrigation. In the years since, the Southern Plains have never experienced such a sustained period of drought, and farmers have increasingly relied on irrigation (*see also* 90–91) to water their crops and anchor their soil. Although flying soil occasionally darkens the region's sky, such

occurrences have been rare. The threat has not necessarily passed, however. Farmers have pinned their hopes of a continuing water supply on the Ogallala aquifer (a large underground lake) that underlies a significant portion of the Southern Plains. The Ogallala is an enormous aquifer, but it has also faced enormous use; between 1960 and 1990, irrigators used more than half a billion acre-feet (enough water to cover an acre of land to a depth of 1 foot [0.3 meter]) of water. Irrigators pump out many acre-feet of water per year; however, replacement water accumulates at a rate of less than 1 acre-inch (103 cubic-meters) per year. Given the finite state of the aquifer, the region's environmental limitations, and farmers' reliance on irrigated agriculture, the potential for another Dust Bowl is very real.

—*Pamela Riney-Kehrberg*

Chemicalization of Agriculture in the United States

From the 1930s to the 1960s, chemicals revolutionized agriculture in the United States. These decades saw exponential growth in the production and use of synthetic chemical fertilizers, pesticides, and herbicides. By the end of the 1960s, the combined forces of the farm economy, the Department of Agriculture, and the chemical industry had established the use of agrichemicals as the dominant practice in U.S. agriculture. However, beginning in the early 1960s, as the environment began to show signs of contamination and degradation, protesters questioned the effects of agricultural chemicals on the health of both wildlife and humans.

Early Chemical Uses. The composition and application of these new chemicals differed greatly from most previous fertilization and agricultural pest control methods. Fertilizers, for example, originally came from the natural by-products of animal manure and other farm waste. Commercial fertilizers, however, were composed primarily of industrial compounds containing nitrogen, calcium phosphate, and potassium chloride. Chemical fertilizers were initially valuable for the production of high-yield crops; farming for high yields, however, leads to crop specialization, or monocultural farming. Crops so fertilized, however, were especially vulnerable to weed and insect infestations. In a vicious cycle, farmers depended on large applications of chemical herbicides and pesticides to preserve the higher yields gained from using artificial fertilizers in the first place.

The 1930s saw the Dust Bowl (*see also* 120–21) and the Great Depression, which caused great suffering in farm country; problems ranged from the environmental (e.g., insect infestations) to economic (e.g., weak markets for crops). Farmers had long used earlier forms of chemical pesticides like copper arsenite and lead arsenate. These pesticides were most effective on produce crops, rather than grains, and, increasingly, consumers and government regulators feared that arsenical pesticide residues were unsafe. The government repeatedly seized shipments of fruit that contained high residues of arsenic.

Growth. The circumstances and chemical technologies of World War II provided new answers. During the early 1940s, the war resulted in increased demand for farm products, especially as war-torn Europe sought U.S. agricultural surpluses. Farmers looked to science and technology to help them meet these demands; farm productivity rose by 11 percent, while the acreage under production rose only 5 percent. Rising productivity was attributable to increased use of chemicals. For example, farmers began to use lime to reduce soil acidity and enhance the action of fertilizers. To increase soil productivity, they began to apply phosphates and nitrogen. Mechanization and hybrid seeds also contributed to rising crop yields. In addition, the burgeoning defense industries generated a revolution in agrichemical technologies. For example, the wartime development and use of DDT to control insects translated into postwar sales of DDT to eager domestic markets, despite early concerns about the pesticide's effects on humans and animals. In general, many of the toxic pesticides, fungicides, and herbicides were derived from the by-products of petrochemical manufacturing.

The pesticide industry also experienced enormous growth after World War II. In 1950, pesticide production registered 300 million pounds (140 million

A rancher sprays cattle with DDT solution, which was used to ward off flies and ticks. (© Corbis)

AGRICULTURE

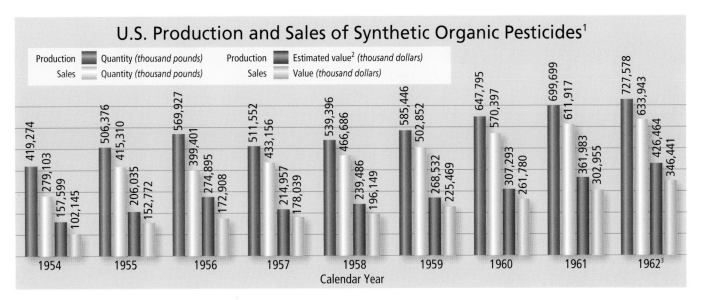

U.S. Production and Sales of Synthetic Organic Pesticides[1]

		Production	Quantity (thousand pounds)		Production	Estimated value[2] (thousand dollars)
		Sales	Quantity (thousand pounds)		Sales	Value (thousand dollars)

1954: 419,274 · 279,103 · 157,599 · 102,145
1955: 506,376 · 415,310 · 206,035 · 152,772
1956: 569,927 · 399,401 · 274,895 · 172,908
1957: 511,552 · 433,156 · 214,957 · 178,039
1958: 539,396 · 466,686 · 239,486 · 196,149
1959: 585,446 · 502,852 · 268,532 · 225,469
1960: 647,795 · 570,397 · 307,293 · 261,780
1961: 699,699 · 611,917 · 361,983 · 302,955
1962[3]: 727,578 · 633,943 · 426,464 · 346,441

Calendar Year

[1]Includes a small proportion of plant hormones and soil conditioners. [2]Calculated from unit sales value, manufacturers' level. [3]Preliminary, at time of reporting.
In the postwar United States, the use and production of chemicals in agriculture increased enormously. For example, between 1954 and 1962 the value of sales of synthetic organic pesticides more than tripled. This rapid growth challenged government regulators' ability to oversee the many new chemicals spreading throughout the environment.
Source: Data from Senate Subcommittee on Reorganization and International Organizations of the Committee on Government Operations, Interagency Coordination in Environmental Hazards, 88th Cong., 1st sess., 1963, 8–9. Underlying data from U.S. Tariff Commission, *Synthetic Organic Chemicals, U.S. Production and Sales* (Washington, D.C.: Government Printing Office, n.d.).

kilograms); by the end of the decade, that figure had doubled. Massive production, limited government supervision, and extensive public use made the 1950s the golden age of pesticides. The political farm bloc, a small elite group of senior senators and representatives from farming regions, stymied attempts to regulate these chemicals. Administrators in the Department of Agriculture also resisted reforms from other arms of the government, such as the Food and Drug Administration and the Public Health Service, while chemical corporations such as DuPont, Monsanto, and Union Carbide forged powerful connections with researchers at various universities and land grant colleges. Government officials, industry representatives, and many research scientists shared the belief that through agricultural chemicals, humans could control nature.

Impact. Over time, the continued use of agricultural chemicals began to reveal its dangers, as new chemical technologies caused large crop surpluses that drove down prices, bankrupted many small farmers, and ultimately created unemployment and economic uncertainty in farm regions. Between 1951 and 1956, operating expenses held steady or increased, while crop prices declined by 23 percent. New and costly agricultural chemicals required different machinery for their application. These expenses weighed down many small farmers with enormous debt, forcing them to look to the government for price supports, marketing aid, and production control programs. Many farmers nevertheless lost their farms. This cycle led to the growth of large corporate ownership of farm operations, a process still ongoing today.

Along with their unexpected long-term impacts on the farm economy, by the 1960s, agricultural chemicals had created other dangers. Rachel Carson's 1962 bestseller *Silent Spring* (*see also* 140–41) inspired a backlash against the indiscriminate use of pesticides, particularly in industrial agriculture. Carson and later environmentalists pointed to the disastrous effects of pesticides on wild and domestic animals, such as during campaigns to eradicate fire ants in the South. Agricultural use of chemicals had spread them widely through the environment (e.g., in rivers, streams, and lakes), raising fears about their long-term effects on human health.

As a result of such problems, gardening without the use of pesticides, or organic farming (*see also* 172–73), gained a following. However, most Americans remained ignorant of problems associated with agricultural chemicals, and, politically, the farm bloc remained in power. Until the last part of the twentieth century, regulation of agrichemicals was basically nonexistent.

—*Maril Hazlett*

Further Reading
Bosso, Christopher. *Pesticides and Politics: The Life Cycle of a Public Issue.* Pittsburgh: University of Pittsburgh Press, 1987.
Hurt, R. Douglas. *Agricultural Technology in the Twentieth Century.* Manhattan, Kan.: Sunflower University Press, 1991.
———. *American Agriculture: A Brief History.* Ames: Iowa State University Press, 1994.
Russell, Edmund. *War and Nature: Fighting Humans and Insects with Chemicals from World War I to Silent Spring.* Cambridge: Cambridge University Press, 2001.

Game Management

ame and wildlife management has gone through two stages of development in Canada and the United States. The first stage began in the 1800s with wildlife preservation (*see also* 96–97) and cataloging, as well as some later attempts at propagation. By the early 1900s, federal and local governments had fully embraced game management practices aimed at producing sustained populations of wild game for recreational hunting and fishing. When the American forester Aldo Leopold developed a broader, ecological outlook on wilderness and game in the 1940s, he formulated the theories upon which the second and present stage is based.

Early Developments. During the first stage of game management, migratory birds were the focus of legislation in both countries. The United States created the first federal wildlife refuge in 1903 specifically for birds; Canada followed suit a dozen years later with its first bird sanctuaries. The two countries signed the Migratory Bird Treaty in 1916. This act recognized the need to protect migratory birds like geese on a continental scale because their ranges often crossed the border between Canada and the United States.

Game management in both countries emphasized propagation (mostly through artificial restocking) to produce game for hunting or for replenishing endangered species. Game management also included controlling or eradicating predators like cougars, wolves, and coyotes to protect game. In the 1910s, this policy led to ecological disasters like the one at the Kaibab Plateau preserve near the Grand Canyon where the government encouraged the elimination of predators. At Kaibab, the protected but uncontrolled deer population increased so much that by 1924, the deer overwhelmed their

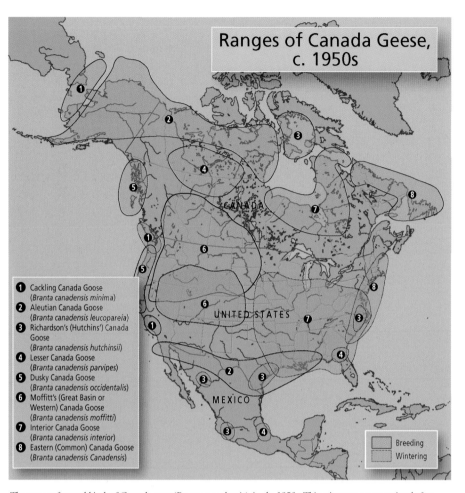

Ranges of Canada Geese, c. 1950s

❶ Cackling Canada Goose (*Branta canadensis minima*)
❷ Aleutian Canada Goose (*Branta canadensis leucopareia*)
❸ Richardson's (Hutchins') Canada Goose (*Branta canadensis hutchinsii*)
❹ Lesser Canada Goose (*Branta canadensis parvipes*)
❺ Dusky Canada Goose (*Branta canadensis occidentalis*)
❻ Moffitt's (Great Basin or Western) Canada Goose (*Branta canadensis moffitti*)
❼ Interior Canada Goose (*Branta canadensis interior*)
❽ Eastern (Common) Canada Goose (*Branta canadensis Canadensis*)

Breeding
Wintering

The ranges of several kinds of Canada geese (Branta canadensis) *in the 1950s. This migratory game animal often breeds in Canada and winters in the United States, thus requiring international cooperation in game management.*
Source: Adapted from Ruben Edwin Trippensee, *Wildlife Management* (New York: McGraw-Hill, 1948–53), Fig. 19–7.

habitat and began starving to death by the thousands because predators no longer kept the deer population in check.

Leopold, while working as a forester for the U.S. Forest Service (*see also* 92–93), began his game management studies in 1915. Leopold left forestry in 1928 to develop the new profession of game management. He modeled it on the profession of forestry and rooted it in the U.S. Forest Service's concepts of wise use (scientific management of natural resources) and sustained yield (a renewable resource, whether an animal or plant, would replenish itself in perpetuity). If the public conserved the habitat of game animals, he argued, game populations could regenerate naturally.

He expressed support for controlling predators in *Game Management* (1933), which helped define the profession's first stage.

U.S. Game Management. In the United States the Wilderness Society and the Wildlife Society worked to increase wildlife populations and wild habitats. With several other citizen groups, they lobbied for the passage of new game management legislation. The Migratory Bird Hunting Stamp Act (1934), commonly known as the Duck Stamp Act, allowed the federal government to use the fees for hunting permits to purchase wetlands. Revenue from the permits helped protect more than 4.5 million acres (1.8 million hectares) of waterfowl habitat, and many of the more than 510 national wildlife refuges in all fifty states have been paid for, all or in part, by Duck Stamp money.

The 1937 Federal Aid in Wildlife Restoration Act (commonly known as the Pittman–Robertson Act) initiated a federal excise tax on sporting arms, handguns, ammunition, and archery equipment to be collected from the manufacturers and allotted annually to the states for projects in wildlife research and land management. During the 1940s, many states used the funds to develop and restock wildlife populations of deer, elk, antelope, and bear; between 1938 and 1948, thirty-eight states acquired almost 900,000 acres (364,000 hectares) of refuges and management areas. In 1950, based on the success of the Pittman-Robertson Act, Congress passed the Federal Aid in Fish Restoration Act to provide similar protection and management to sport fisheries.

As the U.S. government introduced new game management laws during the 1930s and 1940s, Leopold began to recognize that predators were crucial to keeping populations of deer and other browsing game under control. Nature, he realized, maintained its equilibrium when humans did not interfere too much. He made this argument in the important essay, "The Land Ethic," which appeared in his posthumous work, *A Sand County Almanac* (1949). He asserted that humans were "citizens" of the "land-community" who had a moral obligation to respect the land and not let economics or sentimentality drive management decisions that would destroy the ecological balance. Initially overlooked outside conservation circles until the paperback edition came out in 1966, *A Sand County Almanac* provided a catalyst for the environmental movement in the late 1960s and 1970s (*see also* 162–63). By the 1970s, the U.S. government had accepted Leopold's theories on ecological balance and began passing environmental protection laws that moved the nation into the second stage of game management.

Canadian Game Management. During the first stage of game management in Canada, in 1917 the government passed the Migratory Bird Convention Act to enforce the 1916 Migratory Bird Treaty and placed the Migratory Bird section within the Dominion Parks Branch of Canada's Department of Interior. The agency took charge of protecting migratory birds (waterfowl, cranes, rails, shorebirds, doves, insect-eating passerines, and seabirds) and regulated hunting. The agency was also asked to handle all wildlife administration in the Northwest Territories and became the Wild Life Protection Agency (WLPA) in 1918. The main priority of the WLPA until the 1950s would be the cataloging and inventorying of wildlife and other natural resources throughout Canada.

The federal government replaced the WLPA with the Dominion Wildlife Service (DWS) in 1947 as part of a government reorganization. Renamed the Canadian Wildlife Service (CWS) in 1950, its primary mission remains unchanged: administering the Migratory Bird Convention Act and conducting inventories of mammals, birds, and fish. Agency specialists also continued to provide advice on wildlife management to the National Parks Division. The CWS also offered coordination and advice on game management issues to provinces.

The agency faced its first significant challenge in 1949, when Newfoundland and Labrador entered the Canadian Confederation. Residents of Newfoundland relied on seabirds as their only source of fresh meat during the winter months, but

Canada's Migratory Birds Convention Act prohibited them from hunting this food staple. The resulting compromise, which allowed the regulated hunting of the murre, an abundant seabird, established a clear-cut distinction between a traditional harvest of food for subsistence and the practice of market hunting for profit. The former was permissible; the latter was forbidden. The distinction would serve as a foundation of the game policy in Canada thereafter.

In the late 1950s, the CWS began to reexamine its role in wildlife management. Policy slowly began evolving toward one based on ecological principles, one that recognized that human activity, especially hunting, had an impact on wildlife. The CWS not only had to address the effects of pollution on waterways and marine life, but also had to consider the rights and responsibilities of its aboriginal population in the management of wildlife resources. To accommodate expected policy changes and better coordinate fieldwork, the service reorganized itself in 1962 and split into western and eastern regional divisions.

Canada's creation of a system of National Wildlife Areas in 1967 was a tacit recognition of the growing importance of protecting habitats. But the CWS did not formally embrace an ecological approach until the 1970s, around the same time as the United States. Environmental advocates in both countries looked to Leopold's teachings and research for guidance in reformulating policy and made game management an integral part of land management.

—*James G. Lewis*

Further Reading
Burnett, J. Alexander. "A Passion for Wildlife: A History of the Canadian Wildlife Service, 1947–1997." *Canadian Field-Naturalist* 113, no. 1 (1999): 1–183.
Flader, Susan L. *Thinking Like a Mountain: Aldo Leopold and the Evolution of an Ecological Attitude toward Deer, Wolves, and Forests.* Madison: University of Wisconsin Press, 1994.

Leopold, Aldo. *Game Management.* 1933. Reprint, Madison: University of Wisconsin Press, 1986.
———. *A Sand County Almanac and Sketches Here and There.* 1949. Reprint, New York: Oxford University, 1989.
Reiger, John F. *American Sportsmen and the Origins of Conservation.* 3rd ed. Corvallis: Oregon State University Press, 2001.

Sustainable Forestry in British Columbia and Ontario

The unprecedented demand for wood during World War II prompted closer cooperation between provincial governments and private industry in Canada. At the heart of this cooperation lay the relatively new policy of sustainable forestry, which the government of British Columbia defined as "the establishment of a forest yield on a continuous production basis in perpetuity." British Columbia and Ontario both adopted sustainable forestry practices in hopes of keeping the timber industry healthy and capable of providing a permanent source of employment for workers and a steady flow of revenue to government coffers. The desire to keep the industry healthy meant, in reality, helping timber companies find new sources of timber to the detriment of the forests.

Lumber Industry. The stock market crash of 1929 and the Great Depression that followed dealt a crippling blow to the Canadian lumber industry in the early 1930s. But wood pulp soon became the basic material in many new processes: synthetic textiles like rayon; plastics; film; quick-drying lacquers; and packaging materials. By 1935, the lumber industry had stabilized. The outbreak of World War II in 1939 created an unprecedented demand for Canadian wood. During the war, wood harvesting and consumption hit record levels, and the wood industry operated at full capacity. Industry and government leaders alike expected all of this consumption and construction to continue after the war. They soon recognized, however, that the system of unrestrained and unregulated timber exploitation could eventually result in timber shortages and economic catastrophe.

British Columbia. To prevent such outcomes, in 1943 the government of British Columbia appointed Chief Justice Gordon Sloan of that province's supreme court to investigate and report on the forests and forest industry of the province. Sloan examined thirteen issues, the two most important being sustained forestry and forest tenure and licensing. The "Sloan Report" confirmed that sustained, or perpetual, yield from productive forests was essential to the economy. In response to these findings, in 1947 the provincial government passed an amendment to the Forest Act of 1912 with the support of the B.C. Forest Service.

The Forest Act amendment divided timberland into privately and publicly controlled areas. The Forest Service (*see also* 94–95) managed the public lands, but left the responsibility for managing private lands in the hands of the timber industry. The amendment permitted the province's minister of lands and forests, through the issuance of forest management licenses, "to enter into agreement with any person, whereby specified areas of Crown lands are reserved in perpetuity for the use of that person provided he so manages the forests that a sustained yield output will be assured." In other words, the government would own the land, but industry could cut trees as long as it promised to replant them. (Ontario followed suit that same year by passing its own version, called the Forest Management Act.) In

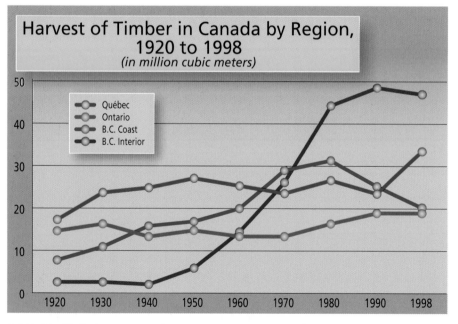

British Columbia has been a provincial leader in sustainable forestry for several decades. The close cooperation between government and industry is reflected in the rise in production of softwood for industrial needs like pulp and paper. Its timber industry expanded after World War II to the interior as newer mills were built closer to standing timber. British Columbia soon replaced Québec as the largest producer of softwood and roundwood. In 1987, it produced 2.7 times as much as Québec, 4 times as much as Ontario, and more than half of the Canadian total. British Columbia's contribution to the softwood harvest has since fallen to around 40 percent.
Source: Adapted from Les Reed, *Two Centuries of Softwood Lumber War between Canada and the United States: A Chronicle of Trade Barriers Viewed in the Context of Saw Timber Depletion* (Montreal: Free Trade Lumber Council, May 2001), 25.

1958, after Sloan issued a second report, the wording of the law was changed from "perpetual" use to a period of twenty-one years, thus giving the provincial government more control over forests. Even privately owned tree farms, operating under tree farm licenses, were to follow sustained yield management practices.

British Columbia's government facilitated forest work by providing funds for roads and other infrastructure but did not closely regulate private activity. Although sustainable forestry was supposed to protect forests, in reality it allowed business and government together to acquire wood to maintain jobs in the mills, while the public paid the cost of industrial expansion and social stability. As a result, lumber towns became even more dependent on business for survival. With the government unwilling or unable to restrain private industry, the system encouraged companies to continually seek new sources of timber. Few at the time realized that clearcutting old growth forests and replacing them with monoculture forests (one species of tree) destroyed biodiversity and created unhealthy forests.

In addition, the requirement to maintain sustainable forestry practices and the licensing system favored larger companies. Major outlays of capital were needed to erect pulp mills and sawmills, as well as to regularly update and modernize them. To remain profitable and competitive, companies merged or combined operations to lower their costs. Integration meant they made the greatest use of the trees cut by taking the waste from sawmills and from mills that produced lumber, plywood, and veneer wood, and shipping the waste to pulp mills to turn it into paper or other pulp products. Companies like Elk Falls, MacMillan-Bloedel, Crown Zellerbach, and B.C. Forest Products Ltd. were created during the 1940s and 1950s through

Further Reading

Apsey, Mike, et al. *The Perpetual Forest: Using Lessons from the Past to Sustain Canada's Forests in the Future*. Vancouver: FORCAST, 2000.

Gillis, R. Peter, and Thomas R. Roach. *Lost Initiatives: Canada's Forest Industries, Forest Policy, and Forest Conservation*. New York: Greenwood Press, 1986.

Marchak, Patricia. *Green Gold: The Forest Industry in British Columbia*. Vancouver: University of British Columbia Press, 1983.

Taylor, G. W. *Timber: History of the Forest Industry in B.C.* Vancouver: J. J. Douglas, 1975.

mergers and takeovers. B.C. Forest, for example, was formed in 1946 after Toronto businessman E. P. Taylor consolidated six different companies. Over the next ten years, Taylor's purchase of several logging and timber-holding companies to assure adequate supplies of timber further transformed the company and made B.C. Forest Products into one of the largest integrated operations in Canada by the 1960s.

Also during this period of consolidation, the lumber industry shifted from building sawmills to emphasizing pulp mills. Hundreds of older, less efficient sawmills were closed between the 1940s and the 1960s. Nevertheless, lumber production increased 50 percent or more during this time as a result of new technologies and the erection of highly automated mills. To supply the mills, company facilities moved closer to new stands of timber. For instance, prior to 1940 Vancouver had been the center of lumber processing, but by 1960 all of the large forestry companies had built new mills outside the Vancouver area where there was more wood. As a result, Port Alberni, located on central Vancouver Island, became a major industrial city devoted entirely to forestry.

Ontario. In Ontario, business needs also influenced government actions and policies. The public paid for infrastructure, while scientific forestry management took a backseat to profits and politics. The 1954 legislative report, "Suggestions for a Program of Renewable Resources Development," exacerbated the problem by documenting the coming shortage in southern Ontario and the need for new

timber sources. Instead of altering or rejecting the exploitative philosophy, the government responded by redirecting lumbering operations from the Ottawa valley to northern areas. In 1962, Ontario sought to undo the damage of the licensing system by passing the Crown Timber Act, which gave responsibility for regeneration to the government, and also launched major initiatives in site preparation, planting, and seeding. Despite its best efforts, Ontario found that regeneration lagged behind cutting and that it was fighting a losing battle.

Policy Changes. The failure of provincial governments to either pay the costs of effective management or force the timber companies to live up to their commitments allowed the shortcomings of sustainable forestry to go unaddressed. The further changes needed in the policies of both provinces to halt the destruction would not come until the 1970s. The 1978 British Columbia Ministry of Forests Act redefined its Forest Service mandate to include management of all aspects of the forest, a move that eventually led other provinces to adopt similar measures. The shift from sustainable forestry toward a more comprehensive ecological approach like that of British Columbia culminated in Ontario's embrace of full ecosystem management in 1994. Ultimately, greater provincial government control (about 95 percent of British Columbia's forests are owned by the province; in Ontario, nearly 90 percent) has benefited provincial forests.

—*James G. Lewis*

Western Dams in the United States

The great age of dam construction in the U.S. West spanned three decades, from the 1930s until the 1960s. It resulted in transformed river systems, strengthened regional economies, and substantial alterations to habitats of fish, birds, and a variety of plants and animals.

Dam Construction. Boulder Dam (renamed the Hoover Dam for Herbert Hoover in 1947) was the first dam built by the federal government during the Great Depression. Authorized by Congress in 1928 during the presidency of Calvin Coolidge, this massive gravity dam was constructed on the lower Colorado River (on the border of Arizona and Nevada) by more than five thousand workers between 1931 and 1935. It provided water and power to Los Angeles, flood control for California's Imperial Valley, and—through Lake Mead, formed by the dammed waters—outdoor recreation (*see also* 138–39) in the desert.

With the banking and construction industries severely affected by the Great Depression, the federal government subsidized Boulder Dam, as well as Grand Coulee Dam on the Columbia River in central Washington and Fort Peck Dam on the upper Missouri in eastern Montana. President Franklin D. Roosevelt knew that construction of these dams would employ thousands of workers. Drawing on funds of the Public Works Administration, he approved the Grand Coulee and Fort Peck Dams in 1933. These large-scale public works projects had twelve-thousand workers laboring on Grand Coulee and 10,500

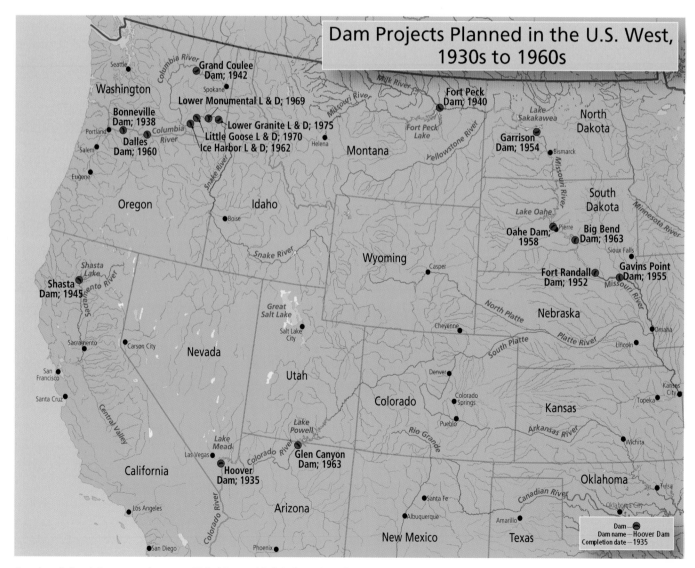

Location of selected dams across the western United States with their dates of completion.
Source: Adapted from Marc Reisner, *Cadillac Desert: The American West and Its Disappearing Water* (New York: Penguin, 1993).

on Fort Peck. Few minorities and no women found employment on these federal construction projects. The men who did toil on the huge dams faced injury and death in scaling cliffs, from falling rock, and from heavy equipment; ninety-six lost their lives while building Boulder Dam, and sixty-five perished at Grand Coulee.

World War II and the Cold War deepened the nation's commitment to water projects by placing a premium on inexpensive hydroelectric power (electricity generated by turbines within a dam). Grand Coulee Dam, which critics had earlier condemned as costly and financially unviable because of an inadequate market for its power, turned a profit and provided electricity during World War II. The electricity from Grand Coulee supported the rapid urban and industrial growth in the Pacific Northwest, particularly the aluminum and aircraft industries that flourished during this era. Other federal projects included Shasta Dam, the northern anchor of the vast Central Valley Project in California, completed in 1945, and several dams along the Missouri River authorized under the Flood Control Act of 1944, including Garrison Dam, Oahe Dam, Big Bend Dam, Fort Randall Dam, and Gavins Point Dam, which were completed in the 1950s and early 1960s.

Effects of Dams. The dams often enriched and stabilized surrounding cities and regions. For instance, Hoover Dam served greater Los Angeles with water and power (700,000 kilowatts in 1940) and the Missouri River dams eliminated destructive floods. These dams transformed free-flowing rivers, widely regarded as wasted natural resources, into human-controlled waterways that could supply water for irrigation (*see also* 90–91) to arid land and hydroelectric power to growing communities. The

reservoirs behind the dams offered fishing, boating, and swimming.

Although some areas benefited greatly, other areas, especially Native American communities, were harmed. In 1953, Garrison Dam on the Missouri River flooded 152,000 acres (61,500 hectares) belonging to the Three Affiliated Tribes in central North Dakota, lands on which native people gathered plants, cultivated gardens, and buried their dead. In 1940, on the Columbia River, the Grand Coulee Dam inundated a fishing site of the Colville tribe at Kettle Falls; in 1956, the Dalles Dam did the same at Celilo Falls in Oregon.

Many other dams had adverse environmental effects. Completion of Grand Coulee in 1942 blocked 1,000 miles (1,600 kilometers) of salmon habitat on the upper Columbia River, causing salmon populations to decline (*see also* 154–55). By the mid-1940s, a growing body of research showed that many juvenile salmon swimming downstream perished in the turbines of Bonneville Dam, located on the border of Oregon and Washington. In response, the U.S. Bureau of Reclamation and U.S. Army Corps of Engineers began transporting salmon in trucks around the Bonneville and Grand Coulee Dams, but salmon populations continued to decline. This raised concerns about the impact of the dams proposed on the Snake River (which empties into the Columbia River in Washington state), such as Ice Harbor, Lower Monumental, Little Goose, and Lower Granite dams. Nevertheless, the dams were eventually constructed over the objections of scientists who predicted further damage to salmon populations between 1962 and 1975 because business interests wanted to establish Lewiston, Idaho, as a deepwater port.

Public Opposition. In the 1940s and 1950s, several proposed dams threatened

Further Reading

Martin, Russell. *A Story That Stands Like a Dam: Glen Canyon and the Struggle for the Soul of the West.* Salt Lake City: University of Utah Press, 1999.

Pitzer, Paul C. *Grand Coulee: Harnessing a Dream.* Pullman: Washington State University Press, 1994.

Reisner, Marc. *Cadillac Desert: The American West and Its Disappearing Water.* New York: Penguin, 1993.

Stevens, Joseph E. *Hoover Dam: An American Adventure.* Norman: University of Oklahoma Press, 1988.

Taylor, Joseph E., III. *Making Salmon: An Environmental History of the Northwest Fisheries Crisis.* Seattle: University of Washington Press, 1999.

scenic areas, prompting public campaigns against them. Conservationists successfully challenged proposed dams in the Selway–Bitterroot Primitive Area in eastern Idaho, in the Cloud Peak Primitive Area of the Big Horns of Wyoming, and near Echo Park (*see also* 146–47) inside of Dinosaur National Monument. However, the Colorado River Storage Project Act of 1956, which authorized Glen Canyon Dam in northern Arizona, was not stopped. River runners and conservationists soon discovered the wondrous inner gorge of Glen Canyon, and deeply regretted the dam's construction, which flooded priceless archaeological sites and drowned miles of unmatched scenery.

The environmental opposition to dams in the western United States gained strength with passage of the National Environmental Policy Act of 1969, which mandated environmental impact statements on federally funded projects. As environmentalists continued to battle against the construction of many dams, a slowing in the national economy, coupled with high inflation in the 1970s and the lack of ideal dam sites, brought the great age of dam building to an end.

—*Mark Harvey*

The Atom Bomb and Nuclear Power

Atomic energy and its harnessing was one of the defining discoveries and developments of the twentieth century—an era of nuclear-powered warships and electricity that promised to be cheaper than power produced by coal and oil (*see also* 102–05). The darker legacy of the atomic age included not just the 1945 atomic explosions at Hiroshima and Nagasaki, but also the environmental impact of weapons testing and nuclear waste, and the risk of proliferation as nuclear technology spread around the world.

Early Experiments. The nuclear age began in 1919 when British physicist Ernest Rutherford split the atom, demonstrating that huge amounts of energy can be released when atoms are broken up. In 1942, Italian physicist Enrico Fermi proved the potential of nuclear energy when he successfully demonstrated the chain reaction (an avalanche of atom-splitting nuclear reactions that generates energy) inside the world's first nuclear "pile" or reactor (the heart of a nuclear power plant where chain reactions

take place). During World War II, fears of Nazi Germany's exploitation of nuclear technology caused the United States to continue nuclear experiments. An initial research grant of $6,000 soon spiraled into the massive $2 billion government-funded Manhattan Project to build a nuclear weapon.

On July 16, 1945, the Manhattan Project exploded its first test bomb at the Alamogordo Air Force Base in New Mexico. With an explosive power equivalent to around 20,000 tons of TNT, the bomb vaporized the tower from which it was detonated, turned the New Mexico desert to glass over a radius of 2 miles (3.2 kilometers), and sent the now familiar mushroom cloud 7.5 miles (12 kilometers) into the air. Within a month, the United States had dropped atom bombs on the Japanese cities of Hiroshima and Nagasaki, killing an estimated 110,000 to 150,000 people and effectively ending Japanese participation in World War II.

Nuclear Proliferation. During the Cold War that followed World War II, the United States competed with the Soviet

Union to develop increasingly powerful nuclear weapons. Tension increased throughout the 1950s and peaked during the October 1962 Cuban missile crisis, a confrontation between the United States and the Soviet Union over the placing of Soviet missiles in Cuba that brought the two nations close to nuclear war. Such incidents heightened public concern about the spread of nuclear weapons and led to the U.N.-sponsored Treaty on the Non-Proliferation of Nuclear Weapons in 1968, originally signed by the United States, the Soviet Union, and sixty other countries (185 nations were signatories as of 2002).

Environmental Concerns. Although the Hiroshima and Nagasaki bombs had demonstrated the destructive power of nuclear weapons, the environmental risks they posed were not experienced outside Japan until 1954. On March 1 of that year, the United States detonated "Bravo," an experimental 15-megaton thermonuclear weapon, at Bikini Atoll, part of the Marshall Islands in the Pacific Ocean. Over 1,000 times more powerful than the Hiroshima bomb, Bravo generated a 3-mile (4.8-kilometer)-wide fireball and spread fallout (radioactive dust and debris) over a vast area, contaminating a Japanese tuna-fishing vessel, *Lucky Dragon*, that was more than 100 miles (160 kilometers) from Bikini and well outside the test zone. All of the crew was hospitalized, several became ill, and one died six months after the blast. The incident prompted a massive public outcry in Japan, partly based on concern that fish stocks had been contaminated and partly because memories of Hiroshima and Nagasaki remained both vivid and painful.

Concern about the incident soon spread throughout the world, and India's Prime Minister Jawaharlal Nehru proposed a ban on nuclear testing later in 1954. The

An Atoms for Peace mobile exhibit promotes the use of nuclear energy. (© Corbis)

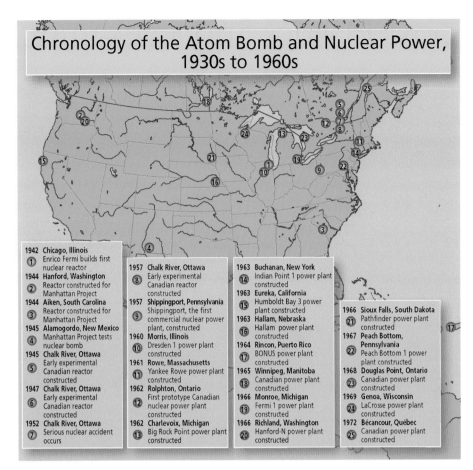

Chronology of the Atom Bomb and Nuclear Power, 1930s to 1960s

1942 Chicago, Illinois
① Enrico Fermi builds first nuclear reactor

1944 Hanford, Washington
② Reactor constructed for Manhattan Project

1944 Aiken, South Carolina
③ Reactor constructed for Manhattan Project

1945 Alamogordo, New Mexico
④ Manhattan Project tests nuclear bomb

1945 Chalk River, Ottawa
⑤ Early experimental Canadian reactor constructed

1947 Chalk River, Ottawa
⑥ Early experimental Canadian reactor constructed

1952 Chalk River, Ottawa
⑦ Serious nuclear accident occurs

1957 Chalk River, Ottawa
⑧ Early experimental Canadian reactor constructed

1957 Shippingport, Pennsylvania
⑨ Shippingport, the first commercial nuclear power plant, constructed

1960 Morris, Illinois
⑩ Dresden 1 power plant constructed

1961 Rowe, Massachusetts
⑪ Yankee Rowe power plant constructed

1962 Rolphton, Ontario
⑫ First prototype Canadian nuclear power plant constructed

1962 Charlevoix, Michigan
⑬ Big Rock Point power plant constructed

1963 Buchanan, New York
⑭ Indian Point 1 power plant constructed

1963 Eureka, California
⑮ Humboldt Bay 3 power plant constructed

1963 Hallam, Nebraska
⑯ Hallam power plant constructed

1964 Rincon, Puerto Rico
⑰ BONUS power plant constructed

1965 Winnipeg, Manitoba
⑱ Canadian power plant constructed

1966 Monroe, Michigan
⑲ Fermi 1 power plant constructed

1966 Richland, Washington
⑳ Hanford-N power plant constructed

1966 Sioux Falls, South Dakota
㉑ Pathfinder power plant constructed

1967 Peach Bottom, Pennsylvania
㉒ Peach Bottom 1 power plant constructed

1968 Douglas Point, Ontario
㉓ Canadian power plant constructed

1969 Genoa, Wisconsin
㉔ LaCrosse power plant constructed

1972 Bécancour, Québec
㉕ Canadian power plant constructed

U.S. nuclear history effectively began in Chicago in 1942 when Enrico Fermi built the first nuclear reactor. Three years later, the world's first atomic bomb was detonated at Alamogordo in New Mexico. During the mid-1940s, experimental reactors were built at a number of sites throughout the United States and Canada. The 1950s saw a shift in emphasis favoring nuclear energy, and power plants were developed in both countries during the 1960s.
Sources: Canadian Nuclear Society. 23 Jan. 2001. <http://www.cns-snc.ca/nuclear_info/canadareactormap.gif>; and U.S. Nuclear Regulatory Commission. 23 Sept. 2002. <http://www.nrc.gov/reactors/operating/map-power-reactors.html>.

United States, however, was intent on developing its nuclear technology; thus it was not until August 1963 that the United States, Britain, and the Soviet Union (soon followed by about one hundred other nations) signed the Nuclear Test-Ban Treaty. The treaty forbade nuclear tests in the atmosphere, at sea, and in space but still allowed underground testing, which was perceived to be safer because it contained the fallout.

Nuclear Energy. Nuclear power (*see also* 156–57) developed initially as a by-product of weapons production. By 1944, large-scale reactors had been built at Hanford, Washington, and Aiken, South Carolina, to produce plutonium (a radioactive element, derived from uranium, used to make nuclear weapons) for the Manhattan Project. U.S.,

Canadian, and British scientists had initially collaborated on that project, but during the 1940s and 1950s, U.S. engineers worked increasingly by themselves, while British and Canadian engineers cooperated to develop nuclear power. The Canadian program experienced one of the world's first major nuclear accidents. On December 12, 1952, a reactor at the Chalk River plant in Ottawa experienced a partial meltdown (a dangerous overheating of the reactor core) and allowed a significant amount of radioactive water to escape into the surrounding environment, requiring a massive cleanup operation.

During the 1950s, the United States and Canada, among other nations began to invest substantially in nuclear energy, promoting it as a source of electricity that would

be "too cheap to meter." U.S. president Dwight D. Eisenhower launched the Atoms for Peace Program with a 1953 speech in which he proposed that atomic energy would be applied "to the needs of agriculture, medicine and other peaceful activities." This program resulted in the world's first large-scale nuclear power plant opening at Shippingport, Pennsylvania, in 1957. Six more U.S. nuclear plants had been commissioned even before Shippingport was complete. After developing three test reactors at Chalk River in the 1940s and 1950s, Canada launched its first prototype nuclear power plant at Rolphton, Ontario, in 1962, with other prototypes constructed at Douglas Point in Winnipeg, Manitoba, and Bécancour in Québec soon afterward.

In theory, the heavily state-subsidized U.S. and Canadian nuclear power programs offered a new, cheap source of energy. In retrospect, their rapid development in the 1950s possibly had as much to do with ensuring plentiful supplies of plutonium for weapons production and making nuclear technology seem more benign to the public. Energy was not, in any case, a purely civilian need: U.S. nuclear plants, for example, were a spin-off from the military program to produce nuclear power for warships and submarines. Regardless of how nuclear power was presented to a skeptical public in the years and decades that followed, it would never quite shake off the controversial legacy of the atom bomb.

—*Chris Woodford*

Further Reading

Duffy, Robert. *Nuclear Politics in America: A History and Theory of Government Regulation.* Lawrence: University Press of Kansas, 1997.

Groves, Leslie. *Now It Can Be Told: The Story of the Manhattan Project.* New York: Da Capo Press, 1983.

Hurst, D.G. et al. *Canada Enters the Atomic Age.* Montreal: McGill-Queen's University Press, 1997.

Consumer Goods: Plastics and Packaging

Plastics have penetrated every part of our lives. Over the last fifty years, plastics have replaced glass, metal, paper, and paperboard (paper packaging), transforming the consumer goods, medical, and especially the food industries in Canada and the United States. Although plastics may have revolutionized contemporary society, our reliance on plastic—along with rising consumption and problems relating to recycling synthetic products—has created an environmental crisis.

Polymers. The changes brought about by the use of plastics for consumer goods and packaging are rooted in the synthetic polymer research discoveries of the first half of the twentieth century. All plastics are called polymers—complex molecules, or macromolecules with a higher molecular weight, that are formed when simpler molecules called monomers, or "mers," link together during a chemical reaction. Most often that chemical reaction is instigated by high heat and pressure. Petroleum-based monomers are used to produce plastic. Currently, about 20 percent of the U.S. annual petroleum supply is dedicated to producing the monomers that create synthetic resins.

Leo Baekeland, a Belgian chemist, produced the first successful synthetic resin, Bakelite, in 1909. The commercial success of his London-based company encouraged initial and significant private investment in synthetic polymer research by large chemical companies throughout the world. As World War II approached, governments around the world worried about possible critical shortages of latex, wool, silk, and, especially, rubber. In an attempt to forestall such shortages, U.S., Canadian, and European governments underwrote basic and applied

research in synthetic polymers conducted by private chemical manufacturers working to develop synthetic polymers.

Plastics. As is often the case in such private–public partnerships during wartime, new commercial products burst onto the market after the war. The 1950s and 1960s were the golden age of plastic consumables in Canada and the United

States. High-strength and lightweight plastics permeated every corner of consumer society: synthetic fibers for clothing, fiberglass car bodies, interior home furnishings, home appliances, telephones, radios, carpets, drapes, wall coverings, water-soluble paints, trash bags, kitchenware, food packaging, plumbing, sinks, bath and shower stalls, and coverings for

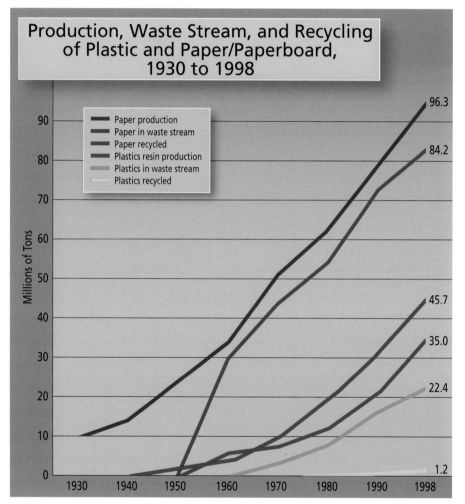

Production, Waste Stream, and Recycling of Plastic and Paper/Paperboard, 1930 to 1998

Legend:
- Paper production
- Paper in waste stream
- Paper recycled
- Plastics resin production
- Plastics in waste stream
- Plastics recycled

(y-axis: Millions of Tons; x-axis: 1930, 1940, 1950, 1960, 1970, 1980, 1990, 1998)

End values: 96.3, 84.2, 45.7, 35.0, 22.4, 1.2

The production of plastic resins began in the 1930s and would explode after the 1960s. At the end of the twentieth century, out of about 22.4 million tons of plastic that had entered the waste stream, only about 1.2 million tons had been recycled. These data are compared with the production, waste stream, and recycling of paper and paperboard (paper packaging) over the twentieth century.

Sources: Plastic resin data compiled by librarians at the Society of the Plastics Industry, Washington, D.C.

U.S. Bureau of the Census, *Statistical Abstract of the United States* (Washington, D.C.: Bureau of the Census, 1938, 1950, 1956, 1960, 1970, 1980, 1990, 2000). Paperboard data compiled from *Statistical Abstract* for years listed.

Waste stream data was collected from: U.S. Bureau of the Census, *Statistical Abstract of the United States* (Washington, D.C.: Bureau of the Census, 2000), Tables 396 and 397.

U.S. Environmental Protection Agency, Office of Solid Waste and Emergency Response, "Characterization of Municipal Solid Waste in the United States: 1992 Update" (Washington, D.C.: Environmental Protection Agency, 1992), 2–2, Table 1; 2–3, Table 2.

electrical wiring. Developed in the 1940s, plastic Tupperware products became a storage staple in many kitchens during the 1950s. Toys were more durable and less likely to break, as mass-produced plastic dolls replaced papier-mâché, wood, and porcelain dolls. Plastics also transformed the medical industry: They were used to develop more effective blood storage in the 1940s, intravenous (IV) containers in the 1950s, balloon catheters in the 1960s, and dialysis treatments in the 1970s.

Packaging. The packaging industry, in particular, benefited from these wartime discoveries. For example, between 1930 and 1937, the U.S. government supported research by companies attempting to develop synthetic rubber products from styrene monomers. Polystyrene, a by-product of this research, later became a key resin in the manufacture of paper plates, hot cups, fast-food containers, and many other common packaging products. Similarly, industry researchers working with ethylene monomers created polyethylene as a potential alternative fuel during World War II. Various forms of polyethylene are now used to make milk containers, water and juice containers, plastic grocery bags, and plastic bottles. Plastic films act as barriers to liquids, oils, and fats, and keep poultry and meats fresh longer, while multilayered plastic containers have replaced metal cans and jars on food shelves, effectively extending the shelf life of many products by months and even years.

After 1950, plastic packaging often complemented or reinforced traditional paper and glass storage in the food industry. The modern milk carton is an example of such hybrid packaging. The paper carton was replaced in the 1960s by a milk container composed of paper and a polyethylene laminated film. A decade later, cartons would replace bottles as high-density polyethylene (HDPE) plastic

Further Reading

Leidner, Jacob. *Plastics Waste, Recovery of Economic Value.* New York: Marcel Dekker, 1981.

Matos, Grecia, and Lorie Wagner. "Consumption of Materials in the United States." *Annual Review of Energy and the Environment* 23 (1998): 107–122.

Meikle, Jeffrey. *American Plastic: A Cultural History.* New Brunswick, N.J.: Rutgers University Press, 1995.

Porro, Jeffrey, and Christine Meller. *The Plastic Waste Primer.* New York: Lyons and Burford, 1993.

Wolf, Nancy, and Ellen Feldman. *America's Packaging Dilemma.* Washington, D.C.: Island Press, 1991.

containers competed for shelf space with the older milk carton. Plastic bottle usage rose from 75 million pounds (34 million kilograms) in 1974 to over 2 billion pounds (0.9 million kilograms) in 1984. By 1985, over eighteen billion plastic bottles were produced in the United States.

Contemporary Concerns. It is not an exaggeration to say that the United States has become a plastic consumption society. Almost 100 billion pounds (45 billion kilograms) of plastic resins are now produced annually to manufacture plastic products. Each individual in the United States discards an average of 4.5 pounds (2 kilograms) of waste daily. Plastics account for about 1.7 pounds (0.8 kilogram) of the waste discarded. Because plastics are light and occupy a lot of space, almost 40 percent of all landfill waste is now plastic and that percentage will continue to grow.

With the exception of recycling plastic bottles, few recycling programs in communities are designed to separate other plastic waste. Whereas over 36 percent of paperboard waste is recycled, only 2.5 percent of all plastic waste is recycled. Breaking down and recycling multilayered packaging, which now accounts for over 40 percent of the plastics entering the waste stream, is even more complex as it requires various protocols to extract and collect the different polymers. The percentage of plastic in our garbage will only increase as plastics used in the building and construction industry twenty-five years ago now begin to enter landfills in large amounts. Plastics are inert and do not decompose, so composting

plastics in a landfill is not an option; rather, they are simply covered and capped and remain buried beneath the soil.

One option for effectively recycling plastic is incineration and the conversion of the heat produced into renewable energy. The technology, however, is expensive. Incinerators need to run at very high temperatures—approximately 1,800°F (980°C)—to successfully burn off all plastics. As most existing incinerators do not burn hot enough to safely destroy plastics, a community would have to invest in new or additional technology. At lower temperatures, unwanted toxic wastes from the plastic residue can enter the fly ash and burn ash and pollute the air.

Since the 1970s, environmental groups have strongly opposed incineration, especially in the wake of dioxin exposure and cancer concerns at toxic waste sites like Love Canal (*see also* 152–53 *and* 158–59). At the same time, the oil embargo in 1973 (*see also* 156–57) triggered a decade or more of high inflation—even if communities had the political will to install new technologies, they could not afford them. Accordingly, most communities still handle plastic waste by dumping the materials into a landfill. Between 1990 and 2000, plastic resin production almost doubled. With no clear ecological solution in sight, plastic-rich landfills are becoming permanent reminders that we have not yet effectively addressed the rapidly growing waste stream created by synthetics.

—*John Ost*

The Evolution of Suburbia and the Federal Aid Highway Act

In Canada and the United States, the development of suburbs, areas of single-family homes that are neither rural farmland nor urban centers, accelerated following World War II, spurred by both government policy and the serious housing shortage encountered by returning war veterans. The growth of suburban living engendered an increase in car ownership, which triggered massive road-building projects to accommodate the ever-growing number of cars and to connect suburban neighborhoods with urban centers.

Housing. In the mid-1930s, both the United States and Canada adopted laws to encourage the construction of new housing, with the United States establishing the Federal Housing Administration in 1934 and Canada adopting the first Dominion Housing Act the following year. These programs were primarily designed to provide construction jobs for the unemployed, but they also contributed to the growth of the suburbs. Both governments eventually agreed to back loans (mortgages) provided by banks to home buyers; this support brought the purchase of a house within the means of many more people. Because of such programs, a new house in the suburbs, purchased with a government-backed loan, could cost a family less each month than rent on an apartment in the city.

Initially, neither housing act had much of an impact because of the severity of the Depression; in addition, the outbreak of World War II in 1939 caused both countries to focus their resources on the war effort. When the war ended in 1945, more than ten million American and Canadian servicemen and women returned home to a housing shortage that lasted throughout the rest of the decade.

Levittown, a new housing development built in the late 1940s on Long Island in New York state, seemed like an answer to the shortage. Using mass-production techniques, the Levittown builders erected a new home every fifteen minutes, turning 1,200 acres (485 hectares) of farmland into an affordable housing development for more than forty thousand people. Levittown became a model for massive suburban development in both the United States and Canada, and during the 1950s more than 1 million acres (0.4 million hectares) were developed every year to accommodate the rising population in suburban areas. While about thirty-one million Americans, less than one-quarter of the U.S. population, lived in suburbs in 1940, by 1960 more than sixty million did—about one-third of the population.

Automobiles. Sales of cars also took off following the war, supported by rising prosperity and the popularity of suburban living. In 1946, twenty-eight million cars were on U.S. roads—only five million more than in 1930. In 1947, more than three million new cars were sold; in 1950, more than six million cars were sold. By 1965, there were seventy million cars on U.S. roads.

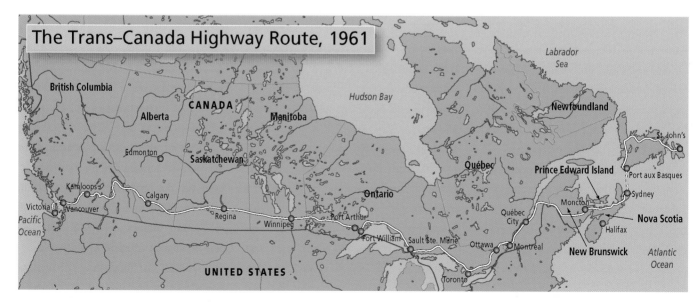

The Trans–Canada Highway Act of 1949 provided funding for a transcontinental highway across Canada. However, unanticipated expenses and construction problems encountered in the Rocky Mountains and in northern Ontario delayed the completion of the highway; at its opening in 1962, more than 1,800 miles (2,900 kilometers) were still unpaved. The trans-Canada highway is the longest national highway in the world and stretches from St. John's, Newfoundland, to Victoria, British Columbia.
Source: Adapted from Donald Kerr et al., eds., *Addressing the Twentieth Century 1891–1961.* Vol. 3 of *Historical Atlas of Canada* (Toronto: University of Toronto Press, 1990), plate 53.

More automobiles led to traffic jams. In response, the United States undertook a massive road-building project with the passage of the Federal Aid Highway Act in 1956. The act created a highway trust fund to provide financing for an interstate highway system, with the federal government picking up 90 percent of the cost of such roads and the states paying the rest. The highway system, which was completed in the early 1980s, consisted of more than 40,000 miles (64,000 kilometers) of roads connecting almost every U.S. city. In addition, the trust fund was used to finance the building of highways outside the interstate highway system, although the share of federal funding for these programs was typically smaller, between 50 and 80 percent. By the early 1980s, the United States had almost 5 million miles (8 million kilometers) of roads, more than twice that of any other country and significantly more than the 800,000 miles (1,290,000 kilometers) of road that crossed Canada.

Although Canada built fewer roads, its federal government took on a larger share of road-building costs. In 1949, under the Trans–Canada Highway Act, the federal government began funding the trans-Canada highway program, which lasted until 1970. Under the program, the federal government paid about half the cost of highway construction, with provincial governments paying the rest. The resulting highway system crosses the entire country, stretching 4,600 miles (7,400 kilometers).

Environmental Impact. The massive road-building projects of this period were seen as crucial to the defense and industry of

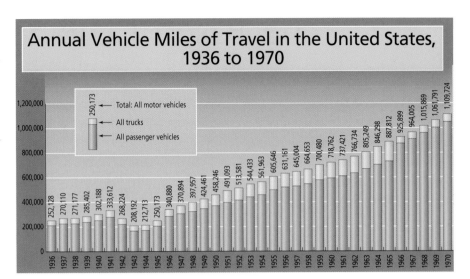

Road-building programs like the 1956 Federal Aid Highway Act, along with an increase in car ownership, contributed to an increase in automobile travel and helped connect communities across the nation. However, new highways also contributed to the spread of suburban development and the loss of natural habitat.
Source: Data from "Highway Statistics Summary to 1995." Federal Highway Administration. U.S. Department of Transportation. 18 Jan. 2002. <http://www.fhwa.dot.gov/ohim/summary95/section5.html>.

both countries. However, even during the 1950s, the environmental impact of this building began to raise alarms, giving rise by the end of the decade to what became known as the open-space movement, which advocated limits to development and the preservation of natural habitat. Suburban and urban development drastically changed the countryside, as more than 40 million acres (16 million hectares) of farmland was developed between 1950 and 1980. Development destroyed woods, wetlands, and other wildlife habitat, threatening species like the Florida panther.

The uncontrolled development of environmentally sensitive wetlands, which vanished at a rate of almost 460,000 acres (186,000 hectares) a year from the mid-1950s to the mid-1970s, soon had a negative effect on suburban communities and public health. Wetlands soak up water during rainstorms, but the paved roads and homes that replaced them were impervious to water and rain would run off, flooding homes on lower-lying land. Likewise suburban development on hillsides caused floods in adjacent valleys. In addition to flooding, water runoff carried the residue of pesticides and fertilizers used in yards and the oil that leaked onto driveways,

causing contamination of water sources downstream. Septic systems, which were commonly used to contain and treat sewage from individual suburban homes, often malfunctioned, contaminating drinking water (*see also* 190–91) with detergents, nitrates (which can cause oxygen depletion in babies), and deadly bacteria.

In addition, the growth of the suburbs and extensive road building encouraged the use of automobiles, which produced pollutants including carbon monoxide, nitrous oxides, and particulates. By 1970, a year in which eighty-nine million of the 193 million cars registered worldwide were found in the United States (seven million were registered in Canada), automobiles were the source of 84 million of the 140 million tons of pollutants spewed into the air every year. Pollutants from automobiles have been linked to everything from smog formation to lung irritation to global warming (*see also* 202–03). Although vehicle emissions standards were tightened in the 1970s, many of the environmental problems that came from the rise of the suburbs and of the car culture remain significant concerns today.

—*Mary Sisson*

Further Reading
Muller, Peter O. *Contemporary Suburban America*. Englewood Cliffs, N.J.: Prentice-Hall, 1981.
Palen, J. John. *The Suburbs*. New York: McGraw-Hill, 1995.
Rome, Adam. *The Bulldozer in the Countryside: Suburban Sprawl and the Rise of American Environmentalism*. Cambridge: Cambridge University Press, 2001.

The Rise of the Sunbelt

Since 1945, no region of the United States has grown with the speed and abandon of the Sunbelt. This loosely defined region, stretching from Florida in the Southeast to California in the West, has experienced remarkable demographic growth and change. Among the most densely populated regions of the nation, more than 90 percent of its population in the West lives in cities. Much of the technological and economic innovation in the postwar United States has originated in the Sunbelt. Federal and, in particular, military spending had no small part in this transformation. The space program was headquartered and run almost exclusively in Texas and Florida; California is the home of Silicon Valley and the computer industry. One major consequence of this growth has been the need to address an array of environmental problems, including water quantity and quality, air pollution, deforestation, and suburban sprawl.

Growth of Military Industries. World War II was the catalyst for change in the Sunbelt. Fighting a war in the Pacific required a comprehensive infrastructure and an entirely new labor force throughout the West. On the heels of the Great Depression and the New Deal, thousands of Americans fled their rural, southern, and even eastern homes for new opportunities in western wartime industries. The federal government built an infrastructure to support the war: Los Alamos, New Mexico, where the atomic bomb was designed (*see also* 130–31); Hanford, Washington, where the bomb was constructed at production facilities; and Richmond, California, which became a center of war manufacturing. The war industries in these cities provided countless jobs but also created an array of environmental problems.

Federal spending surged again with the Cold War and defense contracting and military expenditures became a larger part of the region's economy. Prior to 1940, San Antonio, Texas, and San Diego, California, stood out for their dependence

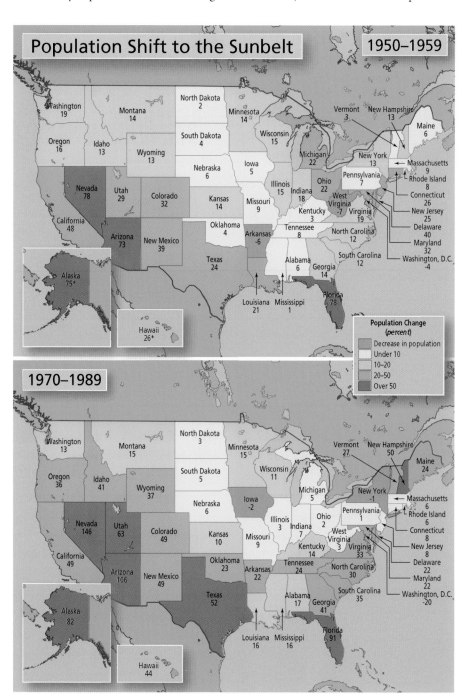

Population Shift to the Sunbelt

1950–1959

1970–1989

Population Change
(percent)
- Decrease in population
- Under 10
- 10–20
- 20–50
- Over 50

* *1959 data.*

Following World War II, the Sunbelt—an area stretching from Florida in the Southeast to California in the West—experienced significant growth as Americans migrated to the region for new economic opportunities and a better quality of life. The region continued to grow in the 1970s and 1980s as it became the center of the technology, military, and aerospace industries.

Source: Adapted from Mary Beth Norton, et al., *A People and a Nation: A History of the United States* (Boston: Houghton Mifflin, 1998), 809, 927. © by Houghton Mifflin Company. Used with permission.

on military spending. After the war, the entire Sunbelt became home to what President Dwight D. Eisenhower labeled the "military-industrial complex." San Antonio, for instance, became home to five major military installations, and received more than $7 billion yearly in federal payments. Other cities benefited similarly, providing workers and their families with unparalleled prosperity, greater economic opportunities, and a rising standard of living. The Sunbelt acquired the title "Gunbelt" as a result of the growth of its military industries.

Population Increase. This prosperity fed a tremendous growth in population. Most of the people who moved to the region for work during World War II stayed. They were joined by millions of others—including retirees—who wanted to take advantage of the postwar boom. After 1965, when American immigration laws became less restrictive, millions more flocked to the Sunbelt from Asia and from Central and South America. California had surpassed New York as the nation's most populous state in 1963, and for most of the succeeding decades grew at roughly twice the rate of the rest of the nation. But every Sunbelt state grew so greatly in population that by 2000 the three most important centers of national electoral power (a system based on U.S. Census population figures) would be Florida, Texas, and California.

Air Pollution. The enormous demographic, economic, social, and environmental change overwhelmed the Sunbelt's infrastructure. Cities expanded geographically, creating new suburbs connected by a tangle of freeways that by 1960 were jammed with cars (see also 134–35). Houston, Texas, ballooned to more than 600 square miles (1,550 square kilometers); by 2001, Houston would have more than 3.7 million cars logging more

Further Reading
Abbott, Carl. *The New Urban America: Growth and Politics in Sunbelt Cities.* Rev. ed. Chapel Hill: University of North Carolina Press, 1987.
Ballard, Steven C., and Thomas E. James, eds. *The Future of the Sunbelt: Managing Growth and Change.* New York: Praeger, 1983.
Fairbanks, Robert B., and Kathleen Underwood, eds. *Essays on Sunbelt Cities and Recent Urban America.* Introduction by Kenneth T. Jackson. College Station: Published for the University of Texas at Arlington by Texas A&M University Press, 1990.
Miller, Randall M., and George E. Pozzetta, eds. *Shades of the Sunbelt: Essays on Ethnicity, Race, and the Urban South.* Boca Raton: Florida Atlantic University Press, 1989.
Mohl, Raymond A., ed. *Searching for the Sunbelt: Historical Perspectives on a Region.* Athens: University of Georgia Press, 1993.
Schulman, Bruce J. *From Cotton Belt to Sunbelt: Federal Policy, Economic Development, and the Transformation of the South, 1938–1980.* Durham, N.C.: Duke University Press, 1994.

70 million daily vehicle miles (113 million kilometers) on local state roads. As of 2001 this Texas metropolis was tied with Los Angeles for having the most polluted air in the country.

The problem of pollution affected a vast portion of the Sunbelt region. By the 1990s, the dense smog of greater Houston and Los Angeles seemed to be permanent, and the $800 million spent yearly on mitigation did little to improve air quality. Despite the introduction in the 1970s of unleaded gasoline and catalytic converters to reduce auto emissions, carbon monoxide levels rose because of the increasing numbers of vehicles on the road and the increasing number of miles they traveled as cities and their surrounding suburbs spread outward. Exacerbating pollution was the need for more and more electrical power, which prompted the construction of coal-fired plants throughout the West in the years after World War II. Ultimately, the emissions of these coal-fired generators extended to and obscured the spectacular vistas of the Grand Canyon. Some argued in the immediate postwar years that bad air quality was a sign of a healthy economy, but that robust economic development came at the cost of environmental and public health.

Water Access. Water, especially in the arid Southwest and West, also became a critical issue with vast urban growth. The rules governing access to water and who had primary rights to it had been established in an earlier agricultural era (see also 100–01). The rise of environmentalism (see also 162–63) in the 1970s put an end to dam construction (see also 128–29), the traditional mode of western water management. After 1980, the decline of agriculture and ranching set the stage for the reallocation of water from rural to urban uses (see also 190–91). By 2001, water that once been used to irrigate cotton outside Yuma, Arizona, had been transferred to accommodate recreational uses in Las Vegas, Nevada, lawn maintenance in Los Angeles, or golf courses outside Phoenix, Arizona.

The transformation of the Sunbelt from the late 1940s to the present represents the latest version of American westward expansion. Like earlier bursts of growth, it was fueled by technology, most prominently air conditioning, and by government spending, especially defense and aerospace. As a result, the Sunbelt developed into the new center of the nation. Home to the powerful computer industry, and characterized by suburban sprawl, increased political power, and rapid surges in population with significant numbers of new immigrants, this region seems most likely to define the United States in the twenty-first century.

—*Hal Rothman*

U.S. Wilderness Recreation

Beginning in the 1920s federally protected wilderness areas (free from roads, logging, mining, and other economic activities) were established on public lands in the United States to protect watersheds, ensure high water quality, maintain valued grazing areas unscathed, and protect wildlife and wilderness parcels. The most important reason, however, was the amazing growth of recreation during the twentieth century, when Americans turned to the outdoors for their leisure activities as never before.

Rise of Wilderness Recreation.

Before the twentieth century, recreation had generally been an upper-class activity, considered a luxury by most. With the development of the automobile as affordable transportation in the early twentieth century, coupled with rising incomes, paid vacations, and an improved standard of living, outdoor recreation opened up to the American middle class. The automobile became a significant component of outdoor recreation, as car camping and auto tourism became popular. Although vacations in resorts with comfortable accommodations remained popular, Americans increasingly began to explore the wild country where they found pleasure in hiking, climbing, canoeing, and appreciating scenic vistas in western national parks like Grand Canyon, Yellowstone, and Yosemite.

Some Americans sought out even more rustic surroundings in the backcountry of the nation's parks and forests. In response to this demand, the United States Forest Service (see also 92–91) began to establish primitive areas during the 1920s. Early wilderness crusaders like Aldo Leopold and Robert Marshall promoted these areas for the spiritual uplift they provided to overstressed city people. Wilderness recreation steadily grew in the Boundary Waters Canoe Area on the U.S.–Canadian border, in many national parks, and in state parks like the Adirondacks in New York.

Conflicts. Outdoor recreation sharply escalated after World War II. Visits to national parks rose from 11.7 million people in 1945 to 25.5 million in 1947; eighteen million people visited national forests in 1941 to camp, fish, hunt, and for general recreation, compared to nearly thirty million in 1951. This trend initially challenged efforts to safeguard wilderness areas. For example, during the war airplanes had carried anglers into the remote boundary waters region of northern Minnesota and Ontario, Canada, disturbing those who cherished the solitude and remoteness of the lakes, islands, and vast forests. Recreation in the boundary waters thus developed into a conflict between those who gained access by planes (and motorboats) and those who preferred canoes. Pressured by wilderness activists Sigurd Olson and Ernest Oberholtzer, President Harry S. Truman in 1949 signed an executive

Wilderness Recreation in Canada

In Canada, the decades from 1930 to 1970 saw growing appreciation of wilderness, increased recreational use, and the onset of problems that necessitated more intensive management. In the 1930s, a relatively small proportion of Canadians used wilderness for recreation. The main traditional uses were hunting and fishing; hiking, boating, and camping in parks were also popular activities. Summer camps and family cottages, especially in Ontario, encouraged outdoor recreation. The Rockies and a few other areas offered mountain climbing, while canoeing on lakes and rivers was popular, especially in northern Ontario.

After World War II, Canadians' money, leisure, and mobility (cars) increased greatly; as a result, outdoor recreation boomed. In response to this growing demand for access to wilderness areas, the government established new national and provincial parks, many with wilderness zones. The number of national parks increased from fourteen in 1930 to twenty-four in 1970. The number of campers in the interior of Algonquin Provincial Park, Ontario, grew from about twenty thousand in 1959 to about forty thousand in 1970. Greater use was made of the Canadian wilderness by people from outside its borders, for example canoeists from the United States in Quetico Provincial Park, Ontario.

Crowding occurred in parks, including Algonquin Provincial Park and Banff National Park in Alberta (see also 113), established in 1885 as Canada's first national park, as well as at facilities like campsites within parks. Some conflicts arose, for example, between motorized (e.g., motor boaters) and nonmotorized travelers (e.g., canoeists) and over the provision of facilities in wilderness areas (e.g., huts and roads). The proposals for the development of an expanded road system and a major ski resort at Lake Louise in Banff National Park were especially controversial because of the disruption of the natural habitat such facilities would involve. Environmental impacts, including destruction of vegetation, increase in forest fires, improper garbage disposal, and human interactions with wildlife, especially bears, became more serious at popular and sensitive wilderness locations.

The response of the federal and provincial governments was to designate more wilderness areas for protection and recreation and to adjust management policies. The government placed restrictions on certain recreational activities (e.g., snowmobiling); limited the number of visitors to certain areas (e.g., on popular canoe routes); and increased education, including warning about the dangers of feeding bears and promoting "no trace camping,"

—John S. Marsh

Further Reading

Frome, Michael. *Battle for the Wilderness*. Rev. ed. Salt Lake City: University of Utah Press, 1997.

Kerasote, Ted, ed. *Return of the Wild: The Future of Our Natural Lands*. Washington, D.C.: Island Press, 2001.

Olson, Sigurd F. *The Meaning of Wilderness: Essential Articles and Speeches*. Edited and with an introduction by David Backes. Minneapolis: University of Minnesota Press, 2001.

Searle, R. Newell. *Saving Quetico-Superior: A Land Set Apart*. St. Paul: Minnesota Historical Society Press, 1977.

order creating an air space reserve over the boundary waters wilderness that prohibited flights below 4,000 feet (1,200 meters). Truman's proclamation was an important milestone in the nation's wilderness history.

Wilderness Protection. From the 1920s until the mid-1960s, primitive, wild, and wilderness areas in the national forests had little security; they were protected only under Forest Service regulations, and the Forest Service could reduce their size to meet demands from private interests for greater timber production. In response, in 1956, the Wilderness Society and other conservation groups began to campaign for a federal law to protect wilderness areas; they would eventually be successful with the passage of the Wilderness Act of 1964 (*see also* 146–47). However, in the following eight years, they met with bitter opposition from commodity industries, such as timber, mining, and ranching, but were aided by rising numbers of hunters and anglers, hikers and rock climbers, dude ranchers and related tourist enterprises. In the 1950s and 1960s wilderness became a valued economic commodity in the American West as hunters and sportsmen flocked to places like the Bob Marshall and Selway–Bitterroot Wilderness Areas in Montana and Idaho. Nearby residents who took to primitive and wilderness areas for their recreation were also an important constituency, in part because they opposed the Forest Service's seeming capitulation to timber interests in the decades after World War II. In 1945, approximately 1.5 billion board feet (3,500 billion cubic centimeters) of timber was harvested in the Pacific Northwest; more than 4 billion board feet (9,400 billion cubic centimeters) was cut there in 1960.

While the wilderness bill made its way slowly through Congress in the late 1950s, the Administration of President Dwight D. Eisenhower established the Outdoor Recreation Resources Review Commission to study the nation's recreational needs. Some opponents of the wilderness bill used the commission to thwart the wilderness campaign, arguing that Congress should not set any new policy for wilderness until the commission completed its review. In 1962 the commission presented its recommendations to President John F. Kennedy; the commission called for expansion of wilderness acreage to meet future recreational demands. Two years later Congress approved and President Lyndon Johnson signed the Wilderness Act into law. The act created the national wilderness system with 9.1 million acres (3.7 million hectares) and initiated a survey by federal land agencies of potential lands to be designated as wilderness areas.

Outdoor recreation continued to fuel expansion of the wilderness system. As the post–World War II economic boom continued through the 1960s and early 1970s, backpacking in national forests and parks increased sharply. Contributing to this increased popularity of wilderness exploration and enjoyment were major improvements in lightweight tents, sleeping bags, and freeze-dried food. In the 1970s, the Forest Service conducted reviews of roadless area that identified nearly three hundred areas suitable for wilderness designation; these reviews became the basis of the many wilderness designations of the 1970s and 1980s. By 2002, the national wilderness system would encompass more than 105 million acres (43 million hectares), with a new generation of environmentalists trying to expand the wilderness system even further (*see also* 184–85). These environmentalists still had traditional opponents in the timber, mining, and grazing industries, as well as new ones—those fond of motorized recreation. They also would face the daunting task of managing wilderness to protect it from the throngs of people who love it so much.

—*Mark Harvey*

Campers on a canoe trip in 1940 in the boundary waters of Superior National Forest, Minnesota, on the U.S.–Canadian border. (© Corbis)

Rachel Carson and *Silent Spring*

With the 1962 publication of her international bestseller *Silent Spring*, scientist and writer Rachel Carson inspired the beginnings of the contemporary environmental movement. The fourth and last book of Carson's successful career, *Silent Spring* examined the disastrous effects of synthetic chemical pesticides on wildlife and human health. Carson's arguments in *Silent Spring* were based on the field of ecology, the scientific investigation of how all members of living communities are interdependent, a concept generally unknown to people at the time of publication. The arguments in her book and the uproar that followed its publication illuminated an important shift in North American attitudes toward nature.

Early Life and Work. Carson's childhood and education introduced her to an ecological perspective early in life. Born Rachel Louise Carson in 1907, she spent much of her youth taking long walks with her mother through the Pennsylvania countryside, identifying and observing various plants and animals. Entering the Pennsylvania College for Women (now Chatham College) in 1925, Carson decided to major in both zoology and English; later, she described the decision as having given her both a subject for lifelong study and a method for expressing her love for nature. After earning a master's degree in zoology from Johns Hopkins University in 1932, Carson went to work for the U.S. Fish and Wildlife Service (then known as the Bureau of Fisheries) as a writer and editor.

Carson's job gave her the freedom to research and write about the natural world that she loved so much, in particular, the mysteries of the sea. After the 1950 publication of her award-winning second book, *The Sea Around Us*, Carson was able to leave her job to focus on writing full time. Her first three books integrated exceptionally beautiful nature writing with thoroughly researched scientific conclusions. This combination earned Carson a large and devoted readership. With *Silent Spring*, Carson made a broad and in-depth indictment of the effects of synthetic chemical pesticides on nature.

Carson's Focus on Pesticides. The rampant use of pesticides had long concerned Carson. The use of increasingly toxic and nonselective (chemicals poisonous to all life forms, not just to target organisms) pesticides such as DDT (dichlorodiphenyltrichloroethane), parathion, and heptachlor had skyrocketed since their introduction to domestic markets after World War II (*see also* 122–23). Wildlife biologists and various citizens had reported the widespread devastation that government spraying campaigns wrought on nontarget animal populations. For example, as casualties of spraying campaigns for Dutch elm disease, robins and other birds were poisoned not only by direct contact with insecticides, but also by accumulation of the poisons within their tissues from their diet of contaminated earthworms and insects.

Already committed to another book project, Carson tried to interest other writers in investigating the additional

Rachel Carson, in 1963, speaking before the Senate Government Operations Subcommittee studying pesticide spraying. (From the collections of the Library of Congress)

dangers of pesticides. Unsuccessful, in 1958 she began the book herself, but what started as a short project lengthened into a four-year odyssey. The delay was caused by Carson's extensive and thorough research, while her declining health, including a diagnosis of breast cancer in 1960, sapped her strength

Release of *Silent Spring.* In the summer of 1962, the *New Yorker* published *Silent Spring* in serial form; the following September, Houghton-Mifflin released the book. An immediate bestseller, *Silent Spring* spent weeks on the *New York Times* bestseller list. In large part the book's impact came from the dramatic conclusions of the text. Toxic pesticide residues, Carson argued, appeared throughout the tissues of all living things and posed unknown risks to the very web of life itself. DDT residues, for example, could be found in everything from human breast milk to the fat of ocean fish; humans and animals were thus equally vulnerable to contamination from pesticides.

The idea that humans should dominate and control nature, rather than respect its often unknown processes, helped contribute to this pervasive toxic threat. Carson argued that the major offenders in this unnecessary and self-defeating battle against nature were not

Reaction to *Silent Spring*

Silent Spring was especially remarkable for the wide range of individuals and groups that it drew into the debate. The grassroots public response was particularly powerful. People wrote Carson, their local papers, or their government representatives, urging the reevaluation of the widespread use of pesticides. Many of these supporters were women, especially those involved in garden clubs, League of Women Voters, and volunteer organizations. The media also gave an enormous amount of coverage to *Silent Spring*, with several newspapers reprinting passages from the book.

While much of this reaction supported Carson, a powerful backlash targeted her work as well. Many pesticide manufacturers attacked Carson's scientific credibility. In particular, they questioned her status as both a woman and a scientist, and described her public supporters as "hysterical." Monsanto, a manufacturer of agricultural pesticides, published a parody titled "A Desolate Year" in a 1962 edition of *Monsanto Magazine* that described the widespread starvation and suffering that would torment a world without pesticides. The National Agricultural Chemicals Association, a pesticide lobbying group in the United States, spent more than $250,000 in a public relations campaign against Carson and *Silent Spring*; the much larger food and chemical industries also lent their support to her attackers. Scientific experts of all sorts, but especially chemists, medical doctors, biologists, and ecologists, debated Carson's conclusions and how best to evaluate the risks posed by pesticides.

Nevertheless, in 1962 President John F. Kennedy appointed a special Science Advisory Committee on pesticides. In 1963, Connecticut senator Abraham Ribicoff convened a special hearing before a U.S. Senate subcommittee, where Carson testified not long before her death. With information gathered by the committee and hearing, the federal government struggled to answer questions about pesticide safety. Ultimately, the committee report validated Carson's conclusions in *Silent Spring*. However, the hearings produced little reform, ultimately closing only a few loopholes in existing pesticide laws, rather than overhauling the regulatory system.

Further Reading

Carson, Rachel. *Silent Spring.* 1962. Reprint, Boston: Houghton Mifflin, 1994.

Gottlieb, Robert. *Forcing the Spring: The Transformation of the American Environmental Movement.* Washington, D.C.: Island Press, 1993.

Lear, Linda. *Rachel Carson: Witness for Nature.* New York: Henry Holt, 1997.

Steingraber, Sandra. *Living Downstream: An Ecologist Looks at Cancer and the Environment.* Reading, Mass.: Addison-Wesley, 1997.

only the chemical industries and agribusiness, but also the government with its short-sighted and fragmented approach to regulation. In the regulation of pesticides, for example, different branches of government held conflicting positions. The U.S. Department of Agriculture supported the widespread use and development of pesticides by and for agribusiness. The U.S. Department of Interior worried about the effects of pesticides on wildlife, while personnel within the U.S. Public Health Service disagreed about the exact effects of pesticides on public health.

The controversy engendered by *Silent Spring* rumbled long past its publication, even after Carson's death from

breast cancer in 1964. Confronted with the reality that, unbeknownst to them, their flesh contained toxic pesticide residues, many members of the public used the ecological arguments of *Silent Spring* to question the directions of science and technology. These reactions to *Silent Spring* laid the groundwork for the development of the contemporary environmental movement (*see also* 162–65), which gained strength through the 1960s and 1970s. By using the principles of ecology to challenge cultural attitudes that sanctioned the domination of nature, Rachel Carson left a legacy that still inspires environmental activists today.

—*Maril Hazlett*

CHAPTER SIX

The Rise of the Environmental Movement
(1960s–1980s)

The 1970s opened with a striking demonstration of the growing importance of the environment in North American politics. In April 1970, the first Earth Day was celebrated, a moment of reflection on the past year's actions on behalf of the global environment. Its significance has grown with the years, attracting larger crowds, political support, and media coverage. But the first Earth Day was of greatest note, if only because it happened at all.

Dire Predictions. The mobilization of support for something as abstract as an "Earth Day" was driven by disturbing, real-world pressures on the natural and built landscape. As world population continued to soar and to concentrate in urban areas that swelled in size, the environmental impact in Canada and the United States was profound: Wetlands disappeared, farmlands were swallowed up, rivers "died" because of the high levels of industrial sludge. Human conflict escalated as well; battles over wealth and power came to be conjoined with racial violence. Those who could flee to the suburbs did so; half of the U.S. population made that trek, as did one-third of Canadians. Left behind were those with few resources, forced to live in inner cities that were abandoned, boarded up, or burned out, including the South Bronx in New York City and the Scarborough Street area in Toronto.

Paul Ehrlich's provocative book, *The Population Bomb* (1968), was one of many apocalyptic screeds that warned of the explosive consequences of unrestrained population growth in an era of finite resources. Although his stark prediction of impending mass starvation and global war between the world's rich and poor failed to materialize, Ehrlich nonetheless identified an issue of undeniable import. One consequence was the subsequent and heavy investment by nations and transnational corporations to develop more sustainable models for agricultural and industrial development.

Rise of Environmentalism. Many middle-class citizens who had grown up in the post–World War II suburbs demanded a more ecologically sensitive economy and a more humane environment. Benefiting from a rising standard of living, they often used their leisure time to hike and camp in U.S. and Canadian national parks, reveling in the glorious natural settings made possible by such legislation as the Wilderness Act of 1964, which required protection and management of public lands in the United States. But the sharp contrast between these pristine wild lands and the rundown central cities around which Americans and Canadians lived prompted North Americans to establish organizations to champion a new environmental vision.

Theirs was an activist creed: to directly challenge those governments and corporations they believed were not responsive enough to the needs of the environment and humanity. Through groups like Canada's Pollution Probe, and the more well-known Greenpeace, initially a joint Canadian–U.S. organization, they confronted those who polluted lakes, oceans, and rivers; publicized the bloody slaughter of seals; and, in their high-speed Zodiac boats, gave chase to, and disrupted, nuclear testing and international whale-hunting expeditions. This new generation of environmentalists also joined with long-exploited groups like indigenous North American peoples to protect free-flowing waterways from hydroelectric dams, burial grounds and sacred lands from desecration, and historic fishing rights from toxic effluent.

In 1971, members of the newly formed group Greenpeace prepare to sail an old fishing boat, also named Greenpeace, *from British Columbia to Amchitka Island in the Aleutian archipelago to prevent the testing of a U.S. nuclear device. The U.S. Coast Guard would intercept the ship and divert it from Amchitka before the blast. (© Bettmann/Corbis)*

Energy Concerns. The number of issues available to protest seemed limitless. The oil crisis of the early 1970s, for instance, forced industrial societies to acknowledge their dependence on foreign "black gold." But proposals to lessen that dependency by building the trans-Alaska pipeline, or by constructing nuclear power plants, sparked a new round of environmental anxieties. The construction of oil production and distribution facilities above the Arctic Circle angered those who suspected they would block animal migration routes and sully the unspoiled tundra. The safety of nuclear energy was in doubt as well, with many fearing that its generation imperiled public health; their fears seemed all-too justified with the 1979 near-meltdown of reactors at Pennsylvania's Three Mile Island complex. Adding to North Americans' jitters was the wrenching discovery of the poisonous wasteland of Love Canal, located in far western New York, near the Canadian border.

Legislation and Regulation. In response, the Canadian and U.S. governments developed new agencies to respond to what appeared to be an endless array of environmental problems. In 1970, President Richard Nixon signed into law the act creating the Environmental Protection Agency (EPA), which was given the power to gather data about the potential environmental consequences of human activity and to punish those who befouled air, land, or water. Its effectiveness has often been circumscribed by reduced budgets and political interference, constraints evident in the EPA's difficulty in enforcing the mandates of the Superfund Act that was passed to expedite cleanup of hazardous waste sites. Its Canadian counterpart, Environment Canada, would be responsible for enforcing the Canadian Environmental Protection Act (1988); it has encountered similarly controversial constraints on its actions.

Shared problems also brought about negotiated settlements. Research had revealed that the central cause of the destruction of riparian and lake habitats was the chemical fallout from coal-fired power plants in both countries. These scientific findings led to intense diplomatic efforts to resolve the conflict. In 1991 Canada and the United States signed an Agreement on Air Quality that established a binational Air Quality Commission charged with reviewing control programs for acid rain, monitoring their effectiveness, and preventing deterioration in air quality.

Emerging Conflicts. Not all environmental tensions that rippled through the U.S. and Canadian political cultures in the late twentieth century were well or easily addressed. In the United States, the so-called Sagebrush Rebellion rose up in opposition to long-standing federal control of public lands and the resources they contained. These anti-environmentalists argued that the individual states, not the federal government, should have sovereignty over such matters, a perspective that challenged the regulatory apparatus that President Theodore Roosevelt had erected at the beginning of the century.

In Canada, a similar east–west political tug-of-war complicated the pursuit of environmental and social justice; making matters more complex still was the emergence of a new, north–south fault line that opened up between the northern First Nations, whose ancestral lands and ancient folkways were threatened by the resource hunger of the southern urban populations. The environment had become a vital political issue in North America, in short, because the Earth had become such a contested terrain.

—*Char Miller*

Population Growth and Consumption

By 1970, the United States and Canada were among the wealthiest nations in the world. Like most affluent nations, the two countries had low birth rates, but immigration from other countries caused their populations to rise. During the 1970s and 1980s, the U.S. population grew from 203 million to 249 million, while Canada's population grew from 22 million to 28 million. The ever-growing population—and rising resource consumption and pollution—became a source of concern to many environmentalists and the public.

Overpopulation Concerns. The possibility that the planet faced an overpopulation crisis came to public notice in 1968 with the publication of *The Population Bomb* by Paul Ehrlich, a Stanford University professor of population studies. The book predicted that global population pressures would soon reach such a level that, in the best-case scenario, fully one-fifth of the three billion people on Earth in 1968 would die of starvation by the late 1970s. Attempts to increase agricultural productivity would only worsen the food shortage in the long run, Ehrlich wrote, because high-yield methods of agricultural production caused erosion and relied too heavily on toxic pesticides (*see also* 122–23) that would eventually damage the soil. To prevent this outcome, Ehrlich recommended programs to coerce people to have fewer children.

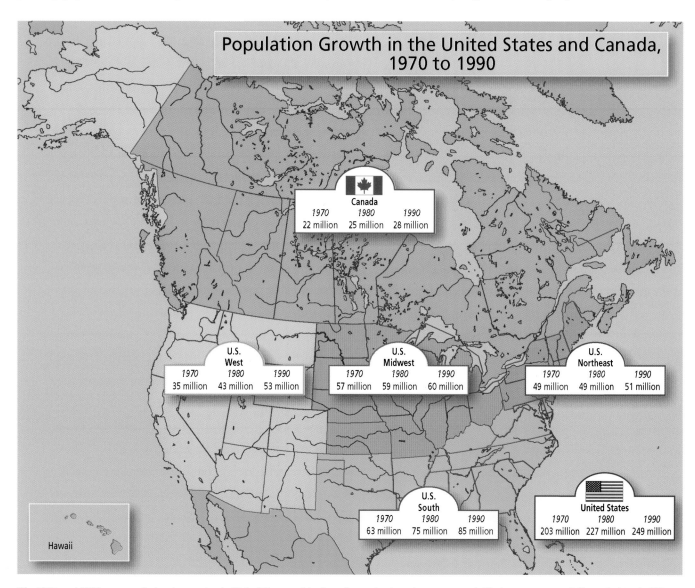

Population Growth in the United States and Canada, 1970 to 1990

Canada		
1970	1980	1990
22 million	25 million	28 million

U.S. West		
1970	1980	1990
35 million	43 million	53 million

U.S. Midwest		
1970	1980	1990
57 million	59 million	60 million

U.S. Northeast		
1970	1980	1990
49 million	49 million	51 million

U.S. South		
1970	1980	1990
63 million	75 million	85 million

United States		
1970	1980	1990
203 million	227 million	249 million

Hawaii

The 1970s and 1980s saw populations increase in the United States and in Canada, continuing a long-term trend. The increase was especially marked in the U.S. South and West (including Alaska and Hawaii), which, combined, gained forty million people in twenty years. By 1990 the U.S. South had more people than the entire United States had in 1900—a year in which the population of the U.S. West was only four million.
Sources: Data from U.S. Census Bureau. 20 Feb. 2003. <http://www.census.gov>; and Statistics Canada. 20 Feb. 2003. <http://www.statcan.ca/start.html>.

In 1972, four years after the publication of Ehrlich's work, an international think tank called the Club of Rome, consisting of industrialists, scientists, and economists, produced a report, *The Limits to Growth*. While more reasoned in tone than Ehrlich's book, the report was no less pessimistic. Working with systems analysts from the Massachusetts Institute of Technology to produce computer models calculating the impact of population growth, the Club of Rome predicted that massive food and resource shortages as well as pollution poisoning would kill off a substantial portion of the world's population well before the year 2100. To prevent this dire outcome, the report recommended a quick halt to both the growth of world population, as well as to global industrialization—a source of dangerous pollutants.

Both Ehrlich and the Club of Rome's serious warnings of global catastrophe generated tremendous attention and controversy, in no small part because the proposed solutions were so extreme. Both were bestsellers, with *The Population Bomb* selling three million copies and *The Limits to Growth*, nine million in the decade following their publication. However, neither an end to industrialization nor population-control programs seemed likely to occur in the United States or Canada; when China adopted a "one-child" policy in 1980, it was condemned in North America as inappropriate government interference in a highly personal decision. Curbing industrialization also was unlikely, as such a policy would seriously hamper economic growth.

Despite Ehrlich's prediction, the global population continued to grow through the 1970s and 1980s, reaching about five billion by 1990. The actual dangers of increasing populations were strongly questioned by those who argued that more efficient use of resources and more environmentally friendly agricultural practices (*see also* 172–73) would allow the planet to support increasing num-

Further Reading
Ehrlich, Paul R. *The Population Bomb*. Rev. ed. New York: Ballantine Books, 1978.
Meadows, Donella H., et al. *The Limits to Growth: A Report for the Club of Rome's Project on the Predicament of Mankind*. 2nd ed. New York: Universe Books, 1974.
World Commission on Environment and Development. *Our Common Future*. New York: Oxford University Press, 1987.

bers of people. While Ehrlich and the Club of Rome dismissed the possibility that technological advances could do more than delay the inevitable, critics argued that developing agricultural methods that relied less heavily on pesticides and preserved topsoil, as well as increasing the energy efficiency and reducing the pollution emissions of the equipment and facilities that people normally used, would benefit the overall environment.

Industrialized Nations. While the doomsday scenarios and draconian solutions of both books generated the most publicity, ultimately the books' more lasting influence came from their criticisms of the overconsumption of industrialized nations. Although people in industrialized countries have far fewer children than people in poorer countries, they use many more resources. *The Limits to Growth* found that the United States alone, with roughly 6 percent of the world's population, consumed 44 percent of the coal, 33 percent of the petroleum, and 63 percent of the natural gas used worldwide.

Additionally, both books highlighted the ever-increasing pollution levels in industrialized nations. *The Limits to Growth* exposed how environmental levels of lead (then commonly used in gasoline), mercury, and other dangerous pollutants were increasing rapidly at sites tested in the United States and Canada—in part because pesticide and fertilizer use was also rapidly increasing. *The Population Bomb* questioned the use of pesticides like DDT, arguing for a stricter regulation of chemicals and the creation of a federal environmental agency in

the United States. Although the U.S. and Canadian governments never addressed population growth as the authors envisioned, regulation of the emission of pollutants and use of pesticides was seriously tightened. DDT was banned by Canada in 1969 and the United States in 1972; the U.S. Environmental Protection Agency was created in 1970 and Canada's Department of the Environment was established in 1971; and both countries began to phase out leaded gasoline in 1975.

Sustainability. Eventually the debate shifted from how to prevent the world's population from growing to how such a large population could enjoy the higher living standards that come with industrialization without creating an environmental catastrophe. What became known as the "sustainable development" or "sustainable growth" movement developed, exploring how efficiency, renewable energy technologies, pollution controls, and agricultural practices could make economic and population growth more environmentally friendly. In 1987 the United Nation's World Commission on Environment and Development published *Our Common Future*, a book on sustainable development. In stark contrast to *The Population Bomb* and *Limits to Growth, Our Common Future* explicitly noted that it was "not a prediction of ever increasing environmental decay, poverty, and hardship" but instead a call for greater international cooperation on environmental issues to ensure "a new era of economic growth, one that must be based on policies that sustain and expand the environmental resource base." While the sustainable growth movement largely focused on economically underdeveloped countries, Canada has also attempted to apply such principles domestically, announcing its Green Plan in late 1990, which focused on preserving wilderness and reducing pollution despite the country's growing population.

—*Mary Sisson*

Wilderness Act of 1964

The Wilderness Act of 1964 stands as a landmark achievement in the protection and management of public lands in the United States. Its passage by Congress was the culmination of years of effort by American wilderness activists to secure the protection of federal law for the nation's wild lands.

Primitive Areas. Since the early colonial period, explorers had identified portions of the American landscape as wild, though designated wilderness areas did not exist within the national forests until the 1920s. These "primitive areas" were roadless tracts administered by the U.S. Forest Service (*see also* 92–93), which maintained them to meet mounting demands by hunters, anglers, conservationists, and recreationists for lands characterized by minimal human impact and presence. After World War II, recreational demands escalated and pressure from water development interests and commodity industries such as timber, mining, and ranching grew sharply; several dams (*see also* 128–29), for example, were proposed on rivers flowing through primitive areas. As a result, conflict increased over the location, size, and boundaries of the primitive areas.

From the 1940s to the early 1960s, the Forest Service reclassified primitive areas into freshly designated wilderness or wild areas, the particular designation depending on the size of the primitive area. Reclassification did not, however, guarantee permanent protection of wilderness because the new areas remained subject to the shifting policies and priorities of the Forest Service and changing demands on national forest lands. For instance, as timber harvesting increased following World War II, the Forest Service reduced the acreage of primitive areas, including in the Three Sisters and Selway–Bitterroot Wilderness Areas of the West.

Introduction of Bill. By 1956, frustrated by the lack of security for areas designated as wilderness, the Wilderness Society, joined by other national organizations and grassroots activists, launched a campaign to safeguard wild lands permanently by an act of Congress. Minnesota senator Hubert Humphrey introduced the first draft of the wilderness bill in the Senate that year. The bill called on the Forest Service and National Park Service to survey their potential wilderness lands and make recommendations to the president, who would subsequently designate new wilderness areas, subject to the approval of Congress.

An intense debate over the bill quickly followed in the American West and Minnesota, where the majority of public land was located. Numerous opponents in the West denounced supporters of the legislation as citified Easterners with no awareness of the rural West's economic dependence on grazing, mining, and timber production. Motorboat users, who sought to maintain motorized access into the boundary waters spanning Minnesota and southwest Ontario, joined the fight. Commodity industries and state water agencies in the West insisted that full development of natural resources was essential to job creation, economic growth, and thus national security during the Cold War. The American Forestry Association contended that the wilderness bill would compromise the Forest

Echo Park

Spanning the border of Utah and Colorado, Dinosaur National Monument has steep-walled canyons through which the Green and Yampa Rivers flow. Echo Park, at the center of the monument where the rivers converge, is a magnificent site flanked by the 800-foot (240-meter)-high Steamboat Rock. In the 1950s, Echo Park became the center of a vociferous debate about wilderness protection.

In the late 1940s, the Bureau of Reclamation proposed several large storage and hydropower dams along the upper Colorado River and its tributaries, one of them on the Green River 2 miles (3.2 kilometers) below Echo Park. The dam would have created a lengthy reservoir within the monument, inundating Echo Park and submerging most of Steamboat Rock. Many residents of the states in the upper Colorado River basin supported the plan, wanting to ensure water and hydroelectric power (electricity generated by turbines within a dam).

American conservationists united against the proposed Echo Park Dam. Led by the National Parks Association, the Wilderness Society, and the Sierra Club, a coalition of organizations pressured the bureau and its supporters in Congress to remove the dam from the plans for the Upper Colorado River Storage Project. They contended that the dam threatened the integrity of the national park system because its presence would violate the National Park Service Act of 1916, which mandated that the parks be preserved unimpaired. Conservationists also stressed the unique beauties of Echo Park and Dinosaur Monument and asserted that the dam would destroy the area's pristine rivers. Faced with strong public pressure to concede the dam, key lawmakers in the Senate did so in 1956. The Colorado River Storage Project Act, signed by President Dwight Eisenhower that same year, stipulated that no dam authorized in the legislation would intrude into any national park or monument. Conservationists viewed this not only as a victory in preserving Echo Park, but also as a sign of strengthened national commitment to the national park system and other threatened wilderness lands.

Green River and Steamboat Rock at Echo Park in Colorado. (© Tom Bean/Corbis)

During the 1970s and 1980s Congress added a number of new areas to the system, which comprises 105 million acres (42.5 million hectares) today.

The Wilderness Act declared that "it is . . . the policy of the Congress to secure for the American people . . . the benefits of an enduring resource of wilderness." It also defined wilderness as "an area where the earth and its community of life are untrammeled by man, where man himself is a visitor who does not remain." Howard Zahniser, the executive director of the Wilderness Society, wrote these words, which were a rallying cry for those who helped in the passage of the Wilderness Act. Zahniser's leadership in its passage was unwavering until his death four months before President Johnson signed the bill into law.

Passage of the Wilderness Act of 1964 was a tremendous achievement for a generation of conservationists. The law embraced and codified an environmental ethic that placed a high value on sustaining natural conditions and plant and animal communities largely unaffected by human influence. It also inspired a new generation of activists who regarded wilderness protection as an essential element of the emerging environmental movement (*see also* 162–63).

—*Mark Harvey*

Service's long-standing multiple-use policy; they argued that "wilderness," the term used in the bill, was by definition a single use and therefore would interfere with the agency's practice of managing its lands for grazing, timber, and fire control. Others warned that the bill would benefit only those able to afford costly trips into the backcountry.

Supporters had their own powerful constituency. After World War II, Americans used their rising incomes and paid vacations to enjoy outdoor recreation (*see also* 138–39). The numbers of visitors to state and federal parks and wilderness lands soared.

Passage of Act. The debate between opponents and supporters of the bill set the stage for a protracted struggle in Congress between 1956 and 1964. Led by Senators Humphrey of Minnesota, James Murray of Montana, Frank Church of Idaho, and Clinton Anderson of New Mexico, the Senate passed the wilderness bill in 1961. The battle shifted to the House of Representatives from 1962 to 1964. Representative Wayne Aspinall of Colorado, chair of the House Interior and Insular Affairs Committee, blocked the legislation until he secured special provisions for the

mining industry that would permit mineral leases and new mining claims to be filed on wilderness lands until December 31, 1983. Aspinall also engineered a key provision that granted Congress sole authority to designate new wilderness areas, instead of merely having a veto power over lands established by the president. The House then passed the bill 374–1 in July 1964, and President Lyndon Johnson signed it into law on September 3 of that year. The Wilderness Act permitted grazing to continue on wild lands already so designated, mineral prospecting for twenty years, and motorboat use in the boundary waters.

Although these compromises bothered wilderness advocates, most were satisfied by the outcome. The act created the national wilderness preservation system with 9.1 million acres (3.7 million hectares) permanently protected from roads, motorized vehicles and equipment such as chain saws, and commercial enterprises. The law also established a review process whereby the Forest Service and National Park Service had ten years to survey their potential wilderness holdings and offer recommendations to Congress about which lands to add to the system.

Further Reading

Allin, Craig. *The Politics of Wilderness Preservation.* Westport, Conn.: Greenwood Press, 1982.

Baker, Richard Allan. *Conservation Politics: The Senate Career of Clinton P. Anderson.* Albuquerque: University of New Mexico Press, 1985.

Frome, Michael. *Battle for the Wilderness.* Rev. ed. Salt Lake City: University of Utah Press, 1997.

Harvey, Mark W. T. *A Symbol of Wilderness: Echo Park and the American Conservation Movement.* Seattle: University of Washington Press, 2000.

Nash, Roderick. *Wilderness and the American Mind.* 4th ed. New Haven, Conn.: Yale University Press, 2001.

The Trans-Alaska Pipeline Dispute

n January 1968 the largest oil field in North American history was discovered at Prudhoe Bay on Alaska's North Slope in the Arctic. Of the various suggested methods (which included ice-breaking supertankers and a pipeline via the Canadian interior) for moving the oil to refineries and markets in the contiguous United States, the proposal that had the support of the oil companies was a 798-mile (1,284-kilometer), subsurface pipeline south to Valdez, North America's northernmost ice-free port. The Trans-Alaska Pipeline System (TAPS) was the most ambitious construction project in American history. By bringing the fate of Alaska's extensive wild lands and wildlife to the forefront of public attention, the

pipeline proposal engendered a four-year public debate unprecedented both in engineering and environmental history.

After Alaska achieved statehood in 1959, the oil industry spearheaded efforts to "open up" the state's relatively unexploited natural resources. Within a decade, oil had replaced fisheries as the state's main source of income. Exploration soon focused on the Arctic and the first leases on state land were sold there in 1964. In June 1969, the TAPS consortium applied to the government for construction permits as most of the proposed pipeline route traversed public lands.

Environmental Concerns. Federal officials were concerned not only about the impact of Alaska's harsh climate and

challenging physical environment on the project but also about its environmental consequences. As permafrost (frozen ground) underlay much of the proposed route, much of the pipe would need to run above ground. Possible oil spills in Prince William Sound after tankers left Valdez presented another potential problem. So did the impact of intrusion by people and construction machinery into the region north of the Yukon—increasingly celebrated as America's "last great wilderness."

Native Alaskan land claims were a further complication. Lawsuits filed by Native Alaskans and environmentalists in the spring of 1970 were found to have a valid basis, creating a major obstacle to authorization of the proposal. The first hurdle was

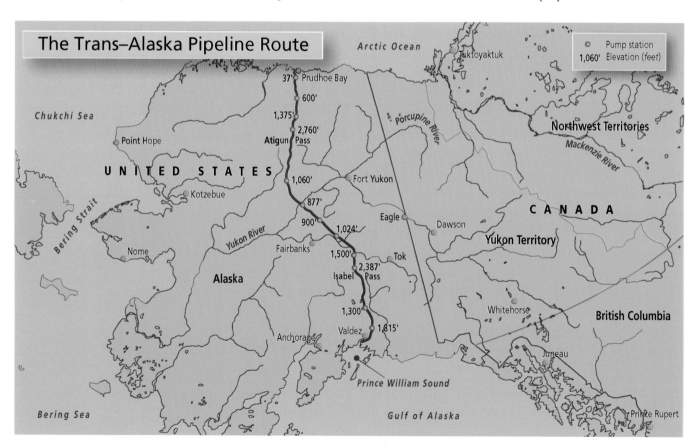

This map shows the route of the Trans–Alaska Pipeline System, which originates in Alaska's North Slope at Prudhoe Bay and travels south to Valdez, on Prince William Sound. Because of the harsh physical conditions of the route, much of the pipeline has been built above ground; the map indicates the elevation of the pump stations.
Source: Adapted from Claus Naske and Herman E. Slotnick, *Alaska: A History of the 49th State* (Norman: University of Oklahoma Press, 1994), 267. Courtesy of the University of Oklahoma Press.

surmounted in December 1971 when the U.S. Congress settled Native Alaskan claims with an act stipulating that if a pipeline corridor was set aside, Native Alaskans could not select lands within it. The settlement also included a $1 billion cash payment, half of which would come from royalties on oil production. Other obstacles included width provisions of the Mineral Leasing Act of 1920, which specified a maximum of 50 feet (15 meters) for rights-of-way across public lands associated with mineral extraction; and the National Environmental Policy Act (NEPA) of 1970, which required consideration of alternatives as part of a public statement of the environmental impact (EIS) of any project involving public lands or federally financed projects.

Public Opposition. Although the government's draft EIS (January 1971) endorsed the project, public hearings demonstrated the extent of opposition. Many remained unconvinced that Alyeska Pipeline Service Company (the TAPS consortium's successor) could build a reliable pipeline, some preferring a Canadian route to the American Midwest that initially followed the Mackenzie River in the Northwest Territories. Others felt that any pipeline, however sensitively designed and built, was profane in principle because this was the last great American wilderness. The proposed terminal at Valdez prompted local fishermen to initiate their own legal action (fearing pollution in coastal British Columbia, the Canadian Wildlife Federation also brought suit). Nevertheless, the final EIS (March 1972) restated the desirability of a trans-Alaska pipeline and in August 1972, the injunction based on noncompliance with NEPA was dissolved.

However, in February 1973, a court sustained the charge that construction permits violated the Mineral Leasing Act and

Further Reading
Berry, Mary Clay. *The Alaska Pipeline: The Politics of Oil and Native Land Claims.* Bloomington: Indiana University Press, 1975.
Coates, Peter. *The Trans-Alaska Pipeline Controversy.* Bethlehem, Penn.: Lehigh University Press, 1991.
———. "The Crude and the Pure: Oil and Environmental Politics in Alaska." In *Politics in the Postwar American West,* edited by Richard Lowitt. Norman: University of Oklahoma Press, 1995.
Strohmeyer, John. *Extreme Conditions: Big Oil and the Transformation of Alaska.* New York: Simon & Schuster, 1993.
Worster, Donald. "Alaska: The Underworld Erupts." In *Under Western Skies: Nature and History in the American West.* Oxford: Oxford University Press, 1993.

the "Canadian alternative" attracted growing public and congressional support. (Midwestern politicians suspected that Alyeska wanted to deliver oil to the West Coast to facilitate export to Japan. Yet the far longer route meant a greater proportion of North American wilderness would have been affected.) The energy crisis of 1973 (*see also* 156–57) broke the stalemate, with Vice President Spiro Agnew using his tie-breaking vote in the Senate to release the project from further court-ordered delay. Caribou protection and the integrity of NEPA seemed a luxury as the pipeline became the flagship of President Richard Nixon's drive to maximize domestic supplies of fuel. Congress passed the final authorization bill in November 1973, construction began in April 1974, and the first oil flowed south in 1977.

Construction. Despite the pipeline's economic benefits and image as an engineering tour de force, its construction was characterized by incompetence, cost overruns, corruption, thievery, and errors. Local communities also suffered considerable upheaval as large numbers of people flocked into the state, driving up the already high cost of housing, placing an enormous strain on public services (e.g., schools, hospitals, police), and bringing higher levels of crime and prostitution. Yet four years of pressure from environmentalists had vastly improved the final product. For example, buried crossings (sag bends) were incorporated in elevated sections at key migration points to prevent potential

delays in the arrival of various caribou herds at their wintering, calving, and summering grounds. No firm conclusions can be drawn about the project's impact on caribou and other wildlife, but vehicle traffic on the adjacent haul road and the human access that the road corridor has facilitated have had a more serious effect on wildlife in general over the short term than the pipeline itself. For instance, animals avoid the pipeline corridor because vehicles can run them down, and better access for hunters has increased levels of illegal trophy hunting of wolves and grizzlies. Caribou cows with calves tend to avoid the corridor just as they would avoid tall shrubs along rivers: The raised roadbed provides concealment for predators.

The pipeline became an integral feature of Alaska's mental and physical landscape; public interest in its future was rekindled in 2001. A few weeks after the attack on the World Trade Center on September 11, 2001, long-standing fears about the pipeline's security were renewed when a bullet from an inebriated hunter caused a temporary shutdown. Above all, the pipeline has remained highly visible through its connection with one of the most contentious environmental issues in America: the oil industry's campaign to drill in the Arctic National Wildlife Refuge (ANWR). North Slope production peaked in 1998 and oil from ANWR would flow to market through the pipeline, prolonging its working life (*see also* 184–85).

—*Peter Coates*

Canadian Dams and River Restorations

R ivers have been fundamental to the national development of Canada. From the early fur trade (*see also* 32–33) and explorations of the interior (*see also* 10–11) between the seventeenth and early twentieth centuries, to industrial and postindustrial development in the later twentieth century, Canada's rivers have contributed to the Canadian economy, either as transportation corridors, hydroelectric producers, or places of rest and recreation (*see also* 138). Fur traders and explorers did little to affect the rivers on which they traveled. Those who followed, including pulp and paper manufacturers, miners, hydroelectric entrepreneurs, and governments that supported economic

development, altered the riverine environment in various ways—often by the construction of dams, which transformed rivers into storage reservoirs, waste ditches, and/or hydroelectric generating stations.

Dam Construction. Industrial dam building in Canada can be divided roughly into two periods. During the first period from the 1890s until the 1960s, dams were located on rivers close to industrial and urban centers (e.g., Montreal, Québec; Toronto, Ontario; and Calgary, Alberta) and were thus often, but not exclusively, located in southern Canada. Dam construction in the second period (the 1960s to the present) was almost entirely on rivers in northern Canada; these areas, considered "frontiers"

for industrial development, were also the homelands of many First Nations (*see also* 48–49) like the Cree, Ojibwa, and Chipewyan. During this period, dams were built on the Saskatchewan River in Saskatchewan, the Churchill and Nelson Rivers in Manitoba, and the La Grande River in northern Québec, which forms part of the James Bay Project launched in 1971 by Québec's premier Robert Bourassa

Northern Dams. The dams developed in northern Canada, all of which involved large-scale water diversions and the creation of vast storage reservoirs, were and continue to be sources of conflict between First Nations and nonnative peoples and between environmentalists and developers because of the damage

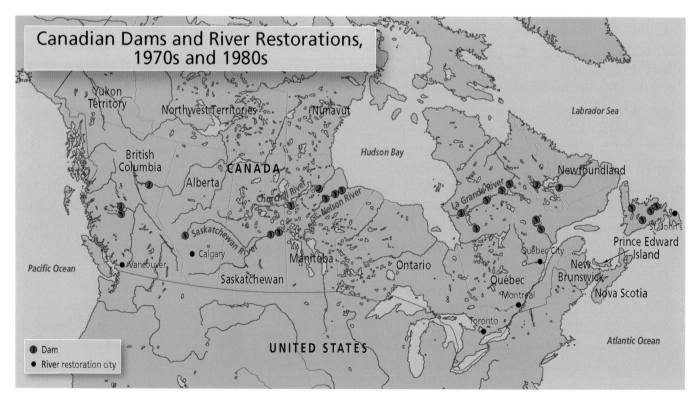

Canadian Dams and River Restorations, 1970s and 1980s

Canadian rivers have been vital to the nation's economic development. This map shows several prominent rivers in Canada that have been dammed to generate hydroelectric energy, as well as the location of Canada's northern hydroelectric dams. It also shows major cities in southern Canada where local citizens are active in restoring rivers to a healthy state.

Source: Adapted from Atlas of Canada. Natural Resources Canada. 18 May 2002. <http://atlas.gc.ca/site/english/maps/freshwater/consumption/hydroelectric>.

Further Reading

McCutcheon, Sean. *Electric Rivers: The Story of the James Bay Project.* Montreal: Black Rose Books, 1991.

Nelles, H. V. *The Politics of Development.* Hamden, Conn: Archon Books, 1974.

Richardson, Boyce. *Strangers Devour the Land.* Toronto: Macmillan of Canada, 1977.

Waldram, James. *As Long as the Rivers Run: Hydroelectric Development and Native Communities in Western Canada.* Winnipeg: University of Manitoba Press, 1988.

they do to the environment. For example, beginning in 1984, the La Grande River was transformed into seven reservoirs, containing diverted waters from four other rivers. As a result, various species of fish lost their spawning beds; trapping areas along shorelines were inundated and never restored; migration routes of large game animals were blocked or disrupted by blasting operations and other construction activities; and nesting sites and feeding zones of wild fowl were wiped out. Finally, when the dams were built, the flooded land contained dangerous levels of mercury that converted into poisonous methylmercury, which can permanently damage the nervous system and the brain. Its concentrations in fish were six times higher after the first La Grande reservoirs were built than they were before the flooding. As a result, the Québec Cree who ate them as a dietary staple had to reduce their consumption of one of their most important foods.

Canada's northern dams and their resulting reservoirs service largely southern needs, creating additional controversy. The transmission lines running out of the La Grande generating station travel south to Montreal, Québec City, and ultimately to the eastern United States. Thus people to the south receive the bulk of the benefits of dam building and the northern First Nations bear the brunt of the ensuing environmental degradation. Environmentalists from both the United States and Canada have cataloged these effects and launched several campaigns to stop further dam construction in northern Québec and the rest of Canada in an effort to preserve the northern riverine ecosystems; the First Nations have also attempted to stop dam construction, but mostly in an effort to preserve their way of life. Neither group has had much success.

River Restoration in the South. In contrast, while rivers in the north were being dammed, some rivers in the south were being restored to their natural conditions after being used as chemical dumps and in manufacturing processes like rinsing agents and coolants. Such restorations, or attempted restorations, have been made in Calgary; Toronto; Vancouver, British Columbia; and St. John's, Newfoundland. Often these attempts were organized by local citizens interested in revitalizing their waterfronts. For example, the Quidi Vidi Rennie's River Development Foundation was formed in 1985 to clean up, beautify, and enhance the Rennie River, which flows through St. John's. This river had become so polluted that its appearance and smell became intolerable. Within ten years, the Rennie was restored to the extent that a rare species of trout returned to the river, and the waterfront area had become a favorite recreational spot for both citizens and tourists. The foundation also established an educational center dedicated to demonstrating the positive effects of citizen activism in promoting environmental stewardship. Similar efforts are being undertaken by the Society for Promotion of Environmental Conservation, in Vancouver but, thus far, with less success.

Canada's rivers remain important to its national development and are the source of many political disputes between First Nation and nonnative citizens, between north and south, and between industrialists and environmentalists. These disputes will likely escalate as water and energy shortages increase and stronger efforts to protect and purify the environment and to meet increased recreational demands are made.

—*Jean L. Manore*

Aerial view of the James Bay Project in Québec. (© Christopher J. Morris/Corbis)

Hazardous Wastes and Toxic Cleanup

The definition of what constitutes a "hazard" has changed considerably. Although historically the term had frequently been used for natural rather than human-made dangers, by the 1970s and 1980s the concept of "hazardous wastes" was used to characterize a waste that threatened human health and wildlife. Policymakers applied the term to certain by-products and wastes resulting from manufacturing processes, medical and scientific procedures and research, and discarded consumer products. In Canada and the United States, the remaining decades of the twentieth century saw governmental and private efforts to clean up polluted sites; many still remain, however.

Industrial Pollution. The industrial hygiene movement of the early twentieth century helped determine the kind of substances that public policy today defines as hazardous. Industrial hygiene focused mainly on substances that workers encountered within the workplace, and its concern with hazardous industrial substances seldom extended beyond factory walls. Although late-nineteenth-century public health auth-orities considered industrial pollution to be a major problem, the focus shifted after the acceptance of the germ theory of disease. Public health officers and sanitary engineers focused on bacterial wastes, especially in water, as the primary threat to human health (*see also* 74--77). They concentrated on the nonpatho-

logical effects of industrial wastes, including the damage they inflicted on fish and shellfish and their interference with water and sewage treatment processes. Only after World War II did professionals begin to pay greater attention to the health and environmental damages of industrial wastes in the ambient environment and not until the 1970s did these areas receive fuller policy recognition.

Waste Storage and Disposal. In the United States, the first federal legislative attention to hazardous waste appeared in the 1970 Solid Waste Act. Section 212 of this act required that the Environmental Protection Agency (EPA; 1970) undertake a comprehensive investigation of the storage and disposal of hazardous wastes. The

U.S. Superfund Sites Listed on the National Priorities List, 2002

CANADA

Washington 48
Montana 13
North Dakota 0
Minnesota 24
Vermont 9
New Hampshire 18
Maine 13
Oregon 11
Idaho 6
Wyoming 2
South Dakota 2
Wisconsin 39
Michigan 67
New York 90
Massachusetts 31
Rhode Island 12
Nevada 1
Utah 16
Colorado 15
Nebraska 10
Iowa 13
Illinois 39
Indiana 28
Ohio 29
Pennsylvania 94
Connecticut 15
New Jersey 113
California 96
Arizona 9
New Mexico 12
Kansas 10
Missouri 23
Kentucky 14
West Virginia 9
Virginia 30
Delaware 16
Maryland 18
Oklahoma 10
Arkansas 12
Tennessee 12
North Carolina 27
Washington, D.C. 1
Mississippi 2
Alabama 13
Georgia 14
South Carolina 25
Texas 40
Louisiana 13
Florida 51
Alaska 7
Hawaii 3
MEXICO

Less than 10
11–20
21–40
41–80
More than 81

Superfund sites on the National Priorities List (NPL) as of 2002. Superfund sites are listed on the NPL after a Hazard Ranking System (HRS) screening and public feedback about the proposed site. Once all comments have been addressed, a site is placed on the NPL.

Source: Data from National Priorities List Sites in the United States. U.S. Environmental Protection Agency. 4 Oct. 2002. <http://www.epa.gov/superfund/sites/npl/npl.htm>.

Further Reading

Colten, Craig E., and Peter N. Skinner. *The Road to Love Canal: Managing Industrial Waste before EPA.* Austin: University of Texas Press, 1996.

Tarr, Joel A. *The Search for the Ultimate Sink: Urban Pollution in Historical Perspective.* Akron, Ohio: University of Akron Press, 1996.

VanNijnatten, Debora L., and Robert Boardman, eds. *Canadian Environmental Policy: Context and Cases.* 2nd ed. Toronto: Oxford University Press, 2002.

EPA's resulting 1974 report to Congress led to the passage, in 1976, of the Resource Conservation and Recovery Act (RCRA). RCRA defined hazardous wastes as solid wastes that can cause serious illness or pose a hazard to human health and to the environment when improperly stored, transported, or managed. In 1980, acting under the RCRA requirements, the EPA announced regulations implementing cradle-to-grave controls for handling hazardous wastes, requiring that such substances be tracked through a manifest system from manufacture, through their use cycles, and then through disposal.

The chemical, primary metals, and tanning industries produced large amounts of wastes in the first decades of the twentieth century. Immediately after World War II, these and other industries began producing a greater amount of hazardous wastes. Much of this waste was disposed of in unlined lagoons, in industrial landfills, and in municipal sanitary landfills. Land disposal of wastes actually increased in the post–World War II period, as states put limits on dumping wastes into water. Older waste-dump sites, in many cases abandoned or closed, posed a special threat to groundwater, which was used by almost half of the U.S. population for drinking (*see also* 190–91). The case of the former chemical waste dump Love Canal (*see also* 158–59) in Niagara Falls, New York, focused public and government attention on the problem in the late 1970s.

Superfund. Congress responded to the danger of these sites in 1980 by approving the Comprehensive Environmental Response, Compensation, and Liability (CERCLA), or Superfund, Act, which provided $1.6 billion for the immediate cleanup of toxic wastes. Under CERCLA, the EPA established procedures of site-specific risk assessments to determine whether the hazardous wastes were a threat to human health. The Superfund Amendments and Reauthorization Act (SARA) in 1986 increased the money available for cleanup to $9.6 billion. The Superfund Act and its amendments sought to cover the costs of cleanup by requiring retroactive liability: those who were responsible for creating hazardous waste sites in the past, including both owners and depositors, were considered liable for the costs of cleanup. The amendments also required that firms that imported, processed, or produced more than 50,000 pounds (22,700 kilograms) per year of any of the EPA's listed chemicals and compounds register and report them in the EPA's annual Toxics Release Inventory. The slow pace of cleanups, however, as well as cumbersome procedures, convinced many experts that the Superfund was not only underfunded but also imposed unreasonable standards of cleanliness where future site uses involved little human interaction, such as parking lots. As of 2000, however, attempts to alter substantially the legislation had failed.

Canadian Issues. Canada has also been affected by industrial hazardous wastes, although on a smaller scale. Canadians were slower to react to these dangers than were U.S. policymakers, partly because their federated governmental system resulted in more decentralization of policy decisions. A special Canadian problem, for instance, involved the transport in the 1990s of U.S. hazardous wastes to disposal destinations in Ontario because of the less-stringent standards of that province. Disposal of hazardous industrial wastes in Ontario increased from about 1.5 million tons in 1990 to over 2.1 million tons in 1997, with declines, however, from 2000 to 2001. Canadian public policy, especially in the provinces, has been attempting to move disposal from land fill and incineration to an emphasis on the "3Rs": reduction, reuse, and recycling. Increasingly, the Canadian federal government has relied upon a policy of impact assessments in an attempt to foresee and prevent hazardous wastes from affecting human health and incurring environmental risks.

—Joel A. Tarr

Medical Wastes

Jacques Cousteau once observed that the "sea is the universal sewer." Confirmation came in 1988 when Long Island and New Jersey beaches were closed after garbage slicks containing needles, syringes, and other medical waste washed ashore. Similar trash also surfaced along the coasts of Canada's Maritime Provinces (Prince Edward Island, Nova Scotia, and New Brunswick), in the Gulf of Mexico, and in the Great Lakes.

Shocked about the illegal or careless handling of some of the then–3.2 million tons of U.S. hospital-generated medical waste, Congress enacted the Medical Waste Tracking Act (MWTA). The MWTA required the Environmental Protection Agency (EPA) to establish a two-year demonstration program to collect data on waste streams, establish management standards for control and disposal of medical wastes, and assess penalties for violators. In 1997, the EPA enacted further regulations governing toxic emissions from medical-waste incinerators and in 1998 entered a voluntary partnership with the American Hospital Association to slash waste volume by 50 percent by 2010, an important first step in protecting oceans and rivers.

Contemporary Native American Land and Resource Rights in the United States

Since the landing of Christopher Columbus in 1492, through the forced removal and relocation of native peoples to reservations in the nineteenth century (*see also* 46–47), Native Americans have fought in various arenas to maintain their independence and rights. With the passage of more favorable legislation, including the Indian Self-Determination and Education Act of 1975, Native American tribes began to reassert claim to their control over water, fishing, and land rights.

Since the 1960s, the 550 federally recognized Native American tribes have controlled more than 56 million acres (23 million hectares) of reservation land, with native Alaskans currently controlling another 44 million acres (18 million hectares). According to the Native American Fish and Wildlife Society, Native Americans possess a natural resource land base of more than 730,000 acres (295,000 hectares) of lakes and impoundments (reservoirs), and over 10,000 miles (16,000 kilometers) of streams and rivers. Thus, control of Native American land and resources is critically important, especially in the West where most reservations are located.

In 1975, Native American tribes officially recognized by the federal government were given semi-sovereign status, meaning they had a great deal of control, but not absolute control, over their reservations. A complicated body of law, including treaties, statutes, and administrative decisions and actions, has developed to define the relationship between tribal governments and federal, state, and local governments. In addition, thousands of cases have been brought before the courts to attempt to interpret these laws on contemporary Native American rights. Some of these cases are still being presented and could drag on for decades, costing millions of dollars in legal fees and never completely addressing or fully resolving the original conflict.

Water Rights. Native Americans won a string of victories, culminating in the landmark *Arizona v. California* U.S. Supreme Court case of 1963, in regard to their reserved water rights (*see also*

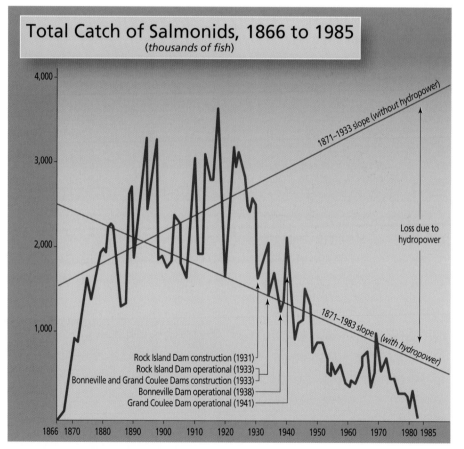

Total Catch of Salmonids, 1866 to 1985
(thousands of fish)

Rock Island Dam construction (1931)
Rock Island Dam operational (1933)
Bonneville and Grand Coulee Dams construction (1933)
Bonneville Dam operational (1938)
Grand Coulee Dam operational (1941)

1871–1933 slope (without hydropower)
Loss due to hydropower
1871–1983 slope (with hydropower)

Native American tribes' fishing rights are protected by treaty. The tribes from the Columbia River Basin point out that their salmon catch has declined precipitously since the government built a series of dams on the river. According to the tribes, the decline has been caused by the construction and operation in the 1930s and 1940s of the Rock Island Dam, Bonneville Dam, and Grand Coulee Dam on the Columbia River, which originates in Canada and forms the boundary between Washington and Oregon. Native Americans consider the dams to be a direct threat to their food supply and a violation of treaties signed by the U.S. government. The U.S. Army Corps of Engineers argues that the dams on the Columbia River are not the principal cause of the salmon decline, and that the returns of salmon to the Columbia River were already in decline prior to the construction of the Bonneville Dam in the 1930s.
Source: Adapted from Center for Columbia River History. <http://www.ccrh.org/comm/river/docs/counts.htm>. Underlying data from Scholz, A., et al. "Compilation of Information on Salmon and Steelhead Total Run Size, Catch and Hydropower Related Losses in the Upper Columbia River Basin, Above Grand Coulee Dam," *Fisheries Technical Report No. 2* (Cheney, Wash.: Upper Columbia United Tribes, Eastern Washington University, Dept. of Biology, 1985).

100–01). The U.S. Supreme Court awarded tribes sufficient water for all the "practicable irrigable acreage" (i.e., enough water to irrigate all land that would benefit from irrigation) on reservations. This victory was followed twenty years later by a series of less favorable decisions. One case, originally filed in 1977 in the state courts of Wyoming, involved reserved water claims of the Wind River Reservation. The Wyoming supreme court, ruling in favor of the Northern Arapahoe and Eastern Shoshone tribes of the Wind River Reservation, granted the tribes a water right to 500,717 acre-feet (617,625,407 cubic-meters) of water (1 acre-foot [1,234 cubic-meters] of water is enough to cover an acre to a depth of 1 foot [0.3 meter], and is equivalent to 325,851 gallons [1,233,444 liters]). However, the court limited the tribes' use of that water to irrigation, making the water virtually useless to the tribes as they could not afford to build an irrigation project, and they preferred to use the water for in-stream flow and fish habitat. By 2002, the disagreement still was unresolved.

Fishing and Hunting Rights. Various treaties between Native American tribes and the U.S. government also granted tribes special fishing and hunting rights. For instance, in the Pacific Northwest, many Native American tribes had signed treaties in the 1850s, known as the Stevens treaties, which permitted them to fish in their "usual and accustomed places." However, conflicts over fishing rights sometimes escalated into violence as local non–Native American fishermen and their supporters in state and local government attempted to prevent Native Americans from exercising these treaty rights. In the upper Midwest, these conflicts involved the right of Native Americans to spearfish—a right denied to non–Native American fishermen. In the 1960s officials

Further Reading
Ambler, Marjane. *Breaking the Iron Bonds: Indian Control of Energy Development.* Lawrence: University Press of Kansas, 1990.
Clow, Richmond, and Imre Sutton. *Trusteeship in Change: Toward Tribal Autonomy in Resource Management.* Boulder: University Press of Colorado, 2001.
McCool, Daniel. *Native Waters: Indian Water Settlements and the Second Treaty Era.* Tucson: University of Arizona Press, 2002.
Utter, Jack. *American Indians: Answers to Today's Questions.* 2nd ed. Norman: University of Oklahoma Press, 2001.

in Washington state resorted to "tear gas and billy clubs" in an effort to stop Native Americans from fishing, according to a 1999 *Seattle Times* article. At anti-Indian protests in the late 1970s, some whites carried signs saying "Spear a pregnant squaw: save a walleye." In 1974 a U.S. district court ruled that the Stevens treaties and other treaty provisions gave tribes the right to one-half of the harvestable run of salmon in the region's rivers. This decision was upheld in 1979 by the U.S. Supreme Court. In recent years, controversy over salmon runs has intensified because of the precipitous decline in salmon numbers over the last century.

Environmental Policy. Water and fishing rights are just two elements in the continuing struggle of Native American nations to control their lands and natural resources. Native American tribes have, since the 1950s, controlled 44 million acres (18 million hectares) of grazing lands, 5.3 million acres (2 million hectares) of commercial forests, 2.5 million acres (1 million hectares) of crop land, 4 percent of the nation's oil and gas reserves, 40 percent of the nation's uranium, and 30 percent of the nation's coal. These resources make Native American tribes significant players in the high-stakes game of environmental policy in the West. Controversies

have also arisen over the dumping of hazardous wastes (*see also* 152–53), including nuclear wastes, on reservations. For example, throughout the 1970s and 1980s, the Navajo nation struggled to deal with the toxic mess created by uranium mining on its reservation, which occupies parts of three states: Arizona, New Mexico, and Utah. Many Navajos became ill as a result of working in the uranium industry or living near uranium mine tailings.

As Native American peoples began to demand control over their own resources in the 1970s, they met with considerable opposition from the Bureau of Indian Affairs (BIA) and state and local governments. However, the federal government gradually recognized the right of tribes to govern their own environment under the terms of the Indian Self-Determination Act. Federal policy now considers Native American tribes to be integral partners in policy making where a policy directly affects Native American lands and resources. Many governing processes previously controlled by the BIA have been transferred to tribes through what is known as the "638 process." In this process, tribes can apply to the secretary of the interior to take over programs administered by the federal government, thus increasing Native American control of their own resources. Federal agencies are required to consult with tribal governments when agency actions affect them, and all levels of government, including state and local, must engage tribes in a government-to-government relationship. These changes have made effectively managing resources and controlling their lands easier for Native Americans. Slowly tribes have taken over the management of their own environment, and now are faced with the delicate task of balancing resource development with the preservation of tribal lands as a permanent homeland.

—*Daniel McCool*

The Energy Crisis and Nuclear Power

Although many experts predicted that the energy crisis in 1974 would produce a rush in orders for new nuclear power plants as a cost-saving, pollution-free alternative to coal and oil (*see also* 102–05), exactly the opposite occurred. Nuclear power construction suffered a complete collapse in the wake of the oil embargo imposed by Middle East oil producers against the United States. The energy crisis and the resulting inflationary pressures made new nuclear power plants both unnecessary and too expensive to build. The energy crisis dealt the fatal blow to an industry that was already struggling with regulatory delays, technical and managerial problems, and rising public opposition.

Energy Consumption. Decades of readily available and cheap oil had made America's energy-hungry economy—dominated by the automobile, high-energy technologies, and consumerism—dangerously dependent on Middle East oil.

Americans used more energy per capita than the citizens of any other nation in the world. But 1970 was a turning point for domestic oil production. Domestic production peaked that year, declining rapidly thereafter. From 1967 to 1973, oil imports jumped from less than 10 percent to 36 percent. With Texas fields no longer able to compensate for disruptions in the international supply, producers in the Middle East recognized that oil could be an economic and political weapon, particularly in the ongoing conflict between Israel—an ally of the United States—and its Arab neighbors.

Americans increased their use of electricity even more than oil, and utilities were hard pressed to meet demand. Between 1945 and 1970, electricity consumption doubled approximately every decade. In the frigid winter of 1969, the country experienced critical power shortages in the East and Midwest and more were predicted. Utility executives

dismissed energy conservation as too restrictive and shunned polluting coal plants. They demanded, and got, larger nuclear power plants. Between 1965 and 1973, utilities ordered twenty-three nuclear power plants each year.

Nuclear Waste. Utility companies were purchasing an untested and unproven technology. Plant designers rushed to build models that were of unknown safety and that lacked the complex support systems needed to create and dispose of nuclear fuel and radioactive components. In addition they were costly to build and operate. Construction expenses were often double the estimates, and maintenance problems were epidemic. The problem of nuclear waste disposal proved far more intractable than the industry had anticipated. Federal and state politicians engaged in a thirty-year battle over where to locate an unpopular long-term waste repository, eventually settling on the politically weak state of Nevada. Meanwhile, radioactive wastes awaiting safe disposal piled up at all the nation's nuclear power plants. Critics of nuclear power, inside and outside the industry, pointed to these problems during regulatory reviews, forcing utilities to abandon plants or make expensive modifications. The time required to license a power plant tripled. Utility company executives slowly realized that they had ordered huge plants that they could not finance, license, or operate efficiently. In 1972, utilities canceled plans for seven nuclear plants, but thirty-eight new orders gave an upbeat image to a troubled industry. The energy crisis turned this minor retreat into a rout.

Oil Embargo. In October 1973, Arab nations announced that they would halt oil

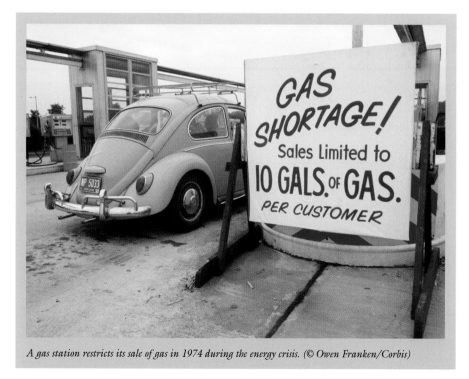

A gas station restricts its sale of gas in 1974 during the energy crisis. (© Owen Franken/Corbis)

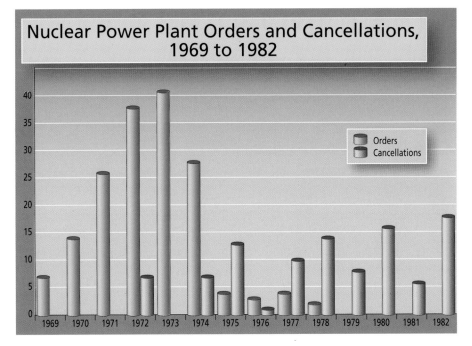

Nuclear Power Plant Orders and Cancellations, 1969 to 1982

Orders
Cancellations

Nuclear power plant orders escalated between 1969 and 1973. Problems in construction and operation, public opposition, and the impact of the energy crisis abruptly halted orders and led to a wave of cancellations.
Source: Data from Energy Information Administration, U.S. Department of Energy, *Nuclear Plant Cancellations: Causes, Costs, and Consequences* (Washington, D.C.: Government Printing Office, 1983).

shipments to the United States and to other countries that supported Israel against Egypt and Syria in the Yom Kippur War that occurred that month. The Arab oil embargo stunned the nation and the scandal-plagued administration of President Richard Nixon, which seemed powerless to end or alleviate the embargo. When Middle East oil producers lifted the ban six months later, the United States was a different nation. The energy crisis created crippling fuel shortages, a national recession, and a decade of high inflation and unemployment; it effectively ended an era in which cheap energy had been the stimulus to national growth. By 1974, the price of oil had risen from $3.65 to $12.25 per barrel. Nixon proposed Project Independence, a program to expand fossil fuel production, to streamline nuclear power regulation, and to promote minimal energy conservation measures. The nuclear power industry warmly endorsed Nixon's plan and eagerly anticipated a desperate public outcry to end restrictions on nuclear power plants. No

public support came. Already weakened by the Watergate scandal, Nixon and, later, President Gerald Ford confronted growing public concerns about reactor safety and could not get legislation passed that supported nuclear power.

Collapse of Nuclear Power. While advocates trumpeted nuclear power as the answer to the energy needs of the United States, public opposition, poor management, and the energy crisis itself proved to be the industry's undoing. Shocked into adopting conservation practices, Americans increased their usage of electricity by only half of what utility officials expected during the 1970s, eliminating the need for many new power plants. The high inflation of the 1970s made construction of nuclear power plants particularly expensive. Interest charges piled up as construction mistakes, new safety systems, and time-consuming litigation by antinuclear activists pushed the average completion time for construction of a power plant to ten years. After 1974,

orders for nuclear plants fell precipitously and many orders were canceled. Often blamed for nuclear power's demise, the 1979 Three Mile Island accident in Pennsylvania (*see also* 158–59) merely delivered the final blow to an already mortally wounded industry. By 1980, the average nuclear plant cost nearly 50 percent more to build than a coal plant, up from 18 percent a decade earlier.

Since the collapse of support for nuclear power, the industry has matured. The nuclear power industry and its regulators have improved the efficiency of existing plants, standardized safer designs, and streamlined the regulatory process. They may yet solve the problem of waste disposal by opening the Yucca Mountain repository in Nevada to store radioactive materials. In forcing a rational reevaluation of atomic energy (*see also* 130–31), the energy crisis may have helped destroy the first nuclear era, but may also have laid the groundwork for a second. Public opinion and the long-term attractiveness of fossil fuels and alternative power sources, such as wind and solar power, will most likely determine if the nuclear industry reemerges.

—Thomas R. Wellock

Further Reading
Bupp, Irvin C., and Jean-Claude Derian. *Light Water: How the Nuclear Dream Dissolved*. New York: Basic Books, 1978.
Campbell, John L. *Collapse of an Industry: Nuclear Power and the Contradictions of U.S. Policy*. Ithaca, N.Y.: Cornell University Press, 1988.
Energy Information Administration, U.S. Department of Energy. *Nuclear Plant Cancellations: Causes, Costs, and Consequences*. Washington, D.C.: Government Printing Office, 1983.
Melosi, Martin V. *Coping With Abundance: Energy and Environment in Industrial America*. New York: Alfred Knopf, 1985.
Wellock, Thomas R. *Critical Masses: Opposition to Nuclear Power in California, 1958–1978*. Madison: University of Wisconsin Press, 1998.

Environmental Disasters

Following World War II, the United States and Canada became increasingly wealthy, largely as a result of industrial growth. Their governments aggressively sought new energy sources (*see also* 130–31 *and* 156–57), while industries disposed of waste cheaply. As the 1960s progressed, however, the cost of such practices became more evident to the public. As a result of greater environmental awareness, calamities that once might have been shrugged off as the inevitable result of industrial development instead riveted public attention, leading to a critical reevaluation of environmentally harmful practices and policies.

Offshore Drilling. During the 1960s, the federal government had strongly encouraged offshore drilling as a way to increase domestic oil production. On January 28, 1969, workers with the Union Oil Company of California accidentally triggered a blowout about 5 miles (8 kilometers) off the coast of Santa Barbara, California. A blowout, or gusher, occurs when natural gas and oil are found together in an underground deposit. When that deposit is drilled into, the pressure from the gas can cause both the gas and oil to shoot out of the well.

The Union Oil workers capped the underwater well, but when the well was plugged, the gas and oil shot out of deep cracks in the ocean bed. Despite efforts to stop the blowout, it continued for two more years, spilling an estimated minimum of 3 million gallons (11 million liters) of oil into the Pacific Ocean. At one point, the resulting oil slick stretched from California's Pismo Beach to the Mexican border, some 250 miles (402 kilometers). Despite intensive rescue efforts, thousands of water birds were killed by the oil. The spill also contaminated fish, so local fishermen were forbidden to fish, thus temporarily destroying their livelihood; tourism also suffered as scenic beaches were fouled with oil.

The Santa Barbara disaster increased public awareness of the potential harms of the practice, which had once seemed like a sensible way to gain access to valuable natural resources. After the spill, public opposition to offshore drilling forced companies to locate wells farther offshore and away from sensitive coastal ecosystems.

Fire on the Cuyahoga. While the Santa Barbara spill raised awareness of the damage being done to the ocean, an incident later that same year put public focus on the health of the nation's rivers. On June 22, 1969, the Cuyahoga River caught fire as it flowed through downtown Cleveland, Ohio. It was not the first time the heavily polluted river had ignited—the river had been catching fire periodically since the first decade of the twentieth century. The fire, which was put out after twenty minutes, was one of the Cuyahoga's smaller fires. The public's reaction was something new, however. That running water was so polluted by

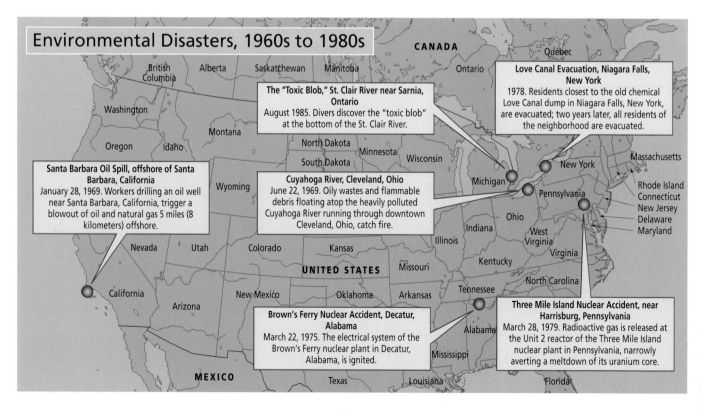

Environmental Disasters, 1960s to 1980s

The "Toxic Blob," St. Clair River near Sarnia, Ontario
August 1985. Divers discover the "toxic blob" at the bottom of the St. Clair River.

Love Canal Evacuation, Niagara Falls, New York
1978. Residents closest to the old chemical Love Canal dump in Niagara Falls, New York, are evacuated; two years later, all residents of the neighborhood are evacuated.

Santa Barbara Oil Spill, offshore of Santa Barbara, California
January 28, 1969. Workers drilling an oil well near Santa Barbara, California, trigger a blowout of oil and natural gas 5 miles (8 kilometers) offshore.

Cuyahoga River, Cleveland, Ohio
June 22, 1969. Oily wastes and flammable debris floating atop the heavily polluted Cuyahoga River running through downtown Cleveland, Ohio, catch fire.

Brown's Ferry Nuclear Accident, Decatur, Alabama
March 22, 1975. The electrical system of the Brown's Ferry nuclear plant in Decatur, Alabama, is ignited.

Three Mile Island Nuclear Accident, near Harrisburg, Pennsylvania
March 28, 1979. Radioactive gas is released at the Unit 2 reactor of the Three Mile Island nuclear plant in Pennsylvania, narrowly averting a meltdown of its uranium core.

oily wastes that it could accidentally ignite caused national outrage.

Nuclear Power Plants. During the 1970s, nuclear accidents—and revelations about shoddy safety practices in nuclear power plants—increased public awareness about the dangers of nuclear power (*see also* 130–31 *and* 156–57), especially the possibility of radiation leaks. On March 22, 1975, for example, a workman's candle, used to detect air leaks, started a fire in the Brown's Ferry nuclear power plant in Decatur, Alabama. The fire spread throughout the plant's electrical system, shorting out the plant's cooling mechanisms. Reactor operators prevented a potentially devastating accident, but the fire caused more than $100 million in damage.

On March 28, 1979, four years after the Brown's Ferry incident, maintenance workers at a reactor at the Three Mile Island nuclear power plant near Harrisburg, Pennsylvania, accidentally cut off the main water supply that cooled the reactor's uranium core. This situation worsened when a drainage valve in the reactor stuck open; because of faulty and inadequate sensors within the reactor itself, the operators were unaware that the reactor needed water. Part of the uranium core then overheated, releasing radioactive gas that was eventually vented outside the plant. After several hours, water was added to the reactor and the core was cooled, but the core came perilously close to a state called meltdown, when the radioactive uranium becomes so hot that it burns through the floor of the plant and into the ground. Publicity surrounding the accident prompted an estimated 140,000 people to flee the area.

Love Canal. A series of events in Niagara Falls, New York, made people look with new suspicion at the very ground they lived on. In 1953 the town's board of education purchased a plot of land for $1 from the Hooker Chemical Company, which for

Further Reading
Easton, Robert. *Black Tide: The Santa Barbara Oil Spill and Its Consequences.* New York: Delacorte Press, 1972.
Ford, Daniel F. *Three Mile Island: Thirty Minutes to Meltdown.* New York: Viking Press, 1982.
Gibbs, Lois Marie. *Love Canal: The Story Continues.* Gabriola Island, B.C.: New Society Publishers, 1998.
Mazur, Allan. *A Hazardous Inquiry: The Rashomon Effect at Love Canal.* Cambridge, Mass.: Harvard University Press, 1998.

more than a decade had dumped toxic chemical wastes on the land. The dump, called the Love Canal, contained at least twenty thousand tons of waste, including carcinogens like dioxin and benzene.

After buying the land, the town built a playground and a school on it, excavated streets, and built homes. During the excavations, rusting metal drums of caustic waste were uncovered. In the mid-1970s, residents nearest to the dump began complaining of smells and black ooze coming out of the ground in their yards and into their basements. Harmful chemicals from the ooze were found in homes by the New York State Department of Health, and publicity generated by the discovery caused home values in the area to plummet.

In 1978, the state and federal governments agreed to buy the homes of those who lived closest to the old dump. But residents in the rest of the neighborhood were also concerned—the value of their homes had decreased, and a series of preliminary studies conducted by groups such as the state health department and the U.S. Environmental Protection Agency appeared to show higher rates of a variety of illnesses and conditions, especially miscarriages and birth defects, among residents of Love Canal. (The studies were later largely discounted as unscientific because many of the preliminary studies were based on small sample sizes or unreliable methods of reporting.) The homeowners began an extensive and impassioned campaign to have their homes bought too; in 1980 the federal government agreed and the entire Love Canal neighborhood was evacuated. The residents' well-publicized crusade inspired many other

communities to examine the environmental threats around them, drew public attention to the previously-ignored problem of toxic waste, and helped give rise to the Comprehensive Environmental Response, Compensation, and Liability Act in 1980 (also known as the Superfund), which mandated the clean up of old toxic waste dumps (*see also* 152–53).

Toxins. In 1985, divers found a mass of black, oily material sitting at the bottom of the St. Clair River near Sarnia, Ontario. Dubbed the "toxic blob," the mass proved to be some 2,500 gallons (9,460 liters) of perchloroethylene, a carcinogenic dry cleaning fluid that had been dumped into the river by Dow Chemical Canada, Inc., and had combined with other toxins, including dioxin, already in the river. The Ontario government fined Dow $16,000 and forced it to clean up the blob, which cost the company more than $1 million. This incident bolstered support for tougher federal laws governing toxins, leading to the adoption of the Canadian Environmental Protection Act (CEPA) in 1988.

The Superfund and CEPA were not the only pieces of legislation prompted by an environmental disaster during this period. Canada adopted clean-water legislation in 1970 and the United States did the same with the Clean Water Act of 1972. The rise of the environmental movement (*see also* 162–65 *and* 188–89) helped bring attention to such calamities; in turn, the publicity surrounding such disasters helped turn environmentalism into a broad-based movement reinforced by extensive laws and regulations.

—Mary Sisson

Collapse of Inner Cities and Industrial Centers

By the end of the 1920s in the United States and Canada, the majority of people lived in or around cities. Sixty years later, however, the future of North American cities seemed to be in doubt. The economy had changed, moving away from the heavy industry that had once sustained cities. Some thirty million jobs were lost because of factory closings in the 1970s alone, and many of those job losses were concentrated in the old industrial cities of the Northeast and Midwest, an area that came to be known as the Rustbelt. Serious riots in the late 1960s—including riots in Newark and Detroit in 1967—riveted public attention on the woes of the inner city, and despite efforts to improve cities and ease poverty, conditions seemed unlikely to get better.

Urban Decline. In the United States in the early 1970s, wealthy and middle-class city dwellers continued to flee to the suburbs (*see also* 134–35). This "hollowing out" of cities was seen to have a strong racial element because most of the people who moved to the suburbs were white. But during the 1980s, wealthier members of racial minorities also moved out of the cities.

U.S. cities in the Northeast and Midwest that were once centers of manufacturing were especially hard hit as the economy shifted from heavy industry and toward the service sector. Certain cities were economically devastated. Detroit, Michigan, once a center of automobile manufacturing, lost fully half its population from 1950 to 1990, with one million people leaving the city in those forty years as the automobile industry declined and jobs vanished. Detroit's economy was so weak by 1990 that one-quarter of its remaining residents were receiving government assistance, and 32 percent were living in poverty, one of the highest poverty rates in the United States.

The tightening of environmental laws during the 1970s restricted urban planning efforts to revitalize cities. Many substances that had been widely used in industry—for example, the lubricant, insulator, and carcinogen polychlorinated biphenyl (PCB), commonly used in the manufacture of electrical components until 1977—were banned during the decade. In addition, the federal Comprehensive Environmental Response, Compensation, and Liability Act, passed in 1980 and better known as the Superfund (*see also* 152–53), required that sites heavily contaminated by toxic substances be cleaned up. Many old manufacturing plants were contaminated, so builders were reluctant to redevelop former factory buildings and sites because they might have to pay the cost of cleanup. As a result, the deserted buildings became eyesores as well as hazards to public safety and health. In Baltimore, for example, by 2000 fully 3,000 (1,200 hectares) of the city's 49,000 acres (19,800 hectares) consisted of vacant or unused former commercial space. Roughly half of that abandoned space consisted of so-called brownfields, former industrial areas believed to be contaminated with toxins in earlier decades.

Pittsburgh

For most of its history, Pittsburgh, Pennsylvania, was synonymous with the manufacture of steel (*see also* 72–73). The city's many steel mills provided well-paying jobs, although they also created so much air pollution that Pittsburgh became known as "The Smoky City." The city cleaned up considerably in the late 1940s, however, thanks to a massive urban renewal project called Renaissance, which rebuilt the city's downtown and restricted the burning of polluting coal. As a result of these improvements, the city flourished during the 1950s.

During the 1970s, however, cheaper steel from other regions and countries began to compete with Pittsburgh's steel, and mills began to close. While the steel industry had employed 150,000 people in the 1950s, by the early 1980s fewer than fifty thousand people worked in steel.

The local government responded with another massive urban renewal project in the late 1970s called Renaissance II. Although the $4.5-billion project provided the city with many new buildings and cultural centers, eventually leading to Pittsburgh's being named in the 1985 *Rand McNally Places Rated Almanac* as the best U.S. city in which to live, it did little to stem the economic slump. By 1989, Pittsburgh's steel industry employed a mere twenty thousand people, and rates of unemployment and poverty in the region were high, even in the suburbs. The city lost some 12 percent of its population from 1970 to 1990, and many of those leaving were young people. The city was slow to adjust to the changing economy—a 1993 report by Carnegie-Mellon University found that of twenty-five metropolitan areas, Pittsburgh had lost the most manufacturing jobs and created the fewest service jobs since 1970. Eventually Pittsburgh attracted high-tech companies, which employed more than fifty thousand people by the mid-1980s, but the city's economy never returned to the glory days of the 1950s.

Suburban Growth. While cities faltered, their surrounding suburbs became increasingly dominant in both the United States and Canada. By the end of the 1980s, almost half of the people in the United States and more than one-third of Canadians lived in suburbs. As the income gap between cities and suburbs grew, suburbs in both countries became more economically independent with the emergence of suburban industrial centers. By the 1970s and 1980s, shopping malls had become common in the suburbs, and more and more companies located facilities there, resulting in a significant shift in where jobs could be found. By 1980 more jobs were located in the suburbs of a typical large northeastern American city than in the city itself. At the same time, the development of suburbs consumed formerly open land, like farms and wetlands, putting pressure on wildlife habitats in many regions.

The movement of jobs to the suburbs made them more attractive to residents with the financial resources to leave the city. But suburban jobs were usually inaccessible to people who remained in the city and did not own cars, often the only way to get to offices in outlying areas. As a result, in some metropolitan areas, poor urban neighborhoods with high unemployment were located only a few miles from suburban areas with labor shortages. For example, by the late 1980s New Jersey had a remarkably low unemployment rate—about 4 percent. The cities of Newark and Trenton, however, had

At an abandoned steel mill in New Jersey, a rusted railway car stands before a storage tank. (© Vince Streano/Corbis)

unemployment rates that were roughly twice as high as the state as a whole—and three to four times as high as the suburbs immediately surrounding them.

Urban Renewal. More dispiritingly, programs undertaken in previous decades to help the urban poor seemed to be ineffective or even to have created new problems. For example, urban renewal efforts in the 1960s had often focused on clearing out slums, which could be infested with vermin or have outdated and unsanitary water and sewer systems, and replacing them with supposedly clean and safe high-rise housing projects. By the 1980s it had become clear that such projects effectively isolated the poor physically, economically, and socially from the rest of the community. Some projects, like the Cabrini Green housing projects in Chicago, became notorious for crime, violent gangs, and drug dealers.

By the end of the 1980s, some policymakers were openly questioning whether cities were worth saving. But amid the gloom and doom, a new strategy of urban renewal was gaining force, often as part of "smart growth" policies that were also designed to curb suburban sprawl and preserve open space. Unlike the massive urban renewal projects of the 1960s, which often involved the razing of entire neighborhoods, these projects focused on renovating existing historic areas, turning former factories into malls, offices, and apartments. One of the earliest was Boston's Faneuil Hall Marketplace, completed in 1976; that project was followed by Baltimore's influential Harborplace in 1980. The two projects, which created scenic shopping locales downtown, proved potent tourist attractions and became models for urban renewal in other cities. While no panacea, these efforts, along with movements to make policing more effective, to replace housing projects with other forms of assistance, and to encourage commerce in urban neighborhoods, would bring new life to cities in the following decade.

—*Mary Sisson*

Further Reading

Bluestone, Barry, and Bennett Harrison. *The Deindustrialization of America: Plant Closings, Community Abandonment, and the Dismantling of Basic Industry.* New York: Basic Books, 1982.

Cozic, Charles P., ed. *America's Cities: Opposing Viewpoints.* San Diego, Calif.: Greenhaven Press, 1993.

Peterson, Paul E. "The Urban Underclass and the Poverty Paradox." In *The Urban Underclass,* edited by Christopher Jencks and Paul E.

Peterson. Washington, D.C.: The Brookings Institution, 1991.

Mercer, John, and Kim England. "Canadian Cities in Continental Context: Global and Continental Perspectives on Canadian Urban Development." In *Canadian Cities in Transition: The Twenty-First Century,* edited by Trudi Bunting and Pierre Filion. 2nd ed. Ontario: Oxford University Press Canada, 2000.

Smith, Arthur G. *Pittsburgh: Then and Now.* Pittsburgh, Penn.: University of Pittsburgh Press, 1990.

The Emergence of the U.S. Environmental Movement

As World War II ended, the conservation movement (*see also* 110–11), having lost much of its earlier gains, was on the way to extinction in the United States. An economic, social, and, within the existing boundaries of the nation, geographic expansion was under way, transforming American life. The concerns of the nation shifted from the elitist conservation agenda of the pre-war era into a more militant environmentalism.

Postwar Growth. A postwar economic boom raised Americans' expectations, and men and women of every race believed that they had earned the right to have a higher standard of living. Industry responded with more of everything.

"New and improved" became a cliché as Americans crowded the marketplace to sample the wares of consumer society. Cars, washing machines, refrigerators, and other "big ticket" items were sold as fast as manufacturers could produce them. Americans consumed, blissfully unaware of the environmental cost of that consumption (*see also* 132–33).

Rapid economic growth had a visible downside, however, that could be measured in the declining quality of air and water that Americans breathed and drank as well as in the despoiling of the American landscape. Wartime industrial expansion accelerated the spread of heavy industry, for example, steel and aluminum manufacturing; this spread had severe

environmental consequences made worse by the effects of chemical and industrial processes on people, land, and water. Sewage flowed untreated into rivers and lakes, industrial waste was disposed of by burial on vacant or rural land (*see also* 152–53), and smokestacks filled the air with sometimes toxic emissions. The oily wastes that polluted the Cuyahoga River, which passed through Cleveland, Ohio, were so profound that the river caught fire more than once (*see also* 158–59).

The problems associated with industrial development presented the nation with a paradox: Industry helped win the war, created tremendous opportunity, and engendered hitherto unseen prosperity. but it also had unanticipated and unplanned for consequences. The growth that allowed Americans to prosper—the factories, chemical plants, and steel mills—reduced their quality of life by fouling their air, polluting their water, and shortening their life expectancy.

Echo Park. The Colorado River Storage Project (CRSP)—a string of nine dams planned to control stream flow; allocate water for agriculture, ranching, and urban use; and create hydroelectric power (electricity generated by turbines within a dam) for Utah, Colorado, New Mexico, and Wyoming—was proposed in the 1940s (and built in the 1950s), with little opposition except to the building of Echo Park Dam (*see also* 146). Echo Park was to be built inside Dinosaur National Monument (located in northwestern Colorado and northeastern Utah); this proposed placement galvanized once quiescent conservationists, transforming them into the modern

Students in St. Louis, Missouri, march through the city's business district in observance of the first Earth Day demonstration in 1970. (© Bettmann/Corbis)

Further Reading

Fox, Stephen. *The American Conservation Movement: John Muir and His Legacy.* Madison: University of Wisconsin Press, 1985.

Harvey, Mark. *A Symbol of Wilderness: Echo Park and the American Conservation Movement.* Albuquerque: University of New Mexico Press, 1994.

Rothman, Hal K. *The Greening of a Nation?: Environmentalism in the U.S. Since 1945.* Fort Worth, Tex.: Harcourt Brace College Publishers, 1998.

environmental movement. Conservationists opposed the Echo Park Dam because it was inside a national park area. The lessons of Hetch Hetchy (*see also* 114)—a valley in Yosemite National Park that was flooded earlier in the century by a dam despite protests from conservationists—had been well learned and Echo Park became a cause célèbre. It pitted development against nature preservation, challenging the ethic of progress for the sake of progress alone. Organizations like the National Parks Association, the Wilderness Society, and the Sierra Club successfully pressured lawmakers in the Senate to block the building of Echo Park Dam. The Colorado River Storage Project Act, signed in 1956, stated that no dam authorized in the legislation would intrude into any national park or monument. Echo Park became a line in the sand, an actual and symbolic challenge to the direction in which American society was headed as well as a moment that signaled the transformation of the conservation movement into the environmental movement.

Rise of Environmentalism. With Echo Park and the 1962 publication by biologist Rachel Carson of *Silent Spring* (*see also* 140–41), a stunning book about the impact of pesticides on the environment and all living beings, the newly revitalized conservation–environmental movement found a new voice and new determination, becoming more political than at any time since the turn of the twentieth century. From these beginnings, modern environmentalism emerged. In 1968,

when the Brookings Institute surveyed the nation about its problems, the environment did not even make the list. One year later, in the same survey, the "environmental crisis" topped all concerns.

The first Earth Day in April 1970, organized by Harvard University law student Denis Hayes, solidified public sentiment about the environment. As people celebrated in the parks and streets of the nation, they demanded of government a

response to the pollution and destruction around them. Politicians gave them a legislative revolution, passing the National Environmental Policy Act in 1970 and creating the Environmental Protection Agency that same year. Direct results included the Clean Air Act of 1970, which set the nation on the road to improved air quality and the Federal Water Pollution Control Act of 1972, which set the stage for the Clean Air Act of 1977. A growing percentage of Americans embraced the ethic of environmentalism, successfully insisting that the government respond to demands for an inhabitable land.

—*Hal Rothman*

The First Earth Day

On April 22, 1970, a public celebration of a new kind occurred all across the United States. The first Earth Day, with ten to twenty million participants, showed how completely many Americans embraced the idea of quality-of-life environmentalism. Combining the tactics of the 1960s, such as marches, rallies, public theater, with a reach across class, generational, and racial lines, Earth Day began as loosely connected environmental teach-ins at colleges, high schools, and community centers throughout the United States. From these disparate origins, Earth Day evolved into public display of support for environmental causes; in recent years, it has been celebrated annually on April 22.

Support for Earth Day came from Senator Gaylord Nelson of Wisconsin, an outspoken advocate of environmental quality, who proposed the idea for a "National Teach-in on the Crisis of the Environment" in a 1969 speech. Nelson recruited 25-year-old Harvard University law student Denis Hayes to serve as the chief organizer. Hayes made it a centrist event by avoiding confrontational politics and seeking to unite rather than polarize participants. Earth Day was a celebration of American society, a search for consensus as well as alternatives to the consumption ethic in American society. This gave it wide appeal to the public, but also undermined the event among activist constituencies, who tended to support more radical change.

Following its 1970 debut, Earth Day became a rousing success, a persuasive and only mildly threatening challenge. Earth Day presented a way to contribute to the renewal of American society, rather than just complain about its demise. It also made participants feel connected to an important cause and reminded them that they could have an impact on their world. This feeling of personal power that so many derived from environmentalism spread its message widely. The symbols of the movement, such as recycling, caught on, and all kinds of Americans made the values of environmentalism their own; businesspeople and activists together talked of the same goals. Legislative action followed, including passage of "bottle bills" that mandated the return of glass containers. For an instant, environmentalism became the center of a new nation, a place where Americans seemed in agreement.

Pollution Probe: The Emergence of the Canadian Environmental Movement

The emergence of an environmental movement in Canada was part of a general shift in the nation's political process that introduced new actors, issues, and tactics, forever altering the life of the country. Environmental groups such as Pollution Probe, one of the first in Canada, helped to shift the debate on the environment from traditional political parties to public pressure groups. Most of these groups emerged from within the university community where a minority of radical students and professors encouraged their more moderate colleagues to address a variety of issues from social justice to gender equality and, late in the 1960s, the environment.

Many of the people who formed the inner core of the Canadian environmental movement had enjoyed outdoor experiences as youths during the outdoor recreation boom of the 1950s (*see also* 138–39). They attended summer camps or vacationed with their families in northern Ontario, which led them to value and appreciate nature. Mounting evidence of ecological imbalance during the 1960s, including that presented in Rachel Carson's 1962 book, *Silent Spring* (*see also* 140–41), first alarmed and then angered these early environmentalists. Polluted air and water not only made the cities in which they lived increasingly unpleasant, but also threatened human health.

Establishment of Pollution Probe.
Pollution Probe was one of the most effective of the first generation of environmental organizations in Canada. Pollution Probe was formed by students and professors at the University of Toronto in 1969 in response to a Canadian Broadcasting Corporation (CBC) television documentary, *The Air of Death,* that highlighted ongoing fluoride

pollution by the Electric Reduction Company at Port Maitland, Ontario. Stunned by the company's aggressive response to the documentary, which spawned an inquiry from the provincial government, the students and professors organized to combat other polluters. In its first year, Pollution Probe was involved in many of the key environmental issues and investigations of the day, from pollution of the Great Lakes (*see also* 166–67) to the struggle to ban the pesticide DDT (*see also* 122–23).

Although Pollution Probe's core members came from the department of zoology, students in all disciplines joined. Soon the group opened membership to the greater Toronto community and by 1970 had grown to about one thousand members. The members deliberately avoided a hierarchical structure, opting instead to divide into

Greenpeace

On September 15, 1971, an old fishing boat, recently rechristened *Greenpeace,* set sail from Vancouver, British Columbia. The goal of those on board was to stop a scheduled test of a 1.2-megaton U.S. nuclear device on Amchitka Island in the Aleutian archipelago, located 765 miles (1,231 kilometers) west of the tip of the Alaskan Peninsula.

On board the *Greenpeace* was a diverse group of Canadian and American activists who also called themselves Greenpeace. Greenpeace had its origins in an earlier group, the "Don't Make a Wave Committee," that was concerned about the Vietnam conflict and the state of the environment; the organization protested nuclear weapons testing by the United States in Amchitka beginning in 1969. The "Don't Make a Wave Committee" recruited influential members of the Vancouver news media, including the Vancouver *Sun's* Bob Hunter and Canadian Broadcasting Corporation's (CBC) Ben Metcalfe.

Committee members worried that the test would elevate Cold War tensions and that the location, on a major fault line, would trigger earthquakes and tsunamis. Influenced by the Quaker tradition of "bearing witness," members decided to sail their ship to the island. They hoped that the coverage of major newspapers and newswire services, such as Toronto's *Globe and Mail* and United Press International as well as national television outlets such as ABC and the CBC, would help bring attention to their quest for global peace. Given their concern about the environment and peace, they decided they were working for a "green peace," and so the group adopted its new name.

The U.S. Coast Guard intercepted the ship *Greenpeace* in late September 1971 and diverted it from Amchitka before the blast. A sister ship, *Greenpeace Too,* was also unable to reach the test site before the blast. However, Greenpeace's media strategy was so successful that they succeeded in publicizing the ecological and military dangers presented by the United States' ongoing weapons testing program. As a result of the negative publicity generated by Greenpeace's efforts, the U.S. government decided to end nuclear testing on the Aleutians. The voyage of *Greenpeace* inspired similar actions against French testing in the South Pacific the following year and created the model for future Greenpeace activity around the world. Over the next thirty years, Greenpeace members would influence decisions ranging from the French decision to end atmospheric nuclear tests in the Pacific (1975), to the imposition of a global moratorium on whaling (1982), to the decision of MacMillan Bloedel, an international resource company, to phase out clearcutting of British Columbia forests (1998).

Group photo of Pollution Probe members and adviser Donald Chant (standing), taken in 1969. (Courtesy of Pollution Probe, Toronto office)

loosely organized work teams responsible for particular issues and projects, such as public education, a newsletter, phosphate detergent pollution, air pollution, and legal affairs. Eventually leaders emerged, among them Tony Barrett, Monte Hummel, Brian Kelly, and Peter Middleton. Pollution Probe also created an advisory board composed of professors and other influential community members who offered the students guidance and expertise. From the beginning, though, Pollution Probe's greatest strength came from the students' youthful enthusiasm, idealism, and energy.

Upon its founding, the group adopted a mandate to investigate all environmental pollution, determine its effects on human health, and mobilize public support for specific remedial measures. Pollution Probe's goals were twofold. First, Probe sought to curtail the negligent actions of corporate polluters through publicity, government pressure, and, where necessary, litigation. Probe's second goal was to empower the public through research-based education and action, presenting the public with the opportunity to make a difference. The students saw themselves as a scientifically advised, grass-roots movement that could mobilize public concern over environmental quality. Among the first projects Probe tackled was the issue of pesticides.

Pesticide Debate. Probe's involvement in the pesticide debate is an example of the group's effective tactics. Although the public furor over the information in *Silent Spring* died down relatively quickly, evidence of danger from persistent pesticides like DDT continued to build. In May 1969, the accidental death of almost thirty waterfowl at Toronto Island, apparently linked to the city Parks Department spraying of the pesticide diazinon, allowed Pollution Probe to rekindle Toronto's public concern about the dangers of pesticides. Probe kept the issue in the press and before the public through the summer of 1969 by creating publicity and monitoring the Toronto Island situation. This included a two-day "Citizens' Inquiry" held at Toronto City Hall that garnered front-page coverage in all the Toronto newspapers. At the inquiry, Probe displayed its scientific expertise, including the residue analyses that zoologist Donald Chant, a primary adviser to the group, and others had conducted on the waterfowl. These tactics established Pollution Probe as the public's voice on this issue. Members were invited to present evidence before the provincial Pesticide Advisory Board, which was responsible for determining future DDT use in the province.

When the provincial government announced extensive restrictions on DDT as well as an outright ban on three other pesticides starting on January 1, 1970, the Toronto media gave overwhelming credit to Pollution Probe. Although other groups and lawmakers had contributed time and effort, Probe had played an essential role by keeping the issue in the media while the Pesticide Advisory Board and the government considered the matter. The organization's success was the result of its ability to combine public education and attention-generating activities with valid science.

Pollution Probe's work on pesticides and other issues signaled a change in the environmental decision-making process in Canada. Resource managers, politicians, and the public at large became aware of a new group seeking influence over the range of issues related to the management of Canada's air, water, and land resources. The pioneering work of groups like Pollution Probe made the environmental decision-making process in Canada more open to public participation.

—Jennifer Read

Further Reading

Killan, Gerald, and George Warecki. "The Algonquin Wildlands League and the Emergence of Environmental Politics in Ontario." *Environmental Review* 16 (Winter 1992):1–27.

Macdonald, Doug. *The Politics of Pollution: Why Canadians Are Failing Their Environment.* Toronto: McClelland & Stewart, 1991.

Owram, Doug. *Born at the Right Time: A History of the Baby Boom.* Toronto: University of Toronto Press, 1996.

Read, Jennifer. "'Let Us Heed the Voice of Youth': Laundry Detergents, Phosphates and the Emergence of the Environmental Movement in Ontario." *Journal of the Canadian Historical Association* 7 (1997): 227–250.

Environmental Diplomacy: The Great Lakes Water Quality Agreement

By the late nineteenth century, pollution from cities and industries in Canada and the United States had created a serious problem. Both nations dumped untreated or lightly treated wastes into the Great Lakes, but the U.S. contribution was much greater. Once released into the water, pollution readily crossed jurisdictional borders. Effective regulation and control of pollution would require joint, international action; this need ultimately influenced the negotiation of the Great Lakes Water Quality Agreement (GLWQA) of 1972 between Canada and the United States.

Attempts to control pollution were complicated by three factors: First, Canadians and Americans expected the Great Lakes to provide clean water for human consumption (*see also* 190–91) and the production of fish, and, at the same time, serve as a sink for wastes; second, the capacity of the Great Lakes to absorb wastes was a "common property resource" barely regulated until the late 1960s and almost freely available to any community or industry that needed a place to dispose of pollutants. As long as the right to dump domestic and industrial wastes in the Great Lakes was widely available, little incentive existed for any level of government to act alone in funding and constructing pollution control facilities. Finally, the Great Lakes were overlain by a grid of jurisdictional subdivisions comprising many cities and towns, one Canadian province (Ontario), eight American states (New York, Pennsylvania, Ohio, Indiana, Illinois, Michigan, Wisconsin, and Minnesota), and two nations.

Boundary Waters Treaty. In 1909, the United States and Britain (representing Canada until 1933) had approved the Boundary Waters Treaty (*see also* 116–17), which addressed the management and pollution of waters along the international boundary. Only pollution that crossed the border and inflicted harm on the other side came under the purview of the new treaty. The treaty also established the International Joint Commission (IJC), which acts in response to joint requests, or references, from the governments of Canada and the United States.

In 1912, the United States and Canada asked the IJC to investigate pollution in the Great Lakes. The IJC's report described the pollution of the Great Lakes as serious in several locations and in violation of the treaty. Concern over pollution of the Great Lakes was largely urban in origin and coalesced around issues related to the threat of disease spread by contaminated drinking water. Building upon the momentum generated by its investigation, the IJC drafted an international convention to address pollution in the Great Lakes, but neither nation ratified it. Communities began to treat their drinking water, which significantly reduced the threat to public health. As public health improved, the popular constituency and political will to reduce pollution also diminished. No further serious initiatives to control pollution of the Great Lakes were undertaken until the 1950s.

Pollution Studies. In 1956, the United States suggested to Canada that they submit a joint reference directing the IJC to

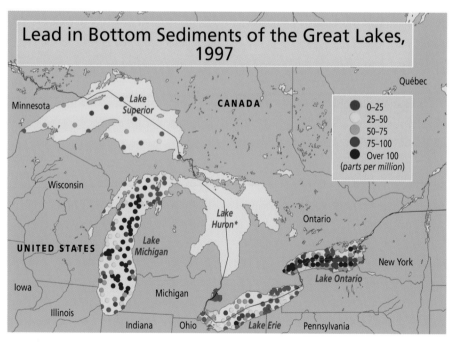

Lead in Bottom Sediments of the Great Lakes, 1997

0–25
25–50
50–75
75–100
Over 100
(parts per million)

*Information for levels in Lake Huron is unavailable.

Building on the success of the GLWQA, the 1997 Great Lakes Binational Toxics Strategy identified Level I Substances as those that are toxic, persistent, and have a tendency to bioaccumulate. Some factors contributing to the selection of these substances include the substances' chemical and physical properties, potential to cause cancer, risk to human health, wildlife, and the environment. Both nations had some variations in their original selection of toxic substances, but the final list reflects the agreement on the nominations from both countries. In 1997, lead—a Level I Substance—was present in bottom sediments of Lake Superior, Lake Michigan, Lake Erie, and Lake Ontario.

Sources: Adapted from Great Lakes Toxic Reduction. U.S. Environmental Protection Agency. 19 August 2002. <http://www.epa.gov/glnpo/p2/bns.html>; and Great Lakes Toxic Reduction. U.S. Environmental Protection Agency. 29 May 2002. "Contaminant Monitoring in the Great Lakes. Water and Sediments: A Multi-Agency Perspective." <http://www.epa.gov/glnpo/bns/meetings/may2002/>.

Further Reading

Boardman, Robert, ed. *Canadian Environmental Policy: Ecosystems, Politics, and Process.* Toronto: Oxford University Press, 1992.

Government of Canada and United States Environmental Protection Agency. *The Great Lakes: An Environmental Atlas and Resource Book.* 3rd ed. Chicago: Great Lakes National

Program Office, 1995. Also at <http://www.epa.gov/grtlakes/atlas>.

Kehoe, Terence. *Cleaning Up the Great Lakes: From Cooperation to Confrontation.* Dekalb: Northern Illinois University Press, 1997.

Willoughby, William R. *The Joint Organizations of Canada and the United States.* Toronto: University of Toronto Press, 1979.

investigate the pollution in Lake Erie, Lake Ontario, and the international sections of the St. Lawrence River (the Lower Great Lakes). Canada responded slowly, partly from concern about splitting the expense with Ontario, and partly because ordinary Canadians seemed to lack a sense of urgency. Not until 1964 did Canada resolve the impasse between the federal and provincial governments over regulatory authority and financial responsibility. Thereafter, the two nations asked the IJC to conduct a study of pollution in the lower Great Lakes. The commission issued reports in 1965, 1968, and 1970; these three reports documented the seriousness of the pollution crisis, especially eutrophication of the comparatively shallow Lake Erie. Eutrophication is an acceleration of the aging process of a body of water brought about by an increase in nutrients. In the case of the Great Lakes, eutrophication was an unintended and unanticipated consequence of the widespread shift from soap powders to phosphate-based detergents after World War II. Phosphates in these detergents stimulated the growth rate of algae, which washed up on shore and created a mess on beaches and lakefront property. Decaying algae depleted dissolved oxygen, added greatly to organic matter in the water, and accelerated the accumulation of a smothering layer of silt on lake bottoms.

Negotiations. Motivated by the findings of the IJC and growing public concern about the environment, in 1970, Canada invited the United States to negotiate an international agreement for regulating pollution and improving water quality in the Great Lakes. The momentum and the initiative for

cleaning up the Great Lakes had passed from the Americans to the Canadians. As Canada attempted to develop an agreement with the United States, it engaged simultaneously in parallel negotiations with Ontario about which level of government would pay for sewage treatment facilities. Given a divided, federal–provincial authority to regulate the environment, the negotiation of the Canada-Ontario Agreement, signed in August 1971, was an essential prerequisite to an agreement between Canada and the United States. The Canadian federal government committed itself to an enhanced and accelerated program of loans and grants that would allow communities in Ontario to pay for construction of municipal sewage treatment plants. Ontario promised to assist with implementation of a joint agreement with the United States.

Water Quality Agreement. The GLWQA was signed on April 15, 1972. For the first time in the history of relations between the two nations, an international, institutional mechanism with the potential for regulating, controlling, and reducing water pollution in the Great Lakes had been created. Both nations committed themselves to creating common water quality objectives, ranging from constructing municipal water treatment facilities to significantly reducing phosphorous loadings in Lakes Erie and Ontario to developing and implementing national programs to achieve those goals. The agreement included provisions for joint monitoring and for enhanced responsibilities for the IJC. The GLWQA also left some difficult issues for further study: pollution of the upper lakes (Huron, Michigan, and Superior), waste discharged from vessels, and pollution from

non-point sources, such as contaminated agricultural runoff. The GLWQA barely noted problems associated with toxic substances. Deposition of heavy metals, including mercury and lead, in sediments, and bioaccumulation of a host of synthetic and organic pesticides (*see also* 122–23) and herbicides emerged as increasingly important problems in the Great Lakes after 1972. A revision of the agreement in 1978 addressed some of these issues.

The agreement succeeded from the moment it was signed. It satisfied Canadian citizens who were worried about environmental degradation and compelled the United States to assign a higher priority to the regulation and control of the massive amount of pollution that it contributed to the Great Lakes. Confronted with a greater volume of pollution and complex, internal political issues, the United States moved more slowly than Canada in the construction of municipal sewage treatment plants and in the reduction of phosphorous; yet, by the early 1980s the United States had met the phosphorus-reduction goals agreed to in 1972. Non-point sources, industrial wastes, and toxic substances continued to present challenges to both nations.

In April 1997, Canada and the United States built on twenty-five years of studying and managing pollution in the Great Lakes under the auspices of the GLWQA when they signed Great Lakes Binational Toxics Strategy, which includes targets for the elimination of a number of persistent, toxic substances. The historical significance of the GLWQA of 1972 rests in the fact that it compelled the United States to commit to a sustained effort to reduce, regulate, and control pollution of the Great Lakes. As Canadians well understood, without that American commitment, there was little hope of ever cleaning up the Great Lakes.

—*Philip V. Scarpino*

Anti-Environmentalism: The Sagebrush Rebellion

The Sagebrush Rebellion, an anti-environmental movement that began in the wide-open spaces of rural Nevada in 1979, was heir to a long tradition that argued for the return of U.S. federal lands (*see also* 184–85) to the jurisdiction of the states in which they were located. With the support in 1980 of U.S. president-elect Ronald Reagan and the naming of James Watt as secretary of the interior in 1981,

the "rebellion" was catapulted to the national stage. Advocating a form of "states' rights," the Sagebrush rebels believed that government should work from the local level up rather than from the federal level down. As a philosophy, states' rights had been consistently questioned since the Civil War, but the emphasis on individual rights during the 1960s, the growing distrust of all levels of government, and the plethora of environmental

regulations enforced in a short period incited a strong reaction against what Westerners perceived was a too-powerful federal government.

The Sagebrush Rebellion resembled previous conflicts (including the resistance to federal forest reservations in the later nineteenth century and the opposition to national monument proclamations in the 1940s) in the West about federal control of public land and of the region's economy. What set this newest incident apart was its claim that federal management in perpetuity, as specified in the Federal Land Policy and Management Act (FLPMA) of 1976, was unconstitutional. This constitutional argument signaled a new legal maneuver in the battle to extend the doctrine of states' rights to the American West.

Nevada Bill. Beginning in the early 1970s in response to complaints of Nevada ranchers about administrative dictates from the Bureau of Land Management (BLM), the Select Committee on Public Lands of the Nevada legislature explored the possibility of transferring federal lands to the state. In 1979, both houses of the Nevada legislature passed a bill that targeted BLM holdings in Nevada. The bill asserted state control over mineral rights and surface access, advocated a multiple-use perspective for management so that all kinds of commercial users would have equal claim to resources, and protected existing leases made by individuals with the federal government. It contained provisions to sell off land to individuals and empowered the state attorney general to pursue the transfer of the lands through legal means.

The Wise Use Movement

In the 1980s, the Wise Use movement came to the fore. A well-financed right-wing effort using corporate funding to fashion a purported grassroots movement in an attempt to derail the environmental movement, Wise Use grew out of the fusion of the ideas of Alan Gottlieb, a conservative thinker, and Ron Arnold. A native of Texas who had once been a member of the Sierra Club, Arnold claimed to be disgruntled by the tactics of the environmental movement. In about 1970, Arnold embarked on a full-scale assault on environmental groups, protected lands, and environmentalism in general. "The National Park Service," Arnold once said of the largely popular federal agency, "is an empire designed to eliminate all private property in the United States." In 1984, Arnold was hired as executive vice president of the Center for the Defense of Free Enterprise. Espousing the philosophy that the only way to defeat one social movement is with another, Arnold began the Wise Use movement.

Arnold and his supporters sought to use public frustration with governmental interference as a way to shape the growing disaffection of the middle class. Arnold used the same tactics as the movement he scorned and presented anti-environmentalism as the greatest use of resources for the greatest number of people in the long run, the very core of American conservation thinking. A direct response to environmentalism, Wise Use was an attempt to turn the huge number of Americans who defined environmentalism as their secular religion against their own beliefs.

The Wise Use movement's assault on government regulations resonated with some sectors of the American public. However, it also depended on corporate money to a much greater degree than did pro-environmental groups, calling into question Arnold's claim to be the initiator of a grass-roots movement. A clearly defined constituency did emerge: It included a small cadre of scientists who regarded environmentalism as part of an antihuman movement; property rights advocates who saw their profits threatened by laws or other regulations that protect wetlands, endangered species, wild and scenic rivers; and various other beneficiaries of industrial and agricultural access to lands and water at below-market costs. The movement remains significant today in its opposition to federal efforts to implement land planning, but it no longer sits at the table on the debate on resource use.

The Nevada bill was based largely on the concept of "culture and custom," the assertion that time-honored patterns of behavior on public land conveyed de facto ownership to long-time users. Opponents of the Nevada bill argued that this idea had no basis in law. Nevada gave up its public lands as a condition of U.S. statehood in 1864, and other western states had never owned the land that they now claimed. This was not local land, as Sagebrush rebels insisted, but was merely "locally located." In most states, BLM land—the target of most of the appropriation strategy—had fallen to that agency because no one else had claimed it. The rebellion voiced and made public the fears of rural Westerners about government intrusion in local affairs.

Political Successes and Failures. In 1980—a decisive year for the Sagebrush Rebellion—legislators in Wyoming, Utah, and New Mexico passed legislation very similar to the Nevada bill that had claimed state sovereignty over BLM lands. Governors Jerry Brown of California and Richard Lamm of Colorado vetoed similar bills, while a measure in Washington state passed the legislature, but was later voided by a 60 percent "no" vote in a statewide referendum. Sagebrush Rebellion bills were also defeated in Montana, Idaho, and Oregon. But the rebellion had attracted a

Secretary of the Interior James Watt during his testimony in 1983 about Native American lands, which he described as a "failed experiment in socialism." (© Bettmann/Corbis)

visible and vocal segment of the population in many western states. Opponents of federal power and jurisdiction, among them libertarians and other advocates of the free market, also joined in, and the Sagebrush Rebellion became an important feature of regional politics in the early 1980s.

The Sagebrush rebels were poised to seize legislative power and implement a political and cultural agenda that would more accurately reflect the territorial era of the nineteenth century, when ranching and mining interests dominated many western states. But for all its legislative success, the movement encountered significant problems. Ranchers were disproportionately represented in a number of state legislatures in the West, but were hardly representative of the increasingly urban and suburban demography of many of these states. Western suburbanites had little in common with ranchers and other proponents of states' rights, and the rebels' opposition to conservationist and

environmental standards also undercut their appeal. To make their case, the Sagebrush rebels had to promote and reinforce the myth of the American West in urban areas throughout the nation. Despite attempts to gain popular support, the Sagebrush rebels' political movement collapsed when, in 1983, Watt was hounded from office after making discriminatory comments.

The rebellion is not over. Court challenges to federal ownership of land and its management, as well as daily harassment of U.S. Forest Service and BLM employees, continue to trouble the West's political landscape in the twenty-first century. Ranchers are becoming less and less powerful in the political arena as the West becomes more and more urban. Yet many in the rural West continue to resent what they perceive as an overreaching federal presence that nonetheless contributes to their livelihood with valuable subsidies.

—*Hal Rothman*

Further Reading

Brick, Philip D., and R. McGreggor Cawley, eds. *A Wolf in the Garden: The Land Rights Movement and the New Environmental Debate.* Lanham, Md..: Rowman & Littlefield, 1996.

Cawley, R. McGreggor. *Federal Land, Western Anger: The Sagebrush Rebellion and Environmental Politics.* Lawrence: University Press of Kansas, 1993.

Helvarg, David. *The War Against the Greens: The "Wise-Use" Movement, the New Right and Anti-environmental Violence.* San Francisco: Sierra Club Books, 1997.

CHAPTER SEVEN

Contemporary Environmentalism
(1980s–Present)

Had the United States, the most powerful nation in the world, reached a point of no return in the last decade of the twentieth century? Was its appetite for energy and natural resources so insatiable that it threatened the survival of human society and the larger biosphere?

Among those who worried about such a calamity was then-senator Al Gore (D-Tennessee). In his much-debated book, *Earth in the Balance* (1992), Gore claimed that the United States had reached a critical juncture. Many, he wrote, have "lost our feeling of connectedness to the rest of nature." To recapture those lost ties would prove difficult for a people so strongly wedded to an urban landscape, industrial efficiency, and a capitalistic economy; our sense of displacement, Gore observed, was perfectly captured by our fervid embrace of the automobile. To make the necessary break from the nefarious trappings of car culture would require renewed spiritual appreciation of the planet or, more precisely, a more humble place in its workings. Although Gore was criticized for what some believed was the accusatory tone of *Earth in the Balance*, he accurately depicted the heavy human impress on the world environment. In the decade following the book's publication, end-of-the-world scenarios no longer seemed implausible.

Forest Fires. Key environmental issues gained in intensity. Take fire. In the western portions of Canada and the United States, a series of annual conflagrations consumed millions of acres, blazes that were among the most widespread and destructive in North American history. These fires were considered to be more dangerous because they swept through what had once been rural landscapes. Because of heavy settlement in areas like Montana's

Bitterroot Valley, or in new suburban subdivisions that thrust out into the mountains, large populations and costly infrastructure were now put at considerable risk. Not everyone was convinced that the best way to fight forest fires was to attack them. Many scientists and environmental analysts argued that long-standing federal and state fire-suppression policies were the cause of the yearly rounds of fire in western forests and that these fires were natural events critical to a forest's capacity to regenerate.

Endangered Species. A similarly heated debate erupted over how or if to save the Pacific salmon. Once present in incalculable numbers, the fish declined following the mid-century construction of mammoth hydroelectric power dams on the Columbia and Snake Rivers in the western United States, and along British Columbia's Columbia tributaries and Peace River. These dams severely disrupted the salmon's migratory pattern that led them from the watersheds in which they were hatched, to the ocean in which they matured, and back to their birth waters in which they would spawn and die.

Chronicling the salmon's demise has been a lot easier than determining how to restore their once-mighty runs up and down Pacific rivers. In both Canada and the United States, various attempts to regenerate the salmon population have been met with considerable distrust and disagreement. Farmers depend on barges that ply now-placid rivers to carry crops to market. Urbanites and industry rely on cheap electricity generated by the dams. Native Americans, whose lives once revolved around the salmon, have successfully sued for redress; one response has been for the United States to spend nearly $1 billion a year to truck salmon around the dams. Environmental activists have offered an alternative, proposing that some of the dams be "decommissioned," that is, torn down so that the salmon may once again swim through rushing waters.

Environmental Politics. A number of other complex matters dominated late-twentieth-century headlines. When the U.S. and Canadian governments radically reduced catch limits of cod to preserve the species, their fishing industries challenged the legitimacy of such regulations. U.S. loggers responded angrily when the Endangered Species Act was invoked to protect the northern spotted owl; the chemical industry fought hard against attempts to protect riparian and marine habitats by regulating industry discharge of effluent into rivers and estuaries. Other fights broke out over the potential threats to the quality of public drinking water, strategies for managing land use in Canada and the United States that damaged the ecological integrity of public lands, and the controversial tactics employed to forestall flooding within the massive Mississippi River watershed. People also clashed over the viability and ethics of alternative agricultural methods, including the production of organic crops and genetically modified foods.

Increasing the volume of these debates was the emergence of new groups that responded to and took advantage of environmentalism as a central force in North American political culture. Perhaps the most cynical development was corporate "greenwashing," public relations campaigns that companies mounted to convince consumers that their products were environmentally friendly while obscuring the devastation their production processes wrought. Battling for attention, too, were inner-city and rural grassroots organizations arguing that minority populations suffered from a disproportionate share of maladies associated with toxic dumps and nuclear waste. Their non-violent demonstrations for environmental justice took place at the same time that eco-radicals advocated a violent defense of Mother Earth. The Earth Liberation Front, founded in 1992, has burned equipment, blown up research laboratories, and ravaged tree farms to inflict economic damage on those corporations and universities it believed were responsible for environmental despoliation.

International Concerns. Complicating the resolution of these varied environmental tensions was the emergence of a more conservative political climate in the United States, whose representatives often came to power based on their anti-environmentalist agenda. One result was the North American Free Trade Agreement (NAFTA), signed by Canada, the United States, and Mexico in 1993; environmentalists were convinced that the treaty lacked substantial environmental regulatory controls. The conservative agenda also helped shape a series of international conferences in the 1990s at which treaties on global warming, ecological preservation, and economic sustainability were negotiated. Although the United States sent representatives to the gatherings in Rio de Janeiro, Brazil; Santiago, Chile; and Kyoto, Japan, it generally refused to sign the protocols or accords that committed signatories to abide by strict environmental controls.

Canada, by contrast, took a leading role in articulating the need for the kind of binding agreements that the United States rejected. Its position was based on a logical assumption: International regulation and mediation are the only ways to tackle complex problems affecting the Earth's atmosphere, land, and seas. This political stance was deftly captured in a popular bumper sticker: Think Globally. Act Locally. Its inversion had become equally true: Think Locally. Act Globally.

—*Char Miller*

An out-of-control forest fire overwhelms a community built in the Seminole Woods in Flagler County, Florida, in 1988. (AP/Wide World Photos)

Alternative Agricultural Methods

The publication of Rachel Carson's *Silent Spring* in 1962 (*see also* 140–41) prompted permanent opposition to the widespread use of pesticides and herbicides. Carson's once-controversial ideas have come to be mainstream public opinion, not least because a variety of alternative agricultural methods have demonstrated that food and other crops can be produced with much less reliance on chemicals.

Impact of Pesticides and Fertilizers.

Largely because of the use of artificial pesticides and fertilizers (*see also* 122–23), agricultural productivity in the United States and Canada roughly quadrupled in the second half of the twentieth century. Fertilizer use in the United States reached its peak of 21 million tons in 1981 and has remained at about the same level since. But the environmental cost of fertilizers has also increased, notably reflected in eutrophication (algal growth, deoxygenation, and loss of freshwater and marine species) of rivers and coastal waters. One spectacular example of eutrophication is the Gulf of Mexico's "dead zone," an area of water devoid of marine life that has appeared each summer off the coast of Louisiana and Texas since 1995 and is now approximately the size of El Salvador (about 7,728 square miles [20,015 square kilometers]).

The dangers of pesticides are much more clearly understood today than in Carson's time. Yet agrichemical use remains pervasive. According to U.S. Environmental Protection Agency figures, some $11,897 million was spent on pesticides in the United States in 1997. Agriculture accounted for about 70 percent of that expenditure, with household use at 17 percent, and industrial and commercial use at 13 percent.

Sustainable Agriculture.

If environmental protection and chemical-fueled growth in agricultural production have often seemed incompatible, the 1980s kindled new interest in sustainable forms of agriculture that offered the best of both worlds. The concept of "sustainable development" was originally defined by the World Commission on Environment and Development in 1987 to mean meeting the needs of the present generation without compromising the ability of future generations to meet their own needs. By 1990, the U.S. Congress had incorporated the idea into the Food, Agriculture, Conservation and Trade Act of 1990 (the "Farm Bill"), defining sustainable agriculture as:

> . . . an integrated system of plant and animal production practices . . . that will, over the long term: satisfy human food and fiber needs; enhance environmental quality and the natural resource base upon which the agricultural economy depends; make

A worker picks berries on an organic farm in Middletown, Maryland. (AP/Wide World Photos)

the most efficient use of nonrenewable resources and on-farm resources and integrate, where appropriate, natural biological cycles and controls; sustain the economic viability of farm operations; enhance the quality of life for farmers and society as a whole.

Opinions have differed on how these "all things to all people" objectives might be achieved. For environmentalists, sustainable agriculture usually means chemical-free organic agriculture. It includes techniques such as permaculture, natural farming, and other low-tillage methods that attempt to maximize yields by disturbing the soil as little as possible. In Canada, organic agriculture is a small but rapidly growing sector of the farming industry. Around 4.9 percent of fruit and vegetable farms are organic and, although organic products accounted for just 1.5 percent of total agricultural sales in 1999, the sector is currently growing at around 20 percent yearly. Some twenty-five hundred organic growers are now in Canada, with 705,000 acres (285,300 hectares) of land under organic cultivation. Organic farming is also growing in the United States. In 1999, the Santa Cruz–based Organic Farming Research Foundation (OFRF) reported that over 77 percent of twelve hundred U.S. organic farmers surveyed intended to increase their organic acreage and the number of organic crops they grow. Yet overall, the impact of organic agriculture remains low. Only 0.2 percent of all U.S. cropland was certified for organic growth in 1997.

In the same survey, OFRF claimed the U.S. Department of Agriculture (USDA) was "woefully out of touch with a new generation of environmentally sound, consumer friendly farmers." Prompting that charge, at least in part, was the controversy over the USDA's handling of the National Organic Program rule—the official definition of what constitutes "organic." Attempts to include genetically modified (GM), irradiated, and other forms of processed food under that umbrella brought a storm of protest and more than a quarter of a million (mostly hostile) responses when the USDA consulted on its proposed organic rule in December 1997.

Genetically Modified Foods. Organic or not, genetically modified foods are one of the most promising yet controversial of alternative agricultural methods. Insect-, virus-, and bacteria-resistant GM plants were first field-tested in 1985. By 1996, the first GM food product, the FlavrSavr tomato, had gained Food and Drug Administration approval for commercial growth and sale. Supporters of genetic engineering point to a range of possible benefits, from high-yield crops that could help to feed the world to disease-resistant strains that could drastically reduce pesticide use. Opponents have been equally vocal about the risks of cross-pollination from GM crops to wild strains of plants and weeds, which could become resistant to herbicides, and the possibility of allergens appearing in GM foodstuffs. The late 1990s brought increased opposition to GM technology, with chemical companies such as Monsanto and food producers such as Campbell's and Kellogg's finding themselves targeted for environmental protest. The USDA has also come under fire for its policies on GM foods. In

U.S. Certified Organic Farmland Acreage and Livestock, 1992 to 1997

Item	Year						Percent Change			
	1992	1993	1994	1995	1996	1997	1992 –97	1995 –97		
U.S. Certified Farmland	Acres								Total U.S. Cropland 1997	Percent Organic 1997
Total	935,450	955,650	991,453	917,894	--	1,346,558	44	47	828,029,449	0.16
Pasture and rangeland	532,050	490,850	434,703	279,394	--	496,385	(7)	78	461,351,095	0.11
Cropland	403,400	464,800	556,750	638,500	--	850,173	111	33	366,678,354	0.23
U.S. Certified Animals	Number									
Beef cows	6,796	9,222	3,300	--	--	4,429	(35)	--		
Milk cows	2,265	2,846	6,100	--	--	12,897	469	--		
Hogs and pigs	1,365	1,499	2,100	--	--	482	(65)	--		
Sheep and lambs	1,221	1,186	1,600	--	--	705	(42)	--		
Layer hens	43,981	20,625	47,700	--	--	537,826	1,123	--		
Broilers	17,382	26,331	110,500	--	--	38,285	120	--		
Unclassified/other	--	--	--	--	--	226,105	--	--		
Total Certified Growers	Number									
	3,587	3,536	4,060	4,856	--	5,021	40			

Note: Numbers may not add due to rounding.
Organic agriculture became one of the fastest growing sectors of the U.S. agricultural industry during the 1990s. For example, cropland under organic cultivation doubled between 1992 and 1997. Nonetheless, the impact of organic agriculture remains low in the United States.
Source: Data from Economic Research Service. U.S. Department of Agriculture. 12 April 2001. <http://www.ers.usda.gov/Emphases/Harmony/issues/organic/table4.htm>. Underlying data from Agricultural Marketing Service. U.S. Department of Agriculture 1992–94; and Agrisystems International (including revision of 1992–94 farmland data), 1995.

February 2002, a U.S. National Research Council report criticized the Department of Agriculture for failing to carry out sufficient checks on GM crops before they are approved for planting.

The development of sustainable agriculture is arguably less of a competition between rival methods than the evolution of a broad range of compatible techniques, each of which has its own strengths and weaknesses. Integrated pest management (IPM) takes this approach, combining physical controls (such as crop rotation), biological controls (including the use of natural predators), and genetic modification (making plants that are resistant to disease and insect infestation), and using reduced amounts of chemical controls (such as pesticides) to complement these other methods. Mixed approaches such as IPM may well form the cornerstone of agricultural production in future.

—*Chris Woodford*

Further Reading
Anderson, Luke. *Genetic Engineering, Food, and Our Environment.* White River Junction, Vt.: Chelsea Green Publishing, 1999.
Hassanein, Neva. *Changing the Way America Farms.* Lincoln: University of Nebraska Press, 1999.

Magdoff, Fred, ed. *Hungry for Profit: The Agribusiness Threat to Farmers, Food, and the Environment.* New York: Monthly Review Press, 2000.
U.S. National Research Council. *Alternative Agriculture.* Washington, D.C.: National Academy Press, 1989.

Sustainable Forestry in the United States

Although the concept of sustainability came into vogue in the late twentieth century, the idea has a long and complex history in the United States. Of its many definitions—scientists and foresters have reached no agreement on the definition of "sustainable forestry"—the most concise is: the act of managing forests to provide the necessities of life. As foresters learn more about forests, they adapt and expand the definition of sustainable forestry to suit the changing demands put upon the forest by those who use it.

Sustained Yield. Sustainable forestry traces its origins to the concept of sustained yield. Gifford Pinchot, who introduced scientific forestry management (*see also* 92–93) to the United States in 1892, believed that sustained yield (harvesting and replanting trees like a crop), along with vigorous fire suppression, would ensure that future generations would have adequate timber for their needs. David Mason, a former U.S. Forest Service forester, changed how foresters and the government defined sustained yield

during the Great Depression. He argued that when private lumber companies had exhausted their supply, they should cut public timber while they grew a new supply on their own land. Mason's new definition of sustained yield became the cornerstone of the Sustained Yield Forest Management Act (1944) and helped assure the survival of many lumber towns in the Pacific Northwest.

In response to growing pressure from preservation and outdoor sporting groups, Congress redefined how the national forests could be used when it passed the Multiple Use–Sustained Yield Act of 1960. This act specified that the term "sustained yield" included wildlife as part of sustainable forestry and required the Forest Service to manage the land and all that lived on it. Although the Forest Service had always practiced multiple use (managing the land for many simultaneous purposes like recreation and logging), the passage of the Multiple Use–Sustained Yield Act made this approach an official policy. In reality, though, the Forest Service favored timber production

over all other uses. Under pressure from lumber companies and politicians to avoid affecting economic prosperity, the Forest Service continually raised the limit of allowable harvests to justify having permitted lumber companies to exceed them.

Influence of Environmentalists. The emergence of the environmental movement (*see also* 162–65) and the science of ecology (the study of the relationships between organisms and their environment and how they are interconnected) in the late 1960s triggered further changes in sustainable forestry. By 1970, foresters and ecologists recognized that forests were part of a larger ecosystem, and that humans needed to change their treatment of the land if this ecosystem were to survive. They attempted to determine the least harmful way to remove the desired natural resources within prescribed limits that would allow the land, wildlife, and people dependent upon the resources to sustain themselves. The Forest Service argued that advances in areas like logging machinery and regeneration would

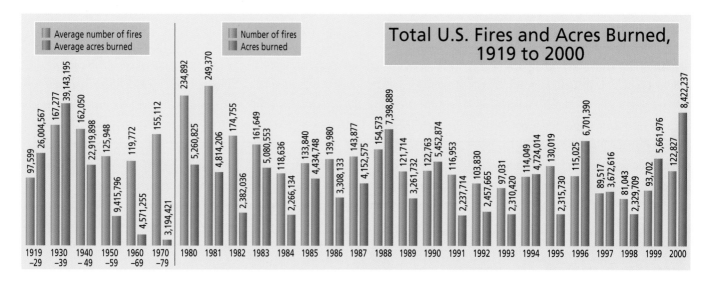

The data for the total U.S. fires and land burned have been gathered from all state and federal land management agencies, including the Bureau of Land Management, the National Park Service, and the U.S. Forest Service, U.S. Fish and Wildlife Service, and their state-level counterparts. Hawaii and Alaska were not included until 1960, one year after they became states. After 1971, the data also include amounts burned by "prescribed burning." From 1995 through 2000, the U.S. Fish and Wildlife Service has burned an average of just over 250,000 acres (101,200 hectares), second only to the Forest Service in total acreage by "prescribed burning."
Source: National Interagency Fire Center. Wildland Fire Statistics. 19 November 2002. <http://www.nifc.gov/stats/wildlandfirestats.html>.

allow it to intensely manage certain parts of a forest and produce higher amounts of timber through clearcutting while leaving other parts of the forest for recreational use. This approach soon led to a clash between environmentalists and the Forest Service, which, despite its rhetoric to the contrary, still favored clearcutting on most lands.

Congress responded with the National Forest Management Act (NFMA) of 1976. To please environmentalists, the law instituted more restrictive rules for determining what lands were "suitable" for timber production; required prompt, successful reforestation after logging; and mandated the maintenance of minimum viable populations of native wildlife and natural vegetation diversity in national forests. The law also required the Forest Service to produce long-term plans for each national forest and release them for public scrutiny. Furthermore, it declared in favor of sustained yield and selective cutting by demanding that "a forest's output of timber must be capable of being sustained perpetually without declines."

The NFMA, however, was so full of loopholes incorporated into the law by the Forest Service and timber company allies in Congress that it actually still permitted clearcutting. The federal government, with few exceptions, had continued to emphasize timber harvests over other aspects of sustainable forestry. The federal government's ability to justify its forestry policies started to unravel in the late 1980s when studies revealed that the Forest Service actually lost tens of millions of dollars on timber sales. Around the same time, controversy over protecting the habitat of the endangered northern spotted owl (*see also* 176–77 *and* 184–85) in the Pacific Northwest erupted. Environmental groups became further enraged by the policies of the Forest Service and the actions of the timber companies.

Ecosystem Management. The controversies from the late 1980s forced the

Further Reading
Coufal, James, and Donald Webster. "The Emergence of Sustainable Forestry." In *The Literature of Forestry and Agroforestry,* edited by Peter McDonald and James Lassoie. Ithaca, N.Y.: Cornell University Press, 1996.
Floyd, Donald W. *Forest Sustainability: The History, the Challenge, the Promise.* Durham, N.C.: The Forest History Society, 2002.
Hirt, Paul W. *A Conspiracy of Optimism: Management of the National Forests Since World War Two.* Lincoln: University of Nebraska Press, 1994.
Pyne, Stephen J. *America's Fires: Management on Wildlands and Forests.* Durham, N.C.: Forest History Society, 1997.
Steen, Harold K. *The U.S. Forest Service: A History.* Seattle: University of Washington Press, 1976.
Wiersum, K. Freerk, "200 Years of Sustainability in Forestry: Lessons from History," *Environmental Management* 19, no. 3 (1995), 321–329.

Forest Service and the timber industry to reexamine their management policies. The Forest Service realized that a species-by-species approach to conservation was not working and adopted the policy it named "Ecosystem Management," which called for "protecting ecosystems, restoring deteriorated ecosystems, and providing multiple benefits for people within the capabilities of ecosystems." The American Forest and Paper Association established its Sustainable Forestry Initiative (SFI) in 1995 and made adherence to its standards a requirement for membership. The association's members own 90 percent of the commercial forestland in the United States and have agreed to a system of principles, objectives, and performance measures audited by a third party that certifies the forests are managed properly.

Prescribed Fire Burning. Another area of dispute is the reintroduction of controlled, or "prescribed" fire burning. The federal government is responsible for approximately 415 million acres (168 million hectares) of fire-adapted land in the contiguous forty-eight states, 200 million acres (81 million hectares) of which are subject to frequent fires. By 1971, both the Forest Service and National Park Service recognized that suppressing fire endangered the health of ecosystems—too many forests were overgrown, diseased, and prone to catastrophic fire. The services wanted to permit naturally occurring fires, like those caused by lightning, to burn themselves out and thus reduce the amount of fuel on the land. After the

devastating fires in Yellowstone National Park in 1988, however, the government temporarily suspended this policy while it reexamined the prescribed burning program. The federal government reinstated the program the next year, but under heavy regulations. The prescribed burning program ran into problems when loggers, grazers, and environmentalists could not agree on where and how much to burn. Wildland fire policy was revised in 1995 and again in 2001 after the nation watched more land burn in 2000 than had burned in the previous half-century.

In 1997, Secretary of Agriculture Dan Glickman assembled a group of scientists to review forest management policies. The group's report, issued two years later, called for making "ecological sustainability" the foundation of national forest management. The Committee of Scientists defined sustainability as "meeting the needs of the present generation without compromising the ability of future generations to meet their needs." Policy had come full circle—Pinchot had said much the same thing ninety years earlier. The committee called for closer cooperation between scientists, the public, and all federal agencies in making decisions about ecosystems, and also called for making those decisions based on local ecological, economic, and social conditions. Just as the debate about the definition of sustainable forestry continues, so do the problems of implementing sustainable forestry policies to the satisfaction of all who use the national forests.

—*James G. Lewis*

Protecting Endangered Species and Habitats

According to *World Resources 2000–01*, 13.1 percent of the land area of the United States and 9.1 percent of the land area of Canada are now protected in national parks and wilderness areas. Nevertheless, many species and habitats remain at great risk. Various initiatives have been launched to combat this decline in biodiversity, but with continuing threats from development—such as highway construction and urban growth—as well as long-term problems like climate change, it has become increasingly apparent that endangered habitats and species can never be completely protected.

Loss of Habitats. By the late 1980s, 85 percent of the primary (virgin) forest that once covered the United States and 90 percent of its ancient woodland had been lost to development, agriculture, and timber harvesting. In contrast, at the beginning of the twenty-first century, Canada retains about 90 percent of its original forest cover and British Columbia alone is home to more than a quarter of the world's temperate rainforest (*see also* 126–27). Yet Canada is also the world's biggest exporter of timber. Half of the old-growth forests in British Columbia have now been felled, and clearcutting still accounts for more than 97 percent of logging in the region. Overall, less than 8 percent of Canadian forests are fully protected from destruction or development.

Sixty percent of U.S. wetlands have also been lost, including large areas of marshes and mangroves (although Alaska retains much of its original 28 million acres [11 million hectares]). About 13 percent of Canada is wetland (this amounts to about a quarter of the world's entire wetland habitat), yet destruction of Canadian wetlands has been drastic, with agriculture accounting for about 85 percent of the losses.

Impact on Species. The gradual disappearance of primary forest, wetlands, and other habitats has had a devastating effect on species in the continent. According to the United Nations Global Environmental Outlook–2000 survey, North America now has an estimated 430 threatened species of mammals, birds, reptiles, amphibians, and fishes. In 2000, some 173 Canadian species, subspecies, or populations of animals and plants were listed as threatened or endangered, with 153 of them at particular risk. The World Wildlife Fund of Canada has estimated that about $400 to $500 million is needed to recover species at risk. Off the east coast of the United States, fish catches have declined from about 2.5 million tons in 1971 to less than 500,000 tons in 1994 (*see also* 178–79).

While the issue of endangered species and habitats may be seen in abstract terms through general statistics such as these, the issue usually becomes more concrete and emotional when specific areas or species are at risk. The logging of old-growth forests in the Northwest became a cause célèbre for campaign groups such as Greenpeace and Earth First! in the 1980s and 1990s, not least because of the plight of species such as the northern spotted owl (*see also* 184–85). Despite setting aside habitat for the owl, its population continues to plummet in Washington state for reasons that remain unclear. The recent controversy over the Bush Administration's proposals to drill for oil in the Arctic National Wildlife Refuge (*see also* 184–85) is another example. Often compared

Threatened Species in the United States and Canada, by Taxonomic Group, 2002

Country	Mammals	Birds	Reptiles	Amphibia
Canada	14	8	2	1
United States	37	55	27	25

	Fishes	Mollusks	Other Invertebrates	Plants
Canada	16	0	10	1
United States	130	256	301	169

Total	
Canada	52
United States	1,000

The United States currently has many more extinct and threatened species than Canada.

Source: Data from 2002 IUCN Red List of Threatened Species. 2002. IUCN/SSC. <http://www.redlist.org>. For more information on specific lists of threatened species in the United States, see <http://endangered.fws.gov/wildlife.html>; for more information on specific lists of threatened species in Canada, see <http://www.cosewic.gc.ca/eng/sct5/index_e.htm>.

to Africa's wildlife-rich Serengeti Plain, the coastal plain of the Refuge—where development is most likely to occur—contains two hundred species of wildlife, including important breeding sites for polar bears and caribou.

Habitat Protection. The strategy of trying to save endangered species by saving their habitats in wilderness and other protected areas has been used throughout North America since the continent's first national park, Yellowstone, was established in 1872 in the United States. According to World Resources Institute figures for 2000–01, some 13.1 percent of U.S. land, amounting to 308 million acres (125 million hectares), is now protected in 3,063 separate areas; 9.1 percent of Canadian land, or 227 million acres (92 million hectares), is protected in 3,083 separate areas. In Canada alone, protected areas increased by around 15 percent between 1990 and 1996. Since the passage of the U.S. Wilderness Act in 1964 (*see also* 146–47) and the Endangered American Wilderness Act in 1978, numerous pieces of legislation have extended the system of protected areas in the United States (including the Alaska National Interest Lands Conservation Act of 1980, which added 56 million acres (23 million hectares), and the California Desert Protection Act of 1994, which added another 7.58 million acres [3.1 million hectares]).

Protection of Species. An alternative strategy to habitat protection, adopted

Further Reading

Heywood, V., ed. *UNEP Global Biodiversity Assessment.* New York & Cambridge: Cambridge University Press, 1995.

World Resources Institute. "National and International Protection of Natural Areas." In *World Resources 2000–01: People and Ecosystems: The Fraying Web of Life.* Washington, D.C.: World Resources Institute, 2001.

Novacek, Michael J., ed. *The Biodiversity Crisis: Losing What Counts.* New York: New Press, 2001.

Wilson, Edward O. *The Future of Life.* New York: Alfred A. Knopf, 2002.

In Ottawa in 2000, members of the International Fund for Animal Welfare participate in a mock debate, urging politicians to pass endangered species legislation in Canada. (© Reuters NewMedia Inc./Corbis)

in the U.S. Endangered Species Act (1973), involves focusing resources on particular species, for example, either by protecting their most important habitats more strictly or by trying to prevent the specific activities that threaten them. Whether the act has been successful is a matter of debate. More than half the species originally listed in the act have recently stopped declining or have recovered population; some, such as the bald eagle, have now been taken off the critical list. Yet many species remain under threat. Some ecologists believe the act would be more effective if it focused on ecosystems (the highly interdependent communities of organisms such as those found in a rainforest or coral reef) rather than individual species, for the conservation of biodiversity requires the preservation of complete ecosystems and all the species that depend on them. Mean-while, controversy continues over whether the Endangered Species Act is too hard on business interests (as landowners claim) or too soft on developments that destroy important habitats (as environmentalists charge).

Issues such as these have been at the forefront of moves to introduce similar legislation in Canada, which lacks federal legislation on endangered species. Originally proposed in 1992, Canada's Species at Risk Act (originally called the Endangered Species Act) has been plagued by political controversy; currently, only four of the country's thirteen provinces have laws protecting endangered species. Without federal legislation, the Committee on the Status of Endangered Wildlife in Canada lacks any real mandate to protect the nation's wildlife.

Future initiatives to protect endangered species and habitats will need to focus not just on local and regional problems, but also on climate change and other global threats (*see also* 202–03). Creating more protected areas, enacting stronger and more consistent legislation, monitoring the status of species and habitats more closely, and focusing on the preservation of entire ecosystems will all be essential if the decline in biodiversity is to be arrested.

—*Chris Woodford*

Canadian Fisheries: Loss of the Cod

Oceans cover 71 percent of Earth's surface and were once thought to be too rich in resources ever to deplete. In 1883, English biologist Thomas Huxley wrote: "I believe that the cod fishery . . . and probably all the great sea fisheries are inexhaustible." About a century later, the dramatic collapse of the cod fisheries off the northeast coast of North America demonstrated a much starker truth: Earth's bounty is finite and humankind can pay a heavy price environmentally, socially, and economically when it abuses and neglects to replenish Earth's resources.

In 1998, Canada's wildlife watchdog, the Committee on the Status of Endangered Wildlife in Canada (COSEWIC), officially added the Atlantic cod (*Gadus morhua*) to its "Special Concern" list of species at risk (*see also* 176–77). This listing was shocking because the cod is not an exotic species that possesses any rare qualities, but a common fish that had survived on Earth for more than

ten million years, most recently in the coastal waters and continental shelves on both sides of the North Atlantic Ocean.

History of Cod Fishery. The cod had not merely survived, it had flourished, being the most abundant and valuable groundfish (a bottom-feeding finfish confined to a fairly well-defined area) in the North Atlantic, with a range extending from Cape Hatteras in North Carolina all the way to Greenland. The origins of the cod fishing industry in North America can be traced to John Cabot, an Italian navigator serving King Henry VII of England, who discovered Newfoundland in 1497; sailors who followed him found that cod could be caught in superabundance simply by lowering baskets over the sides of their ships. Cod became a staple of the European diet and, no less important, a means for Britain and France both to support their own enormous fishing industries and earn foreign revenue by selling the fish they caught to other European nations (*see*

also 12–13). When the 1783 Treaty of Paris ended the American Revolution, U.S. boats were allowed to join in this plunder of the Newfoundland fisheries.

Although catches continued to increase in volume thereafter, cod might have thrived for much longer except for technological advances in the fishing industry in the 1950s and 1960s. Ports and fishing vessels became larger and a new type of "factory ship" was developed; these ships were capable of freezing fish the moment they had been caught, thereby enabling crews to stay out at sea longer and catch more fish. Vastly more cod were suddenly being caught off Newfoundland, many of them by foreign factory ships from the Soviet Union, Japan, and Europe.

Decline of Fish Stocks. By the mid-1970s, stocks of cod and other groundfish like haddock were starting to fall. In 1977, to protect their domestic fishing industries, Canada and The United States declared a 200-mile (320-kilometer) territorial limit off their coasts, effectively preventing foreign fleets from fishing inside that area. In Newfoundland, the Canadian Department of Fisheries and Oceans (DFO) promptly reassessed stocks of cod and, in a politically popular move, issued significantly expanded fishing quotas for the domestic fishing industry, feeling unwarranted confidence that stocks would recover following the banning of foreign fishing fleets. Throughout the 1980s, the DFO continuously overestimated the numbers of cod and Canadian fishing boats overfished what were, in reality, rapidly declining populations.

Despite a significant rise in catches in the early 1980s, which encouraged a belief that stocks were healthy in numbers, catches of cod and other groundfish plummeted from around 500,000 tons in 1988 to around 50,000 tons just five years later—a decline of

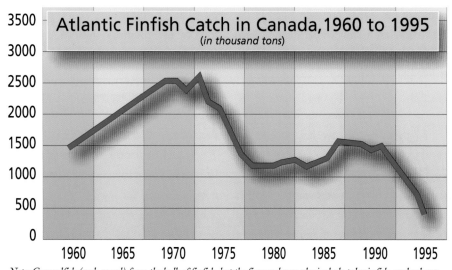

Atlantic Finfish Catch in Canada, 1960 to 1995
(in thousand tons)

3500 3000 2500 2000 1500 1000 500 0

1960 1965 1970 1975 1980 1985 1990 1995

Note: Groundfish (such as cod) form the bulk of finfish, but the figures shown also include pelagic fish and salmon. The introduction of "factory ships" in the 1950s and 1960s led to an increase in Atlantic cod catches throughout the 1960s and early 1970s around Newfoundland, the east coast of Canada, and New England. Catches peaked in 1973 and dropped thereafter until Canada declared a 200-mile (320-kilometer) territorial zone off its coast in 1977. As domestic fishing vessels took advantage of the restriction, yields rose again until 1990. Canada introduced a moratorium on fishing in 1992, causing Canadian fishery to collapse.
Source: Adapted from United Nations Global Environment Outlook–2000. 18 Feb. 2003. <http://www.grida.no/geo2000>. Underlying data from Statistics Canada, National Accounts and Environment Division, System of National Accounts, 1996. (Ottawa: Statistics Canada, n.d.). Adapted with the permission of Statistics Canada.

Atlantic Cod Catch, 1970 to 1994

Catch per Tow
- 1–10
- 11–100
- 101–1,000
- 1,001–10,000
- Over 10,000

Atlantic cod ranges from the Labrador Shelf in Canada to Cape Hatteras in North Carolina.
Source: Adapted from National Oceanic and Atmospheric Administration. *East Coast of North America Strategic Assessment Project: Groundfish Atlas.* Eds. Stephen K. Brown and Robert N. O'Boyle. 26 Oct. 2000. <http://seaserver.nos.noaa.gov/projects/ecnasap/ecnasap.html>.

about 90 percent. According to COSEWIC, the number of spawning fish in various stocks had fallen by almost 98.4 percent since their peak (between 1956 and 1984 depending on the stock). In 1992, the Canadian government had little choice but to announce an immediate two-year moratorium on cod fishing and a package of economic measures to help those who made their living from the cod. Communities in different parts of Newfoundland were estimated to be 80 to 100 percent dependent on groundfish, thus the economic impact was catastrophic: Some thirty thousand to forty thousand people lost their jobs in fishing and related industries. Since the moratorium was imposed, some stocks have shown signs of recovery; others, however, have continued to decline. The Canadian fishing industry has since explored alternatives such as aquaculture (fish farming) and economic diversification in former fishing communities.

Global Concerns. The loss of the cod in Newfoundland reflects a global pattern of overfishing. Several years later in New England, a smaller cod industry was decimated by similar declines in fish stocks. The lessons of Newfoundland were ignored by the U.S. fishing industry. Elsewhere, overfishing has been partly concealed by "fishing down food webs." In a 1998 study of fisheries in 180 countries, Daniel Pauly of the University of British Columbia identified a trend for seeking increasingly lower-level marine organisms as stocks of larger fish are wiped out and commented: "If we keep going like this we will have a sea full of little horrible things that nobody wants to eat. The big things will be gone." Although scientists continue to debate the role of other factors such as global warming, many agree with the authors of a study reported in the July 27, 2001, issue of *Science*, who concluded that overfishing is by far the biggest cause not just of the collapse of fish stocks but of the decimation of entire coastal ecosystems.

—*Chris Woodford*

Further Reading

Bell, K. *COSEWIC Status Report on the Atlantic Cod*, Gadus morhua. Ottawa: Committee on the Status of Endangered Wildlife in Canada, 1998.

Jackson, Jeremy B., et al. "Historical Overfishing and the Recent Collapse of Coastal Ecosystems." *Science* 293 (July 27, 2001): 629–637.

Kunzig, Robert. *Mapping the Deep*. New York: Norton, 2000.

Kurlansky, Mark. *Cod: A Biography of the Fish That Changed the World*. London: J. Cape, 1998.

Pauly, Daniel, et al. "Fishing Down Marine Food Webs." *Science* 279 (February 6, 1998): 860–863.

River Restoration in the United States

For two hundred years the United States government pursued a water policy exclusively focused on controlling rivers with dams, diversions, levees, and other man-made structures (*see also* 128–29). The underlying belief was that more construction and development would solve many of the nation's water problems. However, policymakers now recognize that this construction sacrificed the environmental health of America's rivers, and efforts are currently under way to restore some rivers to a more natural condition.

Water Development Projects. By the 1970s, the U.S. Army Corps of Engineers had constructed 19,000 miles (30,600 kilometers) of waterways, 9,000 miles (14,500 kilometers) of flood control structures, and 7,500 miles (12,100 kilometers) of "improved" channels. The U.S. Bureau of Reclamation had constructed irrigation works (*see also* 90–91) that served 11 million acres (4.5 million hectares). Since the formation of the United States, more than 75,000 dams have been built. The purpose of these projects was to settle the West and spur exploration for and use of the nation's natural resources.

Impact. These agencies built water development projects with little or no regard for their environmental impacts. Consequently, the nation's waterways underwent significant environmental degradation. These projects affected water quality, destroyed fish and wildlife habitat, and replaced natural river scenery with sterile channels and concrete structures. Many of the nation's rivers, including the Colorado, the Columbia, and the Mississippi, became little more than human-made channels, used for barge traffic and water storage.

Policy Changes. The enormous price paid for the single-minded drive to dam, divert, and destroy natural river systems led to a reevaluation of national policy. Beginning in the 1990s, the federal government began a new era in water policy that focused on mitigating past damages and solving water shortages through efficient management and water conservation rather than building new dams. In effect, this new era of water policy will attempt to repair the damage done in previous eras.

Several factors contributed to this fundamental change in policy. The environmental movement sensitized the American public to the value of rivers, which supply water as well as a habitat for fish and wildlife, as critical components of the biosphere. In addition, since the 1970s, recreational use of rivers and lakes has increased tremendously. Whitewater sports have become so popular that government agencies have instituted permit systems on most rivers to control the crowds. For example, private rafters who want to run the Colorado River now go on a waiting list; the wait is now approximately twenty years.

River restoration was also prompted by the Endangered Species Act, passed in 1973, which requires the preservation of habitat for plants and animals listed as endangered (*see also* 176–77). This act has forced government agencies to preserve critical river habitat. For example, the

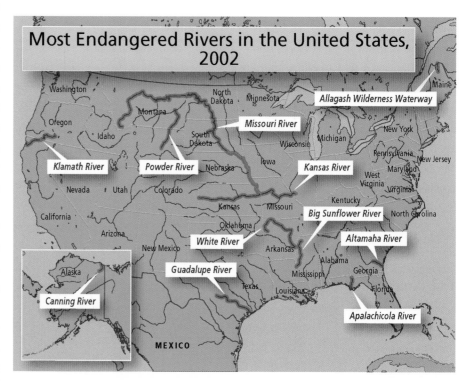

Since 1986, the nonprofit organization *American Rivers* has released an annual report listing America's most endangered rivers. Its 2002 report identifies rivers that are suffering from environmental degradation or that are in danger as a result of proposed water projects.
Source: Adapted from American Rivers. 2 April 2002. <http://www.amrivers.org>. Courtesy of American Rivers.

presence of four endangered fish (the Colorado pikeminnow, the razorback sucker, the humpback chub, and the bonytail chub) found only in the Colorado River and its tributaries has forced water agencies to limit diversions from the river and has stopped several development projects.

Dam Removal. Throughout the country the new federal water policy is rehabilitating natural stream channels and restoring fish habitat and riparian areas (the land alongside the river). The most controversial part of this new policy is the removal of dams, which has the greatest potential for restoring rivers. In the few cases where dams have been removed, a proactive restoration process can assist in returning the affected area to a natural condition. Fish habitat and riparian areas can recover quickly, especially when up- and downstream stretches of the river are still relatively healthy.

However, dam removal also poses the biggest threat to current users, who often prefer the nonnative fish that thrive in reservoirs and want continued access to the water stored behind dams and the hydropower generated by dams. According to the nonprofit organization, American Rivers, 480 dams have been removed in the United States, most of them in the last twenty years. The biggest target, Arizona's Glen Canyon Dam, has been the focus of a concerted political effort for its removal; although this effort is unlikely to succeed in the near future, its growing support indicates how much the public's thinking has changed and is changing.

Major political efforts have also focused on removing the Elwha and Glines Canyon Dams, which were built on the Elwha River in 1913 and 1929, respectively. The Elwha River, which flows through the forests of Washington's Olympic Peninsula, was once a rich source of salmon for the native peoples of the area. The salmon runs on the Elwha were virtually wiped out when the Elwha and Glines Canyon Dams were built on the river to provide hydroelectric power (electricity generated by turbines within a dam). These dams block the passage of the fish up the river, making it nearly impossible for them to spawn.

Beginning in the 1970s, a coalition of Native American tribes, fishermen, and environmental groups began to lobby Congress to remove both dams. The Department of the Interior estimated that, if the dams were removed, the Elwha River would support a wild salmon run of four hundred thousand. The value of those fish far exceeds the value of the electricity generated by the dams. After many years of studies, political maneuvering, and intensive lobbying, the U.S. Congress passed the Elwha River Ecosystem and Fisheries Restoration Act in 1992. In February 2000 the federal government purchased the dams from a private power company. The actual removal of the dams is scheduled for 2004.

Habitat Restoration. In addition to dam removals, innumerable efforts are being made to restore aquatic habitats and river ecosystems. Both the Bureau of Reclamation and the Army Corps of Engineers requested appropriations for fiscal year 2001 to assist with the restoration of ecosystems. The Bureau of Reclamation requested $60 million for the California Bay–Delta Restoration Project, as well as $38.4 million for the Central Valley Project Restoration Fund in California to restore fish and wildlife habitat and populations. The Corps of Engineers' environmental programs accounted for 18.2 percent of its 2001 fiscal budget request of $740 million. The planned projects included $91 million for Columbia River fish mitigation

Further Reading

Bates, Sarah, et al. *Searching Out the Headwaters: Change and Rediscovery in Western Water Policy.* Washington, D.C.: Island Press, 1993.

Gottlieb, Robert. *A Life of Its Own: The Politics and Power of Water.* New York: Harcourt Brace, 1988.

Reisner, Marc. *Cadillac Desert: The American West and Its Disappearing Water.* New York: Penguin, 1993.

to increase fish population survival rates; $158 million to restore, preserve, and protect the Everglades and southern Florida; and $28 million for river restoration. Perhaps the best known of these proposed projects is the $518 million effort to restore the Kissimmee River, as part of the Everglades and southern Florida restoration project.

Restoring rivers and removing dams is both an ecological and political process. These projects often provoke bitter controversy because dams provide water and generate income for some communities. Despite resistance, dams have been removed in nearly every state of the union. Several small streams and rivers have been successfully restored; many of the large-scale, ongoing restoration projects are in the early stages and thus their effects are not yet known. River restoration affects interstate river systems, and even international relations; discussions regarding the Colorado River and the Rio Grande involve Mexico, and the Columbia River crosses the U.S.–Canadian border. Pacific salmon runs in the Columbia Basin and other northwestern rivers affect the fishing industries of many countries.

Through wide-ranging dam removal and ecosystem restoration projects, the federal government is beginning the effort to bring the nation's rivers back to life. A new era of federal water policy has begun.

—Daniel McCool

Mississippi River Watershed

The funnel-like basin or watershed of North America's largest river drains parts of thirty-one states and two Canadian provinces. Covering 1.25 million square miles (3.24 million square kilometers) and exceeded in size only by the watersheds of the Amazon and the Congo, the watershed of the Mississippi is the third-largest river basin on Earth. Nearly 300,000 miles (480,000 square kilometers) of tributary rivers converge to form the river that inspired writer Mark Twain. Called "Messipi" by the Ojibwa Indians of the Lake Superior region, renamed "Rio Escondido" by Spanish explorers, and considered "Father of Waters" by settlers from the expanding United States, the Mississippi rises at Lake Itasca in upper Minnesota. Flowing 2,348 miles (3,779 kilometers), the river more than triples in size where it joins the Ohio River en route to the Gulf of Mexico.

Upper Mississippi. Engineers have traditionally managed the Mississippi as two rivers joined at the confluence of the Ohio at Cairo, Illinois. A diverse fishery, the upper river is home to walleye, northern pike, sauger, bass, perch, crappies, sunfish, and catfish. Forested backwater sloughs sustain otters, beavers, muskrats, minks, and other aquatic mammals. Forty percent of the continent's waterfowl use the upper river's marshes and lakes as a migratory flyway. Songbirds, including finches and warblers, fly the Mississippi corridor south to winter in the Caribbean.

The gateway reach of the Mississippi above St. Louis, Missouri, has long been a hub of interstate commerce. Barge fleets guided by towboats link the great port cities of Pittsburgh via the Ohio River and Chicago via the Illinois River, moving bulk commodities such as coal, gravel, oil, and grain. From St. Louis to St. Paul, Minnesota, twenty-nine gated navigation dams, called locks, pool the river into long reservoirs deep enough to maintain a minimum depth of 9 feet (2.7 meters) during the driest months. Dikes (rock structures that narrow and stabilize the channel) and revetments (rock or concrete mats that line riverbanks, preventing erosion) also facilitate navigation. Annually the barge channel above St. Louis

transports about 130 million tons of products worth $23 billion.

Lower Mississippi. Darker, deeper, and more dangerous than the upper river, the lower Mississippi curves south through a delta region. There, soft alluvial soils spread by the meandering river sustain watery lowlands where cotton, soybeans, rice, sugarcane, timber, feed grain, and hay are grown. Farming on these wetlands, which were reclaimed from the river, depends on a vast federal network of storage reservoirs and spillways with more than 2,000 miles (3,200 kilometers) of levees (earthen embankments). Designed by the U.S. Army Corps of Engineers and authorized in 1928 after the nation's worst flood disaster, the floodway diverts high water away from New Orleans via the Bonnet Carre' Spillway. Another remarkable spillway near the mouth of the Red River above Baton Rouge keeps the Mississippi from jumping west and remaking its delta in the river-swamps of Louisiana's Atchafalaya.

Vanishing wetlands have become a major concern, as these delta lowlands lose valuable marsh in areas where the river once coiled and curved as it flooded through sodden hardwoods. Silt that the river once deposited to nourish these wetlands is now held back by levees. Ship canals pollute and kill freshwater vegetation. Farming, mining, timbering, swamp building, and oil drilling aggravate the natural sinking of land that geologists call subsidence. Deprived of the river's silt, layers of compacted mud weigh down the butter-soft grasslands. An acre of delta marsh disappears every twenty-five minutes. A slab the size of New Orleans subsides every five or six years.

What might be done to restore the vanishing wetlands is an issue clouded by

In Illinois during the summer of 1993, rushing waters from the Mississippi River breach a levee, flooding farmland. The house in the photo was removed from its foundation and carried downstream. (AP/Wide World Photos)

The Mississippi River Drainage Basin

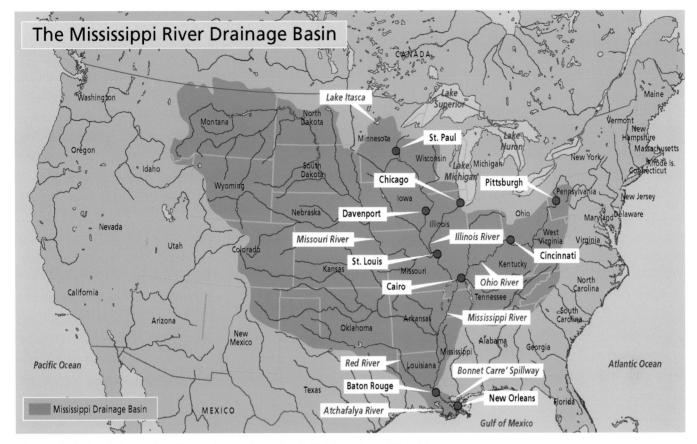

The Mississippi River drains two Canadian provinces and more than half of the continental United States.
Source: Adapted from the Mississippi River Commission. The Great Mississippi River. Project dir. Todd Shallat, et al. U.S. Mississippi Commission, History Center, et al.
<http://www.mvd.usace.army.mil/MRC-History-Center/index.html>. Courtesy of the Mississippi River Commission.

foreboding and doubt. Ecologists claim that dikes and dams alter the pulse of the flood-prone river, causing pollution and habitat loss (*see also* 176–77). Dredging (the mechanical scooping out of mud and sand to deepen a channel for navigation) kills mussels and bottom-feeding aquatic life essential to the river's food chain. Lock pools fill with topsoil, while silt feeds algae blooms and clouds the reedy places that fish need for spawning.

Tributaries. The Mississippi's tributaries are also silted and badly polluted. According to American Rivers, a conservation lobby, the Missouri River has lost 60 percent of its presettlement water surface area and 300,000 acres (120,000 hectares) of sandbars and riparian woodlands. The Ohio River traps enough nitrate-rich farm runoff to endanger the purity of Cincinnati's water supply (*see also* 190–91). Ecologists blame

engineering, in part, for $15 billion in damage that occurred when midwestern rivers breached levees during the summer of 1993, flooding out hundreds of towns. High water devastated Davenport, Iowa, and nearly topped the 52-foot (16-meter) floodwall around St. Louis. Channelization—the dredging and clearing of streams for navigation and drainage—may have contributed to the disaster by compressing river corridors and destroying riparian grasslands that once absorbed seasonal floods.

The new era of public concern for the health of the Mississippi has moved engineering well beyond levees and locks. In Wisconsin, for example, engineers use dredge spoil (excavated mud and sand) to rebuild bird habitat. In Missouri, the U.S. Army Corps of Engineers now cuts notches into dikes so that water can flood over marsh grass. Below New Orleans, a new

spillway keeps plant-killing brine from corroding a freshwater marsh. The environmental challenge is to constrain yet sustain one of the world's great river systems, to restore a buffer of marsh without sinking river commerce, and to respect beauty of water in motion without losing sight of the brute force of a flood (*see also* 180–81).

—*Todd Shallat*

Further Reading

Hunt, Constance Elizabeth. *Down by the River: The Impact of Federal Water Projects and Policies on Biological Diversity.* Washington, D.C.: Island Press, 1988.

Madson, John. *Up On the River: An Upper Mississippi Chronicle.* New York: Penguin Books, 1987.

Palmer, Tim. *America by Rivers.* Washington, D.C.: Island Press, 1996.

Reuss, Martin. *Technology and Politics in the Bayou Country: Water Resources Development in the Atchafalaya Basin, 1790–1990.* Washington, D.C.: Government Printing Office, 1997.

Public Lands: The United States

In general, the public domain in the United States is supervised by four federal agencies: the Department of Agriculture's U.S. Forest Service (*see also* 92–93), the Department of Interior's Bureau of Land Management (BLM), the National Park Service, and the U.S. Fish and Wildlife Service. These four agencies control about 90 percent of public lands. (The Department of Defense, the Bureau of Reclamation, and the Tennessee Valley Authority and other agencies control the balance. Native American reservations, which are federal lands, are not part of the public domain.)

The public domain collectively covers over 1 million square miles (2.6 million square kilometers) and is divided into several units.

The National Wilderness Preservation System, at about 106 million acres (43 million hectares), includes lands that are to be set aside forever as undeveloped areas. All four agencies manage wilderness lands. The National Park System, overseen by the National Park Service, consists of 83 million acres (34 million hectares) of land closed to most forms of economic development, including mining and logging, and available to the public for recreational purposes. The National Wildlife Refuge System, run by the Fish and Wildlife Service, encompasses more than 93 million acres (38 million hectares) and provides habitat for fish, fowl, and mammals. The National Forests, at 191 million acres (77 million hectares), are managed by the Forest Service

using a multiple-use formula that requires a balance of recreation, grazing, timber, and conservation activities. Located primarily in the West and Alaska, the National Rangelands constitute the largest portion of the public domain (403 million acres [163 million hectares]) and vary from grassland and prairie, to desert, to scrub forest and other open space suitable for grazing. The BLM supervises the majority of rangelands, with the Forest Service monitoring the second-largest portion.

Land Use Conflicts. Each of these agencies must work to find the appropriate balance between environmental protection and resource use. Inevitably, such divided responsibility has brought these agencies into conflict with other federal agencies,

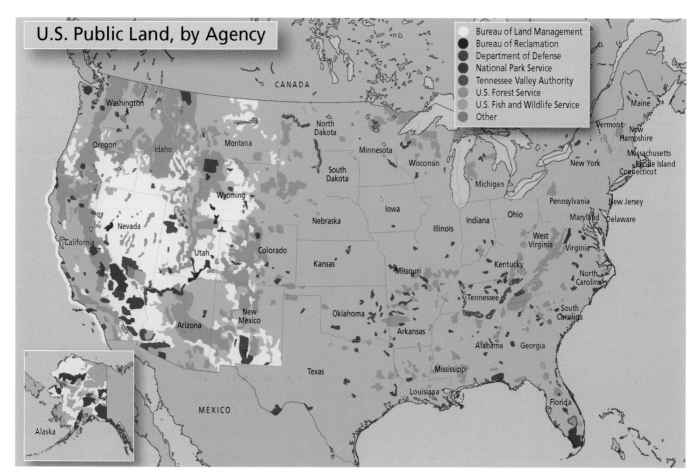

U.S. Public Land, by Agency

- Bureau of Land Management
- Bureau of Reclamation
- Department of Defense
- National Park Service
- Tennessee Valley Authority
- U.S. Forest Service
- U.S. Fish and Wildlife Service
- Other

Public land in the United States is controlled by different federal agencies. Although federal lands comprise one-quarter of the United States, most of the public domain is found in the West. Nevada has the largest percentage of land under federal jurisdiction, with 85 percent.
Source: Adapted from National Atlas of the United States. 27 December 2002. <http://nationalatlas.gov>.

Congress, the White House, environmentalists, and the Wise Use movement—individuals and groups who want access to the land either for profit-making activities or private recreational use (*see also* 168).

In the mid-1980s, the U.S. Forest Service planned to permit the cutting of Oregon's old-growth forests. But the U.S. Fish and Wildlife Service called for the protection of the rapidly disappearing northern spotted owl (*see also* 176–77), whose habitat was located almost exclusively in northwestern old-growth forests stretching from northern California to British Columbia in Canada. Environmental organizations argued that commercial logging would not only adversely affect the owl, but also destroy the ecological balance of the area. Were the spotted owl to be designated an endangered species, the habitat could not be developed, which would force thousands of people in the timber industry out of work. In 1989, a U.S. federal court order declared the northern spotted owl an endangered animal. The controversy prompted the land use agencies to adopt the "ecosystem management" system, which required them to manage ecological systems as a whole.

Controversy also has arisen over the Arctic National Wildlife Refuge (ANWR), where efforts at animal conservation compete with human energy needs (*see also* 148–49). ANWR comprises 19 million acres (8 million hectares) in northeastern Alaska. One of the largest remaining complete ecosystems on the planet, ANWR houses an array of arctic and subarctic habitats and hosts a wide variety of plants and animals. It may also hold as much as 16 billion barrels of recoverable oil, or enough oil to meet the needs of the United States for approximately four years, according to the U.S. Geological Survey. Or it may hold only 3.2 billion barrels, enough for six months, according to some environmentalists. Many environmentalists believe drilling for oil in ANWR is not worth the ecological damage.

Further Reading

Hirt, Paul W. *A Conspiracy of Optimism: Management of the National Forests since World War Two*. Lincoln: University of Nebraska Press, 1994.

Klyza, Christopher McGrory. *Who Controls Public Lands: Mining, Forestry, and Grazing Policies, 1870–1990*. Chapel Hill: University of North Carolina Press, 1996.

McNeill, J. R. *Something New Under the Sun: An Environmental History of the Twentieth-Century World*. New York: W. W. Norton, 2000.

Rosenbaum, Walter A. *Environmental Politics and Policy*. 5th ed. Washington, D.C.: CQ Press, 2002.

Development and drilling in ANWR would threaten the livelihood of the Gwich'in people in Alaska and Canada, who rely for sustenance on the porcupine caribou. The 130,000-head porcupine caribou herd migrates each year from the Yukon in Canada to the coastal plain found within ANWR to calve and graze on the rich vegetation in preparation for winter. Because the herd's migration route extends across the Canada–U.S. border, both nations are affected and any decision making should be joint.

In 1987, Canada and the United States signed an Agreement on the Conservation of the Porcupine Caribou Herd. The agreement committed Canada and the United States to refrain from activities that would damage the herd. But in 2001, the Administration of President George W. Bush proposed opening ANWR to oil drilling. The push by the Bush Administration, the oil industry, and anticonservation groups to drill for oil in ANWR has left the agreement in peril and has created yet another challenge for public land managers.

The coal mining industry struggles with problems similar to those of the oil industry. Coal represents about 90 percent of the remaining U.S. hydrocarbon reserves and could provide a viable alternative to oil for electric utilities and industry. Expanding its use could revive the Appalachian region (*see also* 102–03) and benefit the West and Great Plains, the other two areas with large coal reserves. Extracting coal usually involves strip mining, or removing the top layers of earth, which disturbs the land and the wildlife living on it. Unregulated surface mining in the past left a legacy of sterile land incapable of supporting vegetation. The mining industry has

been hurt by escalating operating costs after the passage of the Surface Mining Control and Reclamation Act of 1977. The law imposed environmental standards on the industry for the first time, including requirements that mined land be returned, as much as possible, to its original contours and use once mining activity had ceased.

Current Issues. At the beginning of the twenty-first century, the Bush Administration has demonstrated a desire to either ease environmental regulations or completely eliminate them. For example, in 2001 the Clinton Administration had closed roughly 60 million acres (24 million hectares) of roadless areas in western National Forests to commercial timbering and road construction. The Bush Administration, supported by a coalition of western logging and snowmobiling interests, filed suit in 2001 to open this acreage up but was rebuffed by the U.S. Court of Appeals in late 2002.

In December 2002, hoping to reduce wildfires after three consecutive years of catastrophic forest fires (*see also* 174–75), the Bush Administration announced that it would curtail environmental reviews and judicial monitoring to speed the cutting of trees and brush in national forests. To make the change without congressional approval, the Administration cited an exemption in administrative regulations for projects that do not have a significant impact on the human environment. Environmentalists charged that the policy is little more than a permit for clearcutting commercial timber. With so many different agendas being promoted, consensus on land-use policies seems unattainable.

—*James G. Lewis*

Public Lands: Canada

During the 1980s and 1990s, Canada first recognized the shortcomings of its public land policies, but faced a constitutional barrier to implementing nationwide changes. Most of the authority to develop and implement public land policies resided with the provinces and territories; the federal government's position was largely advisory and as a funder of research. Nevertheless, Canada's federal government has become a worldwide leader in environmentally sound public land management.

Provincial Role. The provinces and territories currently manage the majority of public lands, including 71 percent of the nation's forests (*see also* 8–9). Each province decides how resources are to be handled on all public land within its jurisdiction. In most cases, the provinces have full authority over land, water, and stationary-source air pollution. British Columbia has fully embraced a policy of sustainable development (*see also* 126–27), while Québec emphasizes resource extraction. Ontario and Alberta established the first provincial departments of the environment in 1971 (the Ontario Ministry of the Environment and Alberta Department of Environment), which provide environmental regulation.

Federal Role. Canada's federal constitution does not explicitly give authority to the federal government for environmental protection, thus creating the conditions for ambiguity, conflict, redundancy, and evasion of responsibility. The federal government has authority over coasts and fisheries (*see also* 178–79), navigable waters, criminal law, and the negotiation of international treaties, but the provinces are responsible for implementing treaty commitments.

To address public land issues and problems of a national scope, the federal government relies on intergovernmental agreements. Federal, provincial, and territorial environmental ministries try to coordinate efforts through the Canadian Council of Ministers of the Environment (CCME), a consultative body organized as a nongovernmental organization in which all members are equal. The ecological effects of logging, mining, fishing,

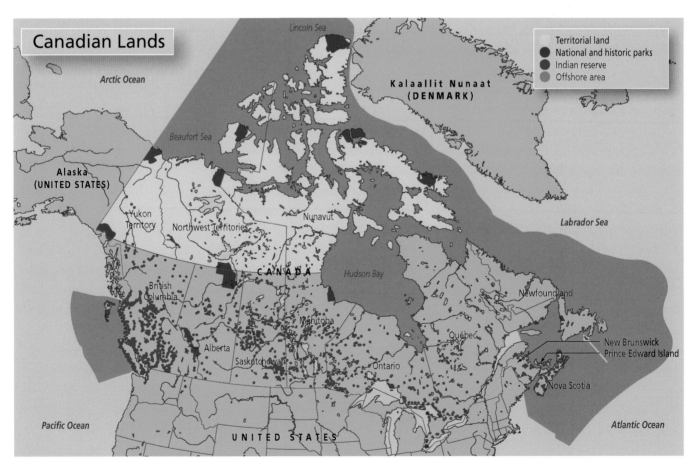

Canadian lands include lands that are held in trust for the people of Canada or specific groups of Canadians, for example, peoples of the First Nations. This includes Indian reserves, national and historic parks, offshore areas, and territorial areas including the Yukon Territory, Northwest Territories, and Nunavut.
Source: Adapted from Geomatics Canada. Natural Resources Canada, Legal Surveys Division. "Canada Lands National Map." 4 December 2002. <http://www.lsd.nrcan.gc.ca/english/canada_lands_national_e.asp>.

forest fires, and acid rain are just a few of the issues that the CCME addresses.

Federal Departments. The federal government also relies on the Natural Resources and Environment Canada departments for public land management. The Canadian Forest Service (*see also* 94–95) and the Earth Sciences Sector are branches of the Natural Resources Department. The Forest Service controls two small research forests totaling less than 50,000 acres (20,240 hectares).

Upon its establishment in 1971, Environment Canada combined and expanded the mandates of existing weather, wildlife, and parks services, and added the Environmental Protection Service. The ministry is predominantly a scientific organization, but does have some regulatory authority. It includes the Environmental Conservation Service (ECS), of which the Canadian Wildlife Service (CWS) is a part. The CWS manages a network of national wildlife areas and migratory bird sanctuaries across Canada that protect about 29 million acres (12 million hectares). The other branches of the ECS work to protect and improve Canada's natural biodiversity, including natural habitat and wildlife, and safeguard the health of large ecosystems like the Great Lakes.

Parks Canada, the national park service, was moved from Environment Canada to the Canadian Heritage Ministry in 1995. The national parks system encompasses about 2 percent of Canada's landmass (94,595 square miles [245,000 square kilometers]), and about 3.5 percent less land that the total landmass of the one thousand provincial parks and nearly fifty territorial parks. However, in October 2002, ten more national parks were proposed, which would bring the total to forty-nine and double the total landmass of the national park system. Most of these lands have been used for oil and gas development, research, mining, hydroelectricity, forestry, agriculture, and private recreation like downhill skiing and

snowmobiling. Resolution of land-use conflicts and jurisdictional issues surrounding these uses need the cooperation of the provinces, territories, indigenous peoples, and all interested parties including local residents.

Resource extraction had long been the dominant use of Canada's public lands until the approval of the 1979 Parks Canada Policy Statement. The policy statement helped set the agenda for all federal land management. It called for support of diverse ecosystems and greater reliance on zoning in individual park plans, which would help control commercial development within a park. It also mandated full consideration of ecological integrity in planning for land use in parks.

The Green Plan. In 1987, the United Nations Brundtland Commission released "Our Common Future," a report that detailed the worldwide problems of environmental degradation and deforestation, and proposed the concept of "sustainable development." The Canadian government quickly embraced this concept, which it defined as "development that meets the needs of the present without compromising the ability of future generations to meet their own needs." Among one of the first countries to begin applying the concept to the management of public land, Canada made sustainable ecosystems the major focus of its Green Plan, a five-year, $3 billion federal conservation strategy.

Passed in 1990, the Green Plan called for, among other things, setting aside 12 percent of the country as protected space with roughly one-third of that figure for national parks (both land and marine parks) by 2000. The protected spaces would serve several different purposes. Parks Canada began using a five-part zoning system, which ranges from small areas designated for intensive recreational use, to wilderness and special protection zones that protect particularly fragile species or areas. A number of recreational activities are permitted, including camping, canoeing, hiking, and cross-country skiing.

With the expiration of the Green Plan in 1995, provincial governments reinserted themselves into the land-management process. In 1998, the CCME guided negotiations that led the federal government, the Yukon and Northwest Territories, and all the provinces except Québec to ratify the Canada-Wide Accord on Environmental Harmonization. The accord sought to eliminate overlap of federal and provincial activities and provided a new framework for cooperation. When federal and provincial laws address the same issue, the provincial law is the one enforced to keep industries from dealing with two different sets of rules and regulating authorities. Federal laws are enforced only in provinces that do not have equivalent provincial laws. Thus, the provinces retain their existing authority, but work with the federal government to improve the coordination of environmental policy.

Despite lofty goals, the national government fell extremely short of its goal of setting aside 12 percent of the land as protected space, having achieved only 87 percent completion by 2002. To compound matters, environmental groups criticized the Green Plan as inadequate, arguing that 12 percent was too small a figure for such a large landmass as Canada.

—James G. Lewis

Further Reading

Environment Canada. *The State of Canada's Environment, 1996.* Ottawa: Minister of Public Works and Government Services, 1996.

Galindo-Leal, Carlos, and Fred L. Bunnell. "Ecosystem Management: Implications and Opportunities of a New Paradigm." *The Forestry Chronicle* 71, no. 5 (September–October 1995): 601–606.

Myre, Pauline. "Changing Forest Values, Forest Legislation and Management in Canada." *The Forestry Chronicle* 74, no. 2 (March–April 1998): 236–240.

Parson, Edward A., ed. *Governing the Environment: Persistent Challenges, Uncertain Innovations.* Toronto: University of Toronto Press, 2001.

VanNijnatten, Debora L., and Robert Boardman, eds. *Canadian Environmental Policy: Context and Cases.* 2nd ed. Toronto: Oxford University Press, 2002.

Industries and Regulatory Strategies

By the end of the 1960s, heavy industries like chemical manufacturing and power generation were responsible for the majority of pollution in North America. As the United States and Canada strengthened environmental regulations, industrial wastes became a major target. Both countries have implemented a variety of regulatory strategies, seeking those that are the most environmentally effective, cost effective, and easiest to manage

U.S. Strategies. In the United States, the Environmental Protection Agency (EPA) was created in 1970 to focus on reducing air and water pollution. The agency attempted to decrease industrial sources of pollution: industrial sewers and factory smokestacks, as well as motor vehicles. More than 80 percent of air pollution (*see also*

106–07) could be traced to smokestacks, vehicles, and industrial processes that leaked toxic gases; the chemical, petroleum, and metal industries were responsible for 90 percent of the continent's toxic waste generation. The pollution laws of the time, including the Clean Air Act of 1970 and the Clean Water Act of 1972, required the EPA to adopt what became known as the command-and-control approach to regulating pollution: Factories were given not only pollution limits, but also the technology and methods of reducing pollution were mandated by law.

Industries found the new regulations extremely intrusive and inflexible. They were required to maintain records of their environmental practices and were inspected by state environmental officials or the EPA. Being required to use certain technology could be expensive, and many

businesses resented not being allowed to experiment with cheaper methods for reducing pollutants.

Relations between the EPA and industry were further strained by the passage, in 1980, of the Comprehensive Environmental Response, Compensation, and Liability Act, commonly known as the Superfund (*see also* 152–53), which addressed the cleanup of old toxic waste dumps that had contaminated the land, running water, and groundwater (*see also* 190–91). The Superfund law directed the government to seek reimbursement from the companies that had dumped the wastes. Because of the high costs the Superfund could impose on a company, businesses had a powerful motivation to fight the EPA in the courts.

During the 1980s, environmental regulators began to focus on determining how much risk a particular pollutant posed to a community, and whether the expense of a cleanup or prevention was justified. This risk assessment or cost-benefit analysis approach helps a regulatory agency ensure the safety of the most people at the lowest cost. In 1987, a risk assessment study argued that the EPA was spending too much money cleaning up old toxic waste dumps while neglecting to address toxic indoor pollution like radon, a radioactive gas that can cause lung cancer.

Although now frequently used by the EPA, risk assessment is not uncontroversial. Risk can be hard to evaluate, and the potential cost of proposed environment regulations is notoriously subjective because such regulations often require significant changes in practices or technology. Groups opposed to new environmental regulations often claim that the compliance would cause economic ruin.

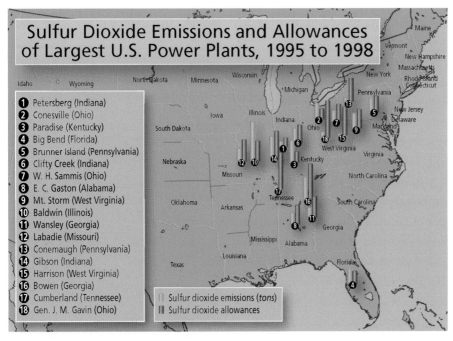

Sulfur Dioxide Emissions and Allowances of Largest U.S. Power Plants, 1995 to 1998

1. Petersberg (Indiana)
2. Conesville (Ohio)
3. Paradise (Kentucky)
4. Big Bend (Florida)
5. Brunner Island (Pennsylvania)
6. Clifty Creek (Indiana)
7. W. H. Sammis (Ohio)
8. E. C. Gaston (Alabama)
9. Mt. Storm (West Virginia)
10. Baldwin (Illinois)
11. Wansley (Georgia)
12. Labadie (Missouri)
13. Conemaugh (Pennsylvania)
14. Gibson (Indiana)
15. Harrison (West Virginia)
16. Bowen (Georgia)
17. Cumberland (Tennessee)
18. Gen. J. M. Gavin (Ohio)

Sulfur dioxide emissions (*tons*)
Sulfur dioxide allowances

In the 1990s, the U.S. Environmental Protection Agency began a program of trading pollution allowances of sulfur dioxide, a pollutant that causes acid rain. Companies can buy or sell allowances, which are essentially the right to emit one ton of sulfur dioxide in a year. Phase I of this acid rain program, which began in 1995 and ended in 1999, required participation by the largest emitters of sulfur dioxide, most of which were coal-burning power plants located in eastern or midwestern states. Phase II of the program, which began in 2000, has introduced stricter emissions limits on participating plants.
Source: Adapted from Byron Swift, "Allowance Trading and Potential Hot Spots—Good News from the Acid Rain Program," Environmental Reporter, 31 (May 12, 2000), 954–959.

Further Reading

Ayres, Robert U., and Leslie W. Ayres. *Industrial Ecology: Towards Closing the Materials Cycle*. Cheltenham, U.K.: E. Elgar, 1996.

Bliese, John R. E. *The Greening of Conservative America*. Boulder, Colo.: Westview Press, 2001.

Shabecoff, Philip. *A Fierce Green Fire: The American Environmental Movement*. New York: Hill and Wang, 1993.

In the 1990s, policymakers continued to address environmental concerns while also considering the financial impact of clean-up efforts. Pollution credits, or allowances, were introduced in hopes of making environmental policy more economically efficient. In a pollution-credit system, overall caps, or limits, determine how much of a particular pollutant can be emitted. If a factory adopts cleaner technology—adding a "scrubber" that removes pollutants to a smokestack, for example—that reduces its emissions of a particular pollutant to below the cap level, that factory is granted a certain number of pollution credits. A second factory that is producing too much of a pollutant can avoid legal penalties by buying pollution credits from the first factory.

Advocates of pollution credits argue that this method provides companies with a financial incentive to adopt more environmentally friendly technology and that it allows businesses to find the most economical way to emit fewer pollutants. Thus, because a company can obtain more credits to sell by further reducing its pollution output, such a system encourages a company to be as clean as it can be rather than doing the bare minimum to comply with the law.

Some environmentalists object to allowing companies to purchase the right to pollute further. In addition, while pollution-credit systems appear to work on a national scale, they are far less effective in addressing local pollution problems and concerns, as a polluting factory or industry in a particular location can buy credits and continue harming the environment and the local population. For example, New York state has long suffered from acid rain (*see also* 196–97) caused by pollutants that are carried into the state on air currents from the south and the west. Pollution produced in-state is less of a problem, because it blows over the Atlantic Ocean, but companies in New York that lowered their emissions were selling their pollution credits to companies in the South and Midwest. While pollutant levels nationwide were falling, they were not decreasing fast enough in New York to significantly reduce acid rain, so in 2000 state legislators passed a bill barring companies located in the state from selling their credits to pollution-emitting companies in other states.

Canadian Strategies. In Canada, the constitutional division of powers limited federal involvement in pollution-control measures through much of the twentieth century. Toward the end of the 1980s, a confluence of domestic and international events—release of the Brundtland Report (1987), concern about the ozone layer and acid rain, and Canadian Supreme Court decisions favoring greater federal intervention—made possible, both politically and constitutionally, a larger role for the federal government in this area. In 1988, the Canadian Environmental Protection Act (CEPA) became law, consolidating several pieces of federal legislation, including the Canada Water Act (1970), the Ocean Dumping Control Act (1975), the Environmental Contaminants Act (1975), and the Clean Air Act (1985). CEPA was designed to address gaps in federal toxic substance legislation and, accordingly, applied to substances not already addressed by existing federal legislation. CEPA also acknowledged provincial pollution control efforts by recognizing existing provincial regulations as equivalent to CEPA regulations, thus giving provinces complete control over toxic substances.

Critics of CEPA 1988 argued that it was inadequate. Federal regulators often were reluctant to supersede provincial authority by aggressively enforcing CEPA. Although CEPA regulations identified fifty or more toxic substances, the regulations were not adequately enforced. In 1999 the law was replaced by a revised CEPA, which included stricter enforcement provisions, required a more aggressive timetable for assessing the toxicity of priority substances, and, most significant, focused on preventing pollution, rather than managing toxic substances once they are in the environment.

Industrial Ecology. In Canada and the United States, the 1990s witnessed the emergence of a movement called industrial ecology, which examines how businesses can use fewer resources and produce less waste by changing their practices and modifying their facilities. Although environmentally sensitive practices are generally assumed to be more expensive, advocates of industrial ecology argue that this is often not the case. For example, Xerox Corp. saved $50 million in 1992 alone after it adopted waste-reduction programs that involved reusing parts in worn-out copy-machine cartridges.

Industry and environmentalists still often find themselves at odds over proposed environmental regulations, common industrial practices, and land use. Nonetheless, environmentalism has moved so far into the mainstream—even the mainstream of the business world—that a company's staff and customers are now quite likely to support ecological practices. Regulations have become more flexible, and business leaders nowadays rarely openly oppose the goals of environmentalism—in fact, many have embraced them.

—*Mary Sisson*

Drinking Water

North America uses more water than any other region in the world. In a year, the average American uses 525,000 gallons (1,987,300 liters) of water, while the average Canadian uses 310,000 gallons (1,173,000 liters). Most of that water is used in industries and agriculture, but the rest is categorized as drinking water. Water is very effective at dissolving solids, which means it can easily be contaminated by harmful chemicals or infected by dangerous microbes. Water shortages as a result of overuse are also a constant concern, especially in the naturally arid western and midwestern United States.

Roughly half of North Americans get their drinking water from surface sources such as rivers, lakes, and reservoirs, while the other half relies on groundwater. Groundwater is pumped up from wells that have been drilled into aquifers—underground pockets of porous, water-bearing rock. Some people in rural areas own their wells, which they usually must monitor for quality themselves. The vast majority of the population gets its water from a public water system, in which water is collected, treated, and pumped out to residences.

Regulation. In the United States, each state is responsible for monitoring the safety of public water systems. Since 1996 states have been required to submit water quality reports to the U.S. Environmental Protection Agency (EPA), which sets limits on more than eighty contaminants, including chemicals like mercury and lead. The EPA was given authority to regulate discharges and implement pollution controls in 1972 with the passage of the Federal Water Pollution Control Act Amendments (commonly known as the Clean Water Act). Since its passage, the act has been revised, most notably in 1977, to recognize

new threats, including those from toxic industrial wastes (*see also* 152–53).

In Canada, the provinces are responsible for setting quality standards and monitoring compliance, a system that has recently been criticized following contamination in 2000 of drinking water in Walkerton, Ontario, by the bacteria *Escherichia coli* that sickened an estimated two thousand people and killed six. In the decentralized Canadian system, each province has different standards regarding water quality, enforcement, and public disclosure; for example, British Columbia and Québec issue dozens of orders that people boil water each year due to suspected bacterial contamination, while the Yukon and Prince Edward Island issue

few or no such orders. In addition, not all provinces keep or disclose records of water quality, making the assessment of Canada's overall water safety difficult.

Water Quality. Contamination of a single public water system (*see also* 74–77) can affect a very large group of people. In the United States, 2 percent of the public water systems serve 75 percent of the population. Such large water systems, which usually provide water to cities, are more likely to be closely monitored for contaminants than smaller systems, but when something goes wrong, more people are affected. For example, in 1993 possible bacterial contamination of two water systems—in New York City and Washington, D.C.—resulted in

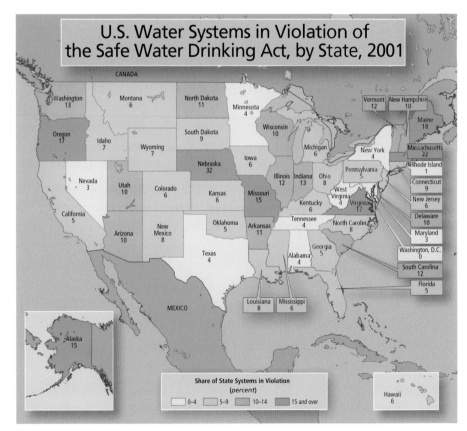

U.S. Water Systems in Violation of the Safe Water Drinking Act, by State, 2001

The percentage of drinking-water systems found to be in violation of U.S. environmental standards in 2001. The majority of such violations result from failures to monitor drinking water or to report the results of such monitoring to the Environmental Protection Agency. Unlike the United States, Canada does not have consistent national standards, nor does its federal government require that provinces keep records on the quality of drinking water. Source: Data from Environmental Protection Agency, Factoids: Drinking Water and Ground Water Statistics for 2001 (Washington, D.C.: Government Printing Office, 2002), 5–7.

local authorities instructing more than seven million people to boil their water.

Surface water is especially vulnerable to pollutants and contaminants from what are called non-point sources—runoff from fields, roads, parking lots, lawns, and farms. Unlike sewers, which are heavily regulated and readily visible, non-point contamination is more diffuse and difficult to prevent. It can transport pesticides (*see also* 122–23) and petroleum products into drinking water sources. Runoff from fertilizers used on lawns and fields can result in high levels of nitrates, which can deplete the oxygen in the bloodstreams of infants, while fecal material in runoff from livestock farms can contain dangerous bacteria. Farm runoff was implicated in the largest outbreak of waterborne disease in the United States, the 1993 contamination of the water supply of Milwaukee, Wisconsin, by the bacteria *Cryptosporidium,* which killed at least fifty people and sickened more than four hundred thousand.

Groundwater is also vulnerable to pollution and contamination. Water can become polluted by percolating through landfills or toxic waste dumps before reaching an aquifer. Underground tanks can leak contaminants into the groundwater; this was the cause of contamination by methyl tertiary butyl ether (MTBE), a carcinogen added to gasoline to reduce smog, which forced the closure of several wells in California in the mid-1990s. When gasoline was stored in underground tanks, the MTBE separated from the gasoline, escaped the tanks, and moved into groundwater supplies.

Some contaminants occur naturally in groundwater. In late 2000, the EPA tightened U.S. standards for the level of arsenic in water, a contaminant found in groundwater in many western states because the water leaches arsenic out of rocks. Arsenic can increase the risk of cancer,

heart disease, and diabetes, but removing it from water can be an expensive process. Such expense led to a much publicized delay in 2000 in implementing the tighter standards, to give the National Academy of Sciences' National Research Council time to review studies of arsenic's health impact. The council concluded that the existing standard of 50 parts per billion was unsafe and that a new standard of 10 parts per billion would provide a significant health benefit and would not be prohibitively expensive to implement.

While both the United States and Canada generally have safe water in comparison to other countries, regulations have continued to be modified to reflect scientific advances and new areas of concern. The Walkerton outbreak gave rise to demands that Canada enact federal water standards, while in the United States the Milwaukee outbreak led to a tightening of existing federal water rules, including several new requirements designed to keep *Cryptosporidium* out of drinking water.

Water Quantity. While the quality of drinking water is an important issue throughout North America, the quantity of drinking water is a major concern, particularly in arid parts of the United States (*see also* 90–91). Some aquifers hold water that is thousands of years old, providing areas that are naturally arid with a "bank" of water. But in the American Southwest and Midwest, many environmentalists worry that

---

Further Reading

De Villiers, Marq. *Water: The Fate of Our Most Precious Resource.* Boston: Houghton Mifflin, 2000.

Michell, John G. "Our Polluted Runoff: Widespread as Rain and Deadly as Poison." *National Geographic* 189, no. 2 (February 1996): 106–125.

Rothfeder, Jeffrey. *Every Drop for Sale: Our Desperate Battle Over Water in a World about to Run Out.* New York: Jeremy P. Tarcher/Putnam, 2001.

---

such water banks may run dry as people pump water out of underground aquifers faster than the aquifers can refill. An estimated one-quarter of the irrigated cropland in the United States is located in areas where wells must be drilled deeper and deeper to find water, indicating that the underlying aquifers contain decreasing amounts of water. In the American West, scarce water supplies were managed for much of the twentieth century by the construction of an extensive network of dams (*see also* 128–29) and canals to capture and transport surface water, but the region has essentially run out of rivers to dam, and western states have engaged in often-acrimonious negotiations to apportion the available water among an ever-growing population.

For example, a series of agreements that date to the early twentieth century have divided the 14 million acre-feet (17,000 million cubic-meters) of water that flows in the Colorado River among Mexico, California, Colorado, Arizona, Utah, Wyoming, New Mexico, and Nevada. However, Nevada, Arizona, and Colorado have requested new agreements that increase their share of the Colorado River to meet the demands of growing populations, while environmentalists argue that the needs of wildlife are not being taken into consideration.

Water, like air, is so pervasive that people tend not to think about it unless something goes wrong—a well runs dry, drinking water begins to smell and taste odd, or terrorists threaten a water system. Nonetheless, environmentalists and, increasingly, regulators are trying to convince people to consider how their daily actions affect water supply and quality. Contamination is much easier to prevent than to clean up, and water conservation in households, industries, and agriculture could help ensure enough water for all.

—*Mary Sisson*

Environmental Justice

In the late 1980s, the concept of "environmental justice" came to the center of the political debate over the environment. First brought to public attention in 1987 by United Church of Christ leader Benjamin Chavis in his Commission for Racial Justice study "Toxic Wastes and Race in the United States," environmental justice claimed that minority communities in the United States were singled out for the siting of environmental hazards (*see also* 152–53), both waste dumps and employment-offering industries, on the basis of the racial makeup of communities.

According to the report, 3 of every 5 black and Hispanic Americans lived in communities with one or more toxic waste sites; more than 15 million African Americans, over 8 million Hispanics, and about 50 percent of Asian/Pacific Islanders and Native Americans lived in communities with one or more abandoned or uncontrolled toxic waste sites. The arguments of environmental justice advocates challenged the existing strategies of large corporations, as well as their motives and behavior.

The public perception of environmental justice brought together a number of similar yet different ideas. Environmental justice was a quest for social equity in environmental matters. Another concept, "environmental racism," argued that racial injustice in American society was as prevalent in environmental issues as in other areas. "Environmental classism" suggested that class played a greater role than race in exposing communities to environmental hazards. Despite their differences, media portrayal quickly lumped all three concepts under environmental justice.

Civil Rights. This concept of environmental justice easily connected with a range of other oppositional voices in American society. It sought to join two modern American fears, nuclear and toxic poisoning, with the greatest of American injustices, racism, in an effort to regain a prominent position for civil rights issues. During the presidency of Ronald Reagan in the 1980s, the traditional strategies that drove civil rights in the United States were weakened. As the economic condition of the country worsened in the recession of 1982, whites in general became noticeably less concerned with the entreaties of the civil rights community. The civil rights movement needed a new strategy, and some of its leaders recognized in the idea of environmental justice an argument so compelling that it might allow civil rights to recapture the moral high ground, high visibility, and priority on the nation's agenda that it had enjoyed during the 1960s.

The concept attracted much attention because it created a powerful moral argument in an era that paid less attention to moral suasion and more attention to cost-benefit analysis. When leaders like

Toxic Poisoning in a Tennessee Community

Outside of Medon, Tennessee, about 70 miles (113 kilometers) from Memphis, a 242-acre (98-hectare) tract was soaked in an ominous witches' brew of chemicals. Beginning in 1964, the Velsicol Corporation of Chicago had been dumping its waste near the cabins and small homes of the rural population. Most of the people were poor, working in whatever jobs they could find and living off the land when they could not find work. They had little political clout and no one to stand up for them.

Velsicol, a major producer of pesticides and chemical products, would be successfully sued in federal court in 1986, but not before seriously harming the community with the waste that it brought to Tennessee. The more than three hundred thousand 55-gallon (208-liter) drums and containers of waste it deposited contained some of the most toxic chemicals in the pesticide industry, heptachlor, endrin, and dieldrin among them. Much of the waste leaked into the groundwater. By the early 1970s, the dump was beginning to affect its neighbors, and in 1973 the state of Tennessee shut down the hazardous operation.

Medical tests in the late 1970s revealed that the region's residents suffered from an array of maladies. Kidney problems, fatigue, respiratory ailments, and other conditions associated with exposure to poisons became common. Birth defects rose to unparalleled levels, paralysis spread among adults, and the area showed signs of toxic poisoning.

Poor and rural, the Medon, Tennessee, area fit the profile of communities typically affected by toxic pollution. But, in this case, some justice was done. In the summer of 1986 Velsicol was prosecuted in the Western District of Tennessee. The company was found liable to the plaintiffs for its negligence in the location, operation, and closure of the site, and failure to protect the community from its chemical dumping. The court held that Velsicol's hazardous waste site offered "a high risk of harm, . . . Velsicol's hazardous waste site was inappropriately located, and activities at the site had no value to the community and thus were outweighed by their dangerous attributes." The court then awarded compensatory damages to the plaintiffs of more than $12.5 million.

Chavis pointed to examples of the siting of toxic dumps based on racial factors, those arguments spoke to and awoke Americans' sympathies for the poor, the defenseless, and the wronged in U.S. society. Although Chavis inserted a moral dimension to this argument, it was woven together with health and safety issues that could affect all citizens.

Class Factors. The environmental justice movement originally surfaced because of concerns about environmental racism; however, in reality, the overwhelming majority of people negatively affected by pollution, toxic chemicals, and nuclear waste in the United States were working-class whites living near industrial plants and factories. The history of pollution had shown one irrefutable fact: people come to the "hazard," a term for the source of industrial pollution. Instances like Love Canal—a former toxic waste site in Niagara Falls, New York (*see also* 158–59)—showed that the beginning of an environmental hazard was often the dumping of toxic chemicals in undeveloped land on which housing was built later. The areas surrounding American factories encountered environmental hazards in equal measure. Throughout the nation, the haze of industrialization hung over the homes of European ethnic immigrants and their children in places like the south side of Chicago; Birmingham, Alabama; and Pittsburgh, Pennsylvania.

Protesters march together in 1982 in demonstration against the siting of a toxic waste dump in Afton, North Carolina. Many believed that the rural community was selected for the site because its residents are black and poor. (© Bettmann/Corbis)

Attorneys who specialized in siting toxic waste dumps freely admitted having a strategy, but it was not one that singled out African Americans or nonwhites in particular. From the point of view of such attorneys, African-American communities were too fractious. Except in specific situations, such as those revealed by sociologist Robert Bullard in his study of Houston, *Dumping in Dixie* (1990), it was difficult to find African-American neighborhoods systematically singled out. Instead, corporations targeted populations with low levels of education, communities that were predominantly Roman Catholic, and areas where the siting of a waste facility would provide needed employment. They used the limited economic advantages of a dump to seduce such communities, admittedly seeking pliant individuals and communities to accept a greater risk than might be acceptable to the public at large. Clearly poorer communities were disproportionately affected and some of those communities included large populations of Hispanics and African Americans. Equally apparent, however, was that the vast majority of people affected by toxic waste in the United States had long been and continued to be lower-middle-class whites.

Federal Action. During the Clinton Administration, environmental justice found executive sanction. In 1994, Executive Order 12898 established the federal Interagency Working Group on Environmental Justice (IWG) to address environmental inequities affecting minority and low-income populations. By 2000, the IWG had begun to implement its goals, releasing the "Integrated Federal Interagency Environmental Justice Action Agenda" in 2000. By then, environmental justice had become an accepted measure within the environmental community.

—*Hal Rothman*

Further Reading

Bullard, Robert D. *Dumping in Dixie: Race, Class and Environmental Quality.* 3rd ed. Boulder, Colo.: Westview Press, 2000.

Bullard, Robert, ed. *Confronting Environmental Racism: Voices from the Grassroots.* Boston: South End Press, 1993.

Rothman, Hal K. *The Greening of a Nation? Environmentalism in the United States since 1945.* Fort Worth, Tex.: Harcourt Brace College Publishers, 1998.

Eco-Radicalism

The rise of radical environmentalism paralleled the success of an environmental legislative agenda that included the Clean Air Act of 1970 and the Clean Water Act of 1972, and the sense of urgency that increasingly came to surround environmental issues. In the 1970s, environmentalists divided into more specialized groups; the Reagan Administration's assault on environmental legislation and the core concepts of environmental protection in the 1980s helped create an audience for radical environmentalism. James Watt's tenure as secretary of the interior did much to foster the development of radical groups. Watt's extreme policies and unwillingness to compromise

caused many environmentalists to embrace more radical approaches.

In response to the anti-environmentalism (*see also* 168–69) of the Reagan Administration, more people became active in the environmental movement, making it both stronger and more diverse. Environmental groups no longer shared the same goals and strategies; instead, they held a broad array of views, advocating discussion, litigation, and even direct action. The Sierra Club, the primary national group since the turn of the nineteenth century, remained central in the environmental movement. It also was one of the more politically mainstream organizations, along with the Audubon Society and the National Parks

and Conservation Association. By the 1980s, however, more than one hundred major conservation and environmental groups competed for membership and the financial support of the public. Some, including the Natural Resources Defense Council (NRDC), experienced spectacular growth during the 1980s. NRDC's willingness to litigate in support of environmental causes appealed to the middle class. Groups like the more staid National Wildlife Federation lost membership between 1979 and 1983, while more activist organizations, such as Greenpeace, founded in 1971, and Earth First!, created in about 1980, blossomed.

Earth First! The first truly radical environmental group, Earth First!, began when

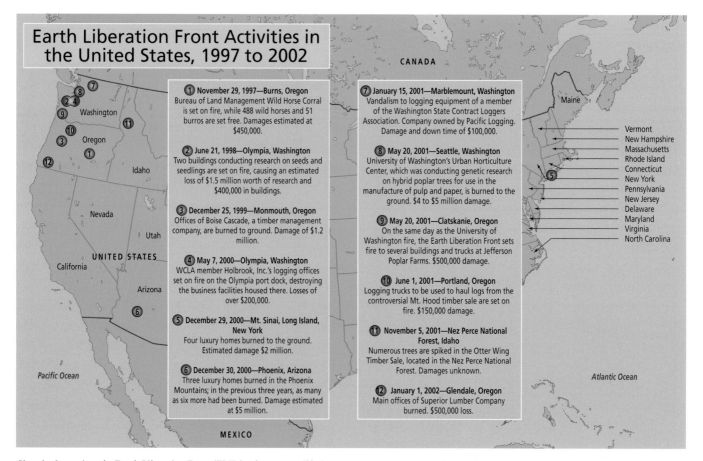

Since its formation, the Earth Liberation Front (ELF) has been responsible for numerous acts of eco-terrorism, including setting fire to logging camps and genetic research facilities. ELF has caused at least $30 million in destruction since 1997. This map shows some actions that have been attributed to the group.

Sources: Frontiers of Freedom Institute,"Recent Actions by the Earth Liberation Front," *Environmental Extremism and Eco-Terrorism: The Costs Imposed on Americans* (Washington, D.C.: Frontiers of Freedom Institute, 2001), 53-54, <http://www.ff.org/media/PDF/ec_conference.pdf>; and Earth Liberation Front. 2003. <http://www.earthliberationfront.com>.

Further Reading

Helvarg, David. *The War Against the Greens: The "Wise-Use" Movement, the New Right and Anti-environmental Violence.* San Francisco: Sierra Club Books, 1997.

Foreman, Dave. *Confessions of an Eco-Warrior.* New York: Harmony Books, 1991.

Rothman, Hal K. *Saving the Planet: The American Response to the Environment in the 20th Century.* Chicago: Ivan R. Dee, 2000.

Zakin, Susan. *Coyotes and Town Dogs: Earth First! and the Environmental Movement.* New York: Viking, 1993.

cofounder Dave Foreman, a former lobbyist for the Wilderness Society, became disgusted by the Forest Service's handling of the wilderness lands it controlled. The agency recommended protecting only 15 million of the 80 million roadless acres (6 million of the 32 million hectares) designated for study on national forest land in the Roadless Area Review and Evaluation (RARE) II process. Wilderness advocates failed in attempts to have the agency rethink its recommendation. After what Foreman regarded as a stunning defeat, he left Washington, D.C., and the Wilderness Society and returned to grass-roots organizing. He believed that the environmental movement (*see also* 162–63) had lost touch with its origins and worried that its moderate tone would fail to achieve results, particularly as increasingly zealous and powerful opponents were attacking wilderness protection. Foreman and a cadre of activists including Howie Wolke, a former Friends of the Earth worker; Susan Morgan, former educational director for the Wilderness Society; Bart Koehler, also from the Wilderness Society; the most overtly left-wing of the group, Mike Roselle; and others disgruntled with the mainstream formed Earth First!

With Watt in office and the Sagebrush Rebellion (*see also* 168–69) gaining momentum during the 1980s, Foreman and Earth First! served as a significant counterweight to extreme forces on the political right. Those who believed environmentalism could remain inside the system of government and still succeed found their numbers diminishing. Although early conservationists (*see also* 110–11) had been responsible for most of the victories of environmentalism,

their tactics seemed increasingly archaic as negotiations with Watt and other anti-environmentalists became almost impossible.

Earth First! carried the banner of anti-establishment direct action. Its slogan, "no compromise in defense of Mother Earth," reflected many of the ideals of the politically turbulent 1960s. Adopting the tactics of the civil rights movement and student protests, the organization believed in an approach to preservation primarily defined by noted environmental author and iconoclast Edward Abbey in his 1975 book, *The Monkey Wrench Gang.* Earth First! attracted media attention to help publicize the environmental cause, with members chaining themselves to trees, blocking bulldozers, and even spiking trees with long nails that could become airborne projectiles if power saws were used to fell the tree. "Monkey wrenching," as spiking and other versions of ecological sabotage (ecotage) were labeled, made confrontation in the wilderness very real. On March 31, 1981, Earth First! made its national debut. The group unfurled a black plastic tarpaulin with a 300-foot (91-meter) painted crack over the Glen Canyon Dam in northern Arizona, the dam that had outraged environmentalists. "Earth First!" shouted Abbey from the walkway atop the dam. "Free the Colorado [River]!" Guerrilla theater, an aggressive stance, and the willingness to do anything to protect wilderness characterized the organization from its outset.

Responses to Eco-Radicalism. To mainstream environmentalists, the radical fringe was a threat. Its actions made environmentalists look unreasonable and threatened the broad public support developed during

the 1960s and 1970s. Even more, the fringe seemed romantic, reflecting the alienation of youth that became common in the 1980s as the nation moved into a newly aggressive phase of material acquisition. It also sapped vitality from conventional environmentalism, even as the numbers of mainstream organizations grew exponentially as Watt's actions drew outraged responses. Despite their small numbers, the radical fringe possessed the greatest creativity and ingenuity within the environmental movement.

Politically, Earth First! anchored the left wing of environmentalism, making the center more palatable to diehard opponents such as Watt. Instead of Foreman of Earth First!, politicians, agency officials, and resource users could sit down with people like Doug Scott, the Sierra Club negotiator. Although radical groups like Earth First! could embarrass mainstream environmental organizations, having a range of groups provided more consistent success.

Underground Environmental Activism. Just as Earth First! was founded by activists frustrated by mainstream environmentalism, so Earth First! would itself be outpaced by more radical activists. In 1992, Earth First! members who advocated direct action and were resistant to the group's desire to become more mainstream founded the international underground group, Earth Liberation Front (ELF). Adopting a form of extreme environmental activism, ELF's goal was to "inflict economic damage on those profiting from the destruction and exploitation of the natural environment." During the 1990s, the battles fought by environmental radical groups were as often internecine as they were with government agencies and corporations. Environmental radicalism became hollow, as much for show as for accomplishment of goals, and like the 1960s radicalism to which it sometimes traced its roots, environmental radicalism faded from prominence.

—Hal Rothman

Environmental Diplomacy: Canada, the United States, and Acid Rain

In the United States and Canada, reductions in nitrogen and sulfur oxide emissions have been achieved in part because of aggressive strategies that include industrial process changes, installation of "scrubbers" to smoke-stacks to remove pollutants, and a switch to cleaner fuels. Pollution generated in one country, however, can cross into the other and be deposited in the form of acid precipitation; thus independent action taken by each country did not eliminate the problem of acid rain. Conflict between Canada and the United States over pollution first emerged in 1925 and persisted until the two nations turned to diplomacy in 1988 to address the transnational issue. Improved cooperation between Canada and the United States in the 1990s has helped to reduce acid precipitation significantly.

Causes of Acid Rain. Scientists have been aware of acid precipitation, more commonly known as acid rain, since the late nineteenth century. The most common chemical sources, or precursors, of acid rain are the emission into the air of sulfur and nitrogen oxide gases resulting from the burning of fossil fuels, mostly by automobiles, coal-burning power plants, and metal-smelting operations. These gases can be picked up by high-altitude winds and transported hundreds of miles from their point of origin. While airborne, these gases become sulfate and nitrate aerosols and join with other airborne chemical compounds, including carbon monoxide, ozone, and hydrogen perox-ide, other volatile chemical compounds, and heavy metals like lead. Those com-pounds mix with water to become complex

chemicals that return to Earth in the form of rain or snow. Based on estimates made in several eastern U.S. watersheds in the late twentieth century, between 60 and 70 percent of acid precipitation found in rain or snow is sulfuric acid and the remainder mostly nitric acid.

The United States discharges about 45 tons of nitrogen and sulfur oxides annually, the most of any nation in the world, largely because of its enormous consumption of fossil fuels. In North America, Canada accounts for much of the rest of the air pollution. Most of the

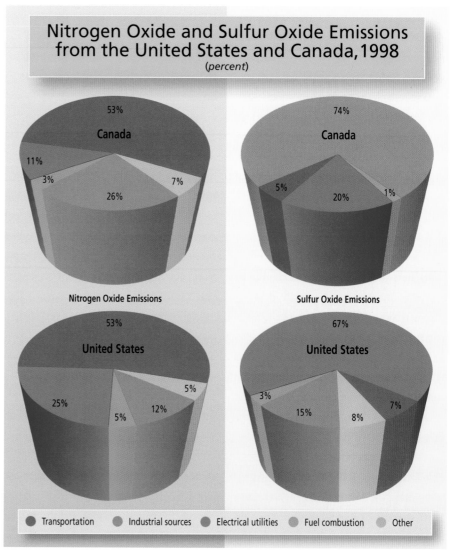

Nitrogen Oxide and Sulfur Oxide Emissions from the United States and Canada, 1998
(percent)

Canada — 53% · 11% · 3% · 26% · 7%
Nitrogen Oxide Emissions

Canada — 74% · 5% · 20% · 1%
Sulfur Oxide Emissions

United States — 53% · 25% · 5% · 12% · 5%

United States — 67% · 3% · 15% · 8% · 7%

● Transportation   ● Industrial sources   ● Electrical utilities   ● Fuel combustion   ● Other

Nitrogen and sulfur oxide emissions are the two major precursors to acid precipitation. The main sources of nitrogen oxide emissions are from motor vehicles, residential and commercial furnaces, industrial and electric-utility boilers and engines, and other equipment. The United States produced 11 times as much as Canada in 1998. Ore smelting, coal-fired power generators, and natural gas processing are the main contributors of sulfur oxide emissions. In 1998, the United States produced over 6 times as much as Canada.

Source: Adapted from The Green Lane™. Environment Canada. 19 December 2002.
<http://www.ec.gc.ca/acidrain/acidfact.html>.

pollution originates in Ontario, both a leading source and victim of acid precipitation. Smelter pollution from Ontario, and to a lesser extent from Québec, descends not only onto eastern Canada but into the New England states as well. Pollutants released in the United States cause acid precipitation in Canada. To compound matters for the United States, prevailing winds move from south to north and can transport pollutants from Mexico into the United States; these pollutants usually affect visibility and air quality.

Agreements and Legislation. In the 1980s, amid growing international disagreement over acid precipitation, the Administration of President Ronald Reagan ignored Canadian complaints about pollution sources in the U.S. Midwest, claiming that evidence linking U.S. pollution sources to Canada's problems was insufficient. As political pressure from environmentalist groups and even northeastern states affected by air pollution grew, the Reagan Administration surprised Canada by entering into an agreement with Mexico while still denying the effects of acid rain on the Canadian environment. In 1983, Mexico and the United States signed the La Paz Agreement, the first transnational air agreement, to help reduce the amount of pollution carried from the smelting plants of the U.S. Southwest and northwestern Mexico to agricultural and populated

areas of the United States. In 1988, the Reagan Administration conceded the seriousness of the problem with Canada and signed an international protocol that declared that nitrogen oxide emissions in the United States would be reduced to 1987 levels by 1994.

In a bold departure from earlier positions, the Administration of President George H. W. Bush agreed in 1990 to add amendments to the Clean Air Act, originally passed in 1977. The amendments committed the United States to reducing sulfur dioxide emissions from electricity generating plants by 10 million tons per year and nitrogen oxides by 2 million tons per year and set a cap on the amount of sulfur oxides emitted by 2000. This goal was easily reached because of the highly successful use of tradable permits, or credits (*see also* 188–99), by electric utilities, which account for roughly 72 percent of sulfur dioxide total emissions.

In 1991, the Bush Administration signed the Canada–U.S. Air Quality Agreement, which committed both nations to reducing sulfur oxide emissions. In the mid-1990s, both nations established successful national acid rain programs; the Canada-Wide Acid Rain Strategy for Post-2000 and the Acid Rain Program in the United States both have brought about further reductions. Although successful in reducing sulfur emissions, Canada and the United States

need to achieve further reductions and also decrease nitrogen emissions if they are to reach acceptable air quality.

British Columbia and Washington State. In Canada, provinces and the federal government share authority in handling air pollution, but in reality the provinces possess greater authority. British Columbia opted to work directly with the state government of Washington to address issues relating to acid rain. In 1992, the province entered into an agreement with Washington state to coordinate action and share information on environmental matters of mutual concern. The British Columbia–Washington Environmental Cooperation Council has become a useful model for bilateral decision making. The council cannot enforce restrictions but provides officials at the subfederal level with a way to share research and coordinate policies before disputes escalate into international problems. For example, when a smelting plant in Trail, British Columbia, was required to redesign its lead smelter because of health concerns in neighboring Washington, Washington officials were asked to collaborate on the plan with officials in British Columbia. In turn, the state spent more than $250,000 in a five-year investigation of long-standing local health concerns in the remote town of Northport, Washington, near the border with British Columbia. Thus, the council enables the provinces to retain power in the Canadian West and also demonstrates the willingness of U.S. state governments to take on some responsibilities for cross-border environmental management. As additional progress in cross-border issues can come only through international cooperation, these examples of cooperation give hope for the future.

—*James G. Lewis*

Further Reading

Alm, Leslie R. *Crossing Borders, Crossing Boundaries: The Role of Scientists in the U.S. Acid Rain Debate.* Westport, Conn.: Praeger, 2000.

Kiy, Richard, and John D. Wirth, eds. *Environmental Management on North America's Borders.* College Station: Texas A&M University Press, 1998.

Rosenbaum, Walter A. *Environmental Politics and Policy.* 5th ed. Washington, D.C.: CQ Press, 2002.

U.S. Department of State. *Environmental Diplomacy: The Environment and U.S. Foreign Policy.* Washington, D.C.: U.S. Government Printing Office, 1997.

VanNijnatten, Debora L., and Robert Boardman, eds. *Canadian Environmental Policy: Context and Cases.* 2nd ed. Don Mills, Ont. and New York: Oxford University Press, 2002.

Wirth, John D. *Smelter Smoke in North America: The Politics of Transborder Pollution.* Lawrence: University Press of Kansas, 2000.

NAFTA and Environmental Side Agreements

The 1990s began a new era in global free trade. Along with the European Union and the Asia Pacific Economic Cooperative Forum (APEC), the 1993 North American Free Trade Agreement (NAFTA) defined a vast area of the world in which trade restrictions that had been imposed in a 1947 umbrella treaty (known as the General Agreement on Tariffs and Trade [GATT], which was replaced by the World Trade Organization [WTO] in 1995) were relaxed. By making free trade more important than the environment, NAFTA became and still is highly controversial. Attempts to incorporate environmental protection into NAFTA through so-called side agreements have proved to be equally controversial. Although some analysts believe that NAFTA paves the way for greater environmental cooperation between the United States, Canada, and Mexico, others argue that the three countries are further away from sustainability than ever.

Free Trade Issues. Even before NAFTA had been signed, it clearly was going to be environmentally controversial. The 1988 Free Trade Agreement (FTA) between the United States and Canada had already demonstrated how one nation's environmental, social, and labor laws can be interpreted as import restrictions and barriers to free trade if another nation lacks similar laws. Shortly after the FTA came into force, the U.S. chemical industry used it to challenge stringent Canadian laws that prevented the United States from exporting pesticides (*see also* 122–23) that were legal in the United States but illegal in Canada.

The NAFTA negotiations in the early 1990s sought to expand the free-trade zone to include Mexico. What soon became apparent was that environmental legislation in all three countries was at risk if such laws threatened the ability of powerful transnational corporations to trade across borders. Advocates of free trade,

consumer protection, and the environment, including public interest activist and corporate critic Ralph Nader, argued that NAFTA and GATT (before it was replaced by the WTO) would lead to the progressive erosion of environmental and social legislation not just across North America but also throughout the world. During his 1992 presidential campaign, Bill Clinton attacked NAFTA's lack of environmental and labor protection and vowed to introduce extra (side) agreements to correct the problem if he was elected.

Side Agreements. During the Clinton Administration, two environmental side agreements to NAFTA were negotiated. The first, the North American Agreement on Environmental Cooperation, was an attempt to build general environmental safeguards into NAFTA by creating a watchdog body called the North American Commission for Environmental Cooperation (CEC). The CEC was designed to promote environmental protection across the region through a mixture of cross-border initiatives, public participation, and transparent decision making. Negotiations over NAFTA had specifically highlighted the problem of polluting industries being exported across the U.S.-Mexico border. Thus the second side agreement, between the United States and Mexico, created a Border Environment Cooperation Commission and a North American Development Bank to increase cooperation and investment in the area.

The environmental side agreements proved to be as controversial as NAFTA. Some nongovernmental organizations (NGOs) argued that by approving the side agreements, environmentalists would make NAFTA's agenda of deregulated trade

Trucks line up in San Diego after crossing into the United States along the U.S.–Mexico border. In compliance with NAFTA, the Administration of George W. Bush proposed to allow Mexican trucks free passage on all U.S. highways, but critics claimed that Mexican trucks do not meet U.S. environmental standards and will contribute to air pollution. (AP/Wide World Photos)

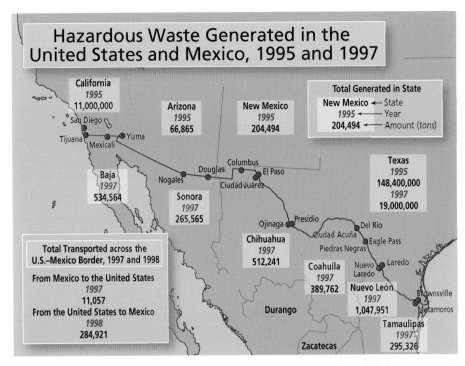

Hazardous Waste Generated in the United States and Mexico, 1995 and 1997

California
1995
11,000,000
San Diego
Tijuana
Mexicali
Yuma

Arizona
1995
66,865

New Mexico
1995
204,494

Total Generated in State
New Mexico ◄— State
1995 ◄— Year
204,494 ◄— Amount (*tons*)

Columbus
Douglas
El Paso
Nogales
Ciudád Juárez

Baja
1997
534,564

Sonora
1997
265,565

Texas
1995
148,400,000
1997
19,000,000

Total Transported across the U.S.–Mexico Border, 1997 and 1998

From Mexico to the United States
1997
11,057
From the United States to Mexico
1998
284,921

Ojinaga
Presidio
Del Rio
Ciudad Acuña
Eagle Pass
Piedras Negras

Chihuahua
1997
512,241

Coahuila
1997
389,762

Nuevo
Laredo
Laredo

Durango

Nuevo León
1997
1,047,951

Brownsville
Matamoros

Tamaulipas
1997
295,326

Zacatecas

Movements of hazardous waste across the U.S.–Mexico border highlight continuing inequalities in environmental protection between the two countries. In 1997, 11,057 tons of hazardous waste was exported from Mexico to the United States, while 284,921 tons of waste crossed the border in the opposite direction the following year.
Source: Adapted from Red Mexicana de Acción Frente al Libre Comercio, *Hazardous Waste Management in the United States–Mexico Border States: More Questions than Answers* (Mexico City and Austin, Tex.: Texas Center for Policy Studies, 2000), 31. Courtesy of Texas Center for Policy Studies.

seem acceptable and environmentally legitimate. Seven large and highly influential U.S. environmental groups, including the World Wildlife Fund, the National Audubon Society, and the Natural Resources Defense Council, supported the side agreements and helped pave the way for NAFTA's passage in 1993.

Since the implementation of NAFTA, opinions vary widely on whether the CEC has proved useful. On the positive side, it has helped to draw attention to continuing environmental discrepancies between the United States, Canada, and Mexico and published several reports monitoring trends in pollution and emissions. On the negative side, critics have argued that the process by which the CEC investigates environmental petitions is too lengthy and complex and basically incomprehensible to the citizens and environmental groups who submit them. Most petitions have taken the CEC a long time to process and few

have resulted in the publication of a "factual record" (the CEC's ultimate adjudication of a complaint). Critics also charge that if the CEC is a watchdog, it lacks teeth: It cannot subpoena documents or inspect environmental sites and its factual records are little more than opinions—they are not legally binding recommendations.

Environmental Debates. Similar uncertainty exists about the wider environmental impacts of NAFTA. In a three-year study concluded in 1997, Joseph DiMento of the University of California determined that the side agreements had at least started a process of cooperation between the three governments to address environmental problems. At a symposium held by the CEC in October 2000, participants concluded that it was overly simplistic to say that free trade damaged the environment, because the effects of free trade on the environment were highly complex. Some cross-border trends have proved to be cautiously

encouraging. In 2000, for example, the CEC reported that Canada was importing 29 percent less hazardous waste and 32 percent less waste for landfill from the United States than in 1999.

Yet environmental problems have worsened on the U.S.–Mexico border where industrialization and urbanization continue apace. For example, the number of maquiladora plants, which employ cheap labor just inside the Mexican border and assemble goods mainly for the U.S. market, has increased by 50 percent since NAFTA was signed and only 11 percent of them dispose of their toxic wastes properly. Moreover, evidence is strong that NAFTA has increased the environmental impact of logging in Mexico's Chihuahua forests. In addition, corporations continue to use NAFTA to challenge environmental laws that restrict their ability to trade. In November 2001, for example, the U.S. Crompton Corp. filed a $100 million lawsuit against the Canadian government for banning the use of the pesticide lindane on canola crops. It is still too early to say whether NAFTA will prove as environmentally disastrous as the green NGOs predicted back in the early 1990s or whether, by starting a process of cooperation among the United States, Canada, and Mexico, the environmental side agreements could be the start of the long and difficult road to sustainability.

—*Chris Woodford*

Further Reading
Athanasiou, Tom. *Divided Planet: The Ecology of Rich and Poor.* Athens: University of Georgia Press, 1998.
MacArthur, John R. *The Selling of "Free Trade": NAFTA, Washington, and the Subversion of American Democracy.* Berkeley: University of California Press, 2001.
Nader, Ralph, ed. *The Case Against Free Trade: GATT, NAFTA, and the Globalization of Corporate Power.* Berkeley, Calif.: North Atlantic Books, 1993.

Corporate "Greenwashing"

"Greenwashing" is the process whereby corporations present an image of being environmentally friendly without necessarily making any changes in their business practices. Long recognized as a tactic by which an enterprise can attempt to profit through environmental concerns, greenwash is now defined in the *Oxford English Dictionary* as: "Disinformation disseminated by an organization so as to present an environmentally responsible public image." Although widely condemned by environmentalists, greenwashing raises disturbing questions not just about the way business responds to environmental issues, but also about the effectiveness of "feel good" environmentalism.

Origin of Greenwashing. Determining when greenwashing began is impossible because pro-industry groups have usually countered charges that industrial activity often damages the planet. Greenwashing may have begun in 1934, when the DuPont Chemical Company set up a public relations group to respond to a U.S. Senate investigation into the harmful effects of its manufacture of gunpowder. Alternatively, greenwashing may have begun with the chemical industry's negative campaign against Rachel Carson's *Silent Spring* in 1962 (*see also* 140–41). Ten years later, Madison Avenue advertising executive Jerry Mander described in *Communication and Arts* magazine how industry had spent over a billion dollars on "ecopornography" (his word for greenwash) to take advantage of burgeoning environmental concerns among the public. A rash of major environmental disasters (*see also* 158–59), such as the 1979 near-meltdown at Metropolitan Edison's Three Mile Island nuclear plant in Pennsylvania and the *Exxon Valdez* oil tanker spillage off the coast of Alaska in 1989, led to the growth of public relations firms specialized in "fire fighting" environmental crises. In response to retail demand and perhaps as an attempt to placate environmentally minded consumers, "ethical" goods and financial services have been offered since at least the early 1970s. According to data from SPINS, a market research firm in San Francisco specializing in the natural products industry, in 1999 alone, sales of environmentally friendly paper products grew 20 percent, of personal care and hygiene products 26 percent, and of household cleaners 30 percent. The eco-friendly market amounts to approximately $8 billion a year in the United States alone.

Greenwashing Strategies. Although some corporations genuinely respect the environment and respond to consumer concerns with legitimate products, the practitioners of greenwashing strive to give the impression that they are environmentally friendly mainly through advertising and public relations campaigns. Transnational corporations (TNCs) embroiled in environmental controversies are most likely to engage in this kind of activity. For instance, DuPont, which manufactured chemicals implicated in ozone destruction, broadcast television advertisements in the early 1990s in which otters, seals, dolphins, and flamingoes cavorted to the finale of Beethoven's Ninth Symphony ("Ode to Joy"). Oil giant BP enthusiastically promotes its tiny solar power offshoot, and Royal Dutch (Shell) points to forestry plantations it supports in countries such as Argentina and Brazil to reduce overall carbon dioxide emissions. Yet both BP and Royal Dutch continue to support major increases in oil production and consumption that will exacerbate global warming (*see also* 202–03). Chemical companies Monsanto and Eli Lilly describe their biotechnology products as an environmentally friendly path to a hunger-free world.

Ambiguously named industry lobby groups are also frequently accused of greenwashing. For example, the U.S. Council for Energy Awareness is a pro–nuclear power lobby group (*see also* 130–31 *and* 156–57);

In 2000, BP Amoco introduced its new logo and announced that it would now be known as BP, standing for "Beyond Petroleum." Many environmentalists have accused the oil giant of corporate greenwashing. (© AFP/Corbis)

Further Reading

Athanasiou, Tom. *Divided Planet: The Ecology of Rich and Poor.* Athens: University of Georgia Press, 1998.

Elkington, John, and Tom Burke. *The Green Capitalists.* London: Victor Gollancz, 1987.

Greer, Jed, and Kenny Bruno. *Greenwash: The Reality Behind Corporate Environmentalism.* Penang, Malaysia: Third World Network, 1996.

Rowell, Andrew. *Green Backlash.* London and New York: Routledge, 1996.

the National Wetlands Coalition in the United States lobbies for mining and other industries that oppose wetlands protection; the Wise Use movement (*see also* 168) broadly opposes environmentally motivated cuts in resource use; and the Global Climate Coalition is less interested in climate protection than in lobbying for oil and automobile companies against measures to prevent global warming. Canada's Business Council on National Issues has played a major role in the advancement of free trade and attacked the Kyoto Protocol (*see also* 202–03) as arbitrary and unrealistic in its approach to tackling climate change. Free-market think tanks are also vociferous critics of environmental regulation and protection. The Cato Institute in Washington, D.C., for example, has published books, among them *Climate of Fear: Why We Shouldn't Worry About Global Warming* (1998), while Canada's Fraser Institute has attacked recycling programs in schools.

Exposing Greenwashing. Some environmental groups have made a specialty of exposing these deceptive claims. In 1992, Greenpeace USA published *Book of Greenwash.* Using a four-point checklist, it suggested a company was probably practicing greenwashing if its core business was fundamentally unsustainable (for example, clearcutting old-growth forests); if it made environmental claims in advertising or in public relations materials or press releases without changing the way it did business; if its research and development budget was not primarily allocated to developing more sustainable activities; or if it lobbied against environmental policies through pro-industry front groups. More recently, U.S. NGO Corporate Watch has given annual Greenwash Awards

"to some of the most polluting corporations on Earth, who use a mixture of images of beautiful nature, the language of the environmental movement, and highly produced, clever advertising to misinform and deceive the public." Similarly, Earth Day Resources (formerly Earth Day 2000) releases "Don't Be Fooled," an annual publication that investigates and reports on greenwashing. Tactics for combating false claims about household products include labeling criteria (such as organic certification) and guides such as the magazine *Whole Earth*, the online source Responsible Shopper, and the guidebook *Shopping for a Better World* (1994), which provide consumers advice about products that are ecologically sound.

If greenwashing raises questions about how companies incorporate environmental concerns into their business practices, it also seems to raise fundamental questions about environmentalism itself. Some critics, such as activist and writer Tom Athanasiou, suggest that "feel good" environmental activities, such as community recycling programs, may also qualify as greenwashing because they prevent calls for more fundamental changes in society, such as reducing consumption or economic growth. Furthermore, in suggesting that superficial solutions, such as changing from aerosol deodorants to roll-ons, can really "save the planet," environmentalists themselves may also be partly to blame for greenwashing. Nonetheless, by confusing the public and obscuring the connection between corporate activities and environmental degradation, corporate greenwashing continues to impede society's progress toward truly sustainable development.

—*Chris Woodford*

Burson-Marsteller

The world's largest public relations firm, New York–based Burson-Marsteller (B-M), describes itself as "an acknowledged leader in the field of corporate social responsibility (CSR) and environmental communication and strategy." According to B-M's 2000 survey "The Responsible Century," companies that possess a good environmental and social record, or appear to, have a new way to make money: "CSR is all about competing beyond technology, quality, service and price—all areas where competitive advantage is fleeting." CSR is good news for PR companies too: The market for corporate anti-environmental PR in the United States is estimated to be worth at least $500 million per year.

Environmental activists portray B-M in less flattering terms as the world's leading practitioner of greenwash, claiming that it has been hired to downplay the risks of cigarettes and genetically modified (GM) foods, among other things. Andrew Rowell, British author of a major study of anti-environmentalism called *Green Backlash* (1996), describes B-M as the "global conductor of the anti-green orchestra." Rowell charges that, in the campaign to help secure the introduction of the controversial cattle drug bovine growth hormone/bovine somatotropin (BGH/BST), B-M was instrumental in defeating legislative proposals to label milk from BST-treated cows and secretly rallied community activists to lobby for the drug's introduction. Critics like Rowell claim B-M has been centrally involved in greenwashing a range of environmental disasters, including the Three Mile Island nuclear accident in 1979 and the *Exxon Valdez* oil spill in 1989. They also charge that B-M helped to found the Business Council on Sustainable Development, which lobbied successfully for corporate interests at the Rio Earth Summit in 1992 (*see also* 202–03).

Globalization: From Rio de Janeiro to Johannesburg

At the dawn of the twenty-first century, the trend toward economic globalization through increasingly deregulated free trade seems to be on a collision course with a parallel trend of "environmental globalization" prompted by problems such as climate change, biodiversity loss, and pollution. Initiatives such as the 1992 UN Conference on Environment and Development (the Rio de Janeiro "Earth Summit") inspired hope that the nations of the world could address environmental problems by acting both locally and globally. Yet more recent attempts, such as the 1997 Kyoto Protocol to limit greenhouse emissions, have illustrated the difficulty of achieving international agreements on environmental problems in a world driven by economic forces.

Rio Earth Summit. In the wake of the 1987 World Commission on Environment and Development (Brundtland Commission) report, *Our Common Future*, which introduced the concept of sustainable development, expectations ran high that the 1992 Rio Earth Summit would truly set the world on the road to sustainability, or the maintenance of a continuous supply of renewable resources. Although numerous nations adopted anti-environmental positions on many of the issues discussed at Rio, the United States, under President George H. W. Bush, emerged as the naysayer, with repeated calls to water down clauses in the summit's key Agenda 21 document and its refusal to sign the convention on biodiversity.

Addressing Climate Change. One of the key treaties negotiated at Rio was the UN Framework Convention on Climate Change (UNFCCC), an international agreement to address global warming by reducing greenhouse emissions, which left the details of how that would be achieved to be worked out at later negotiations. Few believed that the UNFCCC could be successful without the meaningful participation of the United States, the world's biggest emitter of greenhouse gases; however, the election of Bill Clinton as president with Al Gore as vice president in 1992 heartened the treaty's supporters, bringing new confidence that the United States would agree to emissions cuts. Vice President Gore had been an outspoken supporter of emissions cuts while serving in the Senate and had published a manifesto for environmental stewardship, *Earth in the Balance* (1992).

Once in office, however, Clinton and Gore seemed unable to deliver on the environmental rhetoric that had helped to elect them. In 1993, the UNFCCC came into force when formally ratified by fifty nations. However, the Clinton Administration sent a signal of things to come when, that same year, it abandoned plans for a carbon dioxide tax that would have limited its greenhouse gas emissions.

In 1995, industry-funded lobbying groups such as the Global Climate Council effectively stalled progress on emissions reductions at the first UNFCCC negotiating session in Berlin. The following year, the United States and a group of countries (collectively known as JUSCANZ: Japan, United

Aggregate Emissions of Greenhouse Gases (CO_2 Equivalent)[1], 1990 to 1996

	1990[2] (gigagrams)	1991	1992	1993	1994	1995	1996
Australia	415,656	100	101	101	102	105	107
Austria	77,271	106	98	97	97	102	104
Belgium	138,943	103	101	100	104	104	109
Canada	598,099	99	101	103	106	109	112
Czech Republic[3]	192,130	92	85	82	78	79	80
Denmark[3]	71,658	115	108	110	115	110	129
France	557,039	104	102	97	97	98	101
Germany	1,209,107	96	92	91	90	89	90
Greece	105,235	100	101	102	104	107	109
Ireland[4]	56,861	99	100	100	103	104	105
Japan[5]	1,221,707	102	104	103	109	111	
Latvia[3]	35,669	82	72	62	54	54	51
Monaco	111	116	123	125	128	125	131
Netherlands	217,107	103	102	103	104	108	112
New Zealand	72,417	100	101	101	100	100	103
Norway	55,064	96	93	97	101	102	107
Slovakia[4]	72,496	88	81	77	72	75	76
Sweden[3]	65,101	99	101	101	104	103	112
Switzerland[3]	53,749	103	101	98	97	98	99
United Kingdom	757,851	100	97	94	93	92	95
United States	5,999,122	99	101	103	105	106	109

[1]*Excludes land use change and forestry.* [2]*Yearly values relative to 1990, 1990 = 100.* [3]*As estimates for 1990–1995 were not provided in the inventory submission, data from the second national communication are used in this table.* [4]*As estimates for 1990–1994 were not provided in the inventory submission, data from the second national communication are used in this table.* [5]*Estimates were provided only for 1990–95.*
This chart lists the parties to the United Nations Framework Convention on Climate Change, of which both the United States and Canada are members, and indicates the change in emissions for each nation from 1990 to 1996. Despite international pressure to limit production of greenhouse gases, U.S. emissions grew 9.9 percent between 1990 and 1996. Canada had an increase of 12 percent over the same period.
Source: *Data from United Nations Framework Convention on Climate Change. Review of the Implementation of Commitments and of Other Provisions of the Convention. 1998. <http://unfccc.int/resource/docs/cop4/inf09.pdf>.*

States, Canada, Australia, and New Zealand) that supported its position were similarly obstructive at the second negotiating session in Geneva. Canada, for example, wanted to use the carbon dioxide absorbed by its extensive forests as a credit against emissions cuts, thus avoiding politically more aggressive action to reduce carbon dioxide emissions.

Kyoto. The third and most important UNFCCC session, held in Kyoto (Japan) in December 1997, saw a major breakthrough when 150 nations, including the United States and its allies, agreed to the Kyoto Protocol, a legally binding treaty to cut greenhouse gas emissions. During his 2000 election campaign, however, George W. Bush repeatedly signaled his opposition to the Kyoto Protocol. He described it as "ineffective, inadequate, and . . . a bad deal for America and Americans" and, following his election, withdrew the United States from the agreement entirely.

Global Free Trade. Difficulties over global initiatives like Rio and Kyoto have increasingly been linked to mounting concern over economic globalization, for many environmentalists suspect that the political agenda that is advancing global free trade (*see also* 198–99) is the same one opposing global environmental protection. The world's most powerful industries include automobile, oil, and coal producers, all of which potentially stand to suffer from internationally mandated cuts in greenhouse gas emissions. Furthermore, national or regional

Kyoto Protocol, 1997: Article 2

1. Each Party . . . in achieving its quantified emission limitation and reduction commitments . . . in order to promote sustainable development, shall:

(a) Implement and/or further elaborate policies and measures in accordance with its national circumstances, such as:

(i) Enhancement of energy efficiency in relevant sectors of the national economy;

(ii) Protection and enhancement of sinks and reservoirs of greenhouse gases not controlled by the Montreal Protocol, taking into account its commitments under relevant international environmental agreements; promotion of sustainable forest management practices, afforestation and reforestation;

(iii) Promotion of sustainable forms of agriculture in light of climate change considerations;

(iv) Promotion, research, development and increased use of new and renewable forms of energy, of carbon dioxide sequestration technologies and of advanced and innovative environmentally sound technologies;

(v) Progressive reduction or phasing out of market imperfections, fiscal incentives, tax and duty exemptions and subsidies in all greenhouse gas emitting sectors that run counter to the objective of the Convention and apply market instruments;

(vi) Encouragement of appropriate reforms in relevant sectors aimed at promoting policies and measures which limit or reduce emissions of greenhouse gases not controlled by the Montreal Protocol;

(vii) Measures to limit and/or reduce emissions of greenhouse gases not controlled by the Montreal Protocol in the transport sector;

(viii) Limitation and/or reduction of methane through recovery and use in waste management, as well as in the production, transport and distribution of energy . . .

Source: Exerpted from United Nations Framework Convention on Climate Change, *Report of the Conference of the Parties on its Third Session Held at Kyoto from 1 to 11 December 1997.* Kyoto, 1998.

Note: The full text is available at <http://unfccc.int/index.html>.

Further Reading

Athanasiou, Tom. *Divided Planet: The Ecology of Rich and Poor.* Athens: University of Georgia Press, 1998.

Dodds, Felix, ed. *Earth Summit 2002: A New Deal.* London: Earthscan, 2001.

International Forum on Globalization. *Alternatives to Economic Globalization.* San Francisco: IFG, 2002.

Klein, Naomi. *No Logo: Taking Aim at the Brand Bullies.* New York: Picador, 2000.

Leggett, Jeremy. *The Carbon War.* New York: Routledge, 2001.

environmental legislation hinders the ability of transnational corporations (TNCs) to trade their products freely around the world. Concerns about economic globalization are now being expressed along a political spectrum that extends from the San Francisco–based International Forum on Globalization, which published a 250-page critique, *Alternatives to Economic Globalization*, in the spring of 2002, to the crowds of anti-globalization protesters who have picketed and rioted at World Trade Organization summits in Seattle, Genoa, and elsewhere.

Johannesburg. A decade after Rio, world leaders and environmental groups reconvened in Johannesburg, South Africa, in fall 2002 to measure their progress at a summit known as Rio+10. After ten years of

uncertain and largely ineffective action to address and limit climate change, deforestation, and other global problems, and with the planet apparently in worse shape than in 1992, the optimism that preceded the Rio Summit was conspicuously absent. Johannesburg brought a new promise to alleviate poverty and a reiteration of old promises to tackle other global environmental problems. But there was no progress on climate change and a plan to set targets and timetables for the introduction of renewable energy was abandoned. Environmental groups were quick to declare Johannesburg a failure: In their eyes, it seemed "environmental globalization" had been defeated by economic globalization once more.

—*Chris Woodford*

Timeline

9500 B.C.   Ancestors of Native Americans complete their migration to the North American continent.

1000 A.D.   Icelandic explorer Leif Ericson is believed to have reached the coast of Labrador.

1492–1504   Christopher Columbus makes four voyages to the New World, beginning the exchange of plants, animals, and diseases between Europe and the Western Hemisphere.

1497   John Cabot reaches the North American mainland and establishes England's claim to the entire northern continent.

1500–10   European fishermen work the Grand Banks off Canada's eastern shore; many process their catches on the shores of Newfoundland.

1500s   Major breeds of cattle, horses, and hogs arrive in the New World from Europe.

1500s   Disease decimates the Native American population.

1513   Spain sends an expedition to the area now known as Florida in search of gold; the explorers claim the land for the Spanish Crown.

1597   The first atlas devoted exclusively to the New World is produced by Flemish cartographer Cornelius Wyfliet.

1624   English explorer John Smith publishes *General History of Virginia*, which chronicles the difficulties and hardships of the colonists in Jamestown, Virginia.

1629   The king of England charters the Massachusetts Bay Company, composed of Puritan investors, to establish and support a colony in New England.

1670   The Hudson's Bay Company, which would play a dominant role in Canada's fur trade, is organized.

1670s   Slaves or slave traders introduce the African crop of rice to the Carolina lowlands.

1670s   Jacques Cartier begins the lucrative fur trade along the St. Lawrence River in Canada.

1675–76   Growing European populations lead to increasing tensions with Native Americans that culminate in the uprising known as King Philip's War.

1689–1763   The French and Indian Wars between Great Britain and France are fought in Canada, the American West, and the West Indies, slowing the pace of settlement expansion.

1691   The Massachusetts Charter reserves all trees measuring 24 or more inches (0.6 or more meters) in diameter at a height of 3 feet (0.9 meter) from the ground for the British Crown.

1713   The Treaty of Utrecht transfers Acadia, present-day Nova Scotia, from France to England; and British fishermen begin to use its coast to dry fish for sale in the West Indies.

1720   Export markets open in Louisbourg, in present-day Nova Scotia.

1740   Coal becomes the world's premier fuel.

1763   Treaty of Paris ends French and Indian Wars.

1763   Britain takes control of Québec from France and tries to regulate the timber trade by granting licenses to cut timber, but Québec's settlers ignore the law.

1763   Pontiac's Rebellion in the Ohio Valley (in present-day Ohio) occurs when Pontiac, an Ottawa chief, leads a confederacy of tribes against British settlers occupying Native American land.

1763   A Royal Proclamation forbids any private citizen from purchasing land from "the several Nations or Tribes of Indians" within the British colonies. Only the British Crown can obtain land through treaty, and then sell it to settlers.

1772   Virginia outlaws all commercial hunting of white-tailed deer for four years because herds are depleted.

1774   The Québec Act, a British statute, gains the loyalty of French Canadians by affirming French language, religion, and law.

1776–83   The American Revolution is fought, resulting in Britain's colonies in present-day United States gaining independence.

1780–1802   The original thirteen states, notably Virginia, cede their western land claims to the federal government.

1785   The U.S. Land Ordinance turns the U.S. landscape west of the current Pennsylvania–Ohio state line into a vast grid of townships and sections.

1787   The Northwest Ordinance promises Native Americans that their land will not be taken by the U.S. government without the consent of those living on it.

late 1700s   Traders and Native American trappers drive the fur trade inland to hunt beaver.

1790   The Intercourse Act of 1790 attempts to make the cession treaty process in the United States a workable policy by prohibiting individuals and states from purchasing Native American lands, reserving purchase rights to the federal government by treaty.

1791 The colony of Upper Canada is created, constituting what is present-day southern and central Ontario.

1793 Eli Whitney invents the cotton gin.

1796 The U.S. Land Act allows 640-acre (259-hectare) lots of virgin territory to be sold to speculators.

1801 Philadelphia in Pennsylvania becomes the first large U.S. city to construct a municipal waterworks.

1803 The Louisiana Purchase adds 828,000 square miles (2,144,500 square kilometers) to the United States, doubling its public domain.

1815– Britain's Corn (i.e., grain) Laws (1815–46) and
49 Timber Acts (1810–49) establish preferential tariffs that encourage the exploitation of colonial resources and further privatization of public lands in Canada.

1818 U.S. forces push south into Florida, forcing the Spanish to relinquish that territory.

1819 The Adams–Onís Treaty forces Spain to cede all territories north of California to the United States, effectively opening up the West to future annexation.

1819 Canadian federal authorities set aside land for bird sanctuaries, including Point Pelee National Park in Ontario.

1825 The Lachine Canal, Canada's first canal, is completed in Montreal, Québec.

1823 The United States promulgates the Monroe Doctrine, which asserts its control of the Western Hemisphere.

1825 The Erie Canal is completed, running 363 miles (584.2 kilometers) from Albany to Buffalo in New York state.

1827– John James Audubon produces a set of four illustrated
38 volumes, *The Birds of America*, based on his huge oil paintings of all 435 species of North American birds then known.

1830 U.S. Congress passes the Indian Removal Act, which requires most Native American tribes to move beyond the Mississippi River.

1830 In the United States, the Baltimore and Ohio Railroad's first 13-mile (20.9-kilometer) track is completed.

1830, Squatters receive federal protection by U.S.
1841 congressional action.

1831 Cyrus Hall McCormick develops the first successful reaping machine.

1836 American philosopher Ralph Waldo Emerson writes and anonymously publishes his book of essays, *Nature*, describing the mystical unity of man and nature.

1837 John Deere develops a steel plow that automatically cleans away soil.

1837– An armed uprising, the Lower Canadian Resistance,
38 pits French Canadians against the British in Québec.

1839 Fierce competition for white pine along the ill-defined border between Canada and Maine leads to armed conflict, known as the Aroostook War.

1840 Plantations of the U.S. South produce more than 60 percent of the world's cotton.

1840s– The urban park movement in the United States and
50s Canada is successful in having undeveloped land set aside as picturesque pleasure grounds in cities like Boston.

1841 The United States Preemption Act allows squatters to purchase the land they are occupying.

1842 Treaty is signed by the United States and Britain (Canada is still a British territory) settling the Aroostook War and delineating the border between Maine and Canada.

1845 The United States annexes Texas from Mexico.

1846 The British government cedes all territory south of the 49th parallel to the United States.

1848 The utopian Oneida Community is founded by John Humphrey Noyes in New York state.

1848 The Illinois–Michigan Canal is completed.

1849 The Gold Rush to California begins.

1849 Britain drops its protective tariff on Canadian lumber.

1850 The Robinson–Huron and Robinson–Superior Treaties are the first Canadian treaties to recognize explicitly First Nations hunting and fishing rights in exchange for Crown access to other natural resources.

1850 U.S. Commissioner of Indian Affairs proposes a system of reservations for all tribes.

1850s The National Road (now US 40) is completed; it stretches from Baltimore, Maryland, to St. Louis, Missouri.

1850s In the U.S. Pacific Northwest, many Native American tribes sign "Stevens treaties," which permit them to fish in their "usual and accustomed places."

1851 The government of Canada passes An Act for the Better Protection of the Lands and Property of the Indians in Lower Canada (present-day southern Québec).

1852 The Atlantic and St. Lawrence Railroad (known as the St. Lawrence and Atlantic Railroad in Québec) becomes the first cross-border railroad line; it runs between Portland, Maine, and Montreal.

1853 With the Gadsden Purchase, the United States buys from Mexico the southern part of present-day Arizona and New Mexico.

1854 The seigneurial system is abolished in Canada, and habitants are permitted to buy their land from the seigneurs.

1854 Henry David Thoreau's *Walden* is published in the United States.

1855 American poet Walt Whitman publishes his book of poems, *Leaves of Grass.*

1857 Upper Canada's Fisheries Act provides exemptions from fishing restrictions on the Great Lakes for Ojibwa and Iroquois.

1858–59 Petroleum is extracted from Oil Springs, Ontario, and Titusville, Pennsylvania.

1859 Nevada's Comstock silver deposits are discovered.

1859 Charles Darwin publishes *Origin of Species.*

1860 Britain transfers control of First Nations affairs to the province of Canada.

1861–65 U.S. Civil War.

1862 The Homestead Act provides settlers with free farms in the United States.

1862 U.S. president Abraham Lincoln signs the Pacific Railroad Act that eventually cedes to the railroad companies 213 million acres (86.2 million hectares) across much of Minnesota, Iowa, Kansas, Nebraska, Alabama, and across the Rockies and Southwest to the Pacific coast.

1864 Discovery of gold in British Columbia encourages the construction of the famous Cariboo Road, which runs from the Pacific coast to parts of inland Canada.

1864 George Perkins Marsh publishes *Man and Nature*, which questions the destructive human impact on the environment.

1867 The British North America Act establishes Canada as an independent nation.

1867 The federal Bureau of Indian Affairs begins a program of building irrigation projects on Native American reservations in the United States to provide water for farms.

1869 Massachusetts becomes the first U.S. state to create a board of health.

1869 The first transcontinental railroad across the United States is completed.

1870 Waves of immigrants crowd ill-equipped North American cities.

1871–76 Six Numbered Treaties (numbered sequentially starting with one) are signed in Canada with First Nations peoples, protecting First Nations wildlife rights.

1871–1910 Destructive fires repeatedly sweep through the Great Lakes region.

1872 The Mining Law allows private exploitation of "all valuable mineral deposits in lands belonging to the United States" at marginal cost.

1872 Yellowstone becomes the first national park in the United States.

1872 Nebraska establishes the tree-planting holiday, Arbor Day.

1873 U.S. Congress passes the Timber Culture Act, which promotes both tree planting and western settlement; it is repealed in 1891.

1873 The Canadian federal government establishes the Timber, Mineral and Grazing Lands Office within the Department of Interior to issue licenses for harvesting timber, but it does not regulate the actual harvests.

1876 Franklin B. Hough is appointed the first federal forestry agent in the United States.

1881 Congress creates the U.S. Division of Forestry within the Department of Agriculture to conduct scientific research on trees and forests.

1882 The first American Forest Congress convenes in Cincinnati, Ohio.

1882 The Montreal Congress marks the birth of Canadian conservation, introducing conservation concerns to the general public and leading to the creation of forest reserves and tougher fire regulations.

1883 Four North American time zones are created so train timetables can be standardized.

1885 Banff, in Canada's Rocky Mountains, becomes Canada's first national park.

1885 Canada completes its first transcontinental railroad, the Canadian Pacific Railway, which stretches from Montreal to Vancouver.

1886 George Bird Grinnell forms the Audubon Society, a bird preservation group, in the United States.

1887 The speed elevator, which uses steel cables, is perfected, allowing architects to build taller buildings.

1891 U.S. Congress passes the Forest Reserve Act, which allows the president to set aside forests for preservation; however, it does not provide for their protection or management.

1892 John Muir and others organize the Sierra Club, one of the first environmental groups in the United States, to defend the mountain regions of the Pacific Coast.

1894 Under the Carey Act, U.S. Congress offers 1 million acres (0.4 million hectares) of land to any state that will, in partnership with private industry, develop it for irrigation.

1897 The Forest Management Act authorizes the supervised cutting and sale of timber and the protection of forests from fires in the United States.

1898 Beginning in Boston, Massachusetts, metal cylinders are used to tunnel beneath city streets to build the first subways.

1899 Thorstein Veblen criticizes the consumption ethic of the middle and upper class in *The Theory of the Leisure Class*.

1900 The Canadian Forestry Association, an organization of politicians, lumbermen, and public figures who support conservation measures, is founded.

1900– The "City Beautiful" movement in Canada and the
10 United States reaches its height; the movement involves a variety of citizen and professional organizations joining together in a systematic effort to plan, manage, and beautify the industrial-era city.

1901 Oil is discovered at Spindletop, near Beaumont, Texas.

1902 U.S. Congress passes the Reclamation Act, which creates a special fund for irrigation works to reclaim arid and semiarid lands.

1902 The Canadian chief inspector of timber and forestry opens the first forest nursery at Indian Head in Saskatchewan to help with tree planting on the prairies.

1903 Canada and the United States convene an International Waterways Commission to address the question of sharing cross-boundary water resources, including Niagara Falls.

1904– In Canada, the provincial government of Québec sets
08 aside an area larger than the state of California for forest reserves.

1905 The American Bison Society is organized in the United States to save the species from extinction.

1905 Congress establishes the U.S. Forest Service within the Department of Agriculture and transfers the national forests from the Department of Interior.

1905 U.S. president Theodore Roosevelt begins removing millions of acres of public land from private development by placing them under federal control for scientific development.

1906 In the United States, the Hepburn Act prohibits railroads from transporting the coal that they produce, forcing them to divest themselves of their coal interests.

1906 In the United States, the Antiquities Act preserves millions of acres of land as national monuments, federal bird refuges, and game preserves.

1906 The Dominion Forest Reserves Act is passed in Canada, placing 3,459,400 acres (1,400,020 hectares) of prairie forests under scientific management by the federal government.

1908 The U.S. Supreme Court rules that Native Americans' right to water takes precedence over settlers' interests in its landmark *Winters v. U.S.* decision.

1909 The United States, Canada, the British colony of Newfoundland, and Mexico sign the North American Declaration of Principles on Conservation.

1909 Québec establishes the first provincial forestry service to regulate lumbering practices.

1909 Automobile manufacturer Henry Ford introduces the Model T.

1909 The Boundary Waters Treaty and the International Joint Commission it establishes help to resolve water-related disputes between Canada and the United States.

1909 The Canadian Commission of Conservation is formed as an advisory body; it will be abolished in 1921.

1911 U.S. Congress passes the Weeks Act, which authorizes the federal government to purchase land to create new national forests.

1911 The Dominion Parks Branch is established in Canada.

1912 The Ontario legislature passes the Public Heath Act, which creates a public health program that gives the Board of Health authority to address decades of inadequate water systems.

1912 The Forest Act of 1912 gives the new British Columbia Forest Branch jurisdiction over all matters relating to forestry, including revenue collection, fire protection and suppression, logging, reforestation, trade regulation in timber lands and logs, and the ability to enforce statutes.

1913   Despite protests from preservation groups, U.S. Congress approves a proposal to flood the Hetch Hetchy Valley in Yosemite National Park.

1914–18   World War I.

1914   Weyerhaeuser Timber Company, with the cooperation of the U.S. Forest Service, creates the first industrial tree farm.

1914   The largest Canadian irrigation project, the Bow River Scheme, is completed in southern Alberta.

1916   The National Park Service is established in the United States to oversee most of the recreational lands and national monuments once managed by the U.S. Forest Service.

1916   The Migratory Bird Treaty with the United States enables the Canadian federal government to impose closed (no hunt) seasons for hundreds of species of birds.

1918   The Wild Life Protection Agency (WLPA) is established to catalog and inventory wildlife and other natural resources throughout Canada.

1923   The Canadian National Parks Association, a public, preservationist constituency for national parks, is organized.

1924   The U.S. Congress passes the Clark–McNary Act, which creates a partnership between federal, state, and private interests in promoting fire suppression and for other actions, such as acquiring more land for the national forest system.

1929   The U.S. stock market crashes, which launches the Great Depression.

1930s   Kansas, Oklahoma, Texas, New Mexico, and Colorado (the "Dust Bowl") suffer nearly ten years of drought, dust storms, and high temperatures.

1933   U.S. forester Aldo Leopold expresses support for controlling predators in *Game Management*, which helped define the profession's first stage.

1933   The Agricultural Adjustment Administration, a New Deal program to aid farmers, is established in the United States.

1934   The United States establishes the Federal Housing Administration to encourage the construction of new housing.

1935   The Taylor Grazing Act sets aside about 142 million acres (57.5 million hectares) into grazing districts; U.S.

president Franklin D. Roosevelt takes the remaining public domain, more than 165 million acres (66.8 million hectares), off the market.

1935   Canada adopts the first Dominion Housing Act to help create new housing.

1935   The Soil Conservation Service is established in the United States to help farmers implement soil conservation on their farms.

1935   Canada's parliament passes the Prairie Farm Rehabilitation Act, which establishes an agency to coordinate and implement irrigation programs in cooperation with the provinces to address the ecological and economic devastation of the Great Depression.

1936   Archibald Belaney, a pioneering Canadian environmentalist who reinvented himself as the Native American wildlife writer "Grey Owl," publishes *Tales of an Empty Cabin*.

1937   In the United States, the Federal Aid in Wildlife Restoration Act (commonly known as the Pittman–Robertson Act), turns the proceeds of a federal tax on the sale of ammunition and hunting weapons over to the states to restore wild lands and to restock fish and other declining populations of fauna.

1939–45   World War II.

1942   Italian physicist Enrico Fermi proves the potential of nuclear energy when he successfully demonstrates the chain reaction inside the world's first nuclear reactor at the University of Chicago.

1944   The U.S. Congress passes the Sustained-Yield Forest Management Act to help assure the survival of many lumber towns in the Pacific Northwest.

1945   The Manhattan Project explodes its first test nuclear bomb at the Alamogordo Air Force Base near Albuquerque, New Mexico.

1945   The United States drops atom bombs on the Japanese cities of Hiroshima and Nagasaki.

1947   The Canadian federal government establishes the Dominion Wildlife Service.

Late 1940s   The residential community of Levittown is built on Long Island in the United States using mass production techniques.

1949   Under the Trans-Canada Highway Act, the federal government begins funding the trans-Canada highway program.

1949 Aldo Leopold's *A Sand County Almanac*, which would provide a catalyst for the environmental movement in the late 1960s and 1970s, is published posthumously.

1950 U.S. Congress passes the Federal Aid in Fish Restoration Act to provide protection and management of sport fisheries.

1952 A nuclear reactor at the Chalk River plant in Ottawa experiences a partial meltdown and allows a significant amount of radioactive water to escape into the surrounding environment, requiring a massive cleanup operation.

1953 The United States launches the Atoms for Peace Program

1953 The town of Niagara Falls in New York state buys a former toxic waste site called Love Canal and builds a neighborhood including a school and playground on it. Because of concerns about toxic contamination, by 1980 homeowners will force the federal government to evacuate the entire Love Canal neighborhood.

1956 In the United States, the Federal Aid Highway Act creates a highway trust fund to provide financing for the construction of an interstate highway system.

1956 Following pressure from environmental groups wishing to block the building of a dam inside Echo Park in Dinosaur National Monument, lawmakers pass the Colorado River Storage Project Act, which states that no dam authorized in the legislation will intrude into any national park or monument in the United States.

1960 In the United States, the Multiple Use–Sustained Yield Act of 1960 specifies that "sustained yield" includes wildlife as part of sustainable forestry and requires the Forest Service to manage the land and all that live on it.

1962 Rachel Carson publishes *Silent Spring*, which reveals the impact of pesticides on the environment and all living beings.

1962 Ontario legislature passes the Crown Timber Act, which gives responsibility for forest regeneration to the government and also launches major initiatives in site preparation, planting, and seeding.

1963 The United States, Britain, and the Soviet Union (soon followed by about one hundred other nations) sign the Nuclear Test-Ban Treaty, which forbids nuclear tests in the atmosphere, at sea, and in space but still allows underground testing.

1963 In the landmark *Arizona* v. *California* U.S. Supreme Court case, Native Americans win a major victory regarding their reserved water rights.

1964 The Wilderness Act creates a national wilderness system in the United States with 9.1 million acres (3.68 million hectares) and initiates a survey by federal land agencies of potential lands to be designated as wilderness areas.

1967 Canada creates a system of National Wildlife Areas in tacit recognition of the growing importance of protecting habitats.

1968 The U.N.-sponsored Treaty on the Non-proliferation of Nuclear Weapons is signed by the United States, the Soviet Union, and sixty other countries.

1968 Paul Ehrlich publishes *The Population Bomb*, which warns of the impact of global population growth.

1968 The largest oil field in North American history is discovered at Prudhoe Bay on Alaska's North Slope in the Arctic.

1969 Pollution Probe, one of the most effective of the first generation of environmental organizations in Canada, is formed by students and professors at the University of Toronto.

1969 Workers with the Union Oil Company of California accidentally trigger a blowout of natural gas and oil off the coast of Santa Barbara, California.

1969 The heavily polluted Cuyahoga River catches fire as it flows through downtown Cleveland, Ohio, causing public outrage in the United States.

1969 The Trans-Alaska Pipeline System (TAPS) consortium applies to the U.S. government for construction permits to build a 798-mile (1,284-kilometer), subsurface oil pipeline south to Valdez, North America's northernmost ice-free port. Congress will pass the final authorization bill in 1973, construction will begin in 1974, and the first oil will flow south in 1977.

1970 Canada Water Act is signed.

1970 The Toronto provincial government announces extensive restrictions on DDT as well as an outright ban on three other pesticides.

1970 The first Earth Day, organized by Harvard University law student Denis Hayes, is celebrated in April, with ten to twenty million participants across the United States.

1970 U.S. Congress passes the National Environmental Policy Act and creates the Environmental Protection Agency.

1970 The U.S. Congress passes the Clean Air Act.

1970   In the United States, Solid Waste Act provides the first federal legislative regulation of hazardous waste.

1971   Members of the newly formed environmental group Greenpeace set sail from Vancouver, British Columbia, in an unsuccessful attempt to stop a scheduled test of a U.S. nuclear device in the Aleutian archipelago.

1971   Ontario and Alberta establish the first provincial departments of the environment, which provide environmental regulation.

1971   Québec launches the James Bay Project, a hydroelectric power development.

1971   Environment Canada (the federal environment department) is established; it combines and expands the mandates of existing weather, wildlife, and parks services, and adds the Environmental Protection Service.

1972   The Great Lakes Water Quality Agreement between Canada and the United States creates an international, institutional mechanism to regulate, control, and reduce water pollution in the Great Lakes.

1972   The passage of the Federal Water Pollution Control Act Amendments (commonly known as the Clean Water Act) gives the U.S. Environmental Protection Agency authority to regulate discharges and implement pollution controls.

1973   A severe energy crisis occurs in the United States when Arab nations announce that they will halt oil shipments to the United States and to other countries that supported Israel against Egypt and Syria in the Yom Kippur War.

1973   The U.S. Endangered Species Act forces government agencies to preserve habitats critical to particular species.

1975   The Ocean Dumping Control Act and the Environmental Contaminants Act are signed in Canada.

1975   In the Indian Self-Determination and Education Act, Native American claims to control over water, fishing, and land rights in the United States are reaffirmed.

1975   A fire breaks out in the Brown's Ferry nuclear power plant in Decatur, Alabama.

1975   Both Canada and the United States begin to phase out leaded gasoline.

1976   The United States passes the Resource Conservation and Recovery Act, which authorizes the Environmental Protection Agency to control hazardous wastes from the "cradle-to-grave."

1976   The U.S. Congress passes the National Forest Management Act, which institutes restrictive rules for determining what lands are "suitable" for timber production, requires the Forest Service to produce and publicly release long-term plans for each national forest, and demands sustainable forestry practices.

1977   To protect their domestic fishing industries, Canada and the United States declare a 200-mile (320-kilometer) territorial limit off their coasts.

1977   The Surface Mining Control and Reclamation Act imposes environmental standards on the mining industry in the United States.

1977   The U.S. Congress passes the Clean Air Act of 1977, an amendment to the 1970 Clean Air Act.

1978   The British Columbia Ministry of Forests Act redefines its Forest Service mandate to include management of all aspects of the forest, a move that eventually leads other Canadian provinces to adopt similar measures.

1979   The Sagebrush Rebellion, an anti-environmental movement that argues for the return of U.S. federal lands to the jurisdiction of the states in which they are located, begins in Nevada.

1979   The Three Mile Island nuclear accident occurs in Pennsylvania; the core comes close to a meltdown and radioactive gas is released outside the plant.

1980   The U.S. Congress passes the Comprehensive Environmental Response, Compensation, and Liability Act, better known as the Superfund, requiring that sites heavily contaminated by toxic substances be cleaned up.

1981   Earth First! makes its national debut in a protest at the Glen Canyon Dam in northern Arizona, signaling the birth of eco-radicalism.

1982   The Canadian Constitution Act reasserts the exclusive provincial right to legislate in the areas of nonrenewable natural resource exploration, development, conservation, and management.

1983   The United States and Mexico sign the La Paz Agreement, the first transnational air agreement.

1985   Divers discover a "toxic blob" at the bottom of the St. Clair River in Ontario. The blob, 2,500 gallons (9,460 liters) of toxic dry cleaning chemicals that had been dumped earlier that month and combined with other toxins, will cost over $1 million to clean up.

1985   The Clean Air Act is signed in Canada.

1986   The northern spotted owl is designated as endangered by the Committee on the Status of Endangered Wildlife in Canada.

1987 The World Commission on Environment and Development (Brundtland Commission) releases its report, *Our Common Future*, which introduces the concept of sustainable development

1987 Canada and the United States sign an Agreement on the Conservation of the Porcupine Caribou Herd, which commits the nations to refraining from activities that would damage the herd in the Arctic National Wildlife Refuge in northeastern Alaska.

1988 Canada and the United States sign the Free Trade Agreement.

1988 In the United States, Long Island and New Jersey beaches are closed after garbage slicks containing needles, syringes, and other medical waste wash ashore.

1988 The Canadian Environmental Protection Act is adopted; it has tougher federal laws governing toxins.

1988 Devastating fires rage in Yellowstone National Park in the United States.

1989 The *Exxon Valdez* oil tanker spills approximately 11 million gallons (41.6 million liters) of oil off the coast of Alaska.

1989 A U.S. federal court declares the northern spotted owl to be endangered.

1990 The northern spotted owl is listed as threatened under the U.S. Endangered Species Act throughout all of its range in the United States.

1990 The U.S. Congress passes the Food, Agriculture, Conservation and Trade Act (the "Farm Bill"), which incorporates the idea of sustainable agriculture.

1990– The Green Plan in Canada applies the concept of
95   sustainable development to management of public land.

1991 The Canada–U.S. Air Quality Agreement is signed, committing both nations to reducing sulfur oxide emissions.

1992 Canada proposes the Species at Risk Act (originally called the Endangered Species Act).

1992 UN Conference on Environment and Development (the "Earth Summit") convenes in Rio de Janeiro, Brazil.

1993 In the largest outbreak of waterborne disease in the United States, the water supply of Milwaukee, Wisconsin, is contaminated by the bacteria Cryptosporidium, killing at least fifty people and sickening more than four hundred thousand.

1993 The North American Free Trade Agreement relaxes trade restrictions among Canada, Mexico, and the United States.

1993 Midwestern rivers breach levees during the summer, flooding many American towns and causing $15 billion in damage.

1994 North American Agreement on Environmental Cooperation is signed by Canada, Mexico, and the United States as an environmental side agreement to the North American Free Trade Agreement.

1994 The U.S. government establishes the Interagency Working Group on Environmental Justice to address environmental inequities affecting minorities and low-income populations.

1995 Parks Canada, the national park service, is moved from Environment Canada to the Canadian Heritage Ministry

1995 Canada's federal government, the Yukon and Northwest Territories, and all provincial governments except Québec ratify the Canada-Wide Accord on Environmental Harmonization, which provides a new framework for cooperation between the provinces and the federal government.

1997 The United States and Canada sign the Great Lakes Binational Toxics Strategy, which includes targets for the elimination of a number of persistent, toxic substances.

1997 The third session of the UN Framework Convention on Climate Change is held in Kyoto, Japan. Participating nations sign the Kyoto Protocol, a legally binding treaty to cut greenhouse gas emissions. (President George W. Bush will later withdraw the United States from the agreement.)

1998 Canada's Committee on the Status of Endangered Wildlife in Canada adds the Atlantic cod (*Gadus morhua*) to its list of species at risk.

1999 Canada passes a revised version of the 1988 Canadian Environmental Protection Act.

2000 The bacteria *Escherichia coli* contaminates drinking water, sickening approximately two thousand people and killing six in Walkerton, Ontario.

2000 The Environmental Protection Agency tightens U.S. standards for the level of arsenic in drinking water.

2002 World leaders and environmental groups meet for the Earth Summit Rio+10 in Johannesburg, South Africa.

Bibliography

General

Anderson, Luke. *Genetic Engineering, Food, and Our Environment.* White River Junction, Vt.: Chelsea Green Publishing, 1999.

Athanasiou, Tom. *Divided Planet: The Ecology of Rich and Poor.* Athens: University of Georgia Press, 1998.

Bergon, Frank, ed. *The Wilderness Reader.* Reno: University of Nevada Press, 1994.

Bosso, Christopher. *Pesticides and Politics: The Life Cycle of a Public Issue.* Pittsburgh: University of Pittsburgh Press, 1987.

Dodds, Felix, ed. *Earth Summit 2002: A New Deal.* London: Earthscan, 2001.

Ehrlich, Paul R. *The Population Bomb.* Rev. ed. New York: Ballantine Books, 1978.

Greer, Jed and Kenny Bruno. *Greenwash: The Reality Behind Corporate Environmentalism.* Penang, Malaysia: Third World Network, 1996.

Heywood, V., ed. *UNEP Global Biodiversity Assessment.* New York & Cambridge: Cambridge University Press, 1995.

Hoxie, Frederick E., ed. *Encyclopedia of North American Indians.* Boston: Houghton Mifflin, 1996.

Hughes, J. Donald. *North American Indian Ecology.* 2nd ed. El Paso: Texas Western Press, 1996.

Kehoe, Alice B. *North American Indians: A Comprehensive Account.* 2nd ed. Englewood Cliffs, N.J.: Prentice Hall, 1992.

Kehoe, Terence. *Cleaning Up the Great Lakes: From Cooperation to Confrontation.* Dekalb: Northern Illinois University Press, 1997.

Kiy, Richard and John D. Wirth, eds. *Environmental Management on North America's Borders.* College Station: Texas A&M University Press, 1998.

Krech, Shepard, III. *The Ecological Indian: Myth and History.* New York: W.W. Norton, 1999.

Kunzig, Robert. *Mapping the Deep.* New York: Norton, 2000.

Kurlansky, Mark. *Cod: A Biography of the Fish That Changed the World.* London: J. Cape, 1998.

Leggett, Jeremy. *The Carbon War.* New York: Routledge, 2001.

McHugh, Tom. *The Time of the Buffalo.* New York: Alfred A. Knopf, 1972.

McIlwraith, Thomas F. and Edward K. Muller, eds. *North America: the Historical Geography of a Changing Continent.* New York: Rowman and Littlefield Publishers, 2001.

McNeill, J. R. *Something New Under the Sun: An Environmental History of the Twentieth-Century World.* New York: W.W. Norton, 2000.

Meadows, Donella H., et al. *The Limits to Growth: A Report for the Club of Rome's Project on the Predicament of Mankind.* 2nd ed. New York: Universe Books, 1974.

Miller, Char and Hal Rothman, eds. *Out of the Woods: Essays in Environmental History.* Pittsburgh: University of Pittsburgh Press, 1997.

Newton, Norman T. *Design on the Land: The Development of Landscape Architecture.* Cambridge, Mass.: Harvard University Press, 1971.

Novacek, Michael, ed. *The Biodiversity Crisis: Losing What Counts.* New York: New Press, 2001.

Plowden, David. *Bridges: The Spans of North America.* New York: Norton, 2002.

Roe, Frank Gilbert. *The North American Buffalo: A Critical Study of the Species in Its Wild State.* 2nd ed. Newton Abbot, England: David & Charles, 1972.

Rothfeder, Jeffrey. *Every Drop for Sale: Our Desperate Battle Over Water in a World about to Run Out.* New York: Jeremy P. Tarcher/Putnam, 2001.

Rowell, Andrew. *Green Backlash.* London and New York: Routledge, 1996.

Steingraber, Sandra. *Living Downstream: An Ecologist Looks at Cancer and the Environment.* Reading, Mass.: Addison-Wesley, 1997.

Walker, Laurence C. *The North American Forests: Geography, Ecology, and Silviculture.* Boca Raton, Fla.: CRC Press, 1999.

Whitney, Gordon Graham. *From Coastal Wilderness to Fruited Plain: A History of Environmental Change in Temperate North America, 1500 to the Present.* Cambridge and New York: Cambridge University Press, 1994.

Wilford, John Noble. *The Mapmakers.* New York: Alfred A. Knopf, 2000.

Wilson, Edward O. *The Future of Life.* New York: Alfred A. Knopf, 2002.

Wirth, John D. *Smelter Smoke in North America: The Politics of Transborder Pollution.* Lawrence: University Press of Kansas, 2000.

World Commission on Environment and Development. *Our Common Future.* New York: Oxford University Press, 1987.

United States

Abbott, Carl. *The New Urban America: Growth and Politics in Sunbelt Cities.* Rev. ed. Chapel Hill: University of North Carolina Press, 1987.

Albers, Jan. *Hands on the Land: A History of the Vermont Landscape.* Cambridge, Mass.: MIT Press, 2000.

Allin, Craig. *The Politics of Wilderness Preservation.* Westport, Conn.: Greenwood Press, 1982.

Ambler, Marjane. *Breaking the Iron Bonds: Indian Control of Energy Development.* Lawrence: University Press of Kansas, 1990.

Ambrose, Stephen. *Nothing Like It in the World: The Men Who Built the Transcontinental Railroad 1863–1869.* New York: Simon & Schuster, 2000.

Ballard, Steven C. and Thomas E. James, eds. *The Future of the Sunbelt: Managing Growth and Change.* New York: Praeger, 1983.

Baratz, Morton S. *The Union and the Coal Industry.* New Haven, Conn.: Yale University Press, 1955.

Barbour, Barton H. *Fort Union and the Upper Missouri Fur Trade.* Norman: University of Oklahoma Press, 2001.

Bates, Sarah, et al. *Searching Out the Headwaters: Change and Rediscovery in Western Water Policy.* Washington, D.C.: Island Press, 1993.

Berry, Brian J. *America's Utopian Experiments: Communal Havens from Long-Wave Crises.* Hanover, N.H.: University Press of New England, 1992.

Berry, Mary Clay. *The Alaska Pipeline: The Politics of Oil and Native Land Claims.* Bloomington: Indiana University Press, 1975.

Birnbaum, Charles and Robin Karson, eds. *Pioneers of American Landscape Design.* New York: McGraw-Hill, 2001.

Bliese, John R. E. *The Greening of Conservative America.* Boulder, Colo.: Westview Press, 2001.

Bluestone, Barry and Bennett Harrison. *The Deindustrialization of America: Plant Closings, Community Abandonment, and the Dismantling of Basic Industry.* New York: Basic Books, 1982.

Bodnar, John. *The Transplanted: A History of Immigrants in Urban America.* Bloomington: Indiana University Press, 1985.

Boyer, Paul. *Urban Masses and Moral Order in America, 1820–1920.* Cambridge, Mass.: Harvard University Press, 1978.

Brick, Philip D. and R. McGreggor Cawley, eds. *A Wolf in the Garden: The Land Rights Movement and the New Environmental Debate.* Lanham, Md.: Rowman & Littlefield, 1996.

Bullard, Robert D. *Dumping in Dixie: Race, Class and Environmental Quality.* 3rd ed. Boulder, Colo.: Westview Press, 2000.

Bullard, Robert D., ed. *Confronting Environmental Racism: Voices from the Grassroots.* Boston: South End Press, 1993.

Burrows, Edwin G. and Mike Wallace. *Gotham: A History of New York City to 1898.* New York: Oxford University Press, 1999.

Burton, Lloyd. *American Indian Water Rights and the Limits of Law.* Lawrence: University Press of Kansas, 1991.

Campbell, John C. *The Southern Highlander and His Homeland.* 1921. Reprint, Spartanburg, S.C.: Reprint Co., 1973.

Campbell, John L. *Collapse of an Industry: Nuclear Power and the Contradictions of U.S. Policy.* Ithaca, N.Y.: Cornell University Press, 1988.

Carnes, Mark C., John Garraty, and Patrick Williams. *Mapping America's Past: A Historical Atlas.* New York: Henry Holt, 1996.

Carson, Rachel. *Silent Spring.* 1962. Reprint, Boston: Houghton Mifflin, 1994.

Cawley, R. McGreggor. *Federal Land, Western Anger: The Sagebrush Rebellion and Environmental Politics.* Lawrence: University Press of Kansas, 1993.

Chambers, John Whiteclay, II. *The Tyranny of Change: America in the Progressive Era, 1900–1917.* New Brunswick, N.J.: Rutgers University Press, 2000.

Clary, David A. *Timber and the Forest Service.* Lawrence: University Press of Kansas, 1986.

Clow, Richmond and Imre Sutton. *Trusteeship in Change: Toward Tribal Autonomy in Resource Management.* Boulder: University Press of Colorado, 2001.

Coates, Peter. *The Trans-Alaska Pipeline Controversy.* Bethlehem, Penn.: Lehigh University Press, 1991.

Colten, Craig E. and Peter N. Skinner. *The Road to Love Canal: Managing Industrial Waste before EPA*. Austin: University of Texas Press, 1996.

Cowdrey, Albert E. *This Land, This South: An Environmental History*. Rev. ed. Lexington: University Press of Kentucky, 1996.

Cox, Thomas, R. *Mills and Markets: A History of the Pacific Coast Lumber Industry to 1900*. Seattle: University of Washington Press, 1974.

Cox, Thomas R., Robert S. Maxwell, Phillip Drennon Thomas and Joseph J. Malone. *This Well-Wooded Land: Americans, and Their Forests from Colonial Times to the Present*. Lincoln: University of Nebraska Press, 1985.

Cozic, Charles P., ed. *America's Cities: Opposing Viewpoints*. San Diego, Calif.: Greenhaven Press, 1993.

Cranz, Galen. *The Politics of Park Design: A History of Urban Parks in America*. Cambridge, Mass.: MIT Press, 1982.

Cronon, William. *Changes in the Land: Indians, Colonists, and the Ecology of New England*. New York: Hill and Wang, 1983.

Crosby, Alfred W., Jr. *The Columbian Exchange: Biological and Cultural Consequences of 1492*. Westport, Conn.: Greenwood Press, 1972.

Cutright, Paul Russel. *Theodore Roosevelt: The Making of a Conservationist*. Urbana: University of Illinois Press, 1985.

Dale, Edward Everett. *The Range Cattle Industry: Ranching on the Great Plains from 1865 to 1925*. Norman: University of Oklahoma Press, 1960.

Danz, Harold P. *Of Bison and Man*. Niwot: University Press of Colorado, 1997.

Dary, David. *The Buffalo Book: The Full Saga of the American Animal*. Rev. ed. Athens: Swallow Press/Ohio University Press, 1989.

———. *Cowboy Culture: A Saga of Five Centuries*. Lawrence: University Press of Kansas, 1989.

Degler, Carl N. *In Search of Human Nature: The Decline and Revival of Darwinism in American Social Thought*. New York: Oxford University Press, 1991.

De Villiers, Marq. *Water: The Fate of Our Most Precious Resource*. Boston: Houghton Mifflin, 2000.

Dewey, Scott Hamilton. *Don't Breathe the Air: Air Pollution and U.S. Environmental Politics, 1945–1970*. College Station: Texas A&M University Press, 2000.

Dix, Keith. *What's a Coal Miner to Do? The Mechanization of Coal Mining*. Pittsburgh: University of Pittsburgh Press, 1988.

Dorsey, Kurkpatrick. *The Dawn of Conservation Diplomacy: U.S.-Canadian Wildlife Protection Treaties in the Progressive Era*. Seattle: University of Washington Press, 1998.

Duffy, Robert. *Nuclear Politics in America: A History and Theory of Government Regulation*. Lawrence: University Press of Kansas, 1997.

Easton, Robert. *Black Tide: The Santa Barbara Oil Spill and Its Consequences*. New York: Delacorte Press, 1972.

Ekirch, Arthur A., Jr. *Man and Nature in America*. 1963. Reprint, Lincoln: University of Nebraska Press, 1973.

Elkington, John and Tom Burke. *The Green Capitalists*. London: Victor Gollancz, 1987.

Fairbanks, Robert B. and Kathleen Underwood, eds. *Essays on Sunbelt Cities and Recent Urban America*. Introduction by Kenneth T. Jackson. College Station: Published for the University of Texas at Arlington by Texas A&M University Press, 1990.

Fiege, Mark. *Irrigated Eden: The Making of an Agricultural Landscape in the American West*. Seattle and London: University of Washington Press, 1999.

Flader, Susan L. *Thinking Like a Mountain: Aldo Leopold and the Evolution of an Ecological Attitude toward Deer, Wolves, and Forests*. Madison: University of Wisconsin Press, 1994.

Floyd, Donald W. *Forest Sustainability: The History, the Challenge, the Promise*. Durham, N.C.: The Forest History Society, 2002.

Fogarty, Robert S. *Dictionary of American Communal and Utopian History*. Westport, Conn.: Greenwood Press, 1980.

Ford, Daniel F. *Three Mile Island: Thirty Minutes to Meltdown*. New York: Viking Press, 1982.

Foreman, Dave. *Confessions of an Eco-Warrior*. New York: Harmony Books, 1991.

Foster, David R. and John F. O'Keefe. *New England Forests Through Time: Insights from the Harvard Forest Dioramas*. Petersham, Mass.: Harvard Forest, Harvard University, 2000.

Fox, Stephen. *The American Conservation Movement: John Muir and His Legacy*. Madison: University of Wisconsin Press, 1985.

———. *John Muir and His Legacy: The American Conservation Movement*. Boston: Little, Brown, 1981.

Francaviglia, Richard. *Hard Places: Reading the Landscape of America's Historic Mining Districts*. Iowa City: University of Iowa Press, 1991.

Frome, Michael. *Battle for the Wilderness*. Rev. ed. Salt Lake City: University of Utah Press, 1997.

Gates, Paul W. *History of Public Land Law Development*. New York: Arno Press, 1979.

Gibbs, Lois Marie. *Love Canal: The Story Continues*. Gabriola Island, B.C.: New Society Publishers, 1998.

Giedion, Siegfried. *Mechanization Takes Command*. New York: Norton, 1969.

Gottlieb, Robert. *Forcing the Spring: The Transformation of the American Environmental Movement*. Washington, D.C.: Island Press, 1993.

———. *A Life of Its Own: The Politics and Power of Water*. New York: Harcourt Brace, 1988.

Gould, Lewis. *The Presidency of Theodore Roosevelt*. Lawrence: University Press of Kansas, 1991.

Government of Canada and United States Environmental Protection Agency. *The Great Lakes: An Environmental Atlas and Resource Book*. 3rd ed. Chicago: Great Lakes National Program Office, 1995.

Graham, Frank. *The Audubon Ark: A History of the National Audubon Society*. New York: Alfred A. Knopf, 1990.

Gray, Lewis Cecil. *History of Agriculture in the Southern United States to 1860*. 2 vols. Washington, D.C.: Carnegie Institution of Washington, 1933.

Groves, Leslie. *Now It Can Be Told: The Story of the Manhattan Project*. New York: Da Capo Press, 1983.

Hagan, William T. *The American Indian*. Rev. ed. Chicago: University of Chicago Press, 1993.

Harvey, Mark W. T. *A Symbol of Wilderness: Echo Park and the American Conservation Movement*. Seattle: University of Washington Press, 2000.

Hassanein, Neva. *Changing the Way America Farms*. Lincoln: University of Nebraska Press, 1999.

Hawkins, Mike. *Social Darwinism in European and American Thought, 1860–1945*. Cambridge: Cambridge University Press, 1997.

Haynes, Sam. *James K. Polk and the Expansionist Impulse*. 2nd ed. New York: Longman, 2002.

Hays, Samuel P. *Conservation and the Gospel of Efficiency: The Progressive Conservation Movement, 1890–1920*. 1959. Reprint, Pittsburgh: University of Pittsburgh Press, 1999.

Helvarg, David. *The War Against the Greens: The "Wise-Use" Movement, the New Right and Anti-environmental Violence*. San Francisco: Sierra Club Books, 1997.

Hine, Robert V. and John Mack Faragher. *The American West: A New Interpretive History*. New Haven, Conn.: Yale University Press, 2000.

Hirt, Paul W. *A Conspiracy of Optimism: Management of the National Forests since World War Two*. Lincoln: University of Nebraska Press, 1994.

Hofstadter, Richard. *Social Darwinism in American Thought 1860–1915*. Rev. ed. Boston: Beacon Press, 1955.

Hughes, J. Donald. *In the House of Stone and Light: A Human History of the Grand Canyon*. Edited and coordinated by Timothy J. Priehs. Grand Canyon, Ariz.: Grand Canyon Natural History Association, 1978.

Hughes, Robert. *American Visions: The Epic History of Art in America*. New York: Alfred A. Knopf, 1997.

Hundley, Norris, Jr. *The Great Thirst: Californians and Water, 1770s–1990s*. Rev. ed. Berkeley: University of California Press, 2001.

Hunt, Constance Elizabeth. *Down by the River: The Impact of Federal Water Projects and Policies on Biological Diversity*. Washington, D.C.: Island Press, 1988.

Hurley, Andrew, ed. *Common Fields: An Environmental History of St. Louis*. St. Louis: Missouri Historical Society Press, 1997.

Hurt, R. Douglas. *Agricultural Technology in the Twentieth Century*. Manhattan, Kan.: Sunflower University Press, 1991.

———. *American Agriculture: A Brief History*. Ames: Iowa State University Press, 1994.

———. *American Farm Tools from Hand-Power to Steam-Power*. Manhattan, Kan.: Sunflower University Press, 1982.

———. *The Dust Bowl: An Agricultural and Social History*. Chicago: Nelson-Hall, 1981.

———. *The Indian Frontier, 1763–1846*. Albuquerque: University of New Mexico Press, 2002.

Huth, Hans. *Nature and the American: Three Centuries of Changing Attitudes*. 1957. Reprint, with introduction by Douglas H. Strong. Lincoln: University of Nebraska Press, 1991.

Hyde, Charles K. *Copper for America: The United States Copper Industry from Colonial Times to the 1990s*. Tucson: University of Arizona Press, 1998.

Isenberg, Andrew C. *The Destruction of the Bison: An Environmental History, 1750–1920*. Cambridge: Cambridge University Press, 2000.

Jackson, Kenneth T. *Crabgrass Frontier: The Suburbanization of the United States*. New York: Oxford University Press, 1987.

Jackson, W. Turrentine. *Wagon Roads West: A Study of Federal Road Surveys and Construction in the Trans-Mississippi West, 1846–1869*. New Haven, Conn.: Yale University Press, 1964.

Jakle, John H. *Images of the Ohio Valley: A Historical Geography of Travel, 1740 to 1860*. New York: Oxford University Press, 1977.

Jencks, Christopher and Paul E. Peterson, eds. *The Urban Underclass*. Washington, D.C.: The Brookings Institution, 1991.

Kerasote, Ted, ed. *Return of the Wild: The Future of Our Natural Lands*. Washington, D.C.: Island Press, 2001.

Kessell, John L. *Spain in the Southwest: A Narrative History of Colonial New Mexico, Arizona, Texas, and California*. Norman: University of Oklahoma Press, 2002.

Klyza, Christopher McGrory. *Who Controls Public Lands: Mining, Forestry, and Grazing Policies, 1870–1990*. Chapel Hill: University of North Carolina Press, 1996.

Lang, James. *Notes of a Potato Watcher*. College Station: Texas A & M University Press, 2001.

Lear, Linda. *Rachel Carson: Witness for Nature*. New York: Henry Holt, 1997.

Leidner, Jacob. *Plastics Waste, Recovery of Economic Value*. New York: Marcel Dekker, 1981.

Leopold, Aldo. *Game Management*. 1933. Reprint, Madison: University of Wisconsin Press, 1986.

———. *A Sand County Almanac and Sketches Here and There*. 1949. Reprint, New York: Oxford University, 1989.

Licht, Walter. *Industrializing America: The Nineteenth Century*. Baltimore, Md.: Johns Hopkins University Press, 1995.

Lopez, Barry. *Arctic Dreams: Imagination and Desire in a Northern Landscape*. New York: Scribner's, 1986.

Lowitt, Richard, ed. *Politics in the Postwar American West*. Norman: University of Oklahoma Press, 1995.

Lyon, Thomas J., ed. *This Incomparable Land: A Guide to American Nature Writing*. Minneapolis, Minn.: Milkweed Editions, 2001.

MacArthur, John R. *The Selling of "Free Trade": NAFTA, Washington, and the Subversion of American Democracy*. Berkeley: University of California Press, 2001.

Magdoff, Fred, ed. *Hungry for Profit: The Agribusiness Threat to Farmers, Food, and the Environment*. New York: Monthly Review Press, 2000.

Majumdar, Shyamal K. and E. Willard Miller, eds. *Pennsylvania Coal: Resources, Technology and Utilization*. Easton: The Pennsylvania Academy of Science, 1983.

Malone, Michael P. *The Battle for Butte: Mining and Politics on the Northern Frontier, 1864–1906*. Helena: Montana Historical Society Press, 1995.

Mazur, Allan. *A Hazardous Inquiry: The Rashomon Effect at Love Canal*. Cambridge, Mass.: Harvard University Press, 1998.

McCarthy, Michael P. *Typhoid and the Politics of Public Health in Nineteenth-Century Philadelphia*. Philadelphia: American Philosophical Society, 1987.

McCool, Daniel. *Command of the Waters: Iron Triangles, Federal Water Development, and Indian Water*. 1987. Reprint, Tucson: University of Arizona Press, 1994.

———. *Native Waters: Indian Water Settlements and the Second Treaty Era*. Tucson: University of Arizona Press, 2002.

McCusker, John and Russell Menard. *The Economy of British America, 1607–1789*. Chapel Hill: University of North Carolina Press, 1991.

McDonald, Peter and James Lassoie, eds. *The Literature of Forestry and Agroforestry*. Ithaca, N.Y.: Cornell University Press, 1996.

McIntosh, Elaine N. *American Food Habits in Historical Perspective*. Westport, Conn.: Praeger, 1995.

McLynn, Frank. *Wagons West: The Epic Story of America's Overland Trails*. London: Jonathan Cape, 2002.

McPherson, James M. *Battle Cry of Freedom: The Civil War Era*. New York: Ballantine Books, 1989.

Meikle, Jeffrey. *American Plastic: A Cultural History*. New Brunswick, N.J.: Rutgers University Press, 1995.

Meinig, D. W. *The Shaping of America: A Geographical Perspective*. New Haven, Conn.: Yale University Press, 1986.

Melosi, Martin V. *Coping with Abundance: Energy and Environment in Industrial America*. New York: Alfred Knopf, 1985.

————. *The Sanitary City: Urban Infrastructure in America from Colonial Times to the Present.* Baltimore, Md.: Johns Hopkins University Press, 2000.

Merchant, Carolyn. *Ecological Revolutions: Nature, Gender, and Science in New England.* Chapel Hill: University of North Carolina Press, 1989.

Miller, Char. *Gifford Pinchot and the Making of Modern Environmentalism.* Washington, D.C.: Island Press, 2001.

Miller, Char, ed. *Fluid Arguments: Five Centuries of Western Water Conflict.* Tucson: University of Arizona Press, 2001.

Miller, Char and Rebecca Staebler. *The Greatest Good: 100 Years of Forestry in America.* Foreword by William H. Banzhaf; introduction by James E. Coufal. Bethesda, Md.: Society of American Foresters, 1999.

Miller, Randall M. and George E. Pozzetta, eds. *Shades of the Sunbelt: Essays on Ethnicity, Race, and the Urban South.* Boca Raton: Florida Atlantic University Press, 1989.

Mohl, Raymond A., ed. *Searching for the Sunbelt: Historical Perspectives on a Region.* Athens: University of Georgia Press, 1993.

Muir, John. *Our National Parks.* 1901. Reprint, San Francisco: Sierra Club Books, 1991.

Muller, Peter O. *Contemporary Suburban America.* Englewood Cliffs, N.J.: Prentice-Hall, 1981.

Nader, Ralph, ed. *The Case Against Free Trade: GATT, NAFTA, and the Globalization of Corporate Power.* Berkeley, Calif.: North Atlantic Books, 1993.

Nash, Roderick. *Wilderness and the American Mind.* 4th ed. New Haven, Conn.: Yale University Press, 2001.

Nesson, Fern L. *Great Waters: A History of Boston's Water Supply.* Hanover, N.H.: University Press of New England, 1983.

Nordhoff, Charles. *The Communistic Societies of the United States: From Personal Visit and Observation.* 1875. Reprint, New York: Dover Publications, 1966.

Olson, Sherry Hessler. *Depletion Myth: A History of Railroad Use of Timber.* Cambridge, Mass.: Harvard University Press, 1971.

Olson, Sigurd F. *The Meaning of Wilderness: Essential Articles and Speeches.* Edited and with an introduction by David Backes. Minneapolis: University of Minnesota Press, 2001.

Opie, John. *The Law of the Land: 200 Years of American Farmland Policy.* Lincoln: University of Nebraska Press, 1994.

————. *Ogallala: Water for a Dry Land.* 2nd ed. Lincoln: University of Nebraska Press, 2000.

Otto, John Solomon. *Southern Agriculture during the Civil War Era, 1860–1880.* Westport, Conn.: Greenwood, 1994.

Palen, J. John. *The Suburbs.* New York: McGraw-Hill, 1995.

Paludan, Phillip Shaw. *"A People's Contest": The Union & Civil War, 1861—1865.* 2nd ed., with a new preface. Lawrence: University Press of Kansas, 1996.

Paul, Rodman W. *Mining Frontiers of the Far West, 1848–1880.* Rev. ed. Albuquerque: University of New Mexico Press, 2001.

Perkins, Edwin J. *The Economy of Colonial America.* 2nd ed. New York: Columbia University Press, 1988.

Pinchot, Gifford. *Breaking New Ground.* 1947. Reprint, Washington, D.C.: Island Press, 1998.

Porro, Jeffrey and Christine Meller. *The Plastic Waste Primer.* New York: Lyons and Burford, 1993.

Powell, Sumner Chilton. *Puritan Village: The Formation of a New England Town.* Middletown, Conn.: Wesleyan University Press, 1963.

Price, Edward T. *Dividing the Land: Early American Beginnings of Our Private Property Mosaic.* Chicago: University of Chicago Press, 1995.

Prucha, Francis Paul. *The Great Father: The United States Government and the American Indians.* 2 vols. Lincoln: University of Nebraska Press, 1995.

Pyne, Stephen J. *America's Fires: Management on Wildlands and Forests.* Durham, N.C.: Forest History Society, 1997.

————. *Year of the Fires: The Story of the Great Fires of 1910.* New York: Viking, 2001.

Reich, Charles A. *The Greening of America.* New York: Random House, 1970.

Reiger, John F. *American Sportsmen and the Origins of Conservation.* 3rd ed. Corvallis: Oregon State University Press, 2001.

Reisner, Marc. *Cadillac Desert: The American West and Its Disappearing Water.* New York: Penguin Books, 1993.

Riney-Kehrberg, Pamela. *Rooted in Dust: Surviving Drought and Depression in Southwestern Kansas.* Lawrence: University Press of Kansas, 1994.

Robbins, Roy M. *Our Landed Heritage: The Public Domain, 1776–1970.* 2nd ed. Lincoln: University of Nebraska Press, 1976.

Robbins, William G. *American Forestry: A History of National, State, and Private Cooperation.* Lincoln: University of Nebraska Press, 1985.

Rodgers, Andrew, III. *Bernhard Eduard Fernow: A Story of North American Forestry.* New York: Hafner Publishing, 1968.

Rome, Adam. *The Bulldozer in the Countryside: Suburban Sprawl and the Rise of American Environmentalism.* Cambridge: Cambridge University Press, 2001.

Rosenbaum, Walter A. *Environmental Politics and Policy.* 5th ed. Washington, D.C.: CQ Press, 2002.

Rothman, Hal K. *The Greening of a Nation?: Environmentalism in the U.S. Since 1945.* Fort Worth, Tex.: Harcourt Brace College Publishers, 1998.

———. *Saving the Planet: The American Response to the Environment in the 20th Century.* Chicago: Ivan R. Dee, 2000.

Runte, Alfred. *National Parks: The American Experience.* Lincoln: University of Nebraska Press, 1997.

Russell, Edmund. *War and Nature: Fighting Humans and Insects with Chemicals from World War I to* Silent Spring. Cambridge: Cambridge University Press, 2001.

Russell, Howard S. *A Long, Deep Furrow: Three Centuries of Farming in New England.* Hanover, N.H.: University Press of New England, 1982.

Scamehorn, Lee. *Mill and Mine: The CF&I in the Twentieth Century.* Lincoln: University of Nebraska Press, 1992.

Schulman, Bruce J. *From Cotton Belt to Sunbelt: Federal Policy, Economic Development, and the Transformation of the South, 1938–1980.* Durham, N.C.: Duke University Press, 1994.

Scott, Mel. *American City Planning Since 1890.* Berkeley: University of California Press, 1971.

Searle, R. Newell. *Saving Quetico-Superior: A Land Set Apart.* St. Paul: Minnesota Historical Society Press, 1977.

Shabecoff, Philip. *A Fierce Green Fire: The American Environmental Movement.* New York: Hill and Wang, 1993.

Shurts, John. *Indian Reserved Water Rights: The Winters Doctrine in Its Social and Legal Context, 1880s–1930s.* Norman: University of Oklahoma Press, 2000.

Silver, Timothy. *A New Face on the Countryside: Indians, Colonists, and Slaves in South Atlantic Forests, 1500–1800.* Cambridge: Cambridge University Press, 1990.

Slatta, Richard W. *Cowboys of the Americas.* New Haven, Conn.: Yale University Press, 1994.

Smith, Andrew F. *The Tomato in America: Early History, Culture, and Cookery.* Urbana: University of Illinois Press, 2001.

Smith, Arthur G. *Pittsburgh: Then and Now.* Pittsburgh: University of Pittsburgh Press, 1990.

Smith, Duane A. *Mining America: The Industry and the Environment, 1800–1980.* Niwot: University Press of Colorado, 1993.

Starrs, Paul F. *Let the Cowboy Ride: Cattle Ranching in the American West.* Baltimore, Md.: Johns Hopkins University Press, 1998.

Steen, Harold K. *The U.S. Forest Service: A History.* Seattle: University of Washington Press, 1976.

Steinberg, Theodore. *Down to Earth: Nature's Role in American History.* New York: Oxford University Press, 2002.

Stewart, Mart A. *"What Nature Suffers to Groe": Life, Labor, and Landscape on the Georgia Coast, 1680–1920.* Athens: University of Georgia Press, 1996.

Stover, John. *American Railroads.* 2nd ed. Chicago: University of Chicago Press, 1997.

Stover, John and Mark Carnes. *The Routledge Historical Atlas of the American Railroads.* New York: Routledge, 1999.

Stradling, David. *Smokestacks and Progressives: Environmentalists, Engineers, and Air Quality in America, 1881–1951.* Baltimore, Md.: Johns Hopkins University Press, 1999.

Strohmeyer, John. *Extreme Conditions: Big Oil and the Transformation of Alaska.* New York: Simon & Schuster, 1993.

Taniguchi, Nancy J. *Necessary Fraud: Progressive Reform and Utah Coal.* Norman: University of Oklahoma Press, 1996.

Tarr, Joel A. *The Search for the Ultimate Sink: Urban Pollution in Historical Perspective.* Akron, Ohio: University of Akron Press, 1996.

Tarr, Joel A. and Gabriel Dupuy, eds. *Technology and the Rise of the Networked City in Europe and America.* Philadelphia: Temple University Press, 1988.

Thoreau, Henry David. *Walden.* 1854. Reprint, New York: Modern Library, 2000.

Trotter, Joe William, Jr., ed. *The Great Migration in Historical Perspective: New Dimensions of Race, Class, and Gender.* Bloomington: Indiana University Press, 1991.

Udall, Stewart. *The Quiet Crisis.* New York: Avon, 1970.

U.S. National Research Council. *Alternative Agriculture.* Washington, D.C.: National Academy Press, 1989.

Utley, Robert M. *A Life Wild and Perilous: Mountain Men and the Paths to the Pacific.* New York: Henry Holt, 1997.

Utter, Jack. *American Indians: Answers to Today's Questions.* 2nd ed. Norman: University of Oklahoma Press, 2001.

Walker, Laurence C. *The Southern Forest: A Chronicle.* Austin: University of Texas Press, 1991.

Wall, Joseph Frazier. *Andrew Carnegie.* Pittsburgh: University of Pittsburgh Press, 1989.

Ward, David. *Cities and Immigrants: A Geography of Change in Nineteenth-Century America.* New York: Oxford University Press, 1971.

Ward, Geoffrey. *The West: An Illustrated History.* Boston: Little, Brown, 1996.

Warren, Louis S. *The Hunter's Game: Poachers and Conservationists in Twentieth-Century America.* New Haven, Conn.: Yale University Press, 1997.

Weber, David J. *The Spanish Frontier in North America.* New Haven, Conn.: Yale University Press, 1992.

Wellock, Thomas R. *Critical Masses: Opposition to Nuclear Power in California, 1958–1978.* Madison: University of Wisconsin Press, 1998.

White, Richard. *"It's Your Misfortune and None of My Own": A History of the American West.* Norman: University of Oklahoma Press, 1991.

Williams, Michael. *Americans and Their Forests: A Historical Geography.* Cambridge: Cambridge University Press, 1992.

Williamson, Harold F., Ralph L. Andreano, Arnold R. Daum, and Gilbert C. Klose. *The American Petroleum Industry: The Age of Energy, 1899–1959.* Evanston, Ill.: Northwestern University Press, 1963.

Willoughby, William R. *The Joint Organizations of Canada and the United States.* Toronto: University of Toronto Press, 1979.

Wilson, William H. *The City Beautiful Movement.* Baltimore, Md.: Johns Hopkins University Press, 1989.

Winther, Oscar Osburn. *The Transportation Frontier: Trans-Mississippi West, 1865–1890.* Albuquerque: University of New Mexico, 1974.

Wolf, Nancy and Ellen Feldman. *America's Packaging Dilemma.* Washington, D.C.: Island Press, 1991.

Worster, Donald. *Dust Bowl: The Southern Plains in the 1930s.* New York: Oxford University Press, 1982.

———. *Rivers of Empire: Water, Aridity and the Growth of the American West.* New York: Oxford University Press, 1985.

———. *Under Western Skies: Nature and History in the American West.* Oxford: Oxford University Press, 1993.

Worster, Donald, ed. *American Environmentalism: The Formative Period, 1860–1915.* New York: Wiley, 1973.

Yergin, Daniel. *The Prize: The Epic Quest for Oil, Money, and Power.* New York: Simon & Schuster, 1991.

Zaitzevsky, Cynthia. *Frederick Law Olmsted and the Boston Park System.* Cambridge, Mass.: Harvard University Press, 1982.

Zakin, Susan. *Coyotes and Town Dogs: Earth First! and the Environmental Movement.* New York: Viking, 1993.

Canada

Allen, Richard. *The Social Passion: Religion and Social Reform in Canada, 1914–28.* Toronto: University of Toronto Press, 1973.

Apsey, Mike, et al. *The Perpetual Forest: Using Lessons from the Past to Sustain Canada's Forests in the Future.* Vancouver: FORCAST, 2000.

Bell, K. *COSEWIC Status Report on the Atlantic Cod, Gadus morhua.* Ottawa: Committee on the Status of Endangered Wildlife in Canada, 1998.

Boardman, Robert, ed. *Canadian Environmental Policy: Ecosystems, Politics, and Process.* Toronto: Oxford University Press, 1992.

Bunting, Trudi and Pierre Filion, eds. *Canadian Cities in Transition: The Twenty-First Century.* 2nd ed. Ontario: Oxford University Press Canada, 2000.

Dechêne, Louise. *Habitants and Merchants in Seventeenth Century Montreal.* Montreal: McGill-Queen's University Press, 1992.

Dickason, Olive Patricia. *Canada's First Nations: A History of Founding Peoples from Earliest Times.* 3rd ed. New York: Oxford University Press, 2002.

Dorsey, Kurkpatrick. *The Dawn of Conservation Diplomacy: U.S.-Canadian Wildlife Protection Treaties in the Progressive Era.* Seattle: University of Washington Press, 1998.

Eagle, John A. *The Canadian Pacific Railway and the Development of Western Canada, 1896–1914.* Montreal & Kingston: McGill-Queen's University Press, 1989.

Environment Canada. *The State of Canada's Environment, 1996*. Ottawa: Minister of Public Works and Government Services, 1996.

Foster, Janet. *Working for Wildlife: The Beginning of Preservation in Canada*. 2nd ed. Toronto: University of Toronto Press, 1998.

Gaffield, Chad and Pam Gaffield, eds. *Consuming Canada: Readings in Environmental History*. Toronto: Copp Clark, 1995.

Gates, Lillian F. *Land Policies of Upper Canada*. Toronto: University of Toronto Press, 1968.

Gillis, R. Peter and Thomas R. Roach. *Lost Initiatives: Canada's Forest Industries, Forest Policy and Forest Conservation*. New York: Greenwood Press, 1986.

Government of Canada and United States Environmental Protection Agency. *The Great Lakes: An Environmental Atlas and Resource Book*. 3rd ed. Chicago: Great Lakes National Program Office, 1995.

Greer, Allan. *Peasant, Lord, and Merchant: Rural Society in Three Quebec Parishes, 1740–1840*. Toronto: University of Toronto Press, 1985.

Grey Owl. *Tales of an Empty Cabin*. London: L. Dickson, 1936.

Harris, R. Cole and John Warkentin. *Canada Before Confederation: A Study in Historical Geography*. New York: Oxford University Press, 1974.

Harris, Richard Colebrook. *The Seigneurial System in Early Canada: A Geographical Study*. Madison: University of Wisconsin Press, 1984.

Heron, Craig. *Working in Steel, The Early Years in Canada, 1883–1935*. Toronto: McClelland and Stewart, 1988.

Hewitt, Gordon C. *The Conservation of Wildlife in Canada*. New York: Scribner's Sons, 1921.

Historical Atlas of Canada. 3 vols. Toronto, University of Toronto Press, 1987, 1990–93.

Hurst, D. G., et al. *Canada Enters the Atomic Age*. Montreal: McGill-Queen's University Press, 1997.

Jones, Robert Leslie. *History of Agriculture in Ontario: 1613–1880*. Toronto: University of Toronto Press, 1946.

Kain, Roger, ed. *Planning for Conservation*. New York: St. Martin's Press, 1981.

Kerr, Donald, et al., eds. *Addressing the Twentieth Century 1891–1961*. Vol. 3 of *Historical Atlas of Canada*. Toronto: University of Toronto Press, 1990.

Lewis, Robert Davis. *Manufacturing Montreal: The Making of an Industrial Landscape, 1850 to 1930*. Baltimore, Md.: Johns Hopkins University Press, 2000.

Lopez, Barry. *Arctic Dreams: Imagination and Desire in a Northern Landscape*. New York: Scribner's, 1986.

Lothian, W. F. *A Brief History of Canada's National Parks*. Ottawa: Environment Canada Parks, 1987.

Macdonald, Doug. *The Politics of Pollution: Why Canadians Are Failing Their Environment*. Toronto: McClelland and Stewart, 1991.

Marchak, Patricia. *Green Gold: The Forest Industry in British Columbia*. Vancouver: University of British Columbia Press, 1983.

McCutcheon, Sean. *Electric Rivers: The Story of the James Bay Project*. Montreal: Black Rose Books, 1991.

McDonnell, Greg. *The History of Canadian Railroads*. London: Footnote Productions/New Burlington Books, 1985.

Mitchinson, Wendy and Janice Dicken McGinnis, eds. *Essays in the History of Canadian Medicine*. Toronto: McClelland and Stewart, 1988.

Mouat, Jeremy. *Roaring Days: Rossland's Mines and the History of British Columbia*. Vancouver: University of British Columbia Press, 1995.

Nelles, H. V. *The Politics of Development: Forests, Mines & Hydro-electric Power in Ontario, 1849–1941*. Hamden, Conn.: Archon Books, 1974.

Owram, Doug. *Born at the Right Time: A History of the Baby Boom*. Toronto: University of Toronto Press, 1996.

Parson, Edward A., ed. *Governing the Environment: Persistent Challenges, Uncertain Innovations*. Toronto: University of Toronto Press, 2001.

Ray, Arthur J. *I Have Lived Here since the World Began: An Illustrated History of Canada's Native People*. Toronto: Key Porter Books, 1996.

Reaman, G. E. *A History of Agriculture in Ontario*. Vol. 1. Toronto: Saunders, 1970.

Richardson, Boyce. *Strangers Devour the Land*. Toronto: Macmillan of Canada, 1977.

Rodgers, Andrew, III. *Bernhard Eduard Fernow: A Story of North American Forestry*. New York: Hafner Publishing, 1968.

Rogers, Edward S. and Donald B. Smith, eds. *Aboriginal Ontario: Historical Perspectives on the First Nations*. Toronto: Dundurn Press, 1994.

Smith, Donald B. *From the Land of the Shadows: The Making of Grey Owl*. Seattle: University of Washington Press, 1999.

The State of Canada's Forests, 1996–1997: Learning from History. Ottawa: Her Majesty the Queen in Right of Canada, 1997.

Taylor, G. W. *Timber: History of the Forest Industry in B.C.* Vancouver: J. J. Douglas, 1975.

VanNijnatten, Debora L. and Robert Boardman, eds. *Canadian Environmental Policy: Context and Cases*. 2nd ed. Toronto: Oxford University Press, 2002.

Waldram, James. *As Long as the Rivers Run: Hydroelectric Development and Native Communities in Western Canada*. Winnipeg: University of Manitoba Press, 1988.

Wall, Geoff and John S. Marsh, eds. *Recreational Land Use: Perspectives on Its Evolution in Canada*. Ottawa: Carleton University Press, 1982.

Willoughby, William R. *The Joint Organizations of Canada and the United States*. Toronto: University of Toronto Press, 1979.

Wood, J. David. *Making Ontario: Agricultural Colonization and Landscape Re-creation before the Railway*. Montreal: McGill-Queen's University Press, 2000.

Wood, J. David, ed. *Perspectives on Landscape and Settlement in Nineteenth Century Ontario*. Toronto: McClelland and Stewart, 1975.

Wright, J. R. *The Public Park Movement, 1860–1914*. Vol. 2 of *Urban Parks in Ontario*. Toronto: Ministry of Tourism and Recreation, 1984.

Wynn, Graeme. *Timber Colony: A Historical Geography of Early Nineteenth Century New Brunswick*. Toronto: University of Toronto Press, 1981.

ERA BY ERA

European Exploration and the Colonial Era: 1492–1770s

Breen, T. H. *Tobacco Culture: The Mentality of the Great Tidewater Planters on the Eve of the Revolution*. Princeton, N.J.: Princeton University Press, 1985.

Cronon, William. *Changes in the Land: Indians, Colonists, and the Ecology of New England*. New York: Hill and Wang, 1983.

Crosby, Alfred W., Jr. *The Columbian Exchange: Biological and Cultural Consequences of 1492*. Westport, Conn.: Greenwood Press, 1972.

Dechêne, Louise. *Habitants and Merchants in Seventeenth Century Montreal*. Montreal: McGill-Queen's University Press, 1992.

Harris, Richard Colebrook. *The Seigneurial System in Early Canada: A Geographical Study*. Madison: University of Wisconsin Press, 1984.

Jones, Robert Leslie. *History of Agriculture in Ontario: 1613–1880*. Toronto: University of Toronto Press, 1946.

Kessell, John L. *Spain in the Southwest: A Narrative History of Colonial New Mexico, Arizona, Texas, and California*. Norman: University of Oklahoma Press, 2002.

Kulikoff, Allan. *Tobacco and Slaves: The Development of Southern Cultures in the Chesapeake, 1680–1800*. Chapel Hill: University of North Carolina Press, 1986.

McCusker, John and Russell Menard. *The Economy of British America, 1607–1789*. Chapel Hill: University of North Carolina Press, 1991.

Perkins, Edwin J. *The Economy of Colonial America*. 2nd ed. New York: Columbia University Press, 1988.

Powell, Sumner Chilton. *Puritan Village: The Formation of a New England Town*. Middletown, Conn.: Wesleyan University Press, 1963.

Silver, Timothy. *A New Face on the Countryside: Indians, Colonists, and Slaves in South Atlantic Forests, 1500–1800*. Cambridge: Cambridge University Press, 1990.

Stewart, Mart A. *"What Nature Suffers to Groe": Life, Labor, and Landscape on the Georgia Coast, 1680–1920*. Athens: University of Georgia Press, 1996.

Weber, David J. *The Spanish Frontier in North America*. New Haven, Conn.: Yale University Press, 1992.

Expansion and Conflict: 1770s–1850s

Barbour, Barton H. *Fort Union and the Upper Missouri Fur Trade*. Norman: University of Oklahoma Press, 2001.

Berry, Brian J. *America's Utopian Experiments: Communal Havens from Long-Wave Crises*. Hanover, N.H.: University Press of New England, 1992.

Gray, Lewis Cecil. *History of Agriculture in the Southern United States to 1860*. 2 vols. Washington, D.C.: Carnegie Institution of Washington, 1933.

Greer, Allan. *Peasant, Lord, and Merchant: Rural Society in Three Quebec Parishes, 1740–1840*. Toronto: University of Toronto Press, 1985.

Harris, R. Cole and John Warkentin. *Canada Before Confederation: A Study in Historical Geography*. New York: Oxford University Press, 1974.

Haynes, Sam. *James K. Polk and the Expansionist Impulse.* 2nd ed. New York: Longman, 2002.

Hine, Robert V. and John Mack Faragher. *The American West: A New Interpretive History.* New Haven, Conn.: Yale University Press, 2000.

Hurt, R. Douglas. *The Indian Frontier, 1763–1846.* Albuquerque: University of New Mexico Press, 2002.

Isenberg, Andrew C. *The Destruction of the Bison: An Environmental History, 1750–1920.* Cambridge: Cambridge University Press, 2000.

Jakle, John H. *Images of the Ohio Valley: A Historical Geography of Travel, 1740 to 1860.* New York: Oxford University Press, 1977.

Jones, Robert Leslie. *History of Agriculture in Ontario: 1613–1880.* Toronto: University of Toronto Press, 1946.

McHugh, Tom. *The Time of the Buffalo.* New York: Alfred A. Knopf, 1972.

McLynn, Frank. *Wagons West: The Epic Story of America's Overland Trails.* London: Jonathan Cape, 2002.

Nordhoff, Charles. *The Communistic Societies of the United States: From Personal Visit and Observation.* 1875. Reprint, New York: Dover Publications, 1966.

Price, Edward T. *Dividing the Land: Early American Beginnings of Our Private Property Mosaic.* Chicago: University of Chicago Press, 1995.

Robbins, Roy M. *Our Landed Heritage: The Public Domain, 1776–1970.* 2nd ed. Lincoln: University of Nebraska Press, 1976.

Utley, Robert M. *A Life Wild and Perilous: Mountain Men and the Paths to the Pacific.* New York: Henry Holt, 1997.

White, Richard. *"It's Your Misfortune and None of My Own": A History of the American West.* Norman: University of Oklahoma Press, 1991.

Wood, J. David. *Making Ontario: Agricultural Colonization and Landscape Re-creation before the Railway.* Montreal: McGill-Queen's University Press, 2000.

Wood, J. David, ed. *Perspectives on Landscape and Settlement in Nineteenth Century Ontario.* Toronto: McClelland and Stewart, 1975.

Wynn, Graeme. *Timber Colony: A Historical Geography of Early Nineteenth Century New Brunswick.* Toronto: University of Toronto Press, 1981.

Landscape of Industrialization: 1850s–1920s

Ambrose, Stephen. *Nothing Like It in the World: The Men Who Built the Transcontinental Railroad 1863–1869.* New York: Simon & Schuster, 2000.

Baratz, Morton S. *The Union and the Coal Industry.* New Haven, Conn.: Yale University Press, 1955.

Bodnar, John. *The Transplanted: A History of Immigrants in Urban America.* Bloomington: Indiana University Press, 1985.

Burrows, Edwin G. and Mike Wallace. *Gotham: A History of New York City to 1898.* New York: Oxford University Press, 1999.

Burton, Lloyd. *American Indian Water Rights and the Limits of Law.* Lawrence: University Press of Kansas, 1991.

Cox, Thomas R. *Mills and Markets: A History of the Pacific Coast Lumber Industry to 1900.* Seattle: University of Washington Press, 1974.

Dale, Edward Everett. *The Range Cattle Industry: Ranching on the Great Plains from 1865 to 1925.* Norman: University of Oklahoma Press, 1960.

Degler, Carl N. *In Search of Human Nature: The Decline and Revival of Darwinism in American Social Thought.* New York: Oxford University Press, 1991.

Dix, Keith. *What's a Coal Miner to Do? The Mechanization of Coal Mining.* Pittsburgh: University of Pittsburgh Press, 1988.

Eagle, John A. *The Canadian Pacific Railway and the Development of Western Canada, 1896–1914.* Montreal and Kingston: McGill-Queen's University Press, 1989.

Francaviglia, Richard. *Hard Places: Reading the Landscape of America's Historic Mining Districts.* Iowa City: University of Iowa Press, 1991.

Hawkins, Mike. *Social Darwinism in European and American Thought, 1860–1945.* Cambridge: Cambridge University Press, 1997.

Heron, Craig. *Working in Steel, The Early Years in Canada, 1883–1935.* Toronto: McClelland and Stewart, 1988.

Hofstadter, Richard. *Social Darwinism in American Thought 1860–1915.* Rev. ed. Boston: Beacon Press, 1955.

Jackson, W. Turrentine. *Wagon Roads West: A Study of Federal Road Surveys and Construction in the Trans-Mississippi West, 1846–1869.* New Haven, Conn.: Yale University Press, 1964.

Lewis, Robert Davis. *Manufacturing Montreal: The Making of an Industrial Landscape, 1850 to 1930.* Baltimore, Md.: Johns Hopkins University Press, 2000.

Licht, Walter. *Industrializing America: The Nineteenth Century.* Baltimore, Md.: Johns Hopkins University Press, 1995.

Malone, Michael P. *The Battle for Butte: Mining and Politics on the Northern Frontier, 1864–1906.* Helena: Montana Historical Society Press, 1995.

McCarthy, Michael P. *Typhoid and the Politics of Public Health in Nineteenth-Century Philadelphia.* Philadelphia: American Philosophical Society, 1987.

McDonnell, Greg. *The History of Canadian Railroads.* London: Footnote Productions/New Burlington Books, 1985.

McPherson, James M. *Battle Cry of Freedom: The Civil War Era.* New York: Ballantine Books, 1989.

Mouat, Jeremy. *Roaring Days: Rossland's Mines and the History of British Columbia.* Vancouver: University of British Columbia Press, 1995.

Nelles, H. V. *The Politics of Development: Forests, Mines & Hydro-electric Power in Ontario, 1849–1941.* Hamden, Conn.: Archon Books, 1974.

Otto, John Solomon. *Southern Agriculture during the Civil War Era, 1860–1880.* Westport, Conn.: Greenwood, 1994.

Paludan, Phillip Shaw. *"A People's Contest": The Union & Civil War, 1861—1865.* 2nd ed., with a new preface. Lawrence: University Press of Kansas, 1996.

Paul, Rodman W. *Mining Frontiers of the Far West, 1848–1880.* Rev. ed. Albuquerque: University of New Mexico Press, 2001.

Starrs, Paul F. *Let the Cowboy Ride: Cattle Ranching in the American West.* Baltimore, Md.: Johns Hopkins University Press, 1998.

Stover, John. *American Railroads.* 2nd ed. Chicago: University of Chicago Press, 1997.

Stover, John and Mark Carnes. *The Routledge Historical Atlas of the American Railroads.* New York: Routledge, 1999.

Stradling, David. *Smokestacks and Progressives: Environmentalists, Engineers, and Air Quality in America, 1881–1951.* Baltimore, Md.: Johns Hopkins University Press, 1999.

Taniguchi, Nancy J. *Necessary Fraud: Progressive Reform and Utah Coal.* Norman: University of Oklahoma Press, 1996.

Tarr, Joel A. and Gabriel Dupuy, eds. *Technology and the Rise of the Networked City in Europe and America.* Philadelphia: Temple University Press, 1988.

Ward, David. *Cities and Immigrants: A Geography of Change in Nineteenth-Century America.* New York: Oxford University Press, 1971.

Williamson, Harold F., Ralph L. Andreano, Arnold R. Daum, and Gilbert C. Klose. *The American Petroleum Industry: The Age of Energy, 1899–1959.* Evanston, Ill.: Northwestern University Press, 1963.

Wilson, William H. *The City Beautiful Movement.* Baltimore, Md.: Johns Hopkins University Press, 1989.

Winther, Oscar Osburn. *The Transportation Frontier: Trans-Mississippi West, 1865–1890.* Albuquerque: University of New Mexico, 1974.

The Conservation Era: 1880s–1920s

Allen, Richard. *The Social Passion: Religion and Social Reform in Canada, 1914–28.* Toronto: University of Toronto Press, 1973.

Boyer, Paul. *Urban Masses and Moral Order in America, 1820–1920.* Cambridge, Mass.: Harvard University Press, 1978.

Chambers, John Whiteclay, II. *The Tyranny of Change: America in the Progressive Era, 1900–1917.* New Brunswick, N.J.: Rutgers University Press, 2000.

Cutright, Paul Russel. *Theodore Roosevelt: The Making of a Conservationist.* Urbana: University of Illinois Press, 1985.

Dorsey, Kurkpatrick. *The Dawn of Conservation Diplomacy: U.S.-Canadian Wildlife Protection Treaties in the Progressive Era.* Seattle: University of Washington Press, 1998.

Fiege, Mark. *Irrigated Eden: The Making of an Agricultural Landscape in the American West.* Seattle and London: University of Washington Press, 1999.

Foster, Janet. *Working for Wildlife: The Beginning of Preservation in Canada.* 2nd ed. Toronto: University of Toronto Press, 1998.

Fox, Stephen. *John Muir and His Legacy: The American Conservation Movement.* Boston: Little, Brown, 1981.

Gillis, R. Peter and Thomas R. Roach. *Lost Initiatives: Canada's Forest Industries, Forest Policy and Forest Conservation.* New York: Greenwood Press, 1986.

Gould, Lewis. *The Presidency of Theodore Roosevelt.* Lawrence: University Press of Kansas, 1991.

Hays, Samuel P. *Conservation and the Gospel of Efficiency: The Progressive Conservation Movement, 1890–1920.* 1959. Reprint, Pittsburgh: University of Pittsburgh Press, 1999.

Lothian, W. F. *A Brief History of Canada's National Parks.* Ottawa: Environment Canada Parks, 1987.

McCool, Daniel. *Command of the Waters: Iron Triangles, Federal Water Development, and Indian Water.* 1987. Reprint, Tucson: University of Arizona Press, 1994.

Miller, Char. *Gifford Pinchot and the Making of Modern Environmentalism.* Washington, D.C.: Island Press, 2001.

Muir, John. *Our National Parks.* 1901. Reprint, San Francisco: Sierra Club Books, 1991.

Pyne, Stephen J. *Year of the Fires: The Story of the Great Fires of 1910.* New York: Viking, 2001.

Reiger, John F. *American Sportsmen and the Origins of Conservation.* 3rd ed. Corvallis: Oregon State University Press, 2001.

Rodgers, Andrew, III. *Bernhard Eduard Fernow: A Story of North American Forestry.* New York: Hafner Publishing Company, 1968.

Shurts, John. *Indian Reserved Water Rights: The Winters Doctrine in Its Social and Legal Context, 1880s–1930s.* Norman: University of Oklahoma Press, 2000.

Steen, Harold K. *The U.S. Forest Service: A History.* Seattle: University of Washington Press, 1977.

Worster, Donald. *Rivers of Empire: Water, Aridity and the Growth of the American West.* New York: Oxford University Press, 1985.

Wright, J. R. *The Public Park Movement, 1860–1914.* Vol. 2 of *Urban Parks in Ontario.* Toronto: Ministry of Tourism and Recreation, 1984.

Zaitzevsky, Cynthia. *Frederick Law Olmsted and the Boston Park System.* Cambridge, Mass.: Harvard University Press, 1982.

From the Depression to Atomic Power: 1930s–1960s

Abbott, Carl. *The New Urban America: Growth and Politics in Sunbelt Cities.* Rev. ed. Chapel Hill: University of North Carolina Press, 1987.

Carson, Rachel. *Silent Spring.* 1962. Reprint, Boston: Houghton Mifflin, 1994.

Dewey, Scott Hamilton. *Don't Breathe the Air: Air Pollution and U.S. Environmental Politics, 1945–1970.* College Station: Texas A&M University Press, 2000.

Groves, Leslie. *Now It Can Be Told: The Story of the Manhattan Project.* New York: Da Capo Press, 1983.

Hurst, D. G., et al. *Canada Enters the Atomic Age.* Montreal: McGill-Queen's University Press, 1997.

Hurt, R. Douglas. *The Dust Bowl: An Agricultural and Social History.* Chicago: Nelson-Hall, 1981.

Kerr, Donald, et al., eds. *Addressing the Twentieth Century 1891–1961.* Vol. 3 of *Historical Atlas of Canada.* Toronto: University of Toronto Press, 1990.

Lear, Linda. *Rachel Carson: Witness for Nature.* New York: Henry Holt, 1997.

Leopold, Aldo. *Game Management.* 1933. Reprint, Madison: University of Wisconsin Press, 1986.

Martin, Russell. *A Story That Stands Like A Dam: Glen Canyon and the Struggle for the Soul of the West.* Salt Lake City: University of Utah Press, 1999.

Mohl, Raymond A., ed. *Searching for the Sunbelt: Historical Perspectives on a Region.* Athens: University of Georgia Press, 1993.

Pitzer, Paul C. *Grand Coulee: Harnessing a Dream.* Pullman: Washington State University Press, 1994.

Riney-Kehrberg, Pamela. *Rooted in Dust: Surviving Drought and Depression in Southwestern Kansas.* Lawrence: University Press of Kansas, 1994.

Rome, Adam. *The Bulldozer in the Countryside: Suburban Sprawl and the Rise of American Environmentalism.* Cambridge: Cambridge University Press, 2001.

Russell, Edmund. *War and Nature: Fighting Humans and Insects with Chemicals from World War I to* Silent Spring. Cambridge: Cambridge University Press, 2001.

Schulman, Bruce J. *From Cotton Belt to Sunbelt: Federal Policy, Economic Development, and the Transformation of the South, 1938–1980.* Durham, N.C.: Duke University Press, 1994.

Stevens, Joseph E. *Hoover Dam: An American Adventure.* Norman: University of Oklahoma Press, 1988.

Worster, Donald. *Dust Bowl: The Southern Plains in the 1930s.* New York: Oxford University Press, 1982.

The Rise of the Environmental Movement: 1960s–1980s

Berry, Mary Clay. *The Alaska Pipeline: The Politics of Oil and Native Land Claims.* Bloomington: Indiana University Press, 1975.

Bluestone, Barry and Bennett Harrison. *The Deindustrialization of America: Plant Closings, Community Abandonment, and the Dismantling of Basic Industry.* New York: Basic Books, 1982.

Brick, Philip D. and R. McGreggor Cawley, eds. *A Wolf in the Garden: The Land Rights Movement and the New*

Environmental Debate. Lanham, Md.: Rowman & Littlefield, 1996.

Bupp, Irvin C. and Jean-Claude Derian. *Light Water: How the Nuclear Dream Dissolved.* New York: Basic Books, 1978.

Campbell, John L. *Collapse of an Industry: Nuclear Power and the Contradictions of U.S. Policy.* Ithaca, N.Y.: Cornell University Press, 1988.

Cawley, R. McGreggor. *Federal Land, Western Anger: The Sagebrush Rebellion and Environmental Politics.* Lawrence: University Press of Kansas, 1993.

Coates, Peter. *The Trans-Alaska Pipeline Controversy.* Bethlehem, Penn.: Lehigh University Press, 1991.

Colten, Craig E. and Peter N. Skinner. *The Road to Love Canal: Managing Industrial Waste before EPA.* Austin: University of Texas Press, 1996.

Easton, Robert. *Black Tide: The Santa Barbara Oil Spill and Its Consequences.* New York: Delacorte Press, 1972.

Ehrlich, Paul R. *The Population Bomb.* Rev. ed. New York: Ballantine Books, 1978.

Ford, Daniel F. *Three Mile Island: Thirty Minutes to Meltdown.* New York: Viking Press, 1982.

Gibbs, Lois Marie. *Love Canal: The Story Continues.* Gabriola Island, B.C.: New Society Publishers, 1998.

Gottlieb, Robert. *Forcing the Spring: The Transformation of the American Environmental Movement.* Washington, D.C.: Island Press, 1993.

Helvarg, David. *The War Against the Greens: The "Wise-Use" Movement, the New Right and Anti-environmental Violence.* San Francisco: Sierra Club Books, 1997.

Mazur, Allan. *A Hazardous Inquiry: The* Rashomon *Effect at Love Canal.* Cambridge, Mass.: Harvard University Press, 1998.

McCutcheon, Sean. *Electric Rivers: The Story of the James Bay Project.* Montreal: Black Rose Books, 1991.

Rome, Adam. *The Bulldozer in the Countryside: Suburban Sprawl and the Rise of American Environmentalism.* Cambridge: Cambridge University Press, 2001.

Schulman, Bruce J. *From Cotton Belt to Sunbelt: Federal Policy, Economic Development, and the Transformation of the South, 1938–1980.* Durham, N.C.: Duke University Press, 1994.

Wellock, Thomas R. *Critical Masses: Opposition to Nuclear Power in California, 1958–1978.* Madison: University of Wisconsin Press, 1998.

Contemporary Environmentalism: 1980s–Present

Alm, Leslie R. *Crossing Borders, Crossing Boundaries: The Role of Scientists in the U.S. Acid Rain Debate.* Westport, Conn.: Praeger, 2000.

Anderson, Luke. *Genetic Engineering, Food, and Our Environment.* White River Junction, Vt.: Chelsea Green Publishing, 1999.

Athanasiou, Tom. *Divided Planet: The Ecology of Rich and Poor.* Athens: University of Georgia Press, 1998.

Bliese, John R. E. *The Greening of Conservative America.* Boulder, Colo.: Westview Press, 2001.

Bullard, Robert D. *Dumping in Dixie: Race, Class and Environmental Quality.* 3rd ed. Boulder, Colo.: Westview Press, 2000.

Bullard, Robert, ed. *Confronting Environmental Racism: Voices from the Grassroots.* Boston: South End Press, 1993.

De Villiers, Marq. *Water: The Fate of Our Most Precious Resource.* Boston: Houghton Mifflin, 2000.

Dodds, Felix, ed. *Earth Summit 2002: A New Deal.* London: Earthscan, 2001.

Elkington, John and Tom Burke. *The Green Capitalists.* London: Victor Gollancz, 1987.

Foreman, Dave. *Confessions of an Eco-Warrior.* New York: Harmony Books, 1991.

Greer, Jed and Kenny Bruno. *Greenwash: The Reality Behind Corporate Environmentalism.* Penang, Malaysia: Third World Network, 1996.

Hassanein, Neva. *Changing the Way America Farms.* Lincoln: University of Nebraska Press, 1999.

Heywood, V., ed. *UNEP Global Biodiversity Assessment.* New York & Cambridge: Cambridge University Press, 1995.

International Forum on Globalization. *Alternatives to Economic Globalization.* San Francisco: IFG, 2002.

Leggett, Jeremy. *The Carbon War.* New York: Routledge, 2001.

MacArthur, John R. *The Selling of "Free Trade": NAFTA, Washington, and the Subversion of American Democracy.* Berkeley: University of California Press, 2001.

Magdoff, Fred, ed. *Hungry for Profit: The Agribusiness Threat to Farmers, Food, and the Environment.* New York: Monthly Review Press, 2000.

Nader, Ralph, ed. *The Case Against Free Trade: GATT, NAFTA, and the Globalization of Corporate Power.* Berkeley, Calif.: North Atlantic Books, 1993.

Novacek, Michael J., ed. *The Biodiversity Crisis: Losing What Counts.* New York: New Press, 2001.

Parson, Edward A., ed. *Governing the Environment: Persistent Challenges, Uncertain Innovations.* Toronto: University of Toronto Press, 2001.

Pyne, Stephen J. *America's Fires: Management on Wildlands and Forests.* Durham, N.C.: Forest History Society, 1997.

Rothfeder, Jeffrey. *Every Drop for Sale: Our Desperate Battle Over Water in a World about to Run Out.* New York: Jeremy P. Tarcher/Putnam, 2001.

Rowell, Andrew. *Green Backlash.* London and New York: Routledge, 1996.

Wilson, Edward O. *The Future of Life.* New York: Alfred A. Knopf, 2002.

Wirth, John D. *Smelter Smoke in North America: The Politics of Transborder Pollution.* Lawrence: University Press of Kansas, 2000.

Zakin, Susan. *Coyotes and Town Dogs: Earth First! and the Environmental Movement.* New York: Viking, 1993.

THEMATIC CATEGORIES

Agriculture

Anderson, Luke. *Genetic Engineering, Food, and Our Environment.* White River Junction, Vt.: Chelsea Green Publishing, 1999.

Crosby, Alfred W., Jr. *The Columbian Exchange: Biological and Cultural Consequences of 1492.* Westport, Conn.: Greenwood Press, 1972.

Fiege, Mark. *Irrigated Eden: The Making of an Agricultural Landscape in the American West.* Seattle and London: University of Washington Press, 1999.

Gray, Lewis Cecil. *History of Agriculture in the Southern United States to 1860.* 2 vols. Washington, D.C.: Carnegie Institution of Washington, 1933.

Hassanein, Neva. *Changing the Way America Farms.* Lincoln: University of Nebraska Press, 1999.

Hurt, R. Douglas. *Agricultural Technology in the Twentieth Century.* Manhattan, Kan.: Sunflower University Press, 1991.

———. *American Agriculture: A Brief History.* Ames: Iowa State University Press, 1994.

———. *The Dust Bowl: An Agricultural and Social History.* Chicago: Nelson-Hall, 1981.

Jones, Robert Leslie. *History of Agriculture in Ontario: 1613–1880.* Toronto: University of Toronto Press, 1946.

Magdoff, Fred, ed. *Hungry for Profit: The Agribusiness Threat to Farmers, Food, and the Environment.* New York: Monthly Review Press, 2000.

Opie, John. *The Law of the Land: 200 Years of American Farmland Policy.* Lincoln: University of Nebraska Press, 1994.

Reaman, G. E. *A History of Agriculture in Ontario.* Vol. 1. Toronto: Saunders, 1970.

Riney-Kehrberg, Pamela. *Rooted in Dust: Surviving Drought and Depression in Southwestern Kansas.* Lawrence: University Press of Kansas, 1994.

Russell, Howard S. *A Long, Deep Furrow: Three Centuries of Farming in New England.* Hanover, N.H.: University Press of New England, 1982.

U.S. National Research Council. *Alternative Agriculture.* Washington, D.C.: National Academy Press, 1989.

Wood, J. David. *Making Ontario: Agricultural Colonization and Landscape Re-creation before the Railway.* Montreal: McGill-Queen's University Press, 2000.

Wildlife and Forestry

Allin, Craig. *The Politics of Wilderness Preservation.* Westport, Conn.: Greenwood Press, 1982.

Apsey, Mike, et al. *The Perpetual Forest: Using Lessons from the Past to Sustain Canada's Forests in the Future.* Vancouver, B.C.: FORCAST, 2000.

Bell, K. *COSEWIC Status Report on the Atlantic Cod, Gadus morhua.* Ottawa: Committee on the Status of Endangered Wildlife in Canada, 1998.

Clary, David A. *Timber and the Forest Service.* Lawrence: University Press of Kansas, 1986.

Cox, Thomas R., Robert S. Maxwell, Phillip Drennon Thomas, and Joseph J. Malone. *This Well-Wooded Land: Americans and Their Forests from Colonial Times to the Present.* Lincoln: University of Nebraska Press, 1985.

Danz, Harold P. *Of Bison and Man.* Niwot: University Press of Colorado, 1997.

Dary, David. *The Buffalo Book: The Full Saga of the American Animal.* Rev. ed. Athens: Swallow Press/Ohio University Press, 1989.

Flader, Susan L. *Thinking Like a Mountain: Aldo Leopold and the Evolution of an Ecological Attitude toward Deer, Wolves, and Forests.* Madison: University of Wisconsin Press, 1994.

Floyd, Donald W. *Forest Sustainability: The History, the Challenge, the Promise.* Durham, N.C.: The Forest History Society, 2002.

Foster, David R. and John F. O'Keefe. *New England Forests Through Time: Insights from the Harvard Forest Dioramas.* Petersham, Mass.: Harvard Forest, Harvard University, 2000.

Foster, Janet. *Working for Wildlife: The Beginning of Preservation in Canada.* 2nd ed. Toronto: University of Toronto Press, 1998.

Frome, Michael. *Battle for the Wilderness.* Rev. ed. Salt Lake City: University of Utah Press, 1997.

Gillis, R. Peter and Thomas R. Roach. *Lost Initiatives: Canada's Forest Industries, Forest Policy and Forest Conservation.* New York: Greenwood Press, 1986.

Heywood, V., ed. *UNEP Global Biodiversity Assessment.* New York and Cambridge: Cambridge University Press, 1995.

Hirt, Paul W. *A Conspiracy of Optimism: Management of the National Forests Since World War Two.* Lincoln: University of Nebraska Press, 1994.

Isenberg, Andrew C. *The Destruction of the Bison: An Environmental History, 1750–1920.* Cambridge: Cambridge University Press, 2000.

Kurlansky, Mark. *Cod: A Biography of the Fish That Changed the World.* London: J. Cape, 1998.

Marchak, Patricia. *Green Gold: The Forest Industry in British Columbia.* Vancouver: University of British Columbia Press, 1983.

McDonald, Peter and James Lassoie, eds. *The Literature of Forestry and Agroforestry.* Ithaca, N.Y.: Cornell University Press, 1996.

Miller, Char and Rebecca Staebler. *The Greatest Good: 100 Years of Forestry in America.* Foreword by William H. Banzhaf; introduction by James E. Coufal. Bethesda, Md.: Society of American Foresters, 1999.

Novacek, Michael J., ed. *The Biodiversity Crisis: Losing What Counts.* New York: New Press, 2001.

Pyne, Stephen J. *America's Fires: Management on Wildlands and Forests.* Durham, N.C.: Forest History Society, 1997.

Robbins, William G. *American Forestry: A History of National, State, and Private Cooperation.* Lincoln: University of Nebraska Press, 1985.

Roe, Frank Gilbert. *The North American Buffalo: A Critical Study of the Species in Its Wild State.* 2nd ed. Newton Abbot, England: David & Charles, 1972.

The State of Canada's Forests, 1996–1997: Learning from History. Ottawa: Her Majesty the Queen in Right of Canada, 1997.

Steen, Harold K. *The U.S. Forest Service: A History.* Seattle: University of Washington Press, 1976.

Taylor, G. W. *Timber: History of the Forest Industry in B.C.* Vancouver: J. J. Douglas, 1975.

Taylor, Joseph E., III. *Making Salmon: An Environmental History of the Northwest Fisheries Crisis.* Seattle: University of Washington Press, 1999.

Walker, Laurence C. *The North American Forests: Geography, Ecology, and Silviculture.* Boca Raton, Fla.: CRC Press, 1999.

Warren, Louis S. *The Hunter's Game: Poachers and Conservationists in Twentieth-Century America.* New Haven, Conn.: Yale University Press, 1997.

Williams, Michael. *Americans and Their Forests: A Historical Geography.* Cambridge: Cambridge University Press, 1992.

Wynn, Graeme. *Timber Colony: A Historical Geography of Early Nineteenth Century New Brunswick.* Toronto: University of Toronto Press, 1981.

Land Use Management

Ambler, Marjane. *Breaking the Iron Bonds: Indian Control of Energy Development.* Lawrence: University Press of Kansas, 1990.

Bates, Sarah, et al. *Searching Out the Headwaters: Change and Rediscovery in Western Water Policy.* Washington, D.C.: Island Press, 1993.

Berry, Mary Clay. *The Alaska Pipeline: The Politics of Oil and Native Land Claims.* Bloomington: Indiana University Press, 1975.

Burton, Lloyd. *American Indian Water Rights and the Limits of Law.* Lawrence: University Press of Kansas, 1991.

Clow, Richmond and Imre Sutton. *Trusteeship in Change: Toward Tribal Autonomy in Resource Management.* Boulder: University Press of Colorado, 2001.

Coates, Peter. *The Trans-Alaska Pipeline Controversy.* Bethlehem, Penn.: Lehigh University Press, 1991.

Colten, Craig E. and Peter N. Skinner. *The Road to Love Canal: Managing Industrial Waste before EPA.* Austin: University of Texas Press, 1996.

Gates, Lillian F. *Land Policies of Upper Canada.* Toronto: University of Toronto Press, 1968.

Gates, Paul W. *History of Public Land Law Development*. New York: Arno Press, 1979.

Gottlieb, Robert. *A Life of Its Own: The Politics and Power of Water*. New York: Harcourt Brace, 1988.

Klyza, Christopher McGrory. *Who Controls Public Lands: Mining, Forestry, and Grazing Policies, 1870–1990*. Chapel Hill: University of North Carolina Press, 1996.

McCool, Daniel. *Command of the Waters: Iron Triangles, Federal Water Development, and Indian Water*. 1987. Reprint, Tucson: University of Arizona Press, 1994.

———. *Native Waters: Indian Water Settlements and the Second Treaty Era*. Tucson: University of Arizona Press, 2002.

McCutcheon, Sean. *Electric Rivers: The Story of the James Bay Project*. Montreal: Black Rose Books, 1991.

Newton, Norman T. *Design on the Land: The Development of Landscape Architecture*. Cambridge, Mass.: Harvard University Press, 1971.

Opie, John. *Ogallala: Water for a Dry Land*. 2nd ed. Lincoln: University of Nebraska Press, 2000.

Parson, Edward A., ed. *Governing the Environment: Persistent Challenges, Uncertain Innovations*. Toronto: University of Toronto Press, 2001.

Price, Edward T. *Dividing the Land: Early American Beginnings of Our Private Property Mosaic*. Chicago: University of Chicago Press, 1995.

Robbins, Roy M. *Our Landed Heritage: The Public Domain, 1776–1970*. 2nd ed. Lincoln: University of Nebraska Press, 1976.

Shurts, John. *Indian Reserved Water Rights: The Winters Doctrine in Its Social and Legal Context, 1880s–1930s*. Norman: University of Oklahoma Press, 2000.

Waldram, James. *As Long as the Rivers Run: Hydroelectric Development and Native Communities in Western Canada*. Winnipeg: University of Manitoba Press, 1988.

Wall, Geoff and John S. Marsh, eds. *Recreational Land Use: Perspectives on its Evolution in Canada*. Ottawa: Carleton University Press, 1982.

Technology, Industry, and Pollution

Ambrose, Stephen. *Nothing Like It in the World: The Men Who Built the Transcontinental Railroad 1863–1869*. New York: Simon & Schuster, 2000.

Baratz, Morton S. *The Union and the Coal Industry*. New Haven, Conn.: Yale University Press, 1955.

Campbell, John L. *Collapse of an Industry: Nuclear Power and the Contradictions of U.S. Policy*. Ithaca, N.Y.: Cornell University Press, 1988.

Dewey, Scott Hamilton. *Don't Breathe the Air: Air Pollution and U.S. Environmental Politics, 1945–1970*. College Station: Texas A&M University Press, 2000.

Dix, Keith. *What's a Coal Miner to Do? The Mechanization of Coal Mining*. Pittsburgh: University of Pittsburgh Press, 1988.

Duffy, Robert. *Nuclear Politics in America: A History and Theory of Government Regulation*. Lawrence: University Press of Kansas, 1997.

Easton, Robert. *Black Tide: The Santa Barbara Oil Spill and Its Consequences*. New York: Delacorte Press, 1972.

Ford, Daniel F. *Three Mile Island: Thirty Minutes to Meltdown*. New York: Viking Press, 1982.

Gibbs, Lois Marie. *Love Canal: The Story Continues*. Gabriola Island, B.C.: New Society Publishers, 1998.

Heron, Craig. *Working in Steel, The Early Years in Canada, 1883–1935*. Toronto: McClelland and Stewart, 1988.

Hurst, D. G., et al. *Canada Enters the Atomic Age*. Montreal: McGill-Queen's University Press, 1997.

Hyde, Charles K. *Copper for America: The United States Copper Industry from Colonial Times to the 1990s*. Tucson: University of Arizona Press, 1998.

Leidner, Jacob. *Plastics Waste, Recovery of Economic Value*. New York: Marcel Dekker, 1981.

Lewis, Robert Davis. *Manufacturing Montreal: The Making of an Industrial Landscape, 1850 to 1930*. Baltimore, Md.: Johns Hopkins University Press, 2000.

Majumdar, Shyamal K. and E. Willard Miller, eds. *Pennsylvania Coal: Resources, Technology and Utilization*. Easton: The Pennsylvania Academy of Science, 1983.

Mazur, Allan. *A Hazardous Inquiry: The* Rashomon *Effect at Love Canal*. Cambridge, Mass.: Harvard University Press, 1998.

McDonnell, Greg. *The History of Canadian Railroads*. London: Footnote Productions/New Burlington Books, 1985.

Meikle, Jeffrey. *American Plastic: A Cultural History*. New Brunswick, N.J.: Rutgers University Press, 1995.

Melosi, Martin V. *Coping with Abundance: Energy and Environment in Industrial America*. New York: Alfred A. Knopf, 1985.

———. *The Sanitary City: Urban Infrastructure in America from Colonial Times to the Present*. Baltimore, Md.: Johns Hopkins University Press, 2000.

Mouat, Jeremy. *Roaring Days: Rossland's Mines and the History of British Columbia*. Vancouver: University of British Columbia Press, 1995.

Paul, Rodman W. *Mining Frontiers of the Far West, 1848–1880*. Rev. ed. Albuquerque: University of New Mexico Press, 2001.

Porro, Jeffrey and Christine Meller. *The Plastic Waste Primer*. New York: Lyons and Burford, 1993.

Smith, Duane A. *Mining America: The Industry and the Environment, 1800–1980*. Niwot: University Press of Colorado, 1993.

Stover, John and Mark Carnes. *The Routledge Historical Atlas of the American Railroads*. New York: Routledge, 1999.

Stradling, David. *Smokestacks and Progressives: Environmentalists, Engineers, and Air Quality in America, 1881–1951*. Baltimore, Md.: Johns Hopkins University Press, 1999.

Strohmeyer, John. *Extreme Conditions: Big Oil and the Transformation of Alaska*. NewYork: Simon & Schuster, 1993.

Tarr, Joel A. *The Search for the Ultimate Sink: Urban Pollution in Historical Perspective*. Akron, Ohio: University of Akron Press, 1996.

Tarr, Joel A. and Gabriel Dupuy, eds. *Technology and the Rise of the Networked City in Europe and America*. Philadelphia: Temple University Press, 1988.

Wellock, Thomas R. *Critical Masses: Opposition to Nuclear Power in California, 1958–1978*. Madison: University of Wisconsin Press, 1998.

Williamson, Harold F. and Arnold R. Daum. *The American Petroleum Industry: The Age of Illumination, 1859–1899*. Westport, Conn.: Greenwood Press, 1981.

Winther, Oscar Osburn. *The Transportation Frontier: Trans-Mississippi West, 1865–1890*. Albuquerque: University of New Mexico, 1974.

Wolf, Nancy and Ellen Feldman. *America's Packaging Dilemma*. Washington, D.C.: Island Press, 1991.

Human Habitats

Abbott, Carl. *The New Urban America: Growth and Politics in Sunbelt Cities*. Rev. ed. Chapel Hill: University of North Carolina Press, 1987.

Ballard, Steven C. and Thomas E. James, eds. *The Future of the Sunbelt: Managing Growth and Change*. New York: Praeger, 1983.

Bunting, Trudi and Pierre Filion, eds. *Canadian Cities in Transition: The Twenty-First Century*. 2nd ed. Ontario: Oxford University Press Canada, 2000.

Cozic, Charles P., ed. *America's Cities: Opposing Viewpoints*. San Diego, Calif.: Greenhaven Press, 1993.

Dechêne, Louise. *Habitants and Merchants in Seventeenth Century Montreal*. Montreal: McGill-Queen's University Press, 1992.

Dickason, Olive Patricia. *Canada's First Nations: A History of Founding Peoples from Earliest Times*. 3rd ed. Don Mills, Ont.: Oxford University Press, 2002.

Fairbanks, Robert B. and Kathleen Underwood, eds. *Essays on Sunbelt Cities and Recent Urban America*. Introduction by Kenneth T. Jackson. College Station: Published for the University of Texas at Arlington by Texas A&M University Press, 1990.

Greer, Allan. *Peasant, Lord, and Merchant: Rural Society in Three Quebec Parishes, 1740–1840*. Toronto: University of Toronto Press, 1985.

Harris, Richard Colebrook. *The Seigneurial System in Early Canada: A Geographical Study*. Madison: University of Wisconsin Press, 1984.

Hine, Robert V. and John Mack Faragher. *The American West: A New Interpretive History*. New Haven, Conn.: Yale University Press, 2000.

Hurt, R. Douglas. *The Indian Frontier, 1763–1846*. Albuquerque: University of New Mexico Press, 2002.

Jackson, Kenneth T. *Crabgrass Frontier: The Suburbanization of the United States*. New York: Oxford University Press, 1987.

Kessell, John L. *Spain in the Southwest: A Narrative History of Colonial New Mexico, Arizona, Texas, and California*. Norman: University of Oklahoma Press, 2002.

Kulikoff, Allan. *Tobacco and Slaves: The Development of Southern Cultures in the Chesapeake, 1680–1800*. Chapel Hill: University of North Carolina Press, 1986.

Melosi, Martin V. *The Sanitary City: Urban Infrastructure in America from Colonial Times to the Present*. Baltimore, Md.: Johns Hopkins University Press, 2000.

Miller, Randall M. and George E. Pozzetta, eds. *Shades of the Sunbelt: Essays on Ethnicity, Race, and the Urban South*. Boca Raton: Florida Atlantic University Press, 1989.

Mohl, Raymond A., ed. *Searching for the Sunbelt: Historical Perspectives on a Region.* Athens: University of Georgia Press, 1993.

Muller, Peter O. *Contemporary Suburban America.* Englewood Cliffs, N.J.: Prentice-Hall, 1981.

Palen, J. John. *The Suburbs.* New York: McGraw-Hill, 1995.

Powell, Sumner Chilton. *Puritan Village: The Formation of a New England Town.* Middletown, Conn.: Wesleyan University Press, 1963.

Rogers, Edward S. and Donald B. Smith, eds. *Aboriginal Ontario: Historical Perspectives on the First Nations.* Toronto: Dundurn Press, 1994.

Rome, Adam. *The Bulldozer in the Countryside: Suburban Sprawl and the Rise of American Environmentalism.* Cambridge: Cambridge University Press, 2001.

Schulman, Bruce J. *From Cotton Belt to Sunbelt: Federal Policy, Economic Development, and the Transformation of the South, 1938–1980.* Durham, N.C.: Duke University Press, 1994.

Smith, Arthur G. *Pittsburgh: Then and Now.* Pittsburgh: University of Pittsburgh Press, 1990.

Ward, David. *Cities and Immigrants: A Geography of Change in Nineteenth-Century America.* New York: Oxford University Press, 1971.

Weber, David J. *The Spanish Frontier in North America.* New Haven, Conn.: Yale University Press, 1992.

Ideology and Politics

Allen, Richard. *The Social Passion: Religion and Social Reform in Canada, 1914–28.* Toronto: University of Toronto Press, 1973.

Athanasiou, Tom. *Divided Planet: The Ecology of Rich and Poor.* Athens: University of Georgia Press, 1998.

Berry, Brian J. *America's Utopian Experiments: Communal Havens from Long-Wave Crises.* Hanover, N.H.: University Press of New England, 1992.

Boardman, Robert, ed. *Canadian Environmental Policy: Ecosystems, Politics, and Process.* Toronto: Oxford University Press, 1992.

Bullard, Robert, ed. *Confronting Environmental Racism: Voice from the Grassroots.* Boston: South End Press, 1993.

Cawley, R. McGreggor. *Federal Land, Western Anger: The Sagebrush Rebellion and Environmental Politics.* Lawrence: University Press of Kansas, 1993.

Degler, Carl N. *In Search of Human Nature: The Decline and Revival of Darwinism in American Social Thought.* New York: Oxford University Press, 1991.

Dorsey, Kurkpatrick. *The Dawn of Conservation Diplomacy: U.S.-Canadian Wildlife Protection Treaties in the Progressive Era.* Seattle: University of Washington Press, 1998.

Fogarty, Robert S. *Dictionary of American Communal and Utopian History.* Westport, Conn.: Greenwood Press, 1980.

Foreman, Dave. *Confessions of an Eco-Warrior.* New York: Harmony Books, 1991.

Foster, Janet. *Working for Wildlife: The Beginning of Preservation in Canada.* 2nd ed. Toronto: University of Toronto Press, 1998.

Fox, Stephen. *The American Conservation Movement: John Muir and His Legacy.* Madison: University of Wisconsin Press, 1985.

———. *John Muir and His Legacy: The American Conservation Movement.* Boston: Little, Brown, 1981.

Frome, Michael. *Battle for the Wilderness.* Rev. ed. Salt Lake City: University of Utah Press, 1997.

Gottlieb, Robert. *Forcing the Spring: The Transformation of the American Environmental Movement.* Washington, D.C.: Island Press, 1993.

Graham, Frank. *The Audubon Ark: A History of the National Audubon Society.* New York: Alfred A. Knopf, 1990.

Greer, Jed and Kenny Bruno. *Greenwash: The Reality Behind Corporate Environmentalism.* Penang, Malaysia: Third World Network, 1996.

Harvey, Mark. *A Symbol of Wilderness: Echo Park and the American Conservation Movement.* Albuquerque: University of New Mexico Press, 1994.

Hawkins, Mike. *Social Darwinism in European and American Thought, 1860–1945.* Cambridge: Cambridge University Press, 1997.

Haynes, Sam. *James K. Polk and the Expansionist Impulse.* 2nd ed. New York: Longman, 2002.

Hays, Samuel P. *Conservation and the Gospel of Efficiency: The Progressive Conservation Movement, 1890–1920.* 1959. Reprint, Pittsburgh: University of Pittsburgh Press, 1999.

Helvarg, David. *The War Against the Greens: The "Wise-Use" Movement, the New Right and Anti-environmental Violence.* San Francisco: Sierra Club Books, 1997.

Hewitt, Gordon C. *The Conservation of Wildlife in Canada.* New York: Scribner's Sons, 1921.

Hofstadter, Richard. *Social Darwinism in American Thought 1860–1915*. Rev. ed. Boston: Beacon Press, 1955.

Lear, Linda. *Rachel Carson: Witness for Nature*. New York: Henry Holt, 1997.

Lothian, W. F. *A Brief History of Canada's National Parks*. Ottawa: Environment Canada Parks, 1987.

MacArthur, John R. *The Selling of "Free Trade": NAFTA, Washington, and the Subversion of American Democracy*. Berkeley: University of California Press, 2001.

Macdonald, Doug. *The Politics of Pollution: Why Canadians Are Failing Their Environment*. Toronto: McClelland and Stewart, 1991.

Miller, Char. *Gifford Pinchot and the Making of Modern Environmentalism*. Washington, D.C.: Island Press, 2001.

Nader, Ralph, ed. *The Case Against Free Trade: GATT, NAFTA, and the Globalization of Corporate Power*. Berkeley, Calif.: North Atlantic Books, 1993.

Nash, Roderick. *Wilderness and the American Mind*. New Haven, Conn.: Yale University Press, 1982.

Rothman, Hal K. *The Greening of a Nation?: Environmentalism in the U.S. Since 1945*. Fort Worth, Tex.: Harcourt Brace College Publishers, 1998.

———. *Saving the Planet: The American Response to the Environment in the 20th Century*. Chicago: Ivan R. Dee, 2000.

Rowell, Andrew. *Green Backlash*. London and New York: Routledge, 1996.

Runte, Alfred. *National Parks: The American Experience*. Lincoln: University of Nebraska Press, 1997.

Udall, Stewart. *The Quiet Crisis*. New York: Avon, 1970.

Willoughby, William R. *The Joint Organizations of Canada and the United States*. Toronto: University of Toronto Press, 1979.

Wilson, William H. *The City Beautiful Movement*. Baltimore, Md.: Johns Hopkins University Press, 1989.

Zakin, Susan. *Coyotes and Town Dogs: Earth First! and the Environmental Movement*. New York: Viking, 1993.

List of Contributors

Barbour, Barton H.
Department of History, Boise State University, Idaho

Brady, Lisa M.
Department of History (doctoral candidate), University of Kansas

Brunger, Alan G.
Department of Geography, Trent University, Ontario

Calverley, David
Upper School History, Crescent School, Ontario

Coates, Peter
Department of Historical Studies, University of Bristol, United Kingdom

Eber, Ronald
Independent writer on land use and conservation, Salem, Oregon

Girard, Michel F.
Climate Change Bureau, Environment Canada, Ontario

Gorman, Hugh S.
Environmental History and Policy, Department of Social Sciences, Michigan Technological University

Harvey, Mark
Department of History, North Dakota State University

Hazlett, Maril
Department of History (doctoral candidate), University of Kansas

Hurt, R. Douglas
Agricultural History and Rural Studies, Iowa State University

Lewis, James G.
Independent scholar

MacEachern, Alan
Department of History, Queen's University, Ontario

MacLeod, Peter
Canadian War Museum, Ontario

Manore, Jean L.
Department of History, Bishop's University, Québec

Marsh, John S.
Department of Geography, Trent University, Ontario

McCann, Larry
Department of Geography, University of Victoria, British Columbia

McCool, Daniel
Department of Political Science, University of Utah

McIlwraith, Thomas F.
Department of Geography, University of Toronto at Mississauga, Ontario

Mulcahy, Richard P.
Department of History and Political Science, University of Pittsburgh at Titusville, Pennsylvania

Murton, James
Department of History, Queen's University, Ontario

O'Keefe, John F.
Fisher Museum, Harvard Forest, Harvard University, Massachusetts

Opie, John
Department of History (emeritus), New Jersey Institute of Technology

Ost, John
Freelance science writer and teacher, Nashua, New Hampshire

Payne, Sarah
Department of History (doctoral candidate), University of New Mexico; assistant editor of the *New Mexico Historical Review*

Read, Jennifer
Michigan Sea Grant College Program

Riney-Kehrberg, Pamela
Department of History, Iowa State University

Rothman, Hal
Department of History, University of Nevada–Las Vegas

Sanders, Jeffrey
Department of History, University of New Mexico

Scarpino, Philip V.
Department of History, Indiana University

Shallat, Todd
Department of History, Boise State University, Idaho

Silver, Timothy
Department of History, Appalachian State University, North Carolina

Sisson, Mary
Professional writer

Slatta, Richard W.
Department of History, North Carolina State University

Smith, Duane A.
Department of History, Fort Lewis College, Colorado

Stewart, Mart A.
Department of History, Western Washington University

Strelow, Michael H.
Department of English, Willamette University, Oregon

Tarr, Joel A.
Department of History, Carnegie Mellon University, Pennsylvania

Taylor, Matthew D.
Department of History (graduate student), North Dakota State University

Valerio-Jiménez, Omar
Department of History, Clements Center for Southwest Studies, Southern Methodist University, Texas

Warecki, George
Department of Social Sciences, Brescia College, University of Western Ontario

Wellock, Thomas R.
Department of History, Central Washington University

Woodford, Chris
Cofounder, UK Rivers Network, and freelance writer, Staffordshire, United Kingdom

Zimring, Carl
Department of History, Carnegie Mellon University, Pennsylvania

Index

Note: Page numbers in *italic* refer to illustrations. Page numbers in **boldface** indicate main topics.